English Language Assessment and the Chinese Learner

English Language Assessment and the Chinese Learner

Liying Cheng, *Queen's University, Canada*
Andy Curtis, *The Chinese University of Hong Kong*

Routledge
Taylor & Francis Group

NEW YORK AND LONDON

First published 2010
by Routledge
711 Third Avenue, New York, NY 10017

Simultaneously published in the UK
by Routledge
2 Park Square, Milton Park, Abingdon, Oxon OX14 4RN

Routledge is an imprint of the Taylor & Francis Group, an informa business

First issued in paperback 2011

© 2010 Taylor & Francis

Typeset in Minion by Swales & Willis Ltd, Exeter, Devon

Library of Congress Cataloging in Publication Data
Cheng, Liying, 1959–
   English language assessment and the Chinese learner /
   Liying Cheng, Andy Curtis.—1st editon.
   p. cm.
   Includes indexes.
   1. English language—Study and teaching—Chinese speakers
   2. English language—Ability testing. I. Curtis, Andy. II. Title.
   PE1130.C4C54 2008
   428.0071'0951—dc22
   2008043453

ISBN13: 978-0-415-50478-2 (pbk)
ISBN13: 978–0–415–99447–7 (hbk)
ISBN13: 978–0–203–87304–5 (ebk)

To all the Chinese learners, inside and outside China, who have experienced and will experience English language learning and assessment. May English help you realize your goals as it has helped us realize ours.

Contents

Foreword

Lyle F. Bachman

It would appear that, for better or worse, English will continue as the preferred *lingua franca* for international communication well into this century, if not beyond. This, despite the fact that the countries where English is the dominant language are becoming less and less dominant, both economically and politically, and that this century will most certainly see an increasing dominance on the world scene of countries that until now have been classed as "emerging", economically, e.g., Brazil, Russia, India, China, and Korea. English is still the most widely taught foreign or second language in the world, with approximately 2 billion learners expected worldwide by 2010. Furthermore, the bulk of this increase is expected to occur in China and India, both of which are promoting English in primary schools. And to be sure, where English is taught, it will be assessed. This volume thus addresses a very timely and important topic, and the chapters in it provide both broad and in-depth coverage of a number of large-scale English tests in China, including Hong Kong and Taiwan, and about the Chinese Learner.

In their preface, the editors argue that the global scope of English language assessment and the huge scale on which this takes place in China make the particular intersection of language assessment and the Chinese Learner of unique importance. However, I would submit that the language testing issues discussed in the volume are not unique to the assessment of Chinese Learners' English at all. Rather, the enormity of the enterprise in this context magnifies kinds of problems that are faced by language testers everywhere, and makes it more difficult to find justifiable solutions. Thus, one finds some familiar and perennial issues discussed in the chapters: validity of scored-based interpretations, consequences of test use, fairness, washback, and the tensions between the functions of selection and washback, and between assessment for learning and assessment for selection or certification. In addition some very "real-world" issues come through, such as the politics of language assessment development and use and the management of resources as needs and test-taker populations expand. Finally, the chapters also provide some visions for the future of assessing the English of the Chinese Learner.

One message that comes through strong and clear from the descriptions of the high-stakes English tests in China in this volume is that for many of these tests, providing "positive washback" on instruction is explicitly stated as a purpose, in addition to providing information for making various kinds of decisions, such as selection, promotion or certification. The intended consequence of promoting positive washback on instruction is perhaps the single characteristic that distinguishes many of these tests from high-stakes language tests in other parts of the world. In the USA, for example, although much lip-service has been paid to "authentic" and "performance" assessments for high-stakes accountability decisions in school settings, virtually none of the large-scale state assessments of English proficiency, for either English Language Learners or English-only students, claims positive washback on instruction as a goal. This is also the case with tests used for university selection. Thus, in stark contrast with the Hong Kong Advanced Level Examination, neither the SAT nor the ACT in the USA claims to promote positive washback on instruction.

In addition to chapters discussing all of the major high-stakes English tests in China, the volume includes a number of chapters reporting research studies that investigate both specific and general issues in English language testing in China. These chapters provide some very insightful glimpses into the domain of this book—the interaction between English language assessments and Chinese learners. They also take us into the domain of students, teachers, and classroom assessment. Finally, they tell us something about the "Chinese Learner". What I find most fascinating about this group of chapters is that by focusing on a single "type" of learner, they show us once again how complex the interactions are among test-takers, the multifarious facets of test-tasks, and the performance that these tasks elicit. At another level, by focusing on one sociocultural setting, they reveal the complexities of the social, cultural, and political dimensions of the real world in which language assessment takes place.

The world of the Chinese Learner is a particularly complex one that is fraught with inherent tensions, if not conflicts, between traditional Confucian values that honor authority, the family, education, and harmony in society, on the one hand, and a drive to not only compete, but to excel in a modern world in which individualism, personal gain, and corporate profit, even mendacity, seem to be the guiding values, on the other. The "New China" quite legitimately wishes to shed its image as the sick man of Asia, and claim its rightful place as a world leader. However, this rush toward "modernization", which gave China the "Great Leap Forward" and more recently has produced the Three Gorges Dam and the truly amazing buildings for the 2008 Olympics, has also had disastrous consequences for millions of Chinese people. This tension between the benefits and negative consequences of modernization exemplifies, in my view, at the national level, the same tensions and conflicts faced by individual Chinese learners.

Within this context, the assessment of English faces similar tensions. Traditional values of the Chinese society, including a respect for the examination system, pull toward tests that are embedded in the education system, in teaching and learning, and that will lead to decisions that will benefit the society as a whole. This is a culture in which examinations are valued, and decisions that are made on the basis of examination results are generally accepted almost without question, as fair. This explains, in part, why developers of English tests in China begin with the premise that the decisions made on the basis of tests will be beneficial to stakeholders and the society as a whole. Modern psychological and educational measurement, on the other hand, which values qualities such as psychometric reliability, and validity as the predictability of selection decisions, pushes towards tests that can be easily and consistently administered and scored. This is a culture of skepticism, in which test developers and decision-makers must convince an unbelieving public that tests and the decisions made on the basis of test results are justified.

The editors state that "This book, then, attempts to bridge the gap between test validity and test consequences so we can better justify the use of English language assessment to its stakeholders" (Chapter 1), and that it has been structured "in such a way that readers can situate the discussions of the Chinese Learner in relation to English language assessment within a historical, social, political, and economic context in China" (Chapter 19). The bridge between test validity and consequences is long and still largely a vision, not yet a blueprint, let alone under construction, for language assessment, while an understanding of Chinese history and culture is surely a life-long undertaking. Nevertheless, this volume gives us glimpses of both, and thus whets our appetites as researchers, for greater understanding, while stimulating our better instincts, as test-developers, to assure that our assessments of English will promote beneficial consequences, not only for China and the Chinese Learner, but for English learners the world over.

Preface

As noted on the first page of the final chapter of this book, the book is structured "in such a way that the readers can situate the discussions of the Chinese Learner in relation to English language assessment within a historical, social, political, and economic context in China." Interestingly, in relation to the economic context, as we write this preface in July 2008, one of the world's largest and most successful companies, in terms of products and profits, General Motors (GM), is announcing its worst economic losses for more than half-a-century (BBC News Online, July 3, 2008). But what does that have to do with English language assessment and testing?

First, English language assessment and testing is big business, running globally into the millions of US dollars every year, and possibly even more. More importantly, this announcement by GM, together with a great many other indicators, such as the economic recession in America, signals that we may be witnessing, for better and for worse, the beginning of the end of the USA as a global economic, political and military super-power. If so—and assuming the world still needs such super-powers—which country could take on that role? Europe's time in that position appears to have come and gone, and it is still too early for Latin America, although the global growth of the Spanish-speaking world may enable Latin America to take on this role eventually. It is also likely to be too early for the Middle East or Africa. This then leaves, again for better and for worse, China as the most likely contender.

These two factors combined—the multi-million dollar business of English language assessment and testing and rise of The New China, complete with the first ever China Olympic Games under its belt—mean that the impact of English language assessment and testing in China could soon be felt in every part of the world. As noted in the opening chapter: "Currently, more than 27 million Chinese university students are learning English and taking English tests." This is a truly mind-boggling figure, almost beyond comprehension; a figure approaching the entire population of the second largest country in the world (by land mass), Canada, estimated at around 33 million in 2007—and this is only the students in China *at university level*. These, then, are some of the reasons why we started working on this book, which grew out of a conversation during the 2005 Language Testing Research Colloquium (LTRC), held in Ottawa, Canada in July of that year. The conversation was between the two editors in a room at the conference hotel, the Fairmont Château Laurier. As we sat in our hotel room, we asked ourselves: Why, with the massive numbers of Chinese students taking English language exams, and with

China Rising (Goodman & Segal, 1997), is there not a book on this essential aspect of the New China? We then checked to make sure that such a volume did indeed appear to be conspicuous by its absence, and started contacting potential contributors. Four years later, we are finally able to present a comprehensive and up-to-date picture of English language assessment for students in China (mainland China, Hong Kong and Taiwan) and for Chinese Learners of English around the world.

Another reason for bringing this collection together, and one of the recurring themes throughout the book, is that in China, for students to be successful in school means taking numerous tests and examinations in English at every grade. Major public examinations are required to enter junior and senior secondary schools, university, and postgraduate education. Examinations continue to be used for the selection of government officials, for the promotion of academics and professionals, and for obtaining better employment involving international communication. Among these tests and examinations, English is used as the gatekeeper for these purposes. It is therefore essential to understand the Chinese Learner and the Chinese context within which so much of the world's English language assessment is situated.

Another relatively small but significant example, for language testers, of the new world order was the recent LTRC, held for the first time in the organization's 30-year history in June 2008 in mainland China (at Zhejiang University in Hang Zhou). Appropriately, the main accommodation for the conference attendees was the Zhejiang Xizi Hotel, the main block of which is translated into English as 'Villa 1', famous for being the place where Chairman Mao is reported to have stayed 27 times between 1959 and 1975 (according to a bilingual Chinese–English inscription on a boulder just outside Villa 1).

The appropriateness of the venue was inadvertently but fortuitously highlighted by Jianda Liu in Chapter 10 of this collection: "The Cultural Revolution (1966–76) involved a mass mobilization of urban Chinese youth. Schools were closed and students were encouraged to join units which denounced and persecuted Chinese teachers and intellectuals. There were also widespread book burnings and mass relocations. The Cultural Revolution also caused economic disruption. After 10 years, the movement was brought to a close in 1976." That brief, 60-word endnote attempts to summarize, in just a few words, a time of unimaginable turmoil in China's recent history, ending barely 30 years ago—a tiny drop of time in the vast ocean of one of the world's oldest civilizations, dating back more than 5,000 years (see Chapter 1). This, then, was another key reason why we believe that the time has come for a book like this. If China continues to develop over the next 30 years the way it has done over the previous 30, in the near future, English language assessment and testing in China could be driving English language assessment and testing all over the world— assuming it is not already.

In the opening chapter, *The Realities of English Language Assessment and the Chinese Learner in China and Beyond*, the scene is set for the rest of the book by presenting some of the history of English language tests and examinations in China, and by defining the notions of "the Chinese Learner" and "the Chinese context". This opening chapter also gives an overview of the structure of the book, consisting of four major parts and one concluding chapter in part five. We have adopted the term *assessment* to include both examinations and tests.

References

BBC News Online (2008). Dow Jones becomes a bear market. Retrieved July 3, 2008, http://news. bbc.co.uk/go/pr/fr/-/2/hi/business/7486640.stm

Goodman, D. & Segal, G. (1997). *China rising: Nationalism and interdependence.* New York: Routledge.

Acknowledgments

First, we would like to thank the contributors to this book, all of whom are dedicated professionals working with Chinese Learners in the area of English language learning and assessment, producing the best English tests and assessment practices possible, and conducting rigorous research to close the gap between test validation and test consequences, to better support the growth of their learners. Thank you for your patience, persistence and professionalism in working with us over the past 4 years to bring this book to fruition. Without your dedication, there would be no book.

We would also like to thank the three anonymous reviewers who gave such valuable and constructive feedback on the book, as a result of which the book is more clearly conceptualized and focused.

Thanks also go to Naomi Silverman and her team at Routledge: Taylor & Francis Group. Your belief in this book helped make it a reality.

We are also grateful to Terry Milnes and Ying Zheng—doctoral students at Queen's University Faculty of Education—for their work on the final stages of the book's editing.

Last, but not least, we are, as always, very grateful to our family members for their unfailing love and support. They are the sources of our inspiration for all our endeavors.

The Editors

Liying Cheng is an Associate Professor and a Director of the Assessment and Evaluation Group (AEG) at the Faculty of Education, Queen's University. Her primary research interests are the impact of large-scale testing on instruction, and the relationship between assessment and instruction. Her major publications include articles in *Language Testing, Language Assessment Quarterly, Assessment in Education, Assessment & Evaluation in Higher Education*, and *Studies in Educational Evaluation*. Her recent books are *Changing Language Teaching through Language Testing* (Cambridge University Press, 2005); *Washback in Language Testing: Research Contexts and Methods* (co-edited with Y. Watanabe with A. Curtis, Lawrence Erlbaum Associates, 2004); and *Language Testing: Revisited* (co-edited with J. Fox et al., University of Ottawa Press, 2007).

Andy Curtis is the Director of the English Language Teaching Unit at the Chinese University of Hong Kong, China, where he is also an Associate Professor in the Department of Curriculum and Instruction within the Faculty of Education. His main research interests are teacher professional development, managing change in educational systems, and leadership in language education. He has published articles in the *Asian Journal of English Language Teaching*, in the *Asia-Pacific Journal of Teacher Education*, and in the *Asia Pacific Journal of Language in Education*, as well as many other journals. His recent books include *Colour, Race and English Language Teaching: Shades of Meaning* (co-edited with Mary Romney, Lawrence Erlbaum Associates, 2006).

officials, for the promotion of academics and professionals, and for obtaining better employment involving international communication. Among these tests and examinations, English is used most often as the gatekeeper for these purposes in China (Cheng, 2008).

Currently, more than 27 million Chinese university students are learning English and taking English tests (http://www.hnedu.cn/). Chinese students are among the five largest groups of both TOEFL (see Chapter 7) and IELTS (see Chapter 8) test-takers. They are also among the largest groups of international students studying at English medium universities in North America, the UK, Australia, and New Zealand. Given the long history of objective testing and its extensive use in Chinese society, and considering the sheer number of students taking various tests of English in China and elsewhere, an understanding of the impact of English language assessment as illustrated in this book is essential for testing and assessment policy-makers, curriculum designers, researchers, ESL/EFL materials writers, graduate students, and English language teachers/researchers at various levels who are involved in testing and assessment issues in China and elsewhere in the world.

The Chinese Learner and the Chinese Context

China (Traditional Chinese Character: 「中國」; Simplified Chinese Character: 「中国」[1]; Hanyu Pinyin: *Zhōngguó*[2]) is a cultural region, an ancient civilization and a nation in East Asia. It is one of the world's oldest civilizations, consisting of states and cultures dating back more than five millennia. As one of the world's oldest continuous civilizations, China has the longest continuously used written language system of the world. The People's Republic of China, commonly known as China or abbreviated to PRC (Simplified Chinese: 「中华人民共和国」; Traditional Chinese: 「中華人民共和國」; Hanyu Pinyin: *Zhōnghuá Rénmín Gònghéguó*) is a vast geographical region of about 9.6 million square kilometers accommodating more than one-fifth of the world's population (over 1.3 billion in 2008). The majority of China exists today as a country known as the People's Republic of China, but China also represents a long-standing civilization comprising successive states and cultures dating back more than 5,000 years. The chapters in this book come from the testing contexts of mainland China (officially The People's Republic of China), Hong Kong (officially the Hong Kong Special Administrative Region (HKSAR) of The People's Republic of China [香港特別行政區]), and Taiwan (officially The Republic of China), which are treated as geographical rather than political regions. *China* is used in this book to refer to both the People's Republic of China—mainland China[3], but also refers to China in its broadest and most inclusive sense.

The Chinese Learner, as referred to in the title of the book, refers to: "students from Confucian-heritage cultures (CHC) such as China, Hong Kong, Taiwan, Singapore, Korea and Japan, [who] are taught in classroom conditions . . . . [with] large classes, expository methods, relentless norm-referenced assessment, and harsh climate" (Watkins & Biggs, 2001, p. 3). The Chinese Learner defined in this book considers "the Chinese learner as a whole person, not only as a student, and is [are] aware of factors . . . nonetheless important to student outcomes" (Coverdale-Jones, 2006, p. 148). The Chinese Learner in our book consists of mainly Chinese students and test-takers in/

from mainland China, Hong Kong, and Taiwan. These students are studying within the broader Chinese context in China and Asia, and in English-medium of instruction (EMI) universities around the world. These test-takers take English language tests designed and administrated locally in China and internationally. Chinese students and test-takers within the discussion of the book mainly consist of those studying at the school, university, and postgraduate levels. It is, however, not the aim of this book to discuss the cultural, psychological, and pedagogical learning styles of this group of learners (see *Language Culture Curriculum*, 19(1), 2006 for a range of such issues discussed in relation to the Chinese Learner; Rastall, 2004). Rather, the focus of this collection is to portray these Chinese students and test-takers within their English language assessment contexts in and beyond China.

It is essential to point out here to the readers of the book that we have referred to China beyond mainland China in its current state, and the Chinese Learner in a broader sense. When this term is used in singular in this book, it is written as *the Chinese Learner*. When used in the plural, it is written as *Chinese Learners*. In addition, Chinese society and the Chinese Learner also go beyond the political and geographical definition (boundary) of what the People's Republic of China (PRC) is today.

History of English Language Testing and Examinations

The testing and examination history in China can be classified as Ancient, Modern and Current periods (Zhang, 2005). The Ancient examination period, which was dominated by the imperial examinations system「科举制度」, was the longest historical period, stretching from the origins of the examinations around 2200BC until when the imperial examinations were abolished in 1905 (see Chapter 2 for details). The Modern examination period started with the influence of western education and sciences in 1862 and the establishment of the Metropolitan Institute of Foreign Languages「京师同文馆」until the founding of the People's Republic of China (PRC) in 1949, with the Current examination period starting in 1949 and lasting until the present day. All our chapters, except for Chapter 2, discuss the testing and examinations in this Current period (1949–now). The Ancient examination period will be dealt with in Chapter 2. The Modern and Current periods will be discussed below in order to provide the historical, social, and political context for this book.

The Modern Examination Period

The testing of foreign languages in China started around 1862 at the beginning of the Modern examination period, when "the British, American and other western trading empires sought access to Chinese markets and Christian missionaries to the Chinese soul" (Adamson, 2004, p. 21). The first school of foreign languages—the Metropolitan Institute of Foreign Languages (Beijing Normal Language School)「京师同文馆」—was also established around 1862 (Ke, 1986), with British missionary J. C. Burdon as its first English instructor. During its 40-year history, the Beijing Normal Language School taught only five foreign languages: English, French, Russian, German, and Japanese. This tradition of learning (training) and testing of these foreign languages has remained today in mainland China (see Chapter 3), with only Russian being replaced with Spanish in Taiwan (see Chapter 6).

In 1901, the School merged with Beijing Normal University, established in 1898, and was renamed Peking University in 1912 (He, 2001). The early schools of foreign languages were often small in scale and aimed at training diplomats and translators for the Chinese government. Later on, more schools were set up, where foreign languages were taught and assessed, signifying the beginning of foreign language testing in China. Most importantly, the Modern examination period in China witnessed the growing role of English in Chinese society. The increased learning and assessing of English are evidenced by: (1) the Intellectual Revolution where the use of English was a vehicle for exploring Western philosophy and opportunities for study abroad (1911–1923); (2) the use of English was a vehicle for diplomatic, military and intellectual interaction with the West. At the same time, however, English met with resistance from nationalistic scholars and politicians fearing unwanted transfer of culture (1924–1949) (see Adamson, 2004 for details). Although facility in English has since been used for seeking high official positions in China, the status of English (in fact, the status of foreign languages) has been decided by its high or low status since the Ancient period (Ross, 1993), depending on the perceived threat posed by and/or benefits offered by the English language in the political, economic and social systems of China, which has varied during different periods in Chinese history.

The Current Examination Period

As mentioned earlier, the Current examination period started with the establishment of the People's Republic of China (PRC) in 1949. The founding of the PRC marked the end of more than two decades of civil strife between the Chinese Communist Party (CCP 「中国共产党」) and the Chinese Nationalist Party「中国国民党」and the end of the 8-year Japanese occupation of China (1937–1945). With rebuilding the country and its economic infrastructure as its immediate task, China then was also faced with having to find its place in the international arena (Gray, 1991, p. 253). The Current examination period co-existed and interacted with the three major significant historical events below (see Lam, 2005 for details).

1   Soviet influence in the early years of the PRC. This influence was signified by the Treaty of Friendship, Alliances and Mutual Assistance signed on 14 February, 1950 (Lam, 2005) and was followed by the teaching and learning of Russian in schools and universities. However, Russian quickly lost its educational position towards the late 1950s when the relations between China and the Soviet Union turned sour. English thus started to gain higher status as Russian declined. The early 1960s in China was a period of "leadership discussion and economical recovery" (Wang, 1995, p. 24). The national entrance examinations to higher education—the National Unified Enrolment Examinations (NUEE)—were introduced in the 1950s, although these tests appear to have been developed and implemented somewhat haphazardly (Cheng & Qi, 2006; Li, 1990). However, the NUEE still exists (see Chapter 3) and is as powerful as ever and continues to have a tremendous impact on Chinese society (see Chapter 16).

2   The Cultural Revolution (also known as the Great Proletarian Cultural Revolution). The Cultural Revolution was a struggle for power within the Communist Party of China that was manifested in the form of widespread, large-scale social, political, and economic chaos in China, which lasted for about 10 years from 1966–1976. Education was one of the focal points of the Cultural Revolution. Consequently, education at all levels was disrupted and admission to higher education was halted, as were testing and examinations for admission purposes. The teaching of English (and of other foreign languages) virtually ground to a halt, as such activities were treated as some of the "targets of capitalism and imperialism" (Adamson, 2004, p. 127).

3   Deng Xiaoping's Open Door Policy. Deng Xiaoping,[4] the leader of the Chinese Communist Party from 1977 to the 1990s, announced the Policy of Four Modernizations in 1978. This modernization movement soon evolved into the Reform and Opening Policy (Dillion, 1998, p. 109). Around the late 1970s, China re-established the balance between America and the Soviet Union internationally, while domestically China was also "regaining its momentum for educational and economical development after the Cultural Revolution" (Lam, 2005, p. 5). The 1980s saw rapid development in many areas, including English language education. University enrolment resumed in 1977 and the National Unified Enrolment Examinations (NUEE) were reintroduced. This marked the start of China's move towards an international era with the rapid development of its English language education and assessment in particular. The National Matriculation English Test was introduced in 1985, the College English Test in 1987, and the Graduate School Entrance English Examination in 1989. In 1987, the National Education Examinations Authority (NEEA) under the supervision of the Ministry of Education of the People's Republic of China was established—a major step towards official and unified testing and examinations in China (see Chapter 3). On the other hand, without the interruption of the Cultural Revolution in mainland China, the Hong Kong Examinations and Assessment Authority (known as the Hong Kong Examinations Authority or HKEA prior to July 2002) was set up by the Hong Kong Government[5] in 1977. The authority, as a statutory body of the Hong Kong Government, conducts public examinations in Hong Kong (see Chapter 5). In addition, the Language Training and Testing Center, conducting both language training and testing, was also established much earlier in the 1950s in Taiwan[6] (see Chapter 6). Chapters 5 and 6 offer a historical view of English language assessment development, which took a different path compared with the situation in mainland China.

To sum up, as mentioned earlier, the status of foreign languages including English, as well as its assessment, has behaved like a pendulum, swinging according to the political, social and economical winds of change blowing through China at different times. As a result of the economic reforms in China in the late 1970s and the Open Door Policy of China to the outside world, rapid and drastic changes have been brought about in China over the past 30 years. During the same period, there has also been a tremendous boom in foreign language education in China. Foreign language education, especially English language education, has become more and more important for Chinese learners at all levels of education. Since the late 1970s, and early 1980s, foreign experts have been visiting and teaching in China and increasing numbers of students and scholars have been sent abroad (see Lam, 2005). Since the mid-1990s, English has been taught from Grade 3 in primary education. English, as one of the three core subjects together with mathematics and Chinese, is tested for students to enter junior and senior high school. English is a compulsory subject in the national university entrance examinations for all types of universities and colleges. English is also an obligatory subject for all majors in Chinese universities and colleges. Non-English majors are required to take the college English course for at least 2 years. To obtain a bachelor's degree in Chinese universities, these students often need to pass the College English Test—an English language proficiency test (see Chapter 4). English is an examination subject for all students who wish to pursue a graduate degree in China. Apart from English as an academic requirement, English skills are tested for all those seeking promotion in governmental, educational, scientific research, medical, financial, business and other government-supported institutions (He, 2001). Therefore, it is no exaggeration to say that China has the largest English-learning population in the world. In reality, being successful in the various English tests and examinations is one of the keys to success in life for many people in China, and also for many Chinese who wish to pursue their undergraduate and graduate education in English-speaking countries, including the possibility of emigration (see Cheng, 2008; Chapter 8).

Structure of the Book

This book, consisting of four major sections and one concluding chapter, provides an overall framework and context within which to explore and examine the English Language Assessment situation in relation to the Chinese Learner. The theoretical and conceptual framework used in this book is based on Bachman and Palmer's revised framework of *Assessment Use Argument* (Bachman & Palmer, in press; see also Bachman, 2005, 2007). As can be seen from the early part of this chapter (and many chapters of this book), large-scale testing—the traditional and current practices in China—comes with significant consequences for its stakeholders. There is a complex set of relationships, intended and unintended, positive and negative, between testing, teaching and learning. In the field of language testing, however, "the extensive research on validity and validation has tended to ignore test use, on the one hand, while discussions of test use and consequences have tended to ignore validity, on the other" (Bachman, 2005, p. 7). This book, then, attempts to bridge the gap between test validity and test consequences so we can better justify the use of English language assessment to its stakeholders.

Part One sets the scene and provides the background and context within which English Language Assessment is discussed in this book. This section consists of two chapters. Chapter 1 has introduced the broad Chinese context, delineated the concept of the Chinese Learner, offered a brief history of English language education and assessment in China, and provided a roadmap for the readers of this book. Chapter 2 documents the history of the imperial examinations system in ancient China, describes its testing format(s), testing contents/categories, test administration, test candidates and issues of fairness, and discusses the impact of the imperial examinations on Chinese society, on the current examination systems in China, and beyond.

Part Two consists of four chapters, which discuss test validity and validation from the points of view of test designers. Chapter 3 provides a brief introduction to the National Education Examinations Authority under the supervision of the Ministry of Education of the People's Republic of China in relation to its function, its organizational structure, and the way it conducts its examinations. It also describes the main English tests in its charge, such as the National Matriculation English Test and the Public English Test System. Chapter 4 introduces the National College English Testing Committee appointed by the Higher Education Department of the Ministry of Education, the People's Republic of China, and describes the efforts made to provide validation evidence for the College English Test—a national standardized English language test for college and university students in China. Chapter 5 describes the work of the Hong Kong Examinations and Assessment Authority with an emphasis on the developments of English language assessments in the two public examinations—the Hong Kong Certificate of Education Examination and the Hong Kong Advanced Level Examination. Chapter 6 presents the past, present, and future activities of the Language Training and Testing Center (LTTC) in Taiwan, the Republic of China.

Parts Three and Four consist of 12 chapters, which discuss test use and consequences from the points of view of test-users. Chapters 7–12 address test use and consequences by investigating aspects of test quality, such as validity, reliability, and fairness using theoretical and conceptual frameworks. The tests critiqued in these chapters are international tests such as the Test of English as a Foreign Language (TOEFL) (Chapter 7), the International English Language Testing System (IELTS) (Chapter 8), and the Michigan English Language Assessment Battery (MELAB) (Chapter 9); as well as tests issued only to Chinese test-takers, i.e. the Public English Testing System (Chapter 10), the Graduate School Entrance English Examination (Chapter 11), and the General English Proficiency Test (Chapter 12).

Chapters 13–17 present empirical studies conducted within the assessment contexts of English language teaching and learning in relation to Chinese test-takers. Chapter 13 presents a study of the test-driven and culture-specific oral performance by Chinese test-takers on the Cambridge ESOL FCE Speaking Test. Chapters 14 and 15 present studies of the College English Test. Chapter 14 investigates the relationship between Chinese students' perceptions of the classroom assessment environment and their goal orientations, and Chapter 15 investigates the relationship between students' attitudes toward the CET and their CET performance.

Chapters 16 and 17 present studies conducted within the context of the National Matriculation English Test. Chapter 16 presents a study of the functions of the proofreading sub-test of the National Matriculation English Test, and Chapter 17 presents a validation study of the Computerized Oral English Test of the National Matriculation English Test. Chapter 18 presents the preliminary findings of a 2-year longitudinal study of the implementation of the new assessment scheme in 10 Hong Kong secondary schools, which explores some of the issues and problems involved in moving English language teachers and their school communities from a traditional norm-referenced system to a standards-based assessment system.

Taken altogether, the tests and assessment practices discussed in this book are at the society-, university- and school-levels. Society-level tests are those open to all levels of test-takers, whereas the university- and school-level tests are open to students at that

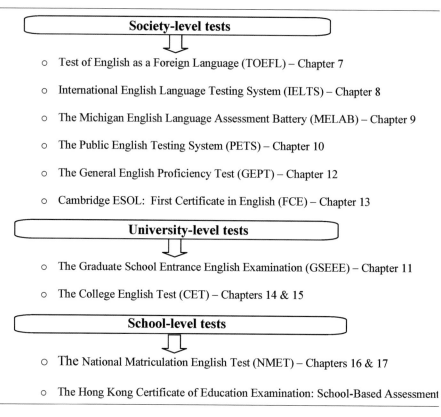

Figure 1.1 Overview of the Tests in this Book

level only. Figure 1.1 illustrates the tests investigated in this book which serves as a visual overview of the book.

The concluding chapter (Chapter 19) draws on the main points from the discussions in each of the chapters in addressing the gap between test validity and validation, and test use and the consequences. This includes a discussion of the extensive use of large-scale assessment/testing on the Chinese Learner in and beyond China and points towards future directions for English language assessment in China.

Notes

1. Chinese characters「汉字」are used to ensure the accuracy of the terms throughout the book. Both simplified and traditional Chinese characters are used depending on the context of the discussion in each chapter and the kind of written system that the contributors are familiar with. Simplified Chinese characters are used in mainland China, whereas traditional Chinese characters are used in Hong Kong and Taiwan. Chinese characters are also used in the format of「汉字」throughout the book.
2. The official system of the phonetic symbol (*Hanyu Pinyin*) of the Chinese characters in China is given in italics throughout the book.
3. *Chinese mainland* and *mainland China* are both used by the contributors of this book to refer to the mainland part of the People's Republic of China.

4. Deng Xiaoping [邓小平] was a prominent Chinese politician, pragmatist and reformer, as well as the late leader of the Chinese Communist Party (CCP). He developed *Socialism with Chinese characteristics* and Chinese economic reform and opened China to the global market.
5. Hong Kong, located on China's south coast, was a dependent territory of the UK from 1842 until the transfer of its sovereignty to the People's Republic of China in 1997. Hong Kong is now a Special Administration Region (SAR) of the People's Republic of China.
6. Following the defeat of the Chinese Nationalist Party by the Chinese Communist Party and the founding of the People's Republic of China in 1949, the Nationalist Party moved to Taiwan—located off the south-eastern coast of mainland China. In 1971, during the Cultural Revolution, the People's Republic of China replaced Taiwan as the official representative of China in the United Nations.

References

Adamson, B. (2004). *China's English*. Hong Kong, China: Hong Kong University Press.

Arnove, R. F., Altback, P. G. & Kelly, G. P. (Eds.). (1992). *Emergent issues in education: Comparative perspectives*. Albany, NY: State University of New York Press.

Bachman, L. F. & Palmer, A. S. (in press). *Language Assessment in the Real World*. Oxford: Oxford University Press.

Bachman, L. F. (2005). Building and supporting a case for test use. *Language Assessment Quarterly: An International Journal, 2*, 1–34.

Bachman, L. F. (2007). Language assessment: Opportunities and challenges. Paper presented at the meeting of the American Association of Applied Linguistics (AAAL), Costa Mesa, CA.

Bray, M. & Steward, L. (Eds.). (1998). *Examination systems in small states: Comparative perspectives on policies, models and operations*. London: Commonwealth Secretariat.

Cheng, L. (2008). The key to success: English language testing in China. *Language Testing, 25*, 15–38.

Cheng, L. & Qi, L. (2006). Description and examination of the National Matriculation English Test in China. *Language Assessment Quarterly: An International Journal, 3*, 53–70.

Coverdale-Jones, T. (2006). Afterword: The Chinese learner in perspective. *Language Culture Curriculum, 19*(1), 148–153.

Dillion, M. (Ed.). (1998). *China: A cultural and historical dictionary*. Richmond, Surrey: Curzon Press.

Eckstein, M. A. & Noah, H. J. (Eds.). (1992). *Examinations: Comparative and international studies*. Oxford: Pergamon Press.

Gray, J. (1991). Liberation. In B. Hook & D. Twitchett (Eds.). *The Cambridge encyclopedia of China* (2nd ed., pp. 253–266). Cambridge: Cambridge University Press.

He, Q. (2001). English language education in China. In S. J. Baker (Ed.), *Language policy: Lessons from global models*. Monterey, CA: Monterey Institute of International Studies, 225–231.

Hu, C. T. (1984). The historical background: Examinations and controls in pre-modern China. *Comparative Education, 20*, 7–26.

Ke, F. (1986). *History of foreign language education in China*. Shanghai, China: Shanghai Foreign Language Education Press

Lai, C. T. (1970). *A scholar in imperial China*. Hong Kong, China: Kelly & Walsh.

Lam, S. L. A. (2005). *Language education in China*. Hong Kong, China: Hong Kong University Press.

Li, X. J. (1990) How powerful can a language test be? The MET in China. *Journal of Multilingual and Multicultural Development, 11*, 393–404.

Rastall, P. (2004). Introduction: The Chinese learner in higher education—Transition and quality issues. *Language Culture Curriculum, 19*(1), 1–4.

Ross, H. A. (1993). China learns English: Language teaching and social change in the People's Republic of China. New Haven: Yale University Press.

Spolsky, B. (1995). *Measured words.* Oxford: Oxford University Press.

Wang, J. C. F. (1995). *Contemporary Chinese politics: An introduction.* Englewood Cliffs, NJ: Prentice Hall.

Watkins, D. & Biggs, J. (Eds.) (2001). *Teaching the Chinese Learner: Cultural, Psychological and Pedagogical Perspectives.* Hong Kong: Comparative Education Research Centre, The University of Hong Kong.

Zhang, Y. Q. (2005). Appraisal of imperial examinations: Standard, field of vision and influence [科举评价: 标准、视野与影响]. *Higher Education,* 10, 81–84.

2   The History of Examinations
Why, How, What and Whom to Select?

Liying Cheng, Queen's University

In China, the history of examinations and the history of the imperial examination 「科举制度」 *are closely related and intertwine throughout history. A review of the imperial examinations informs us of the rationale for when to examine, where to examine, how to examine, what to examine, and who has been permitted to take examinations throughout Chinese history. It is not an exaggeration to say that the imperial examinations have had a tremendous impact on essential aspects of Chinese society. The influence of the imperial examinations on the educational system in China and on the current examination system in particular can still be felt, as the rest of the chapters of this book clearly illustrate. Therefore, it is essential to introduce the history of the examinations (the imperial examinations in particular) so that readers can situate current assessment practices for the Chinese Learner and understand the issues raised in this book within a broader historical, social, and educational setting in Chinese society. This chapter, then, will first briefly document the history of examinations, focusing on the imperial examinations in particular. It will then discuss testing formats, testing contents and categories, test administration, and the issue of fairness related to the imperial examinations as well as provide information on test candidates. The last part of the chapter will discuss the impact of the imperial examinations on Chinese society, on the current examination systems in China, and beyond.*

History of Examinations in China

As indicated in Chapter 1, China represents a long-standing civilization comprising successive states and cultures dating back more than 4,000 years. China is not only the source of some of the world's great inventions, including paper, the compass, gunpowder, and printing: examinations are also one of the inventions of the Chinese people (Liu, Tian, Zhang, & Zheng, 2002). Examinations originated when there was a need to select the best and most capable individuals to run the country. The concept of a country ruled by men of ability and virtue was an outgrowth of Confucian philosophy. Confucius (孔夫子; *Kǒng Fūzǐ*; 551–479BC) was an esteemed Chinese thinker and social philosopher. His philosophy emphasized personal and governmental morality, correctness of social relationships, justice, and sincerity. These Confucian values gained prominence in China over other doctrines, such as Legalism (法家) or Taoism (道家) during the Han Dynasty (206BC–AD220). Confucius' thoughts have been developed into a system of philosophy known as *Confucianism* (儒家). His teachings are known primarily through the *Analects of Confucius* (論語), which were compiled many years after his death. His teachings and philosophy have deeply influenced Chinese, Japanese, Korean, and Vietnamese thought and life. The imperial examination system was an attempt to recruit men on the basis of merit rather than on the basis of family or political connection. Because success in the examination system was the basis of social status and because education was the key to this success, education was highly regarded in traditional China. This is still the case in modern China, as the readers will learn from the chapters in this book.

The history of testing and examination in China can be traced back to the imperial period of the Han Dynasty (206BC–AD220) nearly 2,000 years ago. The imperial examinations (科舉: *kējǔ*) in dynastic China were the first of their kind used to select the highest officials of the country based on talent. Therefore, they are sometimes documented as civil service examinations in Chinese history (Jin, 1990). The contents and categories of the examinations changed over time. The "6 Arts"—music, archery, horsemanship, writing, arithmetic, and ceremonial rites—were tested in 1100BC. The "5 Studies"—civil law, military law, agriculture, taxation, and geography—were tested in 202BC–AD200. By the seventh century AD, the examinations had become a national system by which candidates' ability to remember and interpret Confucian classics was measured (see Higgins & Sun, 2002; H. C. Zhang, 1988).

The testing and examination history in China can be classified into the Ancient, Modern, and Current periods—"three distinct, yet overlapping periods" (Liu et al., 2002, p. 9; Y. Q. Zhang, 2005). The ancient period is the longest one, stretching from the origins of the examinations around 206BC until when the imperial examinations were abolished in 1905 by the Empress Dowager Cixi (慈禧太后) of Qing Dynasty—the last dynasty in China. Because the imperial examination system has the longest history and the greatest influence on the Chinese society, this system is the focus of the discussion of this chapter, and the Modern and Current periods will only be briefly described in the following few paragraphs.

The Modern period started towards the end of Qing Dynasty in 1862—with the influence of Western education and sciences and the establishment of the Metropolitan Institute of Foreign Languages (京师同文馆: *Jing Shi Tong Wen Guan*) until the founding of the People's Republic of China (PRC) in 1949. This period is characterized by the establishment of a series of institutes cultivating talent in foreign languages, the military, technology, and foreign affairs, resulting in modernized methods of examinations. For example, after the fall of the Qing Dynasty in 1911, Dr Sun Yat-sen (孫中山), the leader of the newly-risen Republic of China, developed procedures for the new political system through an institution called the Examination Yuan (考試院; *Kǎoshì Yuàn*). However, this was quickly suspended due to the turmoil in China between the two world wars. During this chaotic period in Chinese history and until the founding of the People's Republic of China (PRC) in 1949, two developments were especially important: the development of achievement testing for various institutes, and the development of proficiency testing for selecting candidates for overseas studies in the West (Y. Q. Zhang, 2002).

The Current examination period is from 1949 until present day, within the context of which the chapters in this book document tests and examinations and their impact on the Chinese Learner today. The Current examination system has developed alongside the development of modern education in China. This period is signified by the development of: (1) national matriculation examinations; (2) achievement testing at various educational/professional levels; (3) a self-taught higher education examination system; (4) Civil Service qualifying examinations; and (5) certificate tests (see Chapter 3 for details). Almost all of these tests are presented and discussed later in this book.

Origins of the Imperial Examinations

As DuBois (1970) has stated, the "[o]rigins of the [examination] system go back to 2200 BC when the Chinese emperor examined his officials every third year to determine their fitness for continuing in office. After three examinations, officials were either promoted or dismissed" (p. 3) (see also Cressey, 1929; Tian, 2002; Wang, 2003). This account came from the description from the classic Chinese history text, the Shi Ji (史记), which was written around 100BC and which mentioned examinations every 3 years under the rule of Shun (舜, 2250BC). However, in the west, the figure of Shun is considered to be mythical without much historical evidence (Bowman, 1989; Waltham, 1971). Most contemporary scholars of ancient China also agree on a later dating of the imperial examinations, i.e., in the early Han dynasty (206BC–AD220) (Liu et al., 2002; Wang, 2003). The birth of the examinations coincided with the abolishment of the governing system by blood (aristocracy), and with the need for more talented men to help the emperor to govern the vast centralized country at that time.

The term *examination* in Chinese consists of two words: Kao (考) and Shi (试), which were first found in a classic work in the dynasty of West Han (206BC–AD24). Although the two words eventually combined to mean examinations, there are two levels of meaning. The first level refers to the evaluation (and selection) of officials. The second level of meaning focuses on the testing of knowledge and ability. This is the purpose served by the majority of tests and examinations, the results of which are still used for various selection purposes in China today (see Tian, 2002).

As mentioned above, the origins of the imperial examination system can be traced back to the imperial period of the Han Dynasty. An edict of Emperor Gao Zu (高祖) in 196BC ordered, for the first time, that feudal princes, powerful ministers, and other officials recommend people of reputation and intelligence from their districts to come to the capital as candidates for official positions (Franke, 1960). Official recommendation (including evaluation) as a way of entering the civil service was used, which "may be considered the forerunner of the examination system" (Pirazzoli-t'Serstevens, 1982, p. 33). In 124BC, the Han Dynasty took another step in the development of the imperial examination system. A number of outstanding young men were selected from all provinces of the empire to be educated by scholarly officials. A year later, these students were examined and given official positions according to their qualifications (Franke, 1960). The practice led to the development of an imperial college called the Tai Xue (太学). The imperial examinations thus engendered a national school system down to the prefectural level during the Song Dynasty (AD960–1279), and further to districts and counties during the Ming Dynasty (1368–1644) and the Qing Dynasty (1644–1912) (Elman, 1989).

The imperial examinations in dynastic China were the first of their kind used to select the highest officials in the country. These examinations determined positions in the civil service based on merit and education, which promoted upward mobility among the population for centuries. Therefore, the term "civil service examinations" is also sometimes used to refer to the imperial examination system in China. These examinations are regarded by many historians as the first standardized tests based on merit (Hu, 1984; Lai, 1970) and constitute the largest contribution that ancient China made to the testing movement (Higgins & Sun, 2002).

Content, Format, Candidature, Administration, and Fairness of the Imperial Examinations

The Contents and Categories of the Examinations

As mentioned earlier, the contents and categories of the imperial examination system changed over time (Higgins & Sun, 2002). For instance, in the Tang Dynasty (618–906), the examinations in different categories (科: *Ke*) were held in the capital. The six most important categories in the examinations were: (1) "cultivated talent" (秀才: *Xiou Cai*) also known as Scholar;[1] (2) "presented scholars" (进士: *Jin Shi*); (3) the Confucian classics (明经: *Ming Jin*); (4) law (明法: *Ming Fa*); (5) calligraphy (and literacy) (明书: *Ming Shu*); and (6) mathematics (明算: *Ming Suan*) (Wang, 2003). There were other minor categories as well. A great majority of candidates chose the Confucian classics (Franke, 1960). In the Song Dynasty (960–1279), the five categories of the examinations were letters (进士: *Jin Shi*), law, history, rituals, and classics (Kracke, 1953; Wang, 2003). A great majority of examination candidates chose the Jin Shi (进士) examination. In the Jin Shi examination, Confucian classics such as the Four Books and Five Classics (四书五经) were basic examination materials. The Four Books were: *The Great Learning* (大学), *The Doctrine of the Mean* (中庸), *The Analects* (论语), and *The Mencius* (孟子). The Five Classics were: *Classic of Changes* (易经), *Classic of Poetry* (诗经), *Classic of Rites* (礼记), *Classic of History* (书经), and *Spring and Autumn Annals* (春秋).

Evolving Testing Formats

The testing formats also varied over the dynasties, and there were five major testing formats in the Tang Dynasty. Oral testing was one of the first methods used that focused on questions and answers. The second and third methods were used when one page of a book was chosen and several lines were omitted: candidates were then required to fill in the missing lines to demonstrate knowledge about the test passages from memory (帖: *Tie*) as well as to summarize the passages (墨义: *Me yi*)—a method similar to cloze testing. Due to the format requiring memorization (帖: *Tie*), being able to recite the work by memory became very important for the candidates. In addition to the above test methods, elucidations of the Confucian classics were the fourth and fifth methods used in the *Jin Shi* examination, which further required candidates to compose a piece of poetry, a poetic description (赋: *Fu*), as well as a dissertation (则: *Ce*) on contemporary affairs and a free discussion (论: *Lun*) of historical and political topics. The increasing number of candidates taking the *Jin Shi* examination led to a gradual eclipse of the other fields. By the Ming Dynasty, the examination systems mostly concentrated on the orthodox interpretation of the Confucian classics (Y. Q. Zhang, 2005, 2006).

A number of important historical factors influenced the imperial examination system. One important step was the transfer of authority over the imperial examinations from the Board of Civil Appointments (吏部; *Lìbù*) to the Board of Rites (禮部; *Lǐbù*). The Board of Civil Appointments dealt with the personnel administration of all civil officials—including evaluation, promotion, and dismissal. The Board of Rites was responsible for all matters concerning protocol at court, which included not just the periodic worshiping of ancestors and various gods by the Emperor to ensure the smooth running of the empire, but also looking after the welfare of visiting ambassadors from tributary nations. The Chinese concept of courtesy (*lǐ*, 禮), as taught by Confucius, was considered an integral part of education. An intellectual was said to know of books and courtesy (rites) (知書達禮). Thus, the Board of Rites's other function was to oversee the nationwide civil examination system for entrance to the bureaucracy.

Later on, the powers of selection and appointment to the civil service were separated. Therefore, the civil service examination system became primarily an institution to enable the emperor and the central government to limit the political power of the hereditary aristocracy in the provinces and the capital. Another factor affecting the imperial examinations was the invention of printing (Chow, 1996; Miyazaki, 1976). In the tenth and eleventh centuries, the invention of printing vastly increased the number of potential candidates for the imperial examinations. One result of this development was to cause the government to make the examinations more difficult and more formal. Candidates aspiring to civil office had to spend many years climbing the social ladder. The other result was the strictly classical content of the questions to be answered in the examinations: candidates' answers had to avoid judgment and originality, which deviated from the standard formula they were expected to produce. The candidates had to concentrate on the narrow scholarship required for success in the imperial examination system.

By the Ming Dynasty (AD1368–1644), the examinations had become extremely elaborate. The initial examinations which required candidates to write poems, articles on state affairs, and essays on the Confucian classics and history became a degenerated format called Ba Gu (eight-legged essays) (八股), invented in 1487. Essays were required to be written in a certain fixed style with a fixed word count and with eight paragraphs, while imitating the tone of the Confucian classics. Ba Gu was viewed as one of the most limited yet demanding forms of writing that channeled the intellectual abilities into a literacy contest of regurgitation and writing according to strictly conventional formats (Yan & Chow, 2002).

Test Candidates

According to historical records, there were several categories of candidates who were not allowed to take part in the examinations at different times in Chinese history. These included merchants, prostitutes/entertainers (the "mean/low" category), people who were in mourning, criminals, clerks, and monks/priests (Lu, 2005).[2] A further example of the social discrimination that existed in the imperial examinations is that women were never allowed to take the examinations (Feng, 1994). In most of the dynasties since the Tang Dynasty, there were also strict regulations on the registered residence (戶籍) requirement, i.e. candidates were only allowed to take the examinations at their place of residence.

For further examples, in the Tang Dynasty, there were two main groups of test candidates. They were graduates (生徒: *Sheng Tu*) who were recommended to take the test by their teachers, and another group of test candidates who were not part of the any institute, i.e., those who were self-taught (乡贡: *Xeng Gong*) (see Sun, 2000; Wang, 2003). In the Yuan Dynasty (蒙古帝國: *Mongolian Empire*), two versions of the imperial examinations were offered: one version was given to the Mongolian (蒙古人) and the Se Mu (色目人) candidates, and the other version was given to the Han (漢人) and the Nan (南人) candidates. The Se Mu (色目人) were the people in the western part of China in the Yuan Dynasty. In the social hierarchy of the Yuan Dynasty, the Se Mu were lower than the Mongolians (蒙古人) (who ruled the dynasty), but above the Han (漢人) and the Nan peoples (南人). The two versions of the examinations were different in content, in the number of the examination questions, and in their level of difficulty. The version for the Han and the Nan candidates was more demanding; however, even when they were successful in the examinations, their official ranks would be one level lower to ensure the Mongolian and the Se Mu candidates were not disadvantaged.

The quota which controlled the ratio of successful versus unsuccessful candidates in different geographic areas and among different ethic groups varied from dynasty to dynasty and from emperor to emperor. A similar system reflecting social discrimination is still in existence in the national matriculation examinations for entrance into a tertiary education in present-day China, where candidates in certain provinces need much higher average scores on the national matriculation examinations compared with those of candidates in other provinces to gain entrance to the same universities.

The number of *presented scholars* (Jin Shi) ranged from a low of several dozen in the Tang Dynasty to a high of 300 annually in late imperial China. For instance, from 1020 to 1057, in the Song Dynasty, there were 8,509 *presented scholars* (Jin Shi) in total with an average of nearly 224 annually (Kracke, 1953). These people, who were considered to be sufficiently qualified, hoped to achieve a distinguished career in government service. The competition in the imperial examinations was extremely intense, and according to Elman's description (1991), about 2 million candidates attended the lowest district examination in 1850, which was held twice every 3 years. Five percent of the 2 million passed the provincial examination; of these, only 300 passed the metropolitan examination. The odds of success at any level of selection were 1 in 6,000 (see also Elman, 2000).

Test Administration and Grading Practices

The book *China's Examination Hell* (Miyazaki, 1976) described in detail the testing administration and the grading practices of the imperial examination system. There were three main levels of examinations: the lowest preliminary examinations in the district (解试: *Xie shi*), the second examination (乡试: *Xiang shi*) in the provincial capital, and the third (会试: *Hui shi*) in the capital of the empire with a final re-examination in the imperial palace (殿试).

Anonymity in testing and grading were demanded to guarantee an equal access to success (Cressey, 1929; Feng, 1994). The names on the examination answer sheets were covered and only the seat number was visible during grading. Raters (often called *readers* in Chinese), mostly magistrates, were required to work day and night judging the papers. Papers were graded and a number of candidates were eliminated after each session. On the day before the qualifying examination, the provincial director of education entered the examination compound and shut himself off completely from the outside world—a practice still used today for those test designers[3] who design the National Matriculation Examination in China.

Early in the morning of the day of the qualifying examination, there was a great throng of people including the candidates, the magistrates of each district, the staff of the district schools, and licentiates. When the gates opened, the candidates, grouped by district, streamed through and lined up at the second gate, where the prefectural clerks searched them looking for reference books, notes, or money, with which they might bribe a clerk. After the inspection, the candidates were allowed though the doors into the examination room. The candidates' identities were authenticated by the guarantors, and then the candidates received their examination papers.

The provincial director of education inspected papers after they had been collected, at the end of each session. His private secretaries helped him select papers with answers that pleased him in style and content. Knowing this was the case, the candidates studied the writings of the director before they took the examination, and composed answers conforming to his views. After grading was completed, the results were announced by seat numbers and the candidates' papers from earlier district and prefectural examinations were used to verify the calligraphy (handwriting). Methods for dealing with such practical problems as cheating and plagiarism were developed. For example, in all three sessions of the qualifying examination, the candidate's name was kept secret, and only his seat number was used to identify him and his answers. The successful candidates whose number was fixed for each district were called Sheng Yuan (生员), or, more colloquially, cultivated talent (秀才: *Xiou Cai*). Those who were successful in the examination at the local level went on to the provincial capital for more extensive examinations.

The qualifying examinations (乡试: *Xiang shi*) were held every 3 years in the provincial capitals under the supervision of one chief examiner and one deputy examiner delegated from the central government. Since the two examiners sent by the central government could not attend to everything, local officials with outstanding scholarship were appointed by the governor to serve as associate examiners, assisting officials, and administrators. There were three portions in the provincial examination and candidates spent days and nights answering papers in the confined space of examination cells.

Again, regulations to prevent cheating and plagiarism were developed and executed. All papers were checked thoroughly. Papers with marks of any sort or which included different inks, missing papers, and incomplete papers were considered in violation of the formal regulations and those candidates were barred from future examinations. The candidates' answers were written in black ink and absolutely no other color was permitted. When the provincial examination had been completed, the black version of the testing papers was first sent to the clerks for copying in yellow ink. This ensured the security of the testing papers and avoided test-irrelevant variance in handwriting. Copyists who copied papers and proofreaders who checked the copies wrote their names on the papers to make clear their roles. Then the copies of the testing papers passed through the hands of the associate examiners who had to carry out the grading in specific, designated places. When they wrote "mediocre" or "without merit", the paper failed. If they wrote "recommended", the paper was delivered to the chief and deputy examiners, who generally only read recommended papers.

As opposed to grading procedures in the previous examinations, the papers for all three sessions in the provincial examination were judged together. When the grading was completed, the results of the examinations in three sessions were averaged and the final decisions were reached. Not knowing the names of the candidates, the examiners used the seat numbers to compile their lists. Then they met with the administrative officials and compared the copies of the testing papers with the original ones. If they matched, the examiners broke the seal and revealed the candidate's name. The successful candidates were called "recommended men" (举人: *Jiu Ren*)—"provincial graduates". After the provincial examination, those with the highest test scores went on to the national capital for a final round of examinations.

The next level after the provincial qualifying examinations was that of the metropolitan examinations (会试: *Hui Shi*), which were arranged every 3 years in the national capital of the Board of Rites under the direction of an examiner especially appointed by the emperor. The metropolitan examination followed the same procedures as those of the provincial examination. The examiners graded the papers, decided on the overall standing of the candidates, and listed them by seat number. Then, the appointed examiner, usually the Minister of Rites as the supervisor of the examination, compared the copies of the candidates' testing papers with their original ones with the assistance of administrative officials. Then the testing papers with the concealed names and personal information were delivered to the higher officials. Each examiner inspected a number of answers and assigned them preliminary grades. "This preliminary grading was extremely important because, even though the opinions of the examiners might differ, as a general rule they did not give grades that were too far apart" (Miyazaki, 1976, p. 80). Above the grade, the examiner wrote his name, clearly taking responsibility for his assessment. After all raters graded a paper, the results were totaled. From several hundred papers, the examiners selected the 10 best papers, ranked them, and presented them to the emperor for his personal decision. However, this process of selection could not be done in a completely fair manner, and this was the source of threat to reliability. In search of objective standards, raters shifted their attention from examining the content of the answers to focusing on writing style.

Immediately after the metropolitan examinations, the successful candidates were summoned to the imperial palace for the re-examination (which was also the final level of the examinations) (殿试: *Dian Shi*) under the personal supervision of the emperor. This palace examination was conducted by the emperor, but high court officials with outstanding literacy abilities were selected as raters. Before the examination, the raters prepared drafts of their questions and had them printed.

During the late Qing dynasty, in order to prevent disputes among examiners, red-ink copies of the 10 best papers were presented to the emperor by the chief examiner so that the emperor himself could rank them and make decisions. The emperor was absolutely free to do as he wished in selecting the best papers. When the emperor finished with the papers, the Minister of Rites verified the copies with the original ones. The best candidates were given the title of presented scholars (进士: *Jin Shi*)—metropolitan graduates, which has been translated as a "doctor" in the western educational system. The candidates entering the final selection were called "regularly submitted names"

(正奏名: Zheng Zou Ming). The three top candidates were called "Zhuang Yuan" (状元), "Bang Yan" (榜眼), and "Tan Hua" (探花).

Fairness Procedures

In ancient Chinese society, class-consciousness was strong and many people from the lower classes had little chance to reach public office, much less to gain a position in the official court. Therefore, the imperial examinations provided the only real opportunity for them to be selected as officials based on their intellectual achievement and talent rather than on birth. Several factors relating to fairness and objectivity were consequently built into the examination system. Impartiality in the civil service examinations was ensured by some important measures described below.

First, candidates' personal information on the written examination papers was covered, including their names and ages, so that the raters did not know whose paper they read. To prevent recognition of candidates' handwriting, all papers had to be transcribed by copyists and proofread by proofreaders. Only these copies were passed to the examiners. The names of the original writers (test-takers) were not disclosed until the raters had read and judged the papers. This regulation regarding the anonymity of test-takers was first introduced to the examinations in the capital and was later extended to the examinations at other levels. If examiners took a bribe or showed favoritism, they were punished most severely and faced the prospect of an immediate loss of their official rank (Cressey, 1929; Feng, 1994; Kracke, 1953; Miyazaki, 1976).

Second, the metropolitan examination candidates were re-examined at the court by the emperor himself. After the palace examination, the successful candidates would be grouped in precise order, according to their achievements. Therefore, the power of the Board of Rites and the Board of Civil Appointments was considerably reduced. "Although these measures could not entirely eliminate correction and favoritism, a high degree of impartiality did seem to have been achieved, subject to the emperor's power of review" (Miyazaki, 1976).

Third, the practice of "examination avoidance" (回避: *Hui Bi*) was implemented in the Qing Dynasty to prevent situations caused by a conflict of interest between the public and private concerns. No family was to have an unfair advantage in examination competition and family connections were not to play any obvious role. Examination avoidance laws, therefore, were designed to prevent office-holding families from abusing their supervisory responsibilities in the imperial examinations by exerting influence and helping their children and relatives towards examination qualifications (Kracke, 1953; Man-Cheong, 1998). The organization of the imperial civil service examination system effectively redesigned and restructured the complicated relationships between social status, state power, and cultural practice in imperial China.

The Impact of the Imperial Examinations

The imperial examinations lasted for about 1,300 years in Chinese history before they were abolished in 1905. The Chinese imperial examination system has had international influence throughout the world. These examinations influenced education systems not only in China, but also in many Asian countries, including Korea, Japan, and Vietnam. A model of the Chinese imperial examination system was adopted by the Goryeo Dynasty and the Joseon Dynasty for the Yangban class in Korea until Korea's annexation by Japan. Similarly, an imperial examination system was used in Vietnam from 1075 to 1919. Japan employed a model of the system in the Heian period; however, its influence was limited and it was replaced by the hereditary system in the Samurai era.

As early as the late sixteenth century, the imperial examination system started to receive attention and consideration in Western publications on China. It is believed that the Jesuits brought the examination system to Europe also around that time (Madaus, 1990). Spolsky (1995, p. 16) further discussed the application of "the Chinese principle" in England in the nineteenth century. The British government adopted a similar system of examinations for its civil service in 1855 (Higgins & Zheng, 2002). Afterwards, the system expanded to the French, German, and American governments (Higgins & Zheng, 2002; Teng, 1943). Miyazaki (1976) argued that "The case for Chinese influence upon the development of civil service examinations in Europe is strong" (p. 124).

However influential the imperial examination system may have been, its limitations were raised in the later period by Chinese critics themselves, who questioned whether the emphasis on writing and reading ability was relevant to the tasks of government civil servants. In particular, the rigid and conventional format of *Ba Gu* (the eight-legged essay) in late imperial China failed to select men who had imagination and creativity. In May 1904, the last examination was held. One year later, an imperial edict ordered the discontinuance of the civil service examination systems at all levels in 1905.

With the abolishment of the imperial examination system, there came the arrival and influence of western modern testing theory on examinations and testing practices in the Modern and Current examination periods in China. This influence has for the most part been reflected in the design of the examinations and tests used in China, as can be seen in many chapters of this book. The function and uses made of examinations and tests in modern-day China, however, still reflect the inheritance of the imperial examinations where examinations are heavily used for selection purpose and are accepted by the general public as a fair selection procedure.

The imperial examinations are not only the products of Chinese traditional culture, but are also one of the bases of Chinese traditional culture. The impact of such an examination system on Chinese society has been far-reaching, multifaceted, and long-standing. Such impact can be recognized from a number of perspectives below.

First, before the imperial examinations, selection and education were two separate systems. Many contemporary Chinese scholars believe that with the advent of the imperial examinations, the selection and education processes overlapped, thus promoting the development of the Chinese educational system (Sun, 2000). Such a belief in a system with dual functions is still evident in the current examination system. For example, the National Matriculation English Test (NMET) has always served as a selection measure for university entrance and at the same time has also tried to have a positive influence on the teaching and learning of English in Chinese schools: the latter was one of the purposes of the test intended by the test developers (see Cheng & Qi, 2006; Qi, 2005; see Chapter 16). The College English Test (CET) tried to resolve the function of the test as an achievement test to assess the requirements of the College English Syllabus while at the same time serve as a norm-referenced testing—"a criterion-related norm-referenced test" (see Chapter 4; Cheng, 2008; Zheng & Cheng, in press).

A second aspect of the impact of the imperial examination system can also be seen in current Chinese testing procedures. For example, the relative access to tertiary education for candidates taking the national matriculation examinations varies by geographic area (provinces) and by ethnic group. In addition, to ensure test security, test designers for each subject area of the national matriculation examinations are "locked" into a location unknown to the public for several weeks every year until after the actual examination in that subject area has been held; this is a procedure which started with the imperial examinations.

The other obvious impact of the imperial examination system is its influence on education in China. "The education by the school is the basis of the imperial examinations. Consequently, the imperial examinations functioned as a traffic wand" (Sun, 2000, p. 167). In this way, the examinations nowadays continue to serve as a magic wand (see Cheng & Qi, 2006, Chapters 4, 16)—with the NMET and the CET serving as a gateway to advancement. This phenomenon, however, is commonly accepted by Chinese society.

The long history of the imperial examinations has molded the tradition of Chinese people trusting in the value of the examinations and regarding them as a fair means to success in life. For example, the tradition originating with the imperial examinations of using examinations for selection purposes is still evident in the current education system in China. A student starts to take examinations as early as the age of 4 years, with the entrance test for kindergarten. Over the years in their primary education (K-Grade 6), secondary education (junior high Grades 7–9, senior high Grades 10–12) and university education (at the undergraduate and postgraduate levels), students take numerous examinations at the school, municipal, provincial, and national levels. Selection by examinations and success or failure have been interrelated and integrated into Chinese society. Examinations continue to enjoy a societal acceptance and recognition in China as a fair measurement for selection of the best talent into the country's social structure. Such fairness (often used to mean "justice" in China) via examination is the foundation upon which testing and examinations function in Chinese society.

Acknowledgment

The author would like to thank Xiaomei Song for her assistance in collecting useful materials in English and in conducting a preliminary review on the imperial examinations.

Notes

1. In the early Tang Dynasty, *cultivated talent* or *Scholar* (Xiou Cai秀才) is a regular examination. This category of the examination was later cancelled and "Scholar" is used to refer to the educated in a broader sense.
2. The rationale behind this decision was very complicated and cannot be explained within the scope of the chapter. For details, please refer to Lu (2005) and Feng (1994).
3. When this book was going through the final stage of editing, around May 2008, two of our contributors were "locked up" without public contact/access to work on the test design. They were released only after the actual 3-day examinations (June 6–9).

References

Bowman, M. (1989). Testing individual differences in Ancient China. *American Psychologist*, 44, 576–578.

Cheng, L. (2008). The key to success: English language testing in China. *Language Testing*, 25, 15–38.

Cheng, L. & Qi, L. (2006). Description and examination of the National Matriculation English Test in China. *Language Assessment Quarterly: An International Journal*, 3, 53–70.

Chow, K (1996). Writing for success: Printing, examinations, and intellectual change in Late Ming China. *Late Imperial China*, 17(1), 120–157.

Cressey, P. F. (1929). The influence of the literacy examination system on the development of Chinese civilization. *The American Journal of Sociology*, 35, 250–262.

DuBois, P. H. (1970). *The history of psychological testing*. Boston: Ally & Bacon.

Elman, B. (1989). Imperial politics and Confucian societies in late imperial China: The Hanlin and Donglin Academics. *Modern China*, 15, 379–418.

Elman, B. (1991). Political, social, and cultural reproduction via Civil Service Examinations in late Imperial China. *Journal of Asian Studies*, 50, 7–28.

Elman, B. A. (2000). *A cultural history of civil examinations in Late Imperial China*. Berkeley, CA: University of California Press.

Feng, Y. (1994). *From the Imperial Examination to the National College Entrance Examination: The dynamics of political centralism in China's educational enterprise.* Paper presented at the 1994 International Pre-Conference of the 19th Annual Meeting of the Association for the Study of Higher Education, Tucson, AZ, November.

Franke, W. (1960). *The reform and abolition of the traditional Chinese examination system.* Cambridge, MA: Harvard University Press.

Higgins, L. T. & Zheng, M. (2002). An introduction to Chinese psychology – Its historical roots until the present day. *Journal of Psychology*, 136, 225–39.

Higgins, L. & Sun, C. H. (2002). The development of psychological testing in China. *International Journal of Psychology*, 37, 246–254.

Hu, C. T. (1984). The historical background: Examinations and controls in pre-modern China. *Comparative Education*, 20, 7–26.

Jin, F. Z. (1990). A comprehensive discussion of China's ancient civil service system. *Social Sciences in China*, XI(2), 35–59.

Kracke, E. A. (1953). *Civil service in early Sung China, 960–1067.* Cambridge, MA: Harvard University Press.

Lai, C. T. (1970). *A scholar in imperial China.* Hong Kong: Kelly & Walsh.

Liu, H. F., Tian, J. R., Zhang, Y. Q. & Zheng, R. L. (2002). *The history of examination in China* [中国考试史]. Wu Han, Hubei, China: The Central China Normal University Press.

Lu, L. Z. (2005). The policy evolution and characteristics of the candidate qualifications of the imperial examinations. *Higher Education*, 12, 100–109.

Madaus, G. F. (1990). *Testing as a social technology.* The inaugural annual Boise lecture on education and public policy. Boston: Boston College.

Man-Cheong, I. D. (1998). Fair fraud and fraudulent fairness: The 1761 examination case. *Late Imperial China*, 18(2), 51–85.

Miyazaki, I. (1976). *China's examination hell: the civil service examinations of imperial China.* (C. Schirokauer, Trans.). New Haven, CT: Yale University Press.

Pirazzoli-t'Serstevens, M. (1982). *The Han civilization of China.* Oxford: Phaidon.

Qi, L. (2005). Stakeholders' conflicting aims undermine the washback function of a high-stakes Test. *Language Testing*, 22, 142– 173.

Spolsky, B. (1995). *Measured words.* Oxford. Oxford University Press.

Sun, P. Q. (Ed.) (2000). *The history of Education in China.* [中国教育史]. Shanghai, China: East China Normal University Press.

Teng, S. (1943). Chinese influence on the Western examination system: I. Introduction. *Harvard Journal of Asiatic Studies*, 7, 268–312.

Tian, J. R. (2002). The origin of examination in China. In H. F., Liu, J. R., Tian, Y. Q., Zhang & R. L., Zheng (Eds.), *The history of examination in China* [中国考试史] (pp. 3–40). Wu Han: The Central China Normal University Press.

Waltham, C. (1971). *Shu Ching: Book of history (A modernized edition of the translation of James Legge of the work of Ssu-ma Ch'ien).* Chicago: Henry Regnery.

Wang, J. J. (2003). *The history of education in China* [中国教育史]. Guangzhou, Guangdong, China: Guangzhou Higher Education Press.

Yan, P. & Chow, J. (2002). On the pedagogy of examinations in Hong Kong. *Teaching and Teacher Education*, 18, 139–149.

Zhang, H. C. (1988). Psychological measurement in China. *International Journal of Psychology*, 23, 101–177.

Zhang, Y. Q. (2002). History of examinations in the modern period. In H. F., Liu, J. R., Tian, Y. Q., Zhang & R. L., Zheng (Eds.), *The history of examination in China* [中国考试史] (pp. 191–312). Wu Han, Hubei, China: The Central China Normal University Press.

Zhang, Y. Q. (2006) On the Cultural Heritage of the Chinese Imperial Examination [论科举文化遗产]. *Journal of Xiamen University*, 2, 20–30.

Zhang, Y. Q. (2005). Appraisal of Imperial Examinations: Standard, Field of Vision and Influence [科举评价: 标准、视野与影响]. *Higher Education*, 10, 81–84.

Zheng, Y. & Cheng, L. (2008). College English Test (CET) in China. *Language Testing*, 25(3), 408–417.

Part II

Validity and Test Validation
Views from Test Designers

3 The National Education Examinations Authority and its English Language Tests

Qingsi Liu, The National Education Examinations Authority

The National Education Examinations Authority (NEEA) is an institution directly under the supervision of the Ministry of Education (MoE) of the People's Republic of China (PRC). Taking advantage of its unique centralized position, the NEEA administers almost all of the nationwide educational tests through the provincial examinations offices and the examinations offices in some of the key universities. The NEEA conducts four main types of tests: university entrance tests; self-taught higher education examination system tests; certificate tests; and overseas-entrusted tests. In each of these four types of tests, English language tests play a key role in accordance with the Chinese government's open-door policy and the urgent needs of Chinese society. The first part of this chapter provides a brief introduction to the NEEA, including its function, its organizational structure, and the way it conducts its examinations. The chapter then goes on to describe the main English tests for which the NEEA is responsible, such as the National Matriculation English Test (NMET) and the Public English Test System (PETS).

The National Education Examinations Authority (NEEA)

The NEEA was established in 1987. After merging in 1994 with the Office of the Self-Taught Higher Education Examinations, which was established in 1983, it was referred to as the National Education Examinations Authority, but with an additional title—the Office of the Self-Taught Higher Education Examinations. The NEEA is appointed by the MoE to exclusively oversee educational examinations and to exercise administrative authority.

Functions of the NEEA

The current NEEA's functions are to:

- participate in the drafting of policies and regulations related to examinations organized by the MoE
- carry out test construction, score analysis, and evaluation for the University Entrance Examinations (UEE)
- perform duties related to the Self-Taught Higher Education Examinations (STHEE) as directed by the relevant State Council and MoE regulations

- provide public testing services, including developing and administering certificate tests, and offering qualifications
- carry out test administration and supervision, including test paper production and distribution, test implementation, and scoring
- administer examinations entrusted by overseas examination organizations with authorization from the MoE
- carry out research in testing and personnel training, with the purpose of making the national testing profession more diversified in designing different tests and standardized in test administration (NEEA, 2006a).

Organizational Structure of the NEEA

The NEEA is usually reorganized every 4 years to meet the emerging requirements of the changing environment in China. In July 2006, the NEEA experienced its fourth re-organization, which resulted in changes to the responsibilities of the four vice presidents and two assistant presidents and the emergence of a new department. Different from what it was 17 years ago (in 1989), in 2006 the NEEA's three test development departments became responsible to the same vice president. The Department of Evaluation and Assessment was newly formed to meet the needs of the NEEA's strategic transfer from an examination authority to an organization conducting both examinations and assessments. Figure 3.1 shows the organizational structure of the NEEA.

Financing of the NEEA

As an institution of the MoE, the NEEA has always committed itself to using its own income to meet its expenditure, since its foundation in 1987. In 1996, the NEEA achieved that goal and established a solid foundation for an efficient testing process. As a non-profit institution, the NEEA collects modest examination fees from the candidates with the approval of the Ministry of Finance and the Commission of Development and Reform of China. The examination fee from most of the programs is tax-free and can only be used to cover the cost of the NEEA's developments and the wages of its staff under the supervision of the Department of Finance of the MoE.

Position of the NEEA within the MoE

According to The Education Law of the People's Republic of China, "the State practices the system of national education examinations. The national education examinations are expected to be defined in terms of their types by the education administrative units of the State Council, and to be overseen by the institutions that have been approved by the State to carry out education examinations" (Education Law of the People's Republic of China, 1998, p. 3). The NEEA is the only educational examinations organization within the MoE, and is responsible to a specific deputy minister of the MoE.

As mentioned above, the NEEA is in charge of the test development and administration of the University Entrance Examinations (UEE) as well as statistical analysis of the data collected. A specific department in the MoE is responsible for policy-making in relation

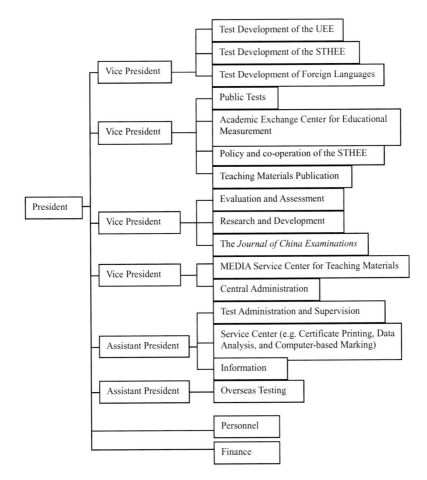

Figure 3.1 Organizational Structure of the NEEA

to the test, that is, how to enroll the candidates into universities based on the results of the test.

To manage the Self-Taught Higher Education Examinations (STHEE), the NEEA carries another two titles known as The Office of the STHEE in the MoE and The Office of the National Committee for the STHEE. The former is an administrative body within the MoE, and the latter serves as the standing office for the STHEE national committee. This national committee is the highest decision-making body for the STHEE, comprised of presidents of universities, ministers of the MoE, the State Planning and Development Commission, the Ministry of Personnel, the Ministry of Finance, the Ministry of Labor and Welfare, leaders from the military and the Youth League, and scholars from several universities.

The NEEA has full responsibility for the public (certificate) tests. Also, the NEEA is authorized to administer overseas tests in mainland China, which have to be approved by the Department of International Development of the MoE.

Research by the NEEA

The Department of Research and Development takes charge of testing research within the NEEA. It carries out the following duties: formulating test research plans; administering test research projects; organizing national public bidding on research projects; managing routine research projects; and organizing research activities and exchanges.

The NEEA values testing research. Every year, a specific budget is drawn up to support this research, which is carried out by both internal staff and external experts in different fields concerned with testing. The research projects mainly focus on policy-making, the application of testing theories in practice such as item analysis, new item type development, test evaluation, and new technologies used in testing. In addition, the NEEA has established a system of statistical analysis and a computer communication network, through which the NEEA is able to collect and analyze data of the sampled candidates, which results in an annual statistical report for each administered test.

Some of the key research projects for the 5 years from 2006 to 2010 are: Research on Reforming the Educational Examinations and the Assessment Policies; University Entrance Examinations Based on the Course Standards; and Assessment and Evaluation of Teaching and Learning in Secondary Schools. The projects concerned with foreign language testing are mainly: Analytical Score Reporting and the Development of the Candidates' English Language Proficiency; Validation Study of the Writing Section in the PETS; and Reliability Study of the Oral Section in the PETS.

Administration of the NEEA Tests

The UEE and the STHEE are administered by the NEEA and local institutions (the provincial admissions office for the UEE and the provincial office of the STHEE). After each test paper is developed by the NEEA, the final proof is sent to the local institutions via a secure system. These institutions print the test paper according to the number of the candidates and deliver them to the lower (county) level of institutions, usually with the help of armed police officers. The county-level institutions organize the examinations according to the regulations drafted by the NEEA. The provincial institutions organize the marking, and issue and send score reports to each of the candidates. The NEEA supervises the whole process.

As for public (certificate) tests such as the PETS and the National Accreditation Examinations for Translators and Interpreters (NAETI), two different approaches are taken. All of the large-scale examinations, that is, tests with over 100,000 candidates, are administered in the same way as the STHEE. The test results of the candidates are, however, transferred to the NEEA, which issues and prints the certificates and asks the provincial institutions to deliver them to the candidates. The NEEA also administers small-scale examinations through the test centers in universities. There are about 40 university test centers approved by the NEEA to administer such examinations. They organize the examinations locally and send the candidates' answer sheets back to the NEEA for marking. The NEEA organizes the marking, prints and issues the certificates and asks these centers to deliver them to the candidates. The NEEA also administers overseas tests such as TOEFL and GRE through the university test centers, which are responsible for organizing the examinations and delivering the score reports.

Opportunities for Further Development and the Challenges Faced by the NEEA

With China undertaking strategic development in all fields, examinations will no doubt experience some changes to meet changing public requirements and the needs of social development in the Chinese context. This is a golden opportunity for development of the NEEA, for the following reasons:

- With new standards being set in almost all fields, such as business and education, various tests are needed and there will be more potential applicants for the NEEA tests.
- In order to build a life-long education system and a learning society, as aimed for by the government, examination agencies like the NEEA are in high demand to provide convenient and diverse services.
- An increasing number of professionals may join the NEEA.
- With more and more foreigners interested in Chinese language and culture, the NEEA will be able to conduct its examinations abroad.

In general, challenges co-exist with opportunities, so the NEEA has to answer the following questions through research and in its daily work in the years to come:

- Ensuring its examinations exhibit more positive washback
- Meeting market demands for scientific, authoritative, and safer tests
- Constructing a more effective management system and training NEEA staff to offer public and professional services.

In early 2006, the NEEA drafted its first 5-year plan, which is called the 11th 5-Year Plan (2006–2010) (NEEA, 2006b) to match the national 11th 5-Year Plan. In this plan, 10 objectives are set for this 5-year period.

1 Constructing a test administration monitoring system to guarantee the safety and justice (including fairness) of the examinations
2 Constructing a national item bank to improve the quality of test development and to ensure the examinations are systematic and authoritative
3 Bringing forth new ideas to enhance the STHEE
4 Expanding public tests and developing high quality tests
5 Developing the capacity to undertake overseas tests and to offer better services
6 Enlarging service space (areas for conducting exams and assessments) and constructing a system of test evaluation and assessment
7 Enhancing scientific research on testing and raising the creative ability of testing services
8 Valuing the use of information technology in the routine work of the NEEA
9 Trying to create a better testing environment through more communication with society
10 Extending international exchange and cooperation.

Based on these 10 objectives, the NEEA drafted five key projects. The first of the five is the construction of the item bank. To ensure that the test development is secure, scientific, and standardized, the NEEA made a strategic decision to construct a national item bank. This will involve most subjects in the UEE and some subjects in the STHEE. A team has been formed, which will take responsibility for software development and coordination between the three test development departments, i.e. Test Development of the UEE, Test Development of the STHEE, and Test Development of Foreign Languages. The test development departments are establishing new working procedures to suit the needs of item banking. Some test papers will be produced from the item bank in the coming years.

The second project is the construction of a command system for test administration. The NEEA will make good use of new technologies, such as digital communication, the Internet, and databases, to establish a digital and informational command system to enable the on-going and the upcoming examinations to be much more secure. This system will be able to reach each of the test centers in mainland China.

The third project is the creation of a preparedness plan in case of emergency. The NEEA takes full responsibility for the administration of almost all of the high-stakes educational examinations in China, covering the procedures of test development, test paper printing, storage and shipping, and the organizing of the examination. Every step requires careful consideration and a back-up plan in case of accidents or emergencies. Experts in relevant fields will be invited to form a working team to draft practical procedures to deal with such emergencies, which will minimize potential harm to the public interest and to social stability.

The fourth project is the building of a secure facility for test development. Dozens of test development meetings, which last from 7–30 days, are held in commercial hotels every year, each of which involves from 30 up to hundreds of item writers. These meetings require a huge budget but security is difficult to ensure. Thus, the NEEA plans to build a multi-function, modern hotel, which will serve as a secure base for test development.

The fifth project is the establishment of a research institute for educational examinations and assessments. As research plays an important role in testing, the NEEA is trying to cooperate with some research institutes and universities to establish a research institute. Testing experts both at home and abroad will be invited to work with the institute on specific research projects.

Testing Programs of the NEEA

The University Entrance Examination to Higher Education (UEEHE; 「普通高等学校招生全国统一考试」)

The UEEHE is the largest examination system in China, which is administered annually between June 7–9th. It is intended to be offered nationwide for admission to general higher educational institutions. Its candidates are mainly high school graduates and others with equivalent educational credentials. In 2006, the candidature was 9.5 million; this increased to 10.1 million in 2007. The tests are mainly classified into two categories: science and liberal arts.

In China, the UEEHE is often nicknamed the "Footslog Bridge" (独木桥) to success, although there are many ways to achieve higher education, such as via the STHEE and the Higher Education for Adults. The reason for this nickname is that the UEEHE is usually seen as the gatekeeper for formal higher education in China. The UEEHE is, undoubtedly, the most visible and important examination system in China. During the examination season each year, secondary schools, universities and even government officials at different levels will focus their attention on the examinations.

The marking of the UEEHE is organized locally by each of the provincial examination and admissions offices. The objective parts are marked using Optical Mark Readers (OMR). The subjective parts are marked on site by invited teachers from universities and secondary schools. Each script is double-marked.

In China, secondary school education, and even the primary school education, is often characterized as examination-oriented (Qi, 2005). The UEEHE is seen as the origin of this orientation because of its specific position in the educational system. Its strong washback leads to a situation commonly known as "what to examine, what to teach" (Yang, 1992) in secondary schools, which the NEEA strongly opposes. Many secondary school teachers are familiar with the textbooks and the examination syllabus but not the teaching curriculum. The exercises of each subject used in the schools follow the format of the examinations. The subjects are grouped into key subjects and regular subjects according to their weighting in the UEEHE. The key subjects are given more attention, i.e., more lessons and more exercises, together with higher status and higher pay to the teachers who are teaching those subjects. In 1992, during an experiment in examination system reform, the subjects of geography and biology were grouped into *optional subjects* in the UEEHE. Some secondary schools reduced the teaching hours or even cancelled the lessons of these two subjects. The NEEA tries to minimize the negative effect of the UEEHE. The examination syllabus is usually published long before the examination date to ensure that every candidate knows the structure and content of the test. The NEEA stresses testing what the teaching curriculum requires and what is taught in the schools. During the current phase of examination system reform, the MoE is encouraging the provinces to give their opinions and carry out a number of experiments. For example, Jiangsu, an east-China province, plans to reduce the number of subjects in the UEEHE from the current four to three (Chinese, Mathematics, and Foreign Language). Students' achievement during the 3 years of senior secondary school learning will be evaluated and given a certain percentage of weighting in the UEEHE.

Before 2004, a single test paper for each subject was used nationwide on the same examination day. In 2004, however, the NEEA was required to develop four sets of papers for each subject, which were used in different provinces to ensure examination security. At the same time, several provinces were required to develop their own matriculation tests. In 2005 and 2006, more provinces were required to do so. The MoE will maintain the status quo in upcoming years, that is, some provinces will develop their own tests and the NEEA will develop tests for the others.

The Graduate School Entrance Examination (GSEE;「研究生入学考试」)

The GSEE covers four subject areas, of which two are common subjects (Political Science and Foreign Language) and the other two are course-related. The two common subject tests are developed by the NEEA and administered uniformly nationwide. At present, the two course-related subject tests are mainly developed by the universities or research institutes enrolling the candidates. The tests are administered in late January or early

February each year. The candidature was 1.28 million in 2007 and 1.2 million in 2008. The candidates take the examination at local test centers. The marking of the common subjects is carried out by the provincial examination and admissions offices, and the course-related subjects by the universities to which the candidates apply. The test results of the common subjects are sent to these universities, which arrange interviews with the candidates whose total scores meet specific requirements.

With increasing competition in the employment market, and the growing number of undergraduates, in spite of the relatively small decline between 2007 and 2008, the candidature for the test is steadily increasing, and the challenge is becoming much greater than before, resulting in a strong washback effect of the test. The positive washback effect is that it leads to the candidates doing more reading and having a stronger desire to advance. The negative effect mainly relates to the extremely large candidature. In order to be successful, undergraduates usually start their preparation quite early, 1 or even 2 years before the examination. During this period of time, they usually focus on the four subjects tested in the GSEE: candidates have many exercises to complete, training courses to attend, and relevant books to read. Consequently, some students may pay less attention to their university undergraduate studies, which are not tested in the GSEE.

Various Admission Tests to Institutions of Higher Education for Adults (ATIHEA; 「各类成人高等学校入学考试」)

These tests are offered on the basis of two educational credentials, namely, secondary schools and vocational schools. They enable candidates with secondary school backgrounds to be admitted to TV universities,[1] higher-level schools for farmers, institutes for managerial cadres, teachers' institutes, institutes for teacher advancement, etc. These tests are taken annually by more than 2 million candidates who are mostly in-service employees. As a gate-keeper for in-service employees to achieve a level of higher education, these tests are very effective in encouraging these employees to continue their studies as part of fulfilling their aspirations. Marking is organized locally by the provincial examination and admissions offices. The objective parts are marked using OMR. The subjective parts are marked on-site by teachers invited from universities.

Self-Taught Higher Education Examination System (STHEE; 「高等教育自学考试」)

The STHEE is designed and offered by the state to provide opportunities for self-taught learners to attain educational credentials. It is a form of higher education that combines self-directed learning, social assistance, and state-administered tests. Each citizen of the People's Republic of China, regardless of his or her sex, age, ethnic group, race, or educational background, is eligible to enter for the examinations according to The Temporary Regulations on the STHEE issued by the State Council (see also Introduction to the National Education Examinations Authority, above). Anyone who passes a subject test receives a subject certificate from a provincial committee or the equivalent level committee of the STHEE. With the completion of the required number of subjects and an essay evaluated and accepted, a candidate is granted a degree by an authorized host institution.

The key feature of this system is its practicality. It offers many specialties which are greatly needed in some specific fields and thus encourages people in these fields to continue their studies. Flexibility is another feature of the system. Self-taught learners can complete their studies themselves according to the reading materials provided and the examination syllabus or they can follow the lessons given by teachers at night schools or weekend training schools, sponsored by colleges or universities. When they feel ready for the test in a certain subject, they enter for it. Therefore, the system brings about a positive washback effect as many people are taking the test not for a degree or certificate, but for the knowledge they are interested in acquiring. The tests are administered four times a year, and are taken by about 4 million candidates each year.

Public (Certificate) Tests 「证书类考试」

To meet growing market demands, the NEEA has designed dozens of public tests since the 1990s, of which the NCRE (National Computer Rank Examination), the PETS, the NIT (National Applied Information Technology Certificate) and the WSK[2] (National Foreign Languages Competence Tests) are the prominent and most promising ones. In total, more than 8 million candidates sit these tests each year.

The NEEA also works with government authorities and industry partners to develop a variety of professional certificate tests, including the Catering Manager Examination Program, the Labor and Social Security Examination Program, and the Chinese Marketing and Sales Certificate Tests.

The effect of these tests is profound and lasting, as all of these tests are designed to meet specific social demands. Some candidates take these to prove their abilities, some for the chance to attend a better school, some for job application purposes, and some for the opportunity for promotion. These multi-functional tests offer the users a standard or level against which they can measure themselves and others. These tests are, therefore, helpful and important in creating a life-long learning society in China.

English Language Tests in NEEA's Charge

Since the introduction of educational reform and an open door policy, China has greatly expanded its communication with the rest of the world. One result of this opening up is that China has had an increasing demand for a large number of professionals and highly qualified personnel in different fields who are able to communicate with non-Chinese professionals. In response to this need, foreign language learning and teaching are prioritized almost everywhere in the country: this is evident in the time allocation given to foreign language learning and teaching in schools and universities; in job applications; and even in the evaluation of professional titles. As a result, the NEEA has been paying special attention to foreign language testing. A foreign language is a compulsory subject in almost all testing programs in the NEEA, and two departments (Test Development of Foreign Languages and Overseas Testing) have been established in the NEEA to carry out language testing. The Test Development of Foreign Languages Department carries out test development for foreign language tests and manages three foreign language test programs (PETS, WSK and NAETI), whereas the Overseas Testing Department is responsible for administering tests entrusted to it by other countries such as the USA, the UK, and Japan.

Entrance Tests

The National Matriculation English Test (NMET)

This test is one of six foreign language tests in the university entrance examination. The other five are Japanese, Russian, German, French, and Spanish. Each of the candidates must select one of these as their foreign language; English is chosen by more than 99 percent of foreign language candidates each year.

The NMET was designed in 1991 and first used in some of the examination-reforming provinces. With more and more provinces undertaking this reform, in 1996, the NMET replaced the MET (the Matriculation English Test, which was introduced into the UEEHE in 1988) and the NMET began to be used nationwide (see also Cheng & Qi, 2006). Since then, the NMET has undergone several changes in its format. Now it exists in three different formats (NEEA, 2007a). The first one is based on the Teaching Curriculum of English and does not have a listening section. The second one is based on the same teaching curriculum but has a listening section. The third one has a listening section but is designed on the basis of the Course Standards of English, which is being promoted in mainland China and is replacing the Teaching Curriculum of English year by year. This test format, which takes Lyle Bachman's 1990 model of communicative language ability (Bachman, 1990) as its theoretical framework, is expected to replace the other two tests by 2012. The detailed format of the test can be found in Tables 3.1 below. All three versions are designed and developed in accordance with the requirements of different provinces.

The impact of NMET can be seen clearly in secondary school English teaching. The format of the NMET has become the format for any English test in schools, and the last semester of the students in secondary school is usually devoted to doing test after test to practice this format (see Chapters 16 and 17 for further information on this test).

The Graduate School Entrance English Examination (GSEEE)

This is one of three foreign language tests in the Graduate School Entrance Examination. The other two are Japanese and Russian, and candidates must take one of these tests to meet the foreign language requirement. The current test format (NEEA, 2007b) was designed in 2004 and first used in 2005, following the removal of a listening section from the examination, in accordance with the official requirement for ease of test administration. The test contains three sections: Use of English, Reading Comprehension, and Writing, with the weighting of these three sections being 10, 60, and 30 percent, respectively.

The section on Use of English focuses on control of formal elements of the language in context, including a wide range of vocabulary, expressions, and structures, as well as recognition of features of discourse relating to coherence and cohesion. Candidates are required to complete a cloze test with 20 multiple-choice (four-option) items.

The Reading Comprehension section consists of three parts focusing on candidates' ability to read and understand written English. In Part A, candidates are tested on their ability to understand detailed information, grasp the gist of a text, deduce the meaning of unfamiliar vocabulary items, and make inferences. They are required to read four texts and demonstrate their understanding by answering 20 multiple-choice (four-option)

Table 3.1 Overview of the NMET Based on the Course Standards of English

Section	Part	Input	Language of Rubric	Task Focus	Item Types	Number of Items	Raw Score
I. Listening Comprehension	A	5 short dialogues (heard once)	Chinese	Simple factual information	MC (3-option)	5	7.5
	B	5 dialogues and monologues (heard twice)	Chinese information	Simple factual	MC (3-option)	15	22.5
II. Use of English	A	15 sentences/dialogues	Chinese	Grammar and vocabulary	MC (4-option)	15	15
	B	1 text (200 words)	Chinese	Vocabulary	MC cloze (4-option)	20	30
III. Reading Comprehension	A	4 texts (over 900 words in total)	Chinese	General and detailed information	MC (4-option)	15	30
	B	1 text (about 300 words)	Chinese	Relationship between sentences or paragraphs	Gap-filling (7-option)	5	10
IV. Writing	A	1 text (100 words)	Chinese	Error correction	Error correction	10	10
	B	prompt (in Chinese)	Chinese	Writing a short text	Guided writing	1	25
Total						85+1	150

items. In Part B, candidates are tested on their understanding of the coherence of the text. They read an incomplete text with five gaps and fill in the gaps with five of the seven choices provided. In Part C, candidates are tested on their accuracy of understanding by reading one text and translating five underlined sections from English into Chinese.

The section on Writing consists of two parts focusing on candidates' writing ability. In Part A, candidates are tested on their ability to write a short text giving some factual information. The input takes the form of pictures, charts, directions in Chinese, etc. In Part B, candidates are required to write an essay in English based on input in the form of guidelines in either Chinese or English.

The impact of the GSEEE is not readily apparent, as no impact reports have yet been published. However, every candidate is aware that knowledge and skills in a foreign language usually plays a key role in admission to graduate studies. Thus, the foreign language requirement attracts candidates' attention. In preparing for the GSEEE, candidates often complete many exercises and may also attend training courses, which mirror the requirements and format of the test (see Chapter 11 for more details).

The English Test for Admission to Institutions of Higher Education for Adults

This is an important test in the Admission Tests to Institutions of Higher Education for Adults (ATIHEA). As with the UEEHE and the GSEE, three foreign language tests are included in the ATIHEA, namely, English, Japanese, and Russian. More than 99 percent of candidates choose the English test. The test format is usually amended every 2–3 years according to feedback from the provincial admissions offices as well as from the candidates themselves. The current test format (NEEA, 2005a) was designed in 2005. The English test contains three sections: Use of English, Reading Comprehension, and Writing. The weighting of these three sections is 40, 30, and 30 percent, respectively.

The section on Use of English consists of three parts focusing on candidates' knowledge of phonology, grammatical structures, vocabulary, and simple expressions. In Part A, candidates are tested on their knowledge of word pronunciation. They complete five items by selecting a word with its underlined part pronounced the same as the underlined part in the word given in the stem. In Part B, candidates complete 15 multiple-choice (four-option) items based on statements or short dialogues in order to demonstrate their knowledge of grammatical structures and simple expressions. In Part C, candidates are tested on their knowledge of vocabulary. They complete a cloze test with 15 multiple-choice (four-option) items.

The Reading Comprehension section focuses on candidates' ability to understand general and detailed information in four different texts. The candidates are required to demonstrate their understanding by answering 15 multiple-choice (four-option) items. The section on Writing consists of two parts. In Part A, candidates must finish an incomplete dialogue based on the information given in the instruction, and in Part B, candidates are tested on their ability to write a short text giving some factual information.

As is the case with the GSEEE, there has not yet been a report published on the impact of the test. However, the candidature of more than 1 million each year and the popularity of the tutoring materials available in bookshops appear to indicate that the test can potentially impact on the English learning and teaching.

Tests for Self-taught Learners

English Test (1) and (2)

These have been designed for non-English-major self-taught learners. These two tests are for candidates who are doing 2 years and 4 years of self-directed learning, respectively. English is a voluntary subject in the 2-year learning program, and approximately 98,000 candidates take the English Test (1) each year. For some of the 4-year learning program candidates, English is a compulsory subject. About 760,000 candidates take the English Test (2) each year. These two tests were designed more than 10 years ago so the test format and content are due to be revised. Both of the current tests contain three sections (NEEA, 2005b): Use of English, Reading Comprehension, and Translation.

Tests for English-major Self-taught Learners

Candidates who are English-majors have to take a battery of tests, including Comprehensive Course of English, English Listening Comprehension, Oral Workshop in English, Basic College Composition, English-Chinese Translation, Modern English Grammar, Modern Linguistics, and English Lexicology. The candidature is approximately 250,000 for the 2-year program and 400,000 for the 4-year degree program each year.

Certificate Tests

The Public English Test System (PETS)

PETS is one of the NEEA's most important certificate tests. When the testing system was designed, the project received financial support from the UK's Department for International Development (DfID), as well as technical and professional support from the University of Cambridge Local Examinations Syndicate (UCLES). The project is included in the inter-governmental program of Sino-British cultural exchange (PETS Working Group, 1999).

This system rationalizes publicly available, criterion-referenced English language tests within a five-level framework ranging from the level of English expected at junior secondary school (after 3 years of English study) to the level required by graduates planning to study or work abroad. It is available to all learners of English, with no restriction on age, profession, or academic background. Each of the five PETS levels is composed of two separate test components. One is the Written Test, which consists of sections assessing listening comprehension, use of English, reading comprehension, and writing. The weighting of these four sections at each level is approximately 30, 20, 30, and 20 percent, respectively, with use of English more heavily weighted at the lower levels and reading comprehension more heavily weighted at the higher levels. The other component is an Oral Test designed to assess candidates' speaking ability. Only candidates who have passed both the Written Test and the Oral Test are granted PETS certificates by the NEEA.

In line with international practice, the NEEA is responsible for the level definition of the testing system while the users have the right to use the test results for their own purposes. Consequently, every level of PETS is multi-functional.

Level 1 is mainly used by the technical colleges to assess students' English language ability. In some cities, the test result is used by junior secondary schools to admit new students and by some companies to hire new employees.

Level 2 is beginning to take the place of English Test (1) in the STHEE program. In some cities, it is used by secondary schools to admit new students and by some companies to hire new employees. In some provinces, the Oral Test at this level functions as the oral test in the UEEHE, which is required for English-major candidates.

Level 3 is beginning to take the place of English Test (2) in the STHEE program. Some secondary school students take it to test their own English language ability, and some non-English-major students from private universities take the test to obtain the PETS Level 3 certificate, which is regarded as authoritative proof of their English language proficiency level.

Level 4 candidates are mainly non-English-major university students. Some of them take the test to prove their English language ability, while others are preparing for the GSEE and take the test as a pre-examination exercise.

Level 5 has become a substitute for the English Proficiency Test (EPT), used to assess candidates seeking government sponsorship for overseas academic development.

Since its introduction to the public in 1999, the PETS system has become increasingly popular in China, with the candidature reaching 1.01 million in 2007 (for more detailed information on the PETS, see Chapter 10).

The National Accreditation Examinations for Translators and Interpreters (NAETI)

This examination system is one for which the NEEA and Beijing Foreign Studies University (BFSU) are jointly responsible. The NEEA is in charge of test development and administration, and the BFSU is responsible for instruction and the writing and publication of training materials.

The NAETI system has three levels (NEEA, 2005c), with Level 1 designed for experienced translators or interpreters, Level 2 for English-major post-graduates, and Level 3 for English-major graduates. Each of the three NAETI levels is composed of two separate tests. One is translation, which consists of two sections: English–Chinese translation and Chinese–English translation. The other is interpretation, which consists of two or three sections, with the candidates assessed on their ability to interpret both from English into Chinese and from Chinese into English. To obtain the Level 1 Certificate of Interpretation, candidates have to pass tests in consecutive interpretation as well as simultaneous interpretation. Candidates who have passed the test at a certain level of the examination are granted the relevant NAETI certificates jointly issued by the NEEA and the BFSU. The NAETI system is available to all learners of English, with no restriction on age, profession, or academic background. This system was introduced to the public in 2003, and approximately 3,000 candidates take the examination each year.

The College English Test (CET)

This test system is one for which the NEEA and the National College English Testing Committee (NCETC) are jointly responsible. The NEEA takes charge of test administration while the NCETC carries out test development and related research. The candidates receive a score report after taking the CET (for details about the CET see Chapters 4, 14, and 15).

Conclusion

As the only education examinations authority under the Ministry of Education, the People's Republic of China, the NEEA takes charge of almost all of the high-stakes education examinations in China. It serves around 38 million candidates each year and is without doubt conducting the largest-scale examinations in the world. The NEEA implements these examinations through its unique test administration system. To serve a huge candidature better and to keep itself flexible and modernized, the NEEA values testing research. As a result, it has set 10 objectives and formed five projects for the 5 years starting in 2006 as mentioned in the earlier part of this chapter. The fulfillment of these tasks has the potential to bring about major changes in the test administration of the NEEA, thus having a significant impact on Chinese society.

Notes

1. A TV university is a type of Open University. After being admitted to the university, the students follow the courses given on television at the local branches of the university.
2. The WSK is an examination used to select professionals for study and training overseas.

References

Bachman, L. F. (1990). *Fundamental considerations in language testing.* Oxford: Oxford University Press.

Cheng, L. & Qi, L. (2006). Description and examination of the National Matriculation English Test in China. *Language Assessment Quarterly: An International Journal, 3,* 53–70.

Education Law of the People's Republic of China. (1998). *Collections of the current education laws and regulations (1990–1995),* 1–5. Beijing, China: People's Education Press.

NEEA. (2005a). *Examination syllabus for admission tests to institutions of higher education for adults.* Beijing, China: Higher Education Press.

NEEA. (2005b). *Examination syllabus for self-taught examination for higher education (English).* Beijing, China: Higher Education Press.

NEEA. (2005c). *Examination syllabus for national accreditation examination for translators and interpreters.* Beijing, China: Higher Education Press.

NEEA. (2006a). *General introduction to national education examinations authority.* Beijing China: NEEA.

NEEA. (2006b). *NEEA's 11th Five-Year Plan (2006–2010).* Beijing, China: NEEA.

NEEA. (2007a). *Examination syllabus for university entrance examination to higher education.* Beijing, China: Higher Education Press.

NEEA. (2007b). *Examination syllabus for the graduate school entrance English examination.* Beijing, China: Higher Education Press.

PETS Working Group. (1999). *China public English test system.* Beijing, China: NEEA.

Qi, L. (2005). Stakeholders' conflicting aims undermine the washback function of a high-stakes test. *Language Testing, 22,* 142–173.

Yang, X. W. (1992). Effects and difficulties of giving the general examination for students. *China Examinations, 1,* 4–6.

4 The National College English Testing Committee

Yan Jin, Shanghai Jiaotong University

The National College English Testing Committee (NCETC) of China is an academic organization appointed by the Higher Education Department of the Ministry of Education, the People's Republic of China. The Committee is in charge of the design and development of the College English Test (CET「大学英语四、六级考试」), a national standardized English language test for college and university students in China. Since its inception in 1987, the CET has attracted an increasing number of test-takers every year, and its population has become the world's largest for any test of English as a Foreign Language (EFL). Members of the current NCETC consist of 25 Chinese university professors whose research areas focus on English language teaching and testing. This chapter will first trace the history of the NCETC from its formation in the mid-1980s, when a group of Chinese language testing experts felt there was a need for an English language test to complement the teaching of English in colleges and universities in China. This chapter will then introduce details of the operational structure of the NCETC, which was designed to ensure the successful development and implementation of this large-scale test. As a well-established EFL test, the quality of the CET is the result, to a large extent, of the Committee's continuous efforts in pursuing the validity, reliability, and practicality of the test. A major part of this chapter will be devoted to the role played by the NCETC in maintaining the test's professional standards. In response to changing social needs and to accommodate changing teaching requirements, the NCETC has made substantial changes to the content and format of the CET and also its score reporting system in recent years. However, the real challenge facing the NCETC is to improve the test's washback and impact on English language teaching and learning at the tertiary level in China. This chapter will end with a discussion of the mission of the Committee in the twenty-first century.

From a Test Design Group to a National Committee

The NCETC is one of a large number of testing groups, organizations, and committees that have sprung up in China within the EFL community since the mid-1980s. The NCETC administers an English language test which was taken by 12.5 million test-takers in 2007, making this the world's largest EFL test and the one that has perhaps attracted the most public attention in China.

Since China began its reform and opening up policy in the late 1970s and resumed its national college and university entrance examination in 1977, great efforts have been made by teachers and students to meet the pressing social and professional requirements of college and university graduates who will need to communicate in English. In the early 1980s, the State Education Commission (now the Ministry of Education) set up a team of language teaching experts to conduct a large-scale survey and identify the social and professional needs for college and university students with respect to their proficiency in English. In accordance with the results of a careful needs analysis based on a survey conducted with 1,700 college and university graduates from 1982 to 1984, the College English Teaching Syllabus (State Education Commission, 1985, 1986), the first national college English teaching syllabus for non-English major college and university students, was published in the mid-1980s.

To promote the implementation of the College English Teaching Syllabus (the Syllabus), the College English Test Design Group was formed in 1986, which consisted of 12 language teaching and testing experts from different universities across China. This group of professionals designed and developed the first standardized English language test for tertiary institutions in China, the College English Test Band 4 (CET-4), for students completing Bands 1–4 of the Syllabus. The test was administered first in 1987 to 100,000 students. In 1989, 60,000 students took the CET Band 6 (CET-6), a higher-level test for students who have completed Bands 5 and 6 of the Syllabus. Since the administration, 20 years ago, of the first CET-4, the CET Design Group (and later the NCETC) has been working continuously to improve the quality of the test and promote the teaching and learning of English as a medium of communication in colleges and universities in China.

The group was formally recognized in 1994 when the Higher Education Department of the State Education Commission established the first National College English Testing Committee to be in charge of the design, development, and administration of the CET. The CET is held twice a year, once in June and again in December or January. Members of the Committee are officially appointed by the Higher Education Department of the Ministry of Education, and the universities concerned are informed of the appointment. As an academic organization, the NCETC members work part-time for the CET and meet on a regular basis for item writing and revision, standard-setting for essay marking, training of markers, score equating and reporting, test revision, policy-making, and so forth. With the active participation of its members, and with Professor Yang Huizhong from Shanghai Jiaotong University as the head of the group from 1987 to 2004, the Committee made a name for itself as a professional test design team. The current Committee, set up in June 2004, at a time when the reform of college English teaching and testing was entering a new stage, is a relatively young team consisting of 25 professors from 23 universities across China; many of these members are heads of their department of English or school of foreign languages. As leading professors at the forefront of applied linguistics research in China, the NCETC members are fully aware of the importance of a healthy relationship between language teaching and testing, especially for a large-scale, high-stakes test like the CET. Senior members of the first and second Committee, Professor Yang Huizhong and Professor Guo Jieke (from South China University of Technology), who have worked for the NCETC for approximately 20 years, now serve as consultants to the Committee. In addition to test design and development, the current

Committee is paying closer attention to policies relating to the use of test results, hence, the division of the Committee into two groups: one mainly responsible for test design and the other for providing advice on CET-related policies.

Language testing researchers and practitioners in China are proud of the fact that examinations originated in China (Sun, 1985). As a system for selective purposes, it has existed in China for more than 1,700 years (see also Chapter 2). But language testing in its modern form is based on psychometrics and modern linguistics, which developed and flourished in the West. Therefore, since the 1990s, with China's further opening up to the outside world, the NCETC has participated in various international conferences and exchange programs in order to learn from the accumulated experience of world-renowned, well-established tests like IELTS and TOEFL, which have a much longer history than the CET. In August 1999, the former President of the Educational Testing Service (ETS) in the USA, Nancy Cole, and her team of senior vice presidents were invited to visit the NCETC. Great interest was shown by the ETS delegation in the rapid development of the CET, and the two groups exchanged views on issues and problems encountered in the process of test development and revision. In 2000, the NCETC's proposal to make a presentation at a symposium at the Language Testing Research Colloquium in Vancouver was accepted, and a delegation of four members was sent to the conference where they gave a 2-hour presentation on the first day of the conference introducing the CET for the first time to the world. In 2002, the NCETC organized and hosted the First International Conference on English Language Testing in China. Testing organizations from countries and regions in Asia, ETS in the USA and the University of Cambridge Local Examinations Syndicate (UCLES) in the UK sent delegates to the conference, which focused on the relationship between language teaching and testing, an area of growing interest in the field of language testing in recent years with the emergence of more and more powerful language tests. At the "Big Tests" Symposium of the 2005 Conference of the International Association of Applied Linguistics in Madison, Wisconsin, delegates from ETS, UCLES, and the NCETC gave presentations on the recent revisions to their tests and exchanged views on ways to improve the washback of large-scale high-stakes tests.

In Asia, the NCETC has held regular exchanges with many key language testing organizations over the past two decades, including, for example, the Hong Kong Examinations and Assessment Authority, the College Entrance Examinations Center in Taipei, the Language Testing and Training Center in Taipei, the Society for Testing English Proficiency in Japan, and the Korean English Language Testing Association. As the initiator of the Academic Forum on English Language Testing in Asia and the organizer of the first and seventh forum, the NCETC is playing a central role in English language testing in Asia.

Operational Structure of the NCETC

Essentially hierarchical with the Higher Education Department of the Ministry of Education at the top, the overall operational structure of the NCETC is a coordinated group of various departments and organizations. In fact, one of the key reasons for the steady development of the CET over the decades is the strong support that the NCETC has received from the Higher Education Departments of the Provincial or Municipal

Education Commissions. The impetus provided by the implementation of the CET to the teaching and learning of English at the tertiary level in China, in return, has convinced government officials that the test has, on the whole, exerted a beneficial washback on the teaching of English as a foreign language in tertiary institutions across China (Wu, 2005).

Under the guidance of the Higher Education Department of the Ministry of Education, the NCETC is responsible for test design and development. The Committee has a qualified team of item writers, essay markers, and oral examiners, who ensure the quality of the test items and the reliability of the marking. The CET Administration Office, set up in the School of Foreign Languages of Shanghai Jiaotong University as the standing body of the NCETC, is in charge of the day-to-day administration of the test, for example, organizing item-setting and revision meetings, score equating meetings, and quality control meetings. The office was responsible for all the administrative work of the test from 1987 to 2005, including the editing of the test papers, the printing and distribution of test materials, as well as the calculation, equating, reporting, and release of the scores. At the provincial and municipal levels, the head of the Higher Education Department of the Provincial or Municipal Education Commission was appointed as the CET chief supervisor. The CET Administration Office had direct contact with the chief supervisors in each province or municipality to ensure the smooth implementation and administration of the test. In colleges and universities of the respective provinces and municipalities, CET supervisors, usually the head of the Academic Affairs Office, were in charge of the administration of the test and relevant administrative issues.

Since China is a vast country, three CET test centers were set up to better manage administrative affairs in the different regions: Center 1 in Tsinghua University, Beijing, Center 2 in Shanghai Jiaotong University, Shanghai and Center 3 in Wuhan University, Wuhan. Test Center 1 was responsible for the regions of North and Northeast China, Test Center 2 for East and South China, and Test Center 3 for the Southwest, North-west and Central China regions.

The CET Administration Office coordinated the administrative affairs of the three centers and organized regular meetings to improve efficiency and solve problems that had arisen. In addition to administrative work, the office staff have been actively involved in research programs related to test administration, test design, and test validation. Over its 20 years of operation, the office has established a strong research base capable of carrying out important, new research in the field of language testing. The base consists of human resources such as research staff, statisticians, and computer programmers and non-human resources such as computing facilities and specialized software, together with a major collection of printed materials on language testing.

The National Education Examinations Authority (NEEA), an institution directly under the supervision of the Ministry of Education and appointed by the Ministry to undertake educational examinations, took over direct responsibility for the administration of the CET in 2006. At present, the focus of the NCETC is on the improvement of test design, control of the quality of test items, and the marking of constructed response items. At the provincial or municipal level, the routine operation of test administration including, for example, registration, test delivery, and coordination of the marking centers, has become the responsibility of the Provincial or Municipal Education Examinations Authorities. The following flowchart (Figure 4.1) illustrates the operational structure for the CET before and after the recent reform in 2006.

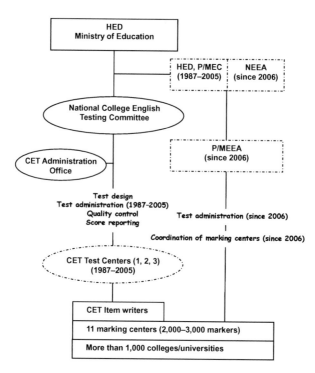

Figure 4.1 The Operational Structure of the NCETC

Notes

The ovals and boxes with dotted lines indicate the parts of the operational structure where changes were made in the recent reform. HED: Higher Education Department; P/MEC: Provincial/Municipal Education Commission; NEEA: National Education Examinations Authority; P/MEEA: Provincial/Municipal Education Examinations Authority.

Efforts to Maintain the Professional Standards of the CET

In the early 1990s, the NCETC's understanding of the most essential qualities of a language test was based on test validity and reliability. The Committee concerned itself in particular with accuracy in measurement as defined by Davis (1990), referring to the relation between the test instrument and the domain to be measured, that is, whether a test is measuring what it is supposed to measure, and to the consistency of measurement, that is, whether a test is measuring in an accurate manner. The CET validation study, a joint research project conducted in conjunction with the British Council, was completed in the late 1990s. The study was the first of its kind in China since large-scale standardized language tests came into being in the mid-1980s. It paid close attention to the construct validity of the test, its content validity, concurrent validity, predictive validity, and face validity. Various types of evidence of the test's validity and marking reliability were collected during the 3-year project, proving the basis for arguing that the CET was a valid and reliable measure of the English proficiency of college and university students in China (see Yang & Weir, 1998).

Validity Evidence

The CET has adopted a componential view of the language construct and measures the four major language skills separately, that is, listening, reading, and writing in the CET and speaking in the CET Spoken English Test (CET-SET). Internal correlations show that various components of the CET measure different skills. Factorial structures indicate that one principal component is being measured by the CET, which is interpreted as general linguistic competence.

In a rank order validity study (Yang & Weir, 1998), 50 experienced teachers were invited to provide a rank order list of the English proficiency of the students in their classes and to judge whether a particular student would pass the CET-4. A high correlation between CET-4 scores and teachers' rank order (an average correlation of .7) and satisfactory decision validity (an average agreement of 82 percent) were achieved.

The item-setting process of the CET follows a principled procedure, which consists of stringent control of item difficulty level and discrimination power through pre-testing and a careful check of the coverage of test operations specified in the test specifications. However, it was felt necessary during the validation study to collect evidence and see whether the behavior of the CET test-takers matched the expectations of the test developers. An introspective study was therefore conducted on the CET-4 and CET-6 reading components of the prototype test papers (Jin & Wu, 1997, 1998). A total of 40 students from Fudan University and Shanghai Jiaotong University participated in the experiment, which employed the think-aloud technique. Major findings included: (a) Students using expected reading operations were more likely to arrive at correct answers; (b) when students took the CET reading test, authentic reading behavior was produced, which involves the use of contributory reading strategies in order to facilitate comprehension; and (c) students using non-contributory test-taking strategies were more likely to get the wrong answers.

Marking Reliability

The NCETC has established, over the years, a qualified team of essay markers and a strict system of quality control. Prior to 2006, the Committee and its three Test Centers were responsible for the coordination of the 11 CET marking centers, including the selection and training of markers, and the implementation of all other quality control measures.

Due to the immense scale of the CET, the Committee requires its markers to read an essay once only and to give a holistic impression mark based on the level descriptors. Directors of the 11 CET marking centers are invited by the Committee after each administration of the test to decide on the range-finders (representative essays for each level) and two sets of sample scripts to be used for marker training. In each center, there are 5–10 supervisors, who are responsible for marker training and spot checking of the quality of marking in the center. Each supervisor is in charge of several groups of markers. For each group of markers, there is a group leader who conducts random checking of the essays in his/her group and marks the essays as well.

An investigation of CET marker reliability was conducted during the 1990s validation study (Yang & Weir, 1998), in which 240 markers from six marking centers were required to mark two parallel sets of pre-scored scripts. The results of the study showed that these markers in general were able to keep to the standards, as more than 84 percent of them gave the two parallel scripts marks that fell within the same level, with a higher percentage of agreement for the scripts of low and high scores than for the middle ones. The study also showed that CET markers are over-sensitive to students' grammatical errors, but not sensitive enough to their idiomatic use of English. The findings had important implications for improving the quality of CET marking. In the marker training sessions following the study, CET essay markers were encouraged to reward students' accurate and idiomatic use of English rather than penalize their incorrect grammar.

Starting in December 2006, the National Education Examinations Authority and the Provincial or Municipal Education Examinations Authorities took over responsibility for the coordination of the marking centers, with the NCETC still being responsible for implementing the CET essay marking approach and marking scheme and the quality control of the CET marking. Figure 4.2 shows the system of the CET essay marking and its quality control procedure before and after the reform of the operational structure for the CET in 2006.

Since 2004, the NCETC has successfully experimented with the CET online marking system, which was co-developed with a commercial computer systems provider. Quality control measures tailored to the needs of CET marking were built into the system, making it the only test in China that is working on a one-reading plus spot-checking principle. For the December 2007 administration, more than 7 million CET scripts were

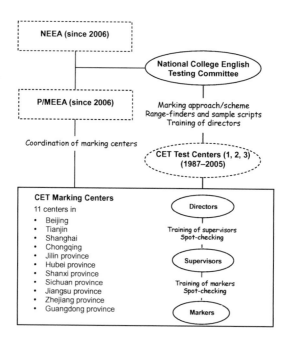

Figure 4.2 The CET Essay Marking System and Quality Control Procedure

Notes
The ovals and boxes with dotted lines indicate the parts of the system where changes were made in the recent reform. For abbreviations, please see Figure 4.1.

marked online, greatly improving the efficiency and quality of marking. Apart from the essays, constructed response items such as dictation, sentence completion, translation, and so forth were also marked using the CET online system.

Washback of the CET

As an assessment tool to see whether college students have met the curriculum requirements of the compulsory College English course of Band 4 or Band 6 as specified in the various versions of the national teaching syllabus (State Education Commission, 1985, 1986; Ministry of Education, 1999), the CET has drawn both teachers' and learners' attention to College English teaching and learning, which was much neglected before the mid-1980s. Students in most of China's colleges and universities are required to take the CET-4 at the end of the foundation stage study (i.e., the first 2 years of college or university study) and some are required to take the CET-6 before graduation.

As a result of the implementation of the CET, resources such as books, audio-visual materials, and so forth are more readily available and language labs more easily accessible to teachers and students. To help teachers and students make further improvements, the NCETC has been exploring ways to provide various types of diagnostic feedback after each administration of the test. Item analysis data, for example, are reported to teachers to help them understand their students' strengths and weaknesses and take appropriate measures in their future teaching. Institutions are given the writing score distribution data, indicating the average writing ability of the students in a university or college. An Average Graded Score is used to indicate the overall proficiency of students in a university, a city, or a province. The data help educational policy-makers at various levels, for example, university authorities, the Higher Education Departments of Provincial or Municipal Education Commissions and the Higher Education Department of the Ministry of Education, make appropriate decisions with respect to English language teaching and learning.

The growing awareness of the importance of the ability to communicate in English and the increasing value attached to the CET test results, coupled with expanded college and university enrolment, have led to sharp increases in the number of CET test-takers in recent years. The average rate of increase has remained between 10 and 20 percent a year since the late 1990s. The annual CET test population climbed to a record number of 12 million in 2006 and soared to 12.5 million in 2007. Now the test is administered in 32 provinces and autonomous regions including Tibet and Macao. Due to its social significance and immense scale, the CET has become a driving force for the development of College English teaching and learning, thus contributing in its way to the steady improvement of the students' performances in the CET. Statistics from different administrations of the test indicate clearly the rapid progress made by college and university students in their English proficiency (Jin & Yang, 2006).

Responding to the Changing Needs of Society: Revisions to the CET

The starting point and the ultimate purpose of such a large-scale test as the CET is to cater to the needs of society. In Bachman's words, "tests are not developed and used in a value-free psychometric test-tube; they are virtually always intended to serve the needs of an educational system or of society at large" (Bachman, 1990, p. 279). With the steady development of China's economy and the government's continuous efforts to further its reform and opening up policy in the past two decades, there has long been a pressing need for college and university graduates with higher levels of English language proficiency. Hence, major revisions were made to the College English Teaching Syllabus (State Education Commission, 1985, 1986) in 1999 and 2004. In the 1985/1986 syllabus, explicit emphasis was placed on students' ability to read in English and to use English as a medium to access information related to their major areas of study. The 1999 version gave more emphasis to listening, speaking, and writing abilities. In the 2004 version of the College English Curriculum Requirements (Ministry of Education, 2004), students are required to further improve their listening and speaking abilities so that "in their future work and social interactions they will be able to exchange information effectively through both spoken and written channels" (p. 24).

Following the revisions of the teaching requirements which aimed at reflecting to a larger extent the changing needs of society, major changes both in content and format have been introduced in the CET to enhance its validity.

Changes in the Test Content and Format

Based on the first College English Teaching Syllabus (State Education Commission, 1985, 1986) and due largely to the Committee's concern with marking reliability in the late 1980s and early 1990s, the predominant form of the test items was the objective item format, namely, multiple choice questions. Subjective items, or constructed response items, accounted for 15 percent in the CET-4 and 25 percent in the CET-6 when the tests were designed (College English Test Design Group, 1994a, 1994b).

To place more emphasis on the use of language, the Committee has gradually shifted its focus from reliability towards validity and introduced to the CET a number of subjective item formats since 1997, including for example, short answer questions, dictation, translation, and sentence completion. Students are required not only to choose a correct or best answer from a number of given options, but also to express ideas in their own words. Meanwhile, items testing knowledge about the language (e.g., structure items) were reduced in 1997 and the Vocabulary and Structure Section was entirely removed in 2006. In the latest version of the CET test, the percentage of constructed response items has risen to 35–45 percent depending on the alternative formats to be adopted for each test. For example, Short Answer Questions and Banked Cloze are alternatively used for testing careful reading; and integrated tasks can be either Cloze or Error Identification and Correction. With regard to the skills being tested, comprehension of longer conversations, expeditious reading (i.e., skimming and scanning), understanding the contextual meaning of vocabulary in a reading passage (banked cloze), and translation from Chinese to English have been assessed in the revised CET since 2006 (National College English Testing Committee, 2006a, 2006b).

The most significant development was the introduction of the CET Spoken English Test (CET-SET) in 1999. With the clear intention of encouraging students to participate more actively in interactive communication, the test adopts the format of face-to-face interviews and includes a monologue, dialogue, and group discussion. Three test-takers form a mini-group in the test, each answering some questions posed by the interlocutor and making a 1.5-minute individual presentation. They are also required to take part in a 4.5-minute discussion of a controversial topic. During the CET-SET, each test-taker is required to talk for approximately 6.5 minutes. Analytical scores on the three criteria, that is, accuracy and range, size and discourse management, flexibility and appropriacy, are given by an interlocutor and an assessor and are then converted to a graded score (National College English Testing Committee, 1999). In the interests of practicality of test administration, the CET-SET is available only to students who have received a CET score above the qualification point set by the Committee. Although the CET-SET is an optional test and a separate certificate is granted, the implementation of the test has provided positive washback on the teaching and learning of English in universities in China (Jin, 2000).

Changes made to the CET test content and format over the past two decades are summarized in Table 4.1.

Changes in the Score Reporting System

With the revisions made to the test content and format, it was hoped that the CET would be a better measure of Chinese college and university students' English language proficiency. A good measure, however, may not necessarily be used in an appropriate way. For a large-scale test, the score reporting system may have a marked effect on the use of the test.

Unlike most other large-scale standardized language tests, which are either norm-referenced or criterion-referenced, the CET is designed as a criterion-related norm-referenced test. The CET assesses students' skills on key aspects of the language as determined in the teaching syllabuses or curriculum requirements and as reflected in the CET test syllabuses; in this way, it is criterion-related. Scores of each administration are equated first using anchored students, who usually take the test for the equating purpose one or two weeks before the actual test administration, and then normalized against a pre-determined norm set up in 1987 (CET-4) and 1989 (CET-6). In this way the test is clearly norm-referenced. The reported score of any student on the CET, therefore, indicates the percentile position of that student as if she or he had been in the norm group, which was composed of about 10,000 students from six top universities: Beijing University, Tsinghua University, Fudan University, Shanghai Jiaotong University, University of Science and Technology of China, and Xi'an Jiaotong University.

Before June 2005, the CET adopted a 100-point score scale, with a mean of 72 and a standard deviation of 12. A cut-off score was set for 60 and a score of 85 or above was labeled as *Distinction*. However, the cut-off line was to some degree misused. For example, in some colleges and universities, students aimed at a narrow pass and stopped learning English after they passed the test. Teachers were often evaluated according to their students' overall pass rate. With a view to promoting the use of CET test results in a more rational manner, the NCETC in the recent revision abandoned the cut-off line in June 2005 and changed the score reporting system. Instead of issuing a certificate indicating whether the test-taker had passed the test or failed, the CET now gives the test-taker a Score Report Form, showing both the overall score and the profile score for each component. Overall scores range from 220 to 710, with a mean of 500 and a

Table 4.1 Changes in CET Test Content and Format

	1987 (CET-4); 1989 (CET-6)	1997	2006
Listening			
Content	20% Short conversations Listening passages	20% Short conversations, Listening passages or Passage dictation	35% Short conversations, Long conversations, Listening passages, Passage dictation
Format	MCQ	MCQ, Dictation	MCQ, Dictation
Reading			
Content	40% Careful reading	40% Careful reading	35% 25% Reading in depth; 10% Skimming and scanning
Format	MCQ	MCQ, SAQ, Translation (English to Chinese)	MCQ, SAQ, Banked cloze, True or false, Sentence completion
Vocabulary and structure			
Content	15% 7.5% Vocabulary 7.5% Structure	15% CET-4: 10% Vocabulary and 5% Structure; CET-6: 15% Vocabulary	–
Format	MCQ	MCQ	
Writing and translation			
Content	15% CET-4: 100 words in 30 min; CET-6: 120 words in 30 min	15% CET-4: 100 words in 30 min; CET-6: 120 words in 30 min	20% 120 (CET-4)/150 (CET-6) words in 30 min; Translation
Format	Guided writing	Guided writing	Guided writing, Translation (Chinese to English)
Integrated tasks			
Content	10% Integrated task	10% Integrated task	10% Integrated task
Format	Cloze, Error identification and correction	Cloze, Error identification and correction	Cloze, Error identification and correction
Speaking (optional)			
Content and Format	—	Since 1999; Question and answer, Individual presentation, Group discussion	

Table 4.2 Changes in the CET Score Reporting System

Starting date	Mean	SD	Score report	Score interpretation
1987/1989	72	12	Pass Distinction 60 85	Percentile position in the norm group (students in the six top universities in
June 2005 December 2006	500	70	No pass or fail; Reporting total and profile scores	China) In the process of setting up a new norm

standard deviation of 70. Profile score ranges vary slightly across the sub-tests. Table 4.2 summarizes the changes in the CET score reporting system over the years.

With changes in the CET score reporting system, university authorities and officials are adjusting their policies with respect to the use of the CET results. While some universities still require their students to obtain a certain score for graduation, others have abandoned the requirement completely. With new formats and content being introduced to the revised CET in 2006, the NCETC is in the process of establishing a new norm so that CET scores will have clearer and more appropriate interpretations.

From Academic Endeavor to Social Ethics: the NCETC's New Mission Statement

Since the late 1980s when the CET was first designed and implemented, the NCETC has paid particular attention to the measurement standards of this large-scale standardized test, pursuing high validity, reliability, and practicality. As a result, the CET has not only gained recognition among university authorities, teachers, and students but has also been well received by the public. With the growing population and importance of the CET, teachers and students are paying more attention to English language teaching and learning, resulting in a steady improvement in students' English language proficiency. As noted by the Vice Minister of Education at the second news conference of the Ministry of Education in 2005 on the revision of the CET,

> The fact that such a large-scale test has been developing steadily in the past 17 years is in itself solid evidence to show that the CET has met social needs, won social recognition, produced beneficial effects on society, and contributed significantly to the continual improvement of the quality of College English teaching in China. (Wu, 2005)

Meanwhile, an increasing number of people and institutions are being involved in test design, item writing, and test administration, allowing for a healthy development of the CET and striving to ensure that the test is not only of high quality but also securely and reliably administered.

The concerted efforts to maintain the quality of the CET in the past two decades have brought the test a good reputation among its test users. The CET is gaining increasing recognition as a reliable indicator of college and university graduates' English language proficiency. Its stakes are also rising because more and more uses, intended or unintended, are being made of the test. The results of a high-stakes test "are seen—rightly or wrongly—by students, teachers, administrators, parents, or the general public, as being used to make important decisions that immediately and directly affect them" (Madaus, 1988, p. 87). In China today, apart from the CET, there are quite a number of large-scale, high-stakes tests, such as (a) the college and university entrance examination; (b) the key high school entrance examination; (c) the graduate school entrance examination; (d) the Public English Testing Systems; and (e) the Test for English Majors. The high stakes associated with these tests have put test designers in a situation that is impossible to win, whereby the higher the stakes, the more the test can influence what goes on in the classroom, and the greater the possibility for the test to be misused, that is, over-used or used for purposes not intended. Although a high-stakes test can be used as "a catalyst for curriculum innovation", "a strategy to promote curricular innovation", or "a mechanism to drive instruction" (Andrews, 2004, pp. 39–42), it may well become a "ferocious master of the educational process" (Madaus, 1988, pp. 84–85) or "an unethical and undemocratic way of making policy" (Shohamy, 2000, p. 11).

In the case of the CET, one of the most worrisome problems is teaching to the test. In a country with a long history of examinations, teaching to testing is a phenomenon which is prevalent, especially when the test has high stakes. Prior to the abandonment of the CET cut-off line in June 2005, many universities required their students to pass the CET-4 in order to graduate or get their undergraduate degrees. In the competitive job market, a CET certificate with a pass grade or a good test score in many cases has become one of the prerequisites for employment adopted by personnel departments when recruiting college or university graduates. In major cities like Beijing and Shanghai, university graduates are required to pass the CET-4 in order to be granted a residence permit. A recent doctoral study of the washback of the CET on college English teaching and learning (Gu, 2004) shows that in some universities, English textbooks gave way to CET mock tests and classroom activities were replaced by the training of students in test-taking strategies.

Therefore, changes in the CET test content and format are not made just for the sake of test validity. The implied intent is to make the test serve teaching more effectively. As Messick (1996) rightly pointed out, "construct under-representation" and "construct-irrelevant variance" are potential sources of negative washback (p. 252). In a similar fashion, changes in the score reporting system are not simply meant to prevent the use of the CET certificate as a prerequisite for graduation or a nationally-recognized credential for employment. Instead, this is also a purposeful act with a view to encouraging appropriate use of the test results and, accordingly, improving the test's washback on teaching and learning and its impact on society.

Public examinations are double-edged swords, and the CET is a classic case in point. Through its twenty years of experience in designing and revising this large-scale EFL test, the NCETC has come to realize that a powerful test like the CET can be "both a blessing and a worry" (Jin, 2005) for college English teaching and learning. Around the world, in the field of language testing, the growing concern over the social consequences of language tests and the awareness of language testers' social responsibilities have given rise to the need for an extension of the concept of test validity to embrace the facet of the test's washback effect on teaching and learning and its impact on society (e.g., Bachman & Palmer, 1996; Bailey, 1996; Cheng, Watanabe, & Curtis, 2004; Jin, 2006; Kunnan,

2004; McNamara, 2000; Messick, 1996; Weir, 2005). As echoed in Principle 9 of the Code of Ethics for the International Language Testing Association, "Language testers shall regularly consider the potential effects, both short and long term, on all stakeholders of their projects, reserving the right to withhold their professional services on the grounds of conscience" (International Language Testing Association, 2000, p. 6).

The mission of the NCETC in the new millennium is, therefore, to explore ways that will maintain the highest possible quality of the test and at the same time bring about anticipated beneficial washback. As a purely academic organization that has limited control over the use of the test results, however, the NCETC is facing a daunting challenge in its efforts to address the social consequences of the CET and to ensure that the test is playing a positive role in English language teaching at the tertiary level in China as originally intended by its designers. To this end, the NCETC has begun a thorough investigation of the washback and impact of the CET. In the meantime, the Committee is exploring the relationship between language teaching and testing. As vividly described by Li and Zeng (2002) at the First International Conference on English Language Testing in China sponsored and organized by the NCETC in 2002, the nature of the relationship between testing and teaching, instead of being a one-way dog-wags-tail or tail-wags-dog relationship, should be a vigorous interaction that would help drive both teaching and testing forward in step with each other. Providing diagnostic feedback is one way to achieve this interaction, and stressing the importance of combining formative assessment and summative tests in language teaching is also considered to be a potentially effective solution. At the technical level, the NCETC will investigate the possibility and potential benefits of making a large-scale test like the CET a criterion-referenced test. Another major step forward for the NCETC in improving the design and delivery of the CET is to make the best use of modern technology and develop an internet-based version of the test. Whatever the measures that need to be taken, the future of the CET lies in its role as an impetus to English language teaching and learning at the tertiary level in China.

References

Andrews, S. (2004). Washback and curriculum innovation. In L. Cheng, Y. Watanabe, & A. Curtis (Eds.), *Washback in language testing: Research contexts and methods* (pp. 37–50). Mahwah, NJ: Lawrence Erlbaum.

Bachman, L. F. (1990). *Fundamental considerations in language testing*. Oxford: Oxford University Press.

Bachman, L. F. & Palmer, A. S. (1996). *Language testing in practice*. Oxford: Oxford University Press.

Bailey, K. M. (1996). Working for washback: A review of the washback concept in language testing. *Language Testing*, 13, 257–279.

Cheng, L., Watanabe, Y. & Curtis, A. (Eds.). (2004). *Washback in language testing: Research contexts and methods*. Mahwah, NJ: Lawrence Erlbaum.

College English Test Design Group. (1994a). *College English Test Band Four Syllabus and Sample Tests* (Rev. ed.). Shanghai, China: Shanghai Foreign Language Education Press.

College English Test Design Group. (1994b). *College English Test Band Six Syllabus and Sample Tests* (Rev. ed.). Shanghai, China: Shanghai Foreign Language Education Press.

Davis, A. (1990). *Principles of language testing*. Oxford: Blackwell.

Gu, X. (2004). Positive or negative? An empirical study of CET washback on College English teaching and learning in China. Unpublished doctoral dissertation, Shanghai Jiaotong University, Shanghai, China.

International Language Testing Association. (2000, March). *Code of Ethics for ILTA.* Adopted at the annual meeting of the International Language Testing Association, Vancouver, British Columbia, Canada.

Jin, Y. (2000). Backwash effect of CET-SET on teaching EFL in China. *Foreign Language World,* 4, 56–61.

Jin, Y. (2005, July). The National College English Test. In L. Hamp-Lyons (Chair), *Big Tests.* Symposium at the annual meeting of the International Association of Applied Linguistics, Madison, WI.

Jin, Y. (2006). On the improvement of test validity and test washback: The CET washback study. *Foreign Language World,* 6, 65–73.

Jin, Y., & Wu, J. (1997). An application of introspection in research on testing of reading. *Foreign Language World,* 4, 56–59.

Jin, Y., & Wu, J. (1998). Examining the validity of CET reading comprehension by introspection. *Foreign Language World,* 2, 47–52.

Jin, Y., & Yang, H. (2006). The English proficiency of college and university students in China: As reflected in the CET. *Language, Culture and Curriculum,* 19, 21–36.

Kunnan, A. (2004). Test fairness. In M. Milanovic, C. Weir, & S. Bolton (Eds.), *Europe language testing in a global context: Selected papers from the ALTE conference in Barcelona* (pp. 27–48). Cambridge: Cambridge University Press.

Li, X. & Zeng, Y. (2002, September). *Language testing and teaching: Is the tail wagging the dog?* Paper presented at the First International Conference on English Language Testing in China, Shanghai, China.

Madaus, G. F. (1988). The influence of testing on the curriculum. In L. Tanner (Ed.), *Critical issues in curriculum: Eighty-seventh yearbook of the National Society for the Study of Education* (pp. 83–121). Chicago: University of Chicago Press.

McNamara, T. (2000). *Language testing.* Oxford: Oxford University Press.

Messick, S. (1996). Validity and washback in language testing. *Language Testing,* 13, 241–256.

Ministry of Education. (1999). *National College English Teaching Syllabus* (Rev. ed.). Shanghai, China: Shanghai Foreign Language Education Press.

Ministry of Education. (2004). *College English Curriculum Requirements (For Trial Implementation).* Shanghai, China: Shanghai Foreign Language Education Press.

National College English Testing Committee. (1999). *CET-SET Test Syllabus and Sample Test Paper.* Shanghai, China: Shanghai Foreign Language Education Press.

National College English Testing Committee. (2006a). *CET-4 Test Syllabus and Sample Test Paper* (Rev. ed.). Shanghai, China: Shanghai Foreign Language Education Press.

National College English Testing Committee. (2006b). *CET-6 Test Syllabus and Sample Test Paper* (Rev. ed.). Shanghai, China: Shanghai Foreign Language Education Press.

Shohamy, E. (2000). Using language tests for upgrading knowledge. *Hong Kong Journal of Applied Linguistics,* 5(1), 1–18.

State Education Commission. (1985). *College English Teaching Syllabus (For College and University Students of Science and Technology).* Shanghai, China: Shanghai Foreign Language Education Press.

State Education Commission. (1986). *College English Teaching Syllabus (For College and University Students of Arts and Science).* Shanghai, China: Shanghai Foreign Language Education Press.

Sun, Y. (1985). *Collected works of Sun Yat-sen.* Volume 5. Beijing, China: Zhong Hua Book Company.

Weir, C. J. (2005). *Language testing and validation: An evidence-based approach*. New York: Palgrave Macmillan.

Wu, Q. (2005). *On the revision of the CET*. Second news conference of the Ministry of Education. Retrieved February 25, http://www.moe.edu.cn.

Yang, H., & Weir, C. J. (1998). *The CET validation study*. Shanghai, China: Shanghai Foreign Language Education Press.

5 Developments of English Language Assessment in Public Examinations in Hong Kong

Chee-cheong Choi and Christina Lee, Hong Kong Examinations and Assessment Authority

The Hong Kong Examinations and Assessment Authority (HKEAA) is a statutory body established in May 1977 to conduct public examinations for Hong Kong students at the end of various key stages of their secondary education. These statutory responsibilities currently cover the Hong Kong Certificate of Education Examination (HKCEE;「香港中學會考」) for Secondary 5 school leavers and the Hong Kong Advanced Level Examination (HKALE;「香港高級程度會考」) for Secondary 7 leavers seeking admission to universities. The HKEAA also conducts many other examinations and assessments on behalf of overseas as well as local institutions, including examining boards, professional bodies and the Hong Kong Special Administrative Region Government. This chapter describes the work of the HKEAA with an emphasis on the development of English language assessments in two public examinations—the HKCEE and HKALE. It describes how they have interfaced with the communicative approach of the school curriculum, how they have strived to generate positive washback effects, and to meet the needs of major users of examination results, namely, schools, employers, and universities. The chapter also describes how the format of the examinations has been designed to meet the primary qualities of sound language assessments, namely, validity, reliability, authenticity, practicality, equity, and positive washback effects on learning.

Introduction to the HKEAA

The Hong Kong Examinations and Assessment Authority (known as the Hong Kong Examinations Authority or HKEA prior to July 2002) is a statutory body set up by the Hong Kong Government in 1977 to conduct public examinations in Hong Kong. It is a self-financing organization established under the Hong Kong Examinations and Assessment Authority Ordinance. The governing body, the Authority Council, currently has 17 members coming from the school sector, tertiary institutions, and government bodies, including persons experienced in commerce, industry, or a profession. All non-ex-officio members are appointed by the Chief Executive of the Hong Kong Special Administrative Region (HKSAR) Government. The Council is responsible for formulating examination policies and monitoring the work of the Authority, and the 340-member Secretariat is the executive arm of the Authority, responsible for serving its committees and making arrangements for the conduct of examinations.

Hong Kong currently adopts a 3+2+2 secondary school system, i.e., 3 years of junior secondary (S.1–S.3); 2 years of senior secondary (S.4–S.5); and 2 years of sixth form (S.6–S.7). There is no public examination at the end of the first key stage of secondary education. Students take the HKCEE at the end of S.5 (usually around the age of 17), and approximately one-third of them are able to proceed to sixth form in the public sector financed by the Government. They take the HKALE at the end of S.7 (usually aged around 19). Depending on the results of the examination, they seek admission to universities, which normally offer 3-year programs. Commencing September 2009, S.3 students will proceed to a new 3+3+4 system (3 years of junior secondary as before; 3 years of senior secondary; followed by 4-year degree programs). The HKCEE and HKALE will be replaced by the new Hong Kong Diploma of Secondary Education (HKDSE) Examination, which will be administered by the HKEAA for the first time in 2012. This new examination will certify achievements of secondary school leavers in addition to selecting them for university education.

The Examination Landscape Prior to 1977

Prior to 1977, there were three main public examinations in Hong Kong. The HKCEE, taken by Secondary 5 students, was conducted by the Education Department of the Hong Kong Government. The Chinese University Matriculation Examination (CUME), taken by Secondary 6 students (normally aged around 18) completing the 1-year sixth-form course, or at the end of year 1 of the 2-year sixth-form course, as well as some Secondary 7 students following the 2-year sixth-form course, was conducted by The Chinese University of Hong Kong (CUHK). The Hong Kong University Advanced Level Examination (HKUALE) taken by Secondary 7 students was conducted by The University of Hong Kong (HKU).

The HKCEE was a device for selection to sixth form in Hong Kong secondary schools. It also certified the basic education qualification of Secondary 5 students for junior employment. The CUME was solely for admission to CUHK, which was at that time offering 4-year programs. All tertiary institutions running 3-year programs admitted students based on the results of the Advanced Level Examination. CUHK also admitted some Secondary 7 students based on their A-level results when it offered 4-year programs. Candidates who acquired specified CE (i.e., HKCEE) and A-level qualifications could also apply for mid-level posts in the civil service of the Hong Kong Government.

Birth of an Independent Examinations Authority

The Authority was established with a view to achieving better co-ordination, standardization, and resource utilization in public examinations in Hong Kong. The statutory responsibility of the new organization is to conduct all public examinations. It is financially independent but the Hong Kong Special Administrative Region (HKSAR) Government provides premises and non-recurrent subsidies for special initiatives relating to enhancing the processing of public examinations. The Authority works closely with the Curriculum Development Institute of the Education and Manpower Bureau of the Government (renamed the Education Bureau in July 2007).

The HKEA assumed responsibility for the conduct of the HKCEE, the CUME and the HKUALE in 1978, 1979, and 1980, respectively. The two matriculation examinations became public examinations and were renamed the Hong Kong Higher Level Examination (HKHLE) and the Hong Kong Advanced Level Examination (HKALE), respectively. In addition, the Authority conducted the Use of English Examination, an English language proficiency examination required for admission to HKU. The Authority also conducted more than 100 examinations of different kinds on behalf of overseas and local educational and professional bodies as well as examination boards, including the Associated Board of the Royal Schools of Music, the London Chamber of Commerce and Industry Examinations Board, Educational Testing Service, the National Education Examinations Authority of China, the Association of Chartered Certified Accountants, and the Hong Kong Society of Accountants.

Reforming Sixth-form Education

In June 1989, the Working Group on Sixth-form Education (WG) appointed by the Government published its report (Hong Kong Government, 1989). Based on the recommendations of the WG, the Government decided to offer only the 2-year sixth-form course from September 1992 onwards. As all government-funded tertiary institutions had to offer 3-year programs from September 1994 onwards, the HKHLE was conducted for the last time in 1992, and a host of AS-level (advanced supplementary) subjects were introduced to the HKALE to broaden the sixth-form curriculum. Beginning in 1994, students seeking admission to tertiary institutions had to have scored at least grade E in the two new AS-level subjects, Use of English and Chinese Language & Culture. In 1993, the statutory responsibility of the HKEA was revised to conduct the two public examinations, the HKCEE and the HKALE. The Use of English Examination was incorporated into the HKALE in 1994 as one of the newly-introduced AS-level subjects.

Two High-Stakes English Language Examinations

The Authority was renamed the Hong Kong Examinations and Assessment Authority in July 2002 following the necessary amendment of the HKEA Ordinance, giving it a broader portfolio to conduct assessment activities. These include the Language Proficiency Assessment for Teachers (LPAT) and the Territory-Wide System Assessment (TSA) commissioned by the HKSAR Government. Both have an English language component, but Use of English in the HKALE and English Language in the HKCEE have remained the two most important English language assessments conducted by the HKEAA: these examinations are taken by more than 130,000 candidates annually. The primary function of the English language examinations in the HKCEE and the HKALE has been to assess the English proficiency of students at the end of a key stage in their education in order to gauge whether they are adequately prepared for the next stage, where English is frequently used as the medium of instruction.

Hong Kong is a cosmopolitan city and sets great store by high English proficiency, so the importance of these two English language qualifications in Hong Kong cannot be over-emphasized. A grade E (or Level 2, as of 2007) in HKCEE English Language is a pre-requisite for entering sixth form and a grade E in Use of English is a minimum language requirement for university admission. Results of all subjects in both HKCEE and HKALE are reported as six grades, from A to F, with the exception of HKCEE Chinese Language and English Language which have adopted standards-referenced reporting since 2007. Results below grade F are not reported. High English proficiency is also a gateway to securing desirable employment in Hong Kong. This chapter thus focuses on the major developments in English language assessments in HKCEE and HKALE since the inception of the HKEAA.

Assessment Strategy of the HKEAA

The Authority's principal assessment strategy in testing English skills has been to support the English language curriculum which has adopted a communicative approach since the early 1980s. Since its inception, the Authority has aimed at developing its English language assessments for public examinations to meet the criteria of quality language assessments: validity, reliability, authenticity, operational practicality, equity, and above all, the generation of a positive washback effect on English learning in school.

The main targets for designing the assessments have been: (1) to use test materials selected from authentic sources (newspapers, magazines, and the Internet); (2) to test productive and receptive skills in an integrated form; and (3) to require candidates to perform contextualized authentic tasks which they may need to carry out in everyday situations. For example, grammar is not tested using discrete items, but in a contextualized manner; composition topics are given a context so that students know the purpose and the audience for which they are writing.

HKCEE: Syllabus A and Syllabus B

The Hong Kong School Certificate Examination was first introduced in 1937, primarily for Anglo-Chinese school students, and the first school certificate examination for Chinese secondary school students was introduced in 1952. These two examinations were amalgamated in 1974 giving birth to the current HKCEE. Two syllabuses— Syllabus A and Syllabus B—were devised for the subject of English Language to cater to the needs of two cohorts of students with discernible disparity in English language standards. In general, Syllabus A was designed for Chinese secondary school students and Syllabus B for Anglo-Chinese school students. In reality, individual schools and students were allowed to make their own choice based on their own expectations and the original demarcation blurred over the years. In fact, there has always been a single English Language teaching curriculum for senior secondary students.

Traditionally, a grade C in Syllabus A is recognized as equivalent to a grade E in Syllabus B by local universities. The Authority formalized the equivalence in 1987 by adopting approximately 20 common items in the multiple-choice papers. While a Syllabus B grade C has been recognized as the equivalent of an "O-level pass" in an overseas General Certificate of Education (GCE) Examination, Syllabus A grades do not enjoy such overseas recognition. However, a grade E in Syllabus A helps a student meet the minimum English language requirement for sixth-form admission.

In the early years, the formats of these two examinations and the skills tested were quite different. For example, there was a translation component in Syllabus A until 1978 but no oral examination until 1986. Listening tests were introduced into both syllabuses in 1986. In 1996, there was a major redesigning of the English Language syllabuses aiming to bring about further positive washback on the English language education in Hong Kong secondary schools (Cheng, 1997, 2005). The first change was an integration of the listening test and the directed writing paper in the Syllabus B English Language examination, which involved the candidates listening to spoken materials, reading written texts, and then completing written tasks. This revised listening test assessing integrated skills posed a great challenge to all parties: test developers, teachers, and students. A less exacting but similar test was designed for Syllabus A. The second major change was introducing a group interaction component into the two oral tests. The two syllabuses adopted the same assessment format in terms of paper structure and skills tested, with the only difference being in the level of difficulty.

The year 2007 saw the HKCE English Language examination morph into a new shape, in order to be aligned with the 1999 English Language Teaching Syllabus for Secondary Schools prepared by the Curriculum Development Council (appointed by the HKSAR Chief Executive to advise the Government on primary and secondary curricular matters, with the Curriculum Development Institute providing administrative and professional support). The two syllabuses, A and B, were amalgamated and major changes made, which involved the introduction of school-based assessment and the adoption of standards-referenced reporting (see Davison, 2007; Chapter 18). The two syllabuses were combined because one examination provides a fairer assessment for all students based on the same set of standards. In addition, the negative labeling effect was removed, so schools would not feel compelled to opt for the more demanding—and therefore more prestigious—Syllabus B, regardless of the English standards of their students.

Some background information about the candidatures of the two syllabuses will provide a context for the decision to eliminate the two-syllabus approach. The ratio of Syllabus A to Syllabus B candidates had always been disproportionately small when compared to the number of Chinese-medium versus English-medium schools. Between the late 1980s and 2006 the combined Syllabus A and Syllabus B candidature fluctuated between 117,000 and 136,000, depending on demographic changes and the number of private candidates.[1] Syllabus A candidates constituted less than 5 percent of the combined candidature in the late 1980s but increased gradually to around 10 percent in the late 1990s. There was then a relatively large increase to 14 percent in 2000, due to the medium of instruction policy implemented in 1998, when 114 of the over 500 secondary schools were officially granted English medium of instruction (EMI) status. In 2006, the last year when both Syllabus A and Syllabus B were offered, about one-third of the 120,000 HKCEE English Language candidates opted for Syllabus A. The implementation of a single HKCEE English Language Examination has helped to remove any doubts about the choice of syllabus and provides a more level playing field for all candidates. The 2007 candidature was about 103,000, with the reduction largely due to the decrease in the number of private candidates, who are usually not keen to take part in examinations with new formats.

The school-based assessment component (SBA) takes the form of a reading/viewing program where students read books or watch films and take part in group discussions with classmates or make individual presentations on the texts they have read/viewed and respond to their teacher's questions (see HKEAA, 2005 for details of the SBA handbook). The assessment is based on the students' oral performance. The SBA has been introduced for a variety of reasons, the most important being the desire to improve the validity and reliability of the oral assessment. SBA is also expected to generate beneficial washback on the teaching and learning of English, and in particular to promote extensive reading/viewing. Also, there will be less reliance on a one-off public oral examination and less formulaic practice based on the public examination format. In addition, SBA is designed to offer teachers an opportunity for professional development and to empower them to become part of the assessment process.

The adoption of standards-referenced reporting (SRR) means that candidates' results will be reported against described levels of typical performance. Descriptors spelling out the standards required for different levels of performance are provided, along with examples of assessment tasks and samples of typical candidate performance to illustrate the requirements at different levels. End-users should therefore be able to better understand what candidates know and can do. SRR also facilitates teaching and learning by making explicit what a student has to do in order to reach a given level. An additional benefit is that standards can be better maintained over time. HKCEE Chinese Language has also adopted SRR since 2007 and this method of reporting will be implemented across the board for all HKDSE subjects with effect from 2012. Details of the assessment formats over the years can be found in the relevant HKCEE Regulations and Syllabuses Handbooks published by the HKEAA.

HKALE: Use of English

The Use of English (UE) examination was originally the exam used to measure the English proficiency of students seeking admission to the University of Hong Kong (HKU). The UE syllabus in the 1980s began with the following statement: "There will be one written paper and a listening test. These will examine the ability of candidates to understand and write English at the standard needed for pursuing courses in the University of Hong Kong" (HKEA, 1978, p. 83). The reference to HKU in the syllabus disappeared in 1989 when the UE examination was redesigned to measure a wider range of abilities. The aims and objectives of the examination became: "to foster the development of students' English language skills in order to equip them for tertiary education and/or employment" (HKEA, 1987, p. 190). These have remained unchanged up to today. The Authority conducted the UE examination on behalf of HKU between 1980 and 1993. In order to avoid confusing UE with an A-level subject, a separate UE certificate was issued during this period. The UE results have been recorded on the HKALE certificate since 1994 as an AS-level subject.

The main changes to the UE examination after the Authority took over the examination were: (1) the range of abilities tested has been expanded and (2) the assessments have been made more authentic by using more everyday tasks. In 1983, a working group was set up comprising academics from local tertiary institutions and Rex King, the then Senior Subject Officer who headed the Subjects Division (currently the Assessment Development Division) of the Authority, together with his team of English language subject officers (now known as Managers-Assessment Development). After several years of hard work, including consultation with schools, seminars for teachers, and the preparation of sample papers, the final version of the syllabus was published in May 1987 and the new examination took place in 1989.

The new examination consisted of four sections. Sections A and B focused on listening and writing skills, while Section C, called *Reading and Language Systems*, tested reading comprehension and language usage. Section D was entitled *Practical Skills for Work and Study*. For Hong Kong, this was quite revolutionary, as it tested candidates on their practical communicative skills through simulated work and study situations. It was essentially a paper testing the integrated skills of writing and reading, requiring candidates to perform everyday tasks based on authentic materials selected from newspapers, magazines, and the Internet. However, there was no assessment of oral skills until 1994, when the UE examination became an AS-level subject. To emphasize the importance of speaking skills, the oral component is given a weighting of 18 percent, similar to that of the listening, writing and reading sections, while the Practical Skills section remains the most heavily weighted component, at 28 percent.

The format of the UE examination has remained unchanged since 1994, while its candidature increased from approximately 19,000 in 1989 to nearly 26,000 in 1994, when it became an AS-level subject in the HKALE. This increase was due to the abolition of the HKHLE in 1993, which meant that all sixth-form students had to follow a 2-year course leading to the HKALE. The candidature for the 2008 examination was approximately 36,000.

Major Developments in Assessment Format

To sum up, the major landmarks in the development of English language assessment format over the last 30 years since the inception of the Authority are shown in Table 5.1.

Table 5.1 Major Changes in English Examination Syllabuses

Year	Examination	Development
1986	CE English Language	Introduction of listening tests into Syllabuses A and B. Introduction of oral test into Syllabus A
1989	Use of English	Redesigning the syllabus, becoming a 4-section examination, with an integrated reading and writing paper testing work and study skills
1994	AS-level UE	Introduction of oral test with a group discussion format
1996	CE English Language	Syllabuses A and B test similar skills differing only in difficulty, with a new paper testing integrated skills of reading, listening and writing, and the oral test thoroughly overhauled to include a group interaction component
2007	CE English Language	Introduction of school-based assessment and standards-referenced reporting; no differentiation into Syllabuses A and B

The Hong Kong Diploma of Secondary Education (HKDSE) Examination: English Language

The English language assessment format will undergo a major change in the near future with the implementation of the new senior secondary system in 2009. The HKCEE will be conducted for school candidates for the last time in 2010, and the HKALE in 2012, at which time the new Hong Kong Diploma of Secondary Education (HKDSE) Examination will take place for the first time.

The HKDSE English Language examination will be similar to the 2007 HKCEE, but the levels of performance are expected to be higher to meet university entrance requirements and students will be expected to have learnt more with 3 years' senior secondary education instead of the current 2-year course in preparation for the HKCEE. To cater to the needs of students with a wider range of language abilities after 3 years of senior secondary education, a graded approach will be adopted in the reading paper and in the listening and integrated skills paper. There will be a compulsory section with a medium level of difficulty, an easier section, and a more difficult section in each of these papers. Candidates will be free to choose either the easier or the more difficult section in the examination room, but those choosing the easier section will not be able to attain a top-level score. However, they will still be able to meet the requirement for university admission if they do well in the compulsory and easier sections.

Another radical change in the initial proposal regarding the speaking assessment was that school candidates would have their speaking skills assessed by their own teachers in school through the SBA component only, while the speaking paper would be offered to private candidates only. The major reason for this proposed change is that the SBA is considered a more valid and reliable assessment of speaking skills than a one-off oral examination conducted under stressful conditions with strangers as assessors in public examination settings. The proposed HKDSE assessment framework was finalized in April 2008 after a fourth round of consultation in January 2008, in the light of the 2007 HKCEE experience. Survey results indicated that the majority of school teachers were not in favor of abolishing the oral examination for school candidates, despite evidence that most teachers had been able to assess the speaking ability of their own students accurately and reliably with SBA. As a result, the speaking examination has been retained for school candidates, but given a lower weighting than the SBA. Details of the HKDSE English Language assessment framework can be found on the HKEAA website (www.hkeaa.edu.hk).

Technical Aspects of English Language Assessments

Turning to the technical aspects of examining English language proficiency, it is important to note the following developments which have taken place over the years in Hong Kong.

Reliability in Marking Composition: Double Impression Marking

Traditionally, Hong Kong adopted an analytical approach to marking English compositions for many years. It was very difficult to maintain consistency of marking standards among hundreds of markers as marking compositions was fairly subjective. There was also a tendency for markers to bunch the marks in the middle of the scale, thus reducing the discrimination of the assessment. Markers also found the task tedious as they had to count the number of grammatical and spelling mistakes. English language was a subject with a greater probability of upgrading when candidates lodged an appeal after the release of results. Against this backdrop, the Authority had to look for a more effective and reliable alternative.

Rex King, who headed the English team of subject officers when the Authority was established, was keen to develop a more effective means of assessing English compositions.

He completed a Masters of Education after joining the Authority and chose this as the topic of his thesis (King, 1980). His research showed that double impression marking was more reliable than single analytical marking. The results also indicated that while it would be unrealistic to expect markers to finely discriminate between the scripts on a 100-point scale, markers were able to rank order the scripts globally on a 9-point scale quite consistently. His proposal for double impression marking using a 9-point scale was subsequently implemented in the HKCEE English Language Syllabuses A and B examinations from 1986. This methodology was eventually extended to the marking of the Use of English composition scripts in 1989. The main features of this methodology are described below.

Pattern Marking

For the implementation of pattern marking each marker has to be assigned a random sample of scripts representing a cross-section of the entire candidature. Markers are required to rank the scripts in nine piles based on their holistic assessment of the work of the candidates in two broad dimensions: content and interest (including aspects such as task completion, effective communication and coherence); and technical aspects (e.g., punctuation, spelling, vocabulary, grammar, sentence structure, etc.).

The predetermined pattern chosen was close to the stanine distribution (4-8-12-16-20-16-12-8-4), with the top and bottom 4 percent of a batch being given Point 9 and Point 1, respectively. After ranking the scripts into nine piles, markers are required to carry out a vertical check and a horizontal check to make sure the gradation within and across points is correct. This fine-tuning helps to ensure the correct ranking of the scripts. At the end of the marking process, markers are required to complete a graph showing the number of scripts awarded each point on the scale. Each marker marks two batches of about 300 scripts each. The first marker records the score (1–9) on a flap, which is then detached from the script so that the second marker can carry out an assessment independently. The scripts are sorted into the original candidate number order before being sent back to the Authority, from which each marker is given randomly a second batch. Thus each marker does not know the identity of their marking partner.

Quality Control Measures

The computer compares the marks awarded by each partner within a team. If the discrepancy exceeds a prescribed limit, the scripts are re-marked by a third marker with positive marking statistics. Of the 120,000 candidates taking the English Language Syllabuses A and B examinations in HKCEE 2006 (the last year of double impression pattern marking for the CE writing papers) the number of candidates flagged by the computer for third marking was about 7,000, or approximately 6 percent. This discrepancy marking is an important quality control measure of the marking system.

Normally, the sum of the two markers' marks will be the score for the candidate. In the event of a third marking, the third marker's mark and one of the original two marks, whichever is closer to the third mark, will be adopted. The computer program also correlates the scores awarded by each marker with the scores of an objective paper. The overall correlation between the composition scores and the scores from the objective paper has generally been approximately .80. If the correlation coefficient of a marker is significantly lower than the norm, the marks awarded by this marker for his/her whole batch will be discarded and those given by the reliable partner will be doubled to yield the final scores of the candidates. If both team members have poor statistics, the whole batch will have to be re-marked by a more reliable marker. It is worth pointing out that the Authority takes special measures to ensure that teacher markers will not mark the scripts of candidates from their own schools, a measure which applies to all subjects.

Merits of the Methodology

Double impression marking of composition to a pre-determined pattern has proved satisfactory both for the HKCEE and the HKALE. First, the low-standard-deviation problem has been resolved, and better discrimination has been achieved. Second, marking reliability has improved, with an overall inter-marker correlation coefficient between .70 and .80. The number of successful appeals on the composition paper has been much lower than previously when analytical marking was used. Third, adoption of double impression pattern marking has removed the need for statistical mark adjustment due to strict or lenient marking.

Because of the introduction of SRR to HKCEE English Language in 2007, a new set of assessment guidelines has been developed for the writing paper based on the writing descriptors, and double impression pattern marking is no longer used at the CE level. However, this reliable and efficient marking method will continue to be used for the UE writing paper.

Listening Tests

Use of Headphones

The first large-scale listening test in Hong Kong was held in the Use of English Examination in 1979 using public announcement systems in school halls for a candidature of less than 10,000, with results that left much to be desired. Prior to 1986, there had been no listening test for the HKCE English Language examinations. Therefore, during the early 1980s, the Authority took pains to design a system for the satisfactory delivery of listening tests, and eventually a wireless induction loop system was chosen. Signals from a cassette tape were emitted through an amplifier and picked up by headphones worn by candidates. The capital cost was very large: over 33,000 headphones and over 130 sets of cassette players and amplifiers were purchased. Approximately 130 schools deemed to be suitable for this purpose had to be persuaded to have their school halls looped for examination purposes. Recurring costs for storage, maintenance, and movement of equipment made this approach prohibitively expensive.

The logistics of mounting a large-scale listening test using a wireless induction loop system were daunting. The equipment had to be tested after installation at the centre before the examination, and during the examination, invigilators had to carry spare headphones in case candidates asked for replacements. Teacher-invigilators, in particular the center supervisors, found this a stressful task because the test material would only be played once. Candidates' requests for replacement of headphones had to be attended to promptly and a record made on the replaced headphones for HKEAA's follow-up action. The listening test using headphones was first held for the Use of English Examination in 1984, for the Higher Level listening test in 1985, and for the HKCE English Language Examination (both for Syllabus A and Syllabus B) in 1986.

Choosing between Cost and Uniformity: The Five-Session Syllabus B Test

While the number of headphones was sufficient to meet the HKALE need, it lagged far behind the HKCE English Language (Syllabus B) candidature, which was over 100,000 in 1986. To hold the examination for everyone at the same time would be too expensive both in terms of capital cost and storage. After careful thought, it was decided to meet this challenge by arranging a 2-day examination for the Syllabus B listening test. This involved setting five sets of question papers. Rex King had a concise and precise description of how this task was undertaken:

> For security reasons, the three papers for Day 1 were set on common stimulus material using different but parallel items. The Day 2 versions had different stimulus material from Day 1, but usually with parallel themes. (King, 1994, p. 10)

The setting and moderation tasks were clearly daunting, and the relevant moderation committee, in particular the subject officers concerned, had an unenviable task. Each session was taken by a random subset of the Syllabus B candidature (as testified by their comparable mean scores in the multiple-choice paper) and it was expected that the mean score for each session should be quite comparable. The results were not as satisfactory as one would have liked, and despite the efforts put in by a group of experts, statistical adjustment to whole group mean and standard deviation was carried out for the five sessions in a bid to ensure fairness.

Moving to Radios

This unsatisfactory situation prompted the Authority to look for an alternative arrangement for administering the Syllabus B listening test. After much persuasion, Radio and Television Hong Kong (RTHK) finally agreed to support this operation, using one of its channels to broadcast the listening materials in the two public examinations. Candidates had, then, to bring their own battery-powered radios with earphones.

In 1995, the CE English Language Syllabus B listening test was delivered for the first time by radio broadcast. There was a full-scale trial exercise in the form of a mock examination for all Syllabus B candidates in March of that year in order to ensure that students and teachers, who would serve as invigilators that May, were familiar with the operation. Two years later, this mode of delivery of the listening test was extended to the Use of English exam. No trial was carried out as students had gone through a similar test two years previously, and the use of radio broadcasts was extended to the Syllabus A listening test in 1998.

Exploring Better Alternatives for Delivery

This mode of delivery, although plagued by a plethora of teething problems, is still in operation. The main problem lies in complaints from individual candidates regarding reception problems during the broadcast. If this problem is identified before the test material is broadcast, candidates go to a special room set up for this purpose, listening to a desk-top radio. But if the difficulty emerges during the broadcast of the test material, the situation is problematic because even if candidates rush to the special room, they still miss part of the test. The Authority has had to deal with several hundred cases each year, which represent less than .5 percent of the candidature. Although this figure is not disproportionately high, the Authority has been considering more effective alternatives, but an ideal solution has yet to emerge. RTHK switches from stereo to mono mode when broadcasting the listening tests to improve reception, and technicians are sent to examination centers beforehand to check on reception in a bid to pre-empt problems. However, there are still complaints about radio reception after each test, and much effort has to be spent on investigating these cases before appropriate remedial actions can be taken.

Oral Tests

Hong Kong Certificate of Education English Language Examination

At the CE level, an oral English test was incorporated into the English Language examination in the 1950 Hong Kong School Certificate Examination (for Anglo-Chinese schools) and this feature has been retained for the Syllabus B examination. The format of assessment in the early years consisted of a picture description and a simple dialogue with an examiner, which was then changed to reading aloud a prose passage or a short dialogue, followed by a short conversation with one or both of the examiners based on a picture. An oral component was added to the Syllabus A examination in 1986, with a similar format but less demanding.

There was a major change in assessment format in 1996 for both syllabuses. Part A of the test was a role play (6 min preparation plus 4 min role play). Each candidate was required to perform a task with each examiner based on instructions and information provided. Part B was a group interaction where four candidates grouped together were presented with a situation and a task which they worked on together through discussion. Candidates were assessed on their conversational strategies, overall fluency, and the contribution they made to the interaction, with the emphasis on effective communication rather than on task completion. Following this major change, the weighting for the oral component was increased from 10 to 18 percent; a format continued up to 2006.

The two syllabuses together captured a total candidature of over 130,000. The oral tests had to be conducted on 20 afternoons in June each year, engaging over 600 oral examiners working in pairs, and more than 60 sets of papers had to be set (20 for Syllabus A, 40 for Syllabus B, with two sets being used per day, one for each 90-min session). Special arrangements had to be made so that within each session, candidates having taken the test would not encounter those waiting to be examined.

The Use of English Examination (UE)

The incorporation of an oral component was seriously considered when the UE syllabus was redesigned for the 1989 examination. However, the idea was finally dropped because the logistics for conducting a reasonably long oral assessment for Secondary 7 students using double marking for 2 weeks were considered unmanageable at that time. An adequate supply of competent examiners was also in question in view of the difficulty in recruiting enough examiners for the HKCE oral examinations, as the number of teachers teaching sixth form was much smaller than that teaching at the CE level.

In the early 1990s, the Authority began to plan for the addition of an oral component in the UE examination principally to meet the request of local tertiary institutions for information on the English oral communication skills of Secondary 7 students seeking admission to universities, and to enhance the validity of the examination by addressing the construct-under-representation deficiency of the test (see Messick, 1996). It would also breathe some fresh air into classroom teaching, which hitherto had virtually ignored the training of speaking skills. This move was in line with the Authority's assessment policy to generate a positive washback effect on learning and teaching.

The key to overcoming the envisaged difficulty of recruiting sufficient competent oral examiners was to adopt a test design which would examine candidates in groups of four. The UE oral tests had to be conducted in the evenings for two weeks commencing in mid-March. Choi (2002) described how the Authority decided to introduce an oral test into its Use of English Examination in 1994 despite various constraints, which made a difference in classroom teaching. Choi's paper also reports on the design of the test, the operational details, quality control measures, and preparation for teachers and students.

On-Screen Marking (OSM)

On-screen marking of answer scripts was considered by the Authority in early 2005, principally to enhance marking reliability and efficiency of examination processing. The objectives for implementing On-Screen Marking are:

1   to acquire real-time information on the progress and performance of markers in a bid to achieve better quality control
2   to allocate scripts to markers more efficiently and flexibly (particularly for marking by questions and double marking)
3   to save markers from the chores of sorting scripts in candidate number order and filling in score sheets, clerical work which they dislike, and collecting and returning of scripts to the Authority, which can be physically taxing
4   to economize resources for the checking of unmarked pages and incorrect entry of scores, thereby expediting analyses of markers' statistics and the relevant processing of scores
5   to put an end to the unfortunate incident of losing scripts during the marking process.

While there are merits to adopting OSM, there are also challenges which must be resolved before launching this change, including:

1   teachers' acceptance of this new mode of marking
2   design of answer books for digitization of scripts
3   control measures to ensure accurate data capture and security against malpractice during scanning
4   development of necessary marking software
5   setting up a system for the scanning of scripts
6   setting up the hardware and venues for OSM, as delivery of scripts via an intranet is required to ensure data security.

This is a complex project involving technology, human resources, and change in marker behavior, as well as expertise in assessment and software design. Therefore, the Authority decided to implement the initiative for only two subjects in 2007. HKCEE Chinese Language and English Language were chosen because of the introduction of new syllabuses and the use of SRR in these two subjects. A grant was obtained from the Government in December 2005 to support modernization and the development of examination systems including information technology infrastructure.

Scanning of all answer scripts was implemented in the 2006 HKALE and HKCEE to ensure that no scripts would be lost during the marking process, as well as in preparation for OSM. A pilot study of OSM was conducted in April 2006 and major service providers were requested to submit proposals and demonstrate their capabilities. A pilot OSM centre was set up with 44 workstations and associated facilities. Approximately 40 markers and Chief/Assistant Examiners for four different subjects were invited to take part in this pilot study and their feedback was taken into account when developing policies, procedures, and tender specifications for the OSM system.

The Authority set up a special OSM working group with representatives from the Assessment Development, Information Technology, Research, and Human Resources Divisions to oversee the project. After official tendering procedures, a service provider was selected and work was started in September 2006. User requirement studies were carried out in the first two months of the project, and user acceptance tests, including three load tests involving more than 1,600 testers, were conducted between January and March 2007. A trial run was conducted in April 2007 to ensure the smooth conduct of OSM for the live 2007 examination in May and June.

Three assessment centers, with a total of about 1,000 workstations for OSM, have been set up to provide markers with a comfortable environment for marking; 21-inch LCD monitors, spacious work areas as well as lounge and pantry facilities are provided. The opening hours are long and flexible to cater to the needs of teacher markers who can only mark after school hours, and a day-release arrangement has also been made with the support of the Government, so that teachers can mark during school hours with the permission of their school principals.

To overcome the initial reluctance of experienced markers to switch to OSM, a total of 17 workshops were conducted in December 2006 for about 400 participants. Each session involved a presentation on the benefits of scanning and OSM, a demonstration of OSM functions, followed by hands-on trial marking. This strategy proved to be successful and sufficient qualified applicants were recruited for the 2007 Chinese and English papers marked onscreen. In addition, much work had to be done in connection with marker training, assessment center operation, and acceptance by the education sector and the general public.

OSM was conducted successfully for the 2007 HKCEE Chinese Language and English Language papers, with more than 660,000 scripts marked onscreen, involving approximately 1,000 teacher markers. The system was further enhanced and introduced to more HKCE and some HKAL subjects in 2008. The ultimate goal is to adopt OSM for all appropriate subjects in the HKDSE examination in 2012.

Washback Effect

One of the non-psychometric aims of the Authority in designing its examinations has been to produce a positive washback effect on learning in schools. As regards the English Language examinations, the efforts are reflected in the weighting of the oral test at both CE and AS levels. The weighting for the UE oral was 18 percent when it was first introduced in 1994, and when the format for the CE oral test was changed in 1996, the weighting was increased from 10 percent to 18 percent. This was a considered decision in a bid to motivate students to enhance their spoken English proficiency, as before the introduction of the UE oral, schools virtually ignored this productive skill in the sixth form. Group interaction was incorporated into the oral assessments so as to encourage students to engage in these activities in classrooms. Authentic materials have been chosen as stimuli in the papers, with the hope of helping students to adopt the habit of reading newspapers and magazines. The conduct of oral examinations is both costly and labor-intensive, but if speaking skills are not examined, they are not likely to be taught. This reflects the ingrained examination-oriented culture in Hong Kong. The Authority sees its natural role in taking on this responsibility.

Test Accommodation for Special Candidates

The Authority takes great pains to make its English Language examinations accessible to all candidates who wish to take the examinations, as long as the assessment objectives are not compromised. Special versions of the question papers are prepared for candidates with physical disabilities, including Braille and enlarged versions. Examination sessions are conducted in hospital rooms and special examination centers, so that candidates with special needs can take the examinations with extra time allowances and breaks as appropriate. Trained invigilators are also provided, sometimes on a one-to-one basis, if necessary.

Oral examinations pose a special challenge because of the group discussion/interaction component. In the case of candidates with aural or oral disabilities, special professional candidates[2] are provided as group members to facilitate the group discussion. Extended time allowances are given as necessary, and oral examiners are briefed on the special requirements in advance so these candidates' performance can be assessed fairly. Oral examination sessions are also conducted for prison inmates each year, and a group of oral examiners, waiting room supervisors, and professional candidates, headed by a subject officer, will spend afternoons in top-security prisons conducting oral examinations for the scores of inmates aspiring to gain some useful qualifications before their release.

Special arrangements are made to transfer prisoners from smaller institutions to major ones so as to keep the number of sessions to a manageable minimum.

Looking Ahead

Since the inception of the Authority, the assessment of English language in Hong Kong's public examinations has developed actively with several primary goals: (1) to support the English Language curriculum; (2) to enhance the reliability and discrimination of the assessment; and above all (3) to produce a positive washback effect on the learning and teaching of English in secondary schools in Hong Kong, and although English Language assessment has come a long way in the assessment history of the Authority, this basic assessment strategy is likely to continue. This is attributable to the efforts of a group of English language subject officers and a considerable number of school teachers and university academics in English language education in Hong Kong, who have served the Authority with dedication and commitment over the years. Looking ahead, the forthcoming years should be relatively stable in the wake of a period of flux, making this a time for consolidation and adaptation by schools before the new Hong Kong Diploma of Secondary Education Examination in 2012. In the longer term, the impact of technology on assessment is likely to be the main direction for future refinement of the assessment process.

Notes

1. Private candidates are repeaters or mature candidates who enter the examination as individuals instead of being presented as school candidates by registered schools.
2. Professional candidates are employed by the HKEAA to take part in the group discussion section of the oral examination when random normal grouping of candidates is not possible, for example, in special examination sessions for candidates with disabilities or for prison candidates.

References

Cheng, L. (1997). How does washback influence teaching? Implications for Hong Kong. *Language and Education*, 11, 38–54.

Cheng, L. (2005). *Changing language teaching through language testing: A washback study*. Studies in Language Testing: Volume 21. Cambridge, MA: Cambridge University Press.

Choi, C. C. (2002). *Public Examinations, to Lead or to Follow?—The Use of English Oral Examination*. Paper presented at The International Conference on Language Testing and Language Teaching (September). Shanghai, China.

Davison, C. (2007). Views from the chalkface: School-based assessment in Hong Kong. *Language Assessment Quarterly: An International Journal*, 4, 37–68.

HKEA (1978). Hong Kong Advanced Level Examination, Regulations and Syllabuses 1980. Hong Kong: HKEA.

HKEA (1987). Hong Kong Advanced Level Examination, Regulations and Syllabuses 1989. Hong Kong: HKEA.

HKEAA (2005). 2007 Hong Kong Certificate of Education Examination, English Language, Handbook for the School-based Assessment Component. Hong Kong: HKEAA.

Hong Kong Government (1989). Report of the Working Group on Sixth Form Education. Hong Kong: Hong Kong Government.

King, R. (1980). *An investigation into whether a change to Double Impression Marking in the assessment of English compositions in the HKCEE would lead to greater reliability in marking.* Unpublished master's thesis, The University of Hong Kong, Hong Kong.

King, R. (1994). Historical Survey of English Language Testing in Hong Kong. In J. Boyle & P. Falvey (Eds.) *English Language Testing in Hong Kong* (pp. 3–30). Hong Kong: The Chinese University Press.

Messick, S. (1996). Validity and washback in language testing, *Language Testing* 13, 243–256.

6 The Language Training and Testing Center, Taiwan

Past, Present, and Future

Antony John Kunnan, California State University, Los Angeles

Jessica R. W. Wu, The Language Training and Testing Center

In this chapter, we present the past, present, and future activities of the Language Training and Testing Center (LTTC) in Taipei, Taiwan, Republic of China. Established in 1951 jointly by the US Government Aid Agency and the Executive Yuan's Council on US Aid (CUSA), the LTTC conducted English training for US-bound technical assistance program participants in view of their insufficient English proficiency and also gave them pre-departure orientation. Over the decades, the Center expanded its activities and staff and developed language training programs and proficiency tests in languages such as German, Spanish, French, and Japanese, as well as English. At the 50-year mark, it had further expanded its activities to include the development of its flagship test, the General English Proficiency Test (GEPT), which is used widely around the country. Future plans include constructing the GEPT learner corpora, the mapping of the GEPT onto the Common European Framework of Reference for Languages (CEFR), online scoring as well as the development of technology-enhanced instruction and online teaching and learning resources.

Early History, Mission and Organization

Established in 1951 jointly as *The English Training Center* by the US Government Aid Agency and the Executive Yuan's Council on US Aid (CUSA), the Center conducted English training for US-bound technical assistance program participants and gave them pre-departure orientation. *The English Training Center*[1] (later known as *The English Center*) used only one old classroom on the Medical College campus of National Taiwan University (NTU) and trained only about 100 students per year. A few years later, because of the increase in the number of students and their widely differing English abilities, the Center moved to five classrooms behind the NTU College of Engineering. Meanwhile, CUSA signed a contract with NTU to construct a building on the Medical College campus exclusively for English language training and the Center moved to the new building in 1961.

In 1965, as US Aid was being phased out, the Center was taken over by NTU, and the NTU president invited representatives of relevant Chinese and US organizations to organize a Board of Directors to govern the Center. At the same time, the Center renamed itself *The Language Center* to include language training programs in Japanese, French, German, and Spanish in addition to English, in order to send Taiwanese government officials not only to the USA but also to other developed countries, including Japan and several European countries. The Center was reorganized to become a self-supporting institute under NTU in 1974. Five years later, the Center renamed itself *The Language Training and Testing Center* (LTTC) to distinguish itself from the many private language schools that also called themselves Language Centers. In 1985, due to the expansion of the NTU Medical College, the LTTC moved to the present Modern Languages Building on the NTU main campus. On February 7, 1986, the LTTC was registered with the Ministry of Education as a cultural and educational foundation for the purpose of offering language training and testing to people sponsored by various government agencies, public enterprises, and private firms, as well as individuals, to meet the needs of social and economic development of Taiwan. Since then, the LTTC has supported itself financially by providing a wide range of foreign language training and testing programs.

In terms of organizational structure, the LTTC is under the supervision of a Board of Directors. Currently, the President of NTU, Dr Si-chen Lee, presides as Chair, and the other members of the Board are representatives from the NTU and government department offices, including the Council of Economic Planning and Development, the Ministry of Education, the Ministry of Economic Affairs, the Ministry of Foreign Affairs, and the Foundation for Scholarly Exchange.[2] An Executive Director is appointed by the Board to supervise daily operations. Professor Tien-en Kao of the Department of Foreign Languages and Literatures at NTU has held this position since August 2006. Under the Executive Director, there are six departments: Teaching & Training; GEPT; General Testing; Testing Editorial; IT & Media; and the Department of General Affairs. A total of 154 full-time staff and 50 Chinese and foreign instructors are currently employed (see http://www.lttc.ntu.edu.tw/history4.htm for the organizational chart).

Early Language Training and Testing Activities

Language Training[3]

In the 1960s, the LTTC focused primarily on language training programs, with a special focus on English. According to the Language Center Administrative Report (LTTC, 1968–69), general language training programs were conducted in English, French, and German. In addition, special English language programs were conducted for government executives, English teachers, engineers and technicians, bank employees, and tourist guides. Between 1965 and 1974, there was tremendous growth in student enrollment: from an average of 230 students per term in 1965 to an average of 1,853 per term in 1974. The teaching method was eclectic, according to the LTTC Annual Report (LTTC, 1973–74): "the Center has consistently emphasized auditory perception and oral production . . . reading and writing are introduced concurrently to reinforce spoken language acquisition through dictation, dicto-comps, and other exercises" (p. 7). Additional methods that were used included guided or free conversation, speech practice, and written topic discussion. In terms of teacher training, in 1970–71,

Professor Rudolph C. Troike, a Fulbright professor of linguistics from the University of Texas, assisted in upgrading the Center's teacher training program. All new teachers participated in 3-day seminars before the beginning of each term, followed by 1-hour-per-week workshops on teaching pronunciation, reading, grammar, and writing and on classroom observation.

Language Testing

Prior to 1965, the LTTC administered English language tests developed by the American Language Institute/Georgetown University (ALI/GU) and the English Language Institute of the University of Michigan (ELI/UM). In 1965, it developed the Foreign Language Proficiency Test (FLPT) in English, Japanese, French, German, and Spanish. The test components were Aural, Usage, Vocabulary & Reading, and Oral; the test was used to select candidates for scholarships and fellowships, prospective candidates for technical training programs abroad, and applicants for employment. Between 1965 and 1974, there was tremendous growth in test-takers: from 638 in 1965 to 4,230 in 1974. The LTTC also developed placement tests for placing students into appropriate language class levels and standardized classroom tests to assess student progress in language training programs. Further, it administered written and oral tests to tourist guide candidates in English, Japanese, French, German, and Spanish.

The testing program was impacted by political events in the 1971–72 year. According to the LTTC Annual Report (LTTC, 1971–72), "our withdrawal from the United Nations . . . resulted in the cancellation of all language proficiency tests for UN fellowship candidates" (p. 10). However, the testing program extended its services to new organizations such as the Board of Foreign Trade, the Central Trust of China, and the Central Personnel Administration.

In addition to the above tests developed by the LTTC, it also administered the Test of English as a Foreign Language (TOEFL), which was developed by the Educational Testing Service, Princeton, NJ. According to the Language Center Administrative Report (LTTC, 1968–69):

> In November 1965, the United States Embassy in Taiwan officially designated TOEFL as a regular 'student visa examination' to replace the former 'Visa test' developed by the Language Center . . . In April 1969, the USIS Taipei requested the Language Center to conduct interview tests as a supplementary test for those who had taken the TOEFL within the past two years and received a rating of 'acceptable' or 'conditional' . . . the Center complied with the request and the first group of applicants was interviewed in June 1969. (LTTC, 1968–69, pp. 8–9)

Description of Current Language Testing and Training Activities

In this section, we describe the test development activities related to the General English Proficiency Test, the Foreign Language Proficiency Test (LTTC, 2008), and the College Student English Proficiency Test. We conclude with a brief description of the training programs.

The General English Proficiency Test (GEPT;「全民英檢」*)*[4]

In 1997, the LTTC initiated a project to gauge the ability level of English language learners and to encourage people in all walks of life to study English in Taiwan. Two years later, the Ministry of Education (MOE) in Taiwan recognized that these efforts were in accord with its promotion of life-long learning and therefore supported the development of this test. This test became known as the General English Proficiency Test (GEPT). In terms of the test development sequence, the Intermediate Level was made available in 2000, followed by the Elementary and High–Intermediate Levels in 2001, the Advanced Level in 2002, and the Superior Level in 2004. Test development is carried out using the LTTC test development process which includes item writing and revision; pre-testing; item banking; item compilation based on classical true score and IRT item analyses; and test booklet and CD production.

The test is now administered in five levels (Elementary, Intermediate, High–Intermediate, Advanced, and Superior) with each level incorporating listening, reading, writing, and speaking components. In the first four levels, there are two stages. Test-takers must pass the first stage (generally, listening and reading components) before moving onto the second (generally, writing and speaking), and they need to pass both stages to receive a certificate of achievement. In the Superior level, there are two components, writing and speaking, but only one stage. Test-takers must pass both components to receive a certificate of achievement.[5] While test-takers can register individually for the first four levels, for the Superior level, registration is only available upon the request of sponsoring schools or institutions.

The GEPT is a criterion-referenced test[6] with items and content for each level designed to match specific level criteria which include a general-level description of the overall English proficiency expected at that level and specific skill-level descriptions for the listening, reading, writing, and speaking components. According to the GEPT brochure (LTTC, 2007), the Elementary level is equivalent to that of a junior high school graduate in Taiwan; the Intermediate to that of a senior high school graduate in Taiwan; the High–Intermediate to that of a university graduate in Taiwan whose major is not English; the Advanced to that of a graduate of a Taiwanese university whose major is English, or to that of a graduate of an English-speaking country; and the Superior to that of a graduate with native English-speaking ability.

The test has been used by many institutions for various purposes. For example, the Central Personnel Administration of the Executive Yuan has recognized the GEPT as a criterion for promotion of civil servants, and hundreds of public and private schools, including National Cheng Kung University, National Chiao Tung University, National Taiwan University, and National Tsing Hua University, use it as a criterion for admissions, placement, and/ or graduation. The test is also used by private enterprises throughout Taiwan as a means of determining the English ability of their employees. As a result, to date, approximately 2.6 million people have registered for the GEPT. In addition, Taiwan's premier research institutes, including the Academia Sinica, now use the GEPT to screen international applicants for their English language ability as part of the admission process to graduate programs; most recently, applicants from Vietnam took the GEPT for this purpose.

The GEPT is currently administered as a paper-and-pencil test with the multiple-choice response-format for the listening and reading components and with the extended response-format for the writing and speaking components. While the multiple-choice responses are recorded and scored on machine-scored answer sheets, the extended responses are double-rated with the help of rater training and scoring guidelines to ensure both validity and reliability.

According to Dr Jessica Wu,[7] Head of the Testing Editorial Department, The General English Proficiency Test (GEPT) has become a household name in Taiwan in both educational and professional circles. We are happy to learn that since the launch of the GEPT in 2000, most of its stakeholders have reacted positively to the implementation of the test. Now, scores from the GEPT are used by educational institutions for matriculation or placement purposes, by companies and organizations for the selection or promotion of employees, and by individuals from all walks of life who aspire to meet the challenges of the four-skill English test; it has therefore successfully promoted a shift in English teaching and learning to a more communicative orientation.

The Foreign Language Proficiency Test (FLPT; 「外語能力測驗」)

As mentioned earlier, the FLPT was first developed and administered in 1965. It continues to be developed and revised using the test development process at the LTTC. Currently, the test incorporates listening, usage, vocabulary and reading, and speaking components, and is administered in English, Japanese, French, German, and Spanish. In the listening component, there are three item types (answering questions, short statements, and conversations/long statements); in the vocabulary and reading component, there are two item types (vocabulary and idioms, and reading); and in the speaking component, there are five item types (reading, translation, answering questions, discussion or description, and picture description). The usage component focuses on grammar and sentence structures.[8]

The FLPT is designed as a norm-referenced test[9] and its main purpose is to provide information for decision-making on promotion or selection for work or study overseas. The test is used by many public and private institutions in Taiwan such as the MOE, NTU, Taiwan Power Company, and Chunghwa Telecom Co. Although the test was developed specifically for institutional use, the LTTC decided to open the test to the general public in light of the increasing demand for foreign language tests. The targeted test-takers are defined as adults over 18 years old, and the test is designed with respect to the language functions which would be required of competent speakers of the language.

The first three components of the FLPT, listening, usage, and vocabulary and reading, are paper-based, and the fourth is the simulated oral proficiency interview. The paper-based components are in the multiple-choice response format and test-takers' responses on these items are machine-scored. Test-takers' responses in the interview are recorded in a lab and are double-rated using a holistic scale to ensure validity and reliability.

The College Student English Proficiency Test (CSEPT; 「大學校院英語能力測驗」)

According to the CSEPT brochure (LTTC, 2006), the CSEPT was developed in 1997 for some junior colleges to assess students' progress in English and to evaluate the effects of English teaching. The test measures test-takers' abilities to understand spoken and written English in daily life and campus contexts as well as their knowledge of English grammar and usage.

The CSEPT is administered in two levels: Level 1 is intended for students with elementary to intermediate levels of English proficiency and incorporates two components, listening and usage, plus reading and Level 2 is intended for those with intermediate to advanced levels and incorporates three components, listening, usage, and reading.[10] Test development of the CSEPT is carried out using a test development process similar to that of the GEPT.

The CSEPT is designed as a norm-referenced test. It is a paper-and-pencil test with the multiple-choice response-format for all of its components. Test-takers' responses on these items are machine-scored. While this test is currently used by approximately ten institutes such as the Wenzao Ursulin College of Languages and Southern Taiwan University of Technology, the long-term plan is to incorporate students of all institutes of science and technology in Taiwan as its targeted test-takers.

Other Tests

The LTTC administers the following tests on behalf of other institutions: the Japanese Language Proficiency Test (JLPT); the Cambridge ESOL Exams (Main Suite Exam, Young Learners, BULATS, etc.); the Examination for Japanese University Admission for International Students (EJU); the TestDaF; and computer-based tests including TOEFL, GRE, GED, ICMA, USMLE and the PMI.[11]

Language Training Courses

The LTTC offers language courses in English, Japanese, French, German, and Spanish to students sponsored by government organizations, public institutions, and schools and to individuals over the age of 18 years. Courses from elementary to advanced levels are provided regularly on a 10-week basis, incorporating conversation, listening, reading, writing, grammar/usage, business English, and news English. There are also short-term classes in 10-, 20-, and 30-hour blocks specially designed to meet the needs of sponsoring clients. The LTTC employs approximately 50 experienced Taiwanese and foreign instructors who use an interactive-communicative approach with an emphasis on language use and cross-culture understanding. Class sizes range from around 8–18 students with an average of 14, and students are placed into class levels based on their language proficiency.

In addition to language courses, the LTTC also provides language learning workshops and develops learning resources. Further, the "Japanese Culture Corner", "Riddles in Japanese" and the "English Corner" were designed to add a little spice to language learning by exposing learners to different festivals, customs, and important current events in the target languages. Currently, there are about 2,300 students enrolled in each term with about 70 percent taking courses in English and 20 percent in Japanese.

Research and Publications

The LTTC conducts various types of research studies, training-related projects, and workshops and publishes its research and professional activities. A summary of the activities is provided here.

GEPT Research

Research related to the GEPT has been mainly in the following areas: test validation, reliability, impact, and test-taker corpora. Of the 19 reports that are available, nine are available on the LTTC website in Chinese; the other ten have been published in international conference proceedings and journals.[12] Studies have been conducted on parallel-form reliability (Weir & Wu, 2002), on concurrent validity of the Intermediate and High-Intermediate levels (LTTC, 2003), on English proficiency of students in vocational schools and technical colleges and their learning outcomes (LTTC, 2004), on mapping the GEPT to the Common English Yardstick for English Education in Taiwan (LTTC, 2005), on written language of test-takers (Kuo, 2005), on test impact (Wu & Chin, 2006), and on test form and individual task comparability (Weir & Wu, 2006; see http://www.lttc.ntu.edu.tw/academics/geptreport.htm for a list of reports).

Projects

Research in the areas of curriculum development, technology-enhanced instruction, and language teaching methodologies was conducted. In 2004, the LTTC was commissioned by the Civil Service Development Institute to develop the Civil Servant English Framework to integrate the various English courses provided for civil servants by different language institutes. A four-level curriculum framework, covering both general English skills and core skills for workplace English, was developed with reference to the CEFR can-do statements in three parts: a general description of expected overall English proficiency; specific descriptions for each skill area (i.e., listening, speaking, reading, and writing); and recommended course design guidelines described in terms of the topics, functions, text/discourse types, skills, and strategies covered in each skill area at that level.

In 2005, an e-learning project was launched based on a blended course model. Introductory German and French courses were designed, in which two teaching modes—face-to-face (F2F) and teacher-guided, synchronous online teaching—were blended. To explore the feasibility and effectiveness of this teaching model, a German course and a French course were taught to adult learners. The results indicated that both teaching forms had positive contributions to language learning, and the F2F classroom sessions were found to be irreplaceable. Although the learners preferred the blended teaching mode, they were hesitant to try it in the future due to the need for further technological improvement.

Workshops

From 2001 to 2003, the LTTC was commissioned by the Ministry of Education to host annual CALL (Computer-assisted Language Learning) workshops for teachers of English at vocational colleges in Taiwan. At these workshops, ELT research staff gave presentations on how to utilize Internet resources in language teaching and also trained participants in the use of software.

Publications

The LTTC has developed a detailed Handbook for the GEPT test-takers in Mandarin Chinese. It provides information regarding test registration, test procedures, test structure, sample items, score descriptors, test accommodations for test-takers with disabilities, and score re-rating. In addition, word lists,[13] test preparation kits, and past papers for the Elementary, Intermediate, and High-Intermediate levels are also available. Information sheets for the FLPT and the CSEPT have been prepared in Mandarin Chinese for test-takers.[14] Sample tests for the CSEPT and the FLPT in English, Japanese, French, German and Spanish are also available.

The English and Japanese teaching/research teams have published the following learning materials: *English Pronunciation Practice; English Pronunciation Made Easy; Getting Into English; Shopping: Cash* or *Charge?; Taking a Taxi: Where to?; Reservations Confirmed: English for Hotels and Restaurants; Sentence of the Day: English for Civil Servants; Learn English by Surfing the Internet;* and *Japanese GoGoGo* Books 1 to 4.

Challenges

The LTTC has always perceived that both language training and testing programs are equally important, and one cannot exist without the other. This philosophy is realized through the organizational structure which is divided into two major parts: language teaching and training, and language testing. Under such a parallel structure, each part can extend its own programs and services, while both parts can work collaboratively for pedagogical and research purposes. Like all large-scale language teaching and testing organizations, the LTTC faces a number of challenges:

1 Continue to build a research agenda that includes research on areas including validation, reliability, absence of bias, access and accommodations, administration and security, and social consequences (as suggested in Kunnan, 2000, 2004, 2008; and as per the *Code of Fair Testing Practices in Education*: JCTP, 2004; the *Standards for Educational and Psychological Testing*: APA/AERA/NCME, 1999; and *ETS Standards for Quality and Fairness*: ETS, 2002, 2003). These research studies can help defend the claims of all the LTTC tests with sufficient evidence and convincing argumentation (Bachman, 2005).

2 Develop technical and users' manuals that offer evidence and argumentation to support the claims of the tests and to make them available to test score users and any other stakeholders (as per the *Standards for Educational and Psychological Testing*: APA/AERA/NCME, 1999).

3 Continue to maintain high standards of test operations including pre-testing of test items and building parallel forms using appropriate psychometric and content considerations.

4 Venture into emerging areas such as the use of new technologies in test development, computer-delivery and computer-adaptive testing, online automated scoring, diagnostic feedback in proficiency testing, and the use of multiple response formats and integrated skills testing.

5 Maintain a high profile in the community through information sessions and workshops for teachers, test-takers and other stakeholders.

6 Continue to enhance its foreign language curriculum and teaching methodologies through systematic program evaluation and extensive needs analysis.

7   Develop new e-learning models to help teachers and learners overcome time and space constraints and to facilitate individualized, autonomous learning.
8   Consolidate research efforts in curriculum development, course design, materials development, technology-enhanced instruction, and teaching methodologies.

Moreover, given that Taiwan is also an examination-oriented society like China and Hong Kong (as well as other countries in Asia such as Japan, Korea, and India), where examinations have long been used as tools to facilitate better teaching and learning, the LTTC is seen to occupy an important position as a critical influence between Taiwan's language examinations and language teaching and learning. This dual influence can be noticed through the GEPT since its debut in 2000. Not only has language assessment become a topic of wide discussion in the country now, it has brought about positive washback effects. The most significant washback is that productive skills have received more attention from teachers and learners as reported in an impact study (see Wu & Chin, 2006) and by many students and teachers of English in high schools and universities (Wu, in press). Therefore, in addition to the challenges for testing and teaching/learning listed above, the LTTC will need to adopt a more holistic view with consolidated efforts towards the goal of making testing and teaching/learning work collaboratively and complementarily in more concrete terms.

One example of the projects geared to the integration of testing and teaching/learning is the creation of the Taiwan's English as a foreign language (EFL) Learner Corpora (TELC), according to Dr Jessica Wu, Head of the Testing Editorial Department. The TELC will contain writing and speaking performances by learners taking the GEPT. These data will be transcribed and stored according to proficiency level (elementary to advanced) with relevant information about the learners (e.g., age, gender, major, region, etc.). The scripts then will be tagged and coded for a number of grammatical and lexical errors. The TELC aims to describe the features of learners' spoken and written performances in each of the GEPT levels in terms of the lexico-grammatical components. The descriptions will be very informative to those who are involved in English language teaching in Taiwan. In particular, they can be used as a valuable reference by teachers, curriculum developers, and writers of learning materials. An immediate example of potential uses is that the TELC can be used to support the LTTC projects on Developing EFL Writing Materials (see "New Directions") by providing authentic benchmarked performances for the writing skills of Taiwan's EFL learners. Through efforts like the TELC project, the LTTC hopes that language teaching/learning and testing in Taiwan will be integrated in a more coordinated and complementary way, so that the ultimate goal of upgrading the language proficiency of Taiwan's learners can be achieved.

New Directions

The LTTC has established a research agenda to guide its future development; a few of the projects are described here.

Mapping the GEPT to the CEFR

The LTTC officially registered with the Council of Europe (CoE) in July 2005 to participate in their project on Piloting the Manual for Relating Language Examinations to the Common European Framework of Reference for Languages: Learning, teaching, and assessment. The study was completed and the results of the study were sent to the CoE in September 2006; the LTTC provided the CoE with feedback and suggestions for revisions to the Manual. Employing the qualitative analysis procedures presented in the Manual, various features of the GEPT have been re-examined. Based on the results of the Specification procedure, the GEPT conforms to a widely accepted code of practice, and the GEPT Intermediate Level is situated roughly at the CEFR B1 Level. In 2007, the LTTC conducted the LTTC GEPT-CEFR Calibration Project to relate the GEPT Reading Comprehension Tests to the CEFR by following the methods proposed in the CoE's Manual and the procedures outlined in the Dutch project (Alderson et al., 2006). The results of the study show that the first four levels of the GEPT Reading Comprehension Tests, from Elementary Level to Advanced Level, are situated at the CEFR A2 to C1 levels, correspondingly (Wu & Wu, 2007). The LTTC plans to map other test components of the GEPT onto the CEFR, and the project is expected to be completed in 2 years.

Online Marking of the GEPT Intermediate Level Writing Test

In order to enhance the quality of the GEPT in terms of its rating validity and reliability, the LTTC conducted a trial of an online marking system for the GEPT Elementary Level Writing Test in June 2006 over a local area network (or LAN). In April 2007, the LTTC conducted another pilot study of the same system for the GEPT Intermediate Level Writing Test, using a virtual private network (or VPN) to link the two rating centers located in Taipei and Kaohsiung. In this study, the LTTC aimed to further investigate the relationship between online marking and traditional conference marking in terms of inter-rater and intra-rater reliability and explore the possible benefits which online marking may provide.

Research on the Impact of the GEPT

As the LTTC acknowledges that language tests have become a crucial part of the education system and society, scores from the GEPT are used by educational institutions for matriculation or placement purposes and by companies and organizations for the selection or promotion of employees. For the LTTC, the extensive uses of test scores have two significant implications. First, these scores need to provide credible evidence to demonstrate the reliability of scores derived from the test and to support valid uses and interpretations of the test scores. More importantly, LTTC needs to understand the impact of the test—whether intended or unintended—on the stakeholders involved in the assessment process, e.g., test-takers, test-users, teachers, school administrators, curriculum and materials developers. This project aims to systematically collect test-takers' baseline data, including learning background, motivation, and learning strategy, and investigate the impact of the various levels of the GEPT. Research data will be collected mainly through questionnaires and interviews.

Constructing the GEPT Learner Corpora

The LTTC has been sampling the written and spoken data from the test-taker responses to the Writing and Speaking Tests of each GEPT administration since 2001. In 2007, the LTTC began to create the tagged computer-readable GEPT Learner Corpora.

Ongoing Studies into Possible Revisions to the Format of the GEPT

In the interests of promoting test validity and efficient administration of the GEPT, the LTTC has been conducting studies of possible revisions to the format of the GEPT, including alternative methods of taking the test, such as using computers.

Hosting Teacher Workshops and Providing Online Resources for Teachers

The LTTC now hosts teacher workshops, which are designed to facilitate teachers' understanding of the GEPT and provide hands-on classroom activities and resources for teaching GEPT preparation. According to Dr Jessica Wu, Head of the Testing Editorial Department:

> As a leading testing organization in Taiwan, we are devoted to providing our test users with reliable, valid, and useful tests. Through ongoing research, we aim to ensure that the quality of our tests is properly supported in their various facets. With the help of advanced technologies and statistic methods, we hope to offer more credible evidence to demonstrate the reliability of our tests and to better support valid interpretations of their scores, as well as to further investigate how our tests have affected the educational practices in the context of Taiwan and the stakeholders involved in the assessment process. We will also endeavor to relate the LTTC's tests to other major English language tests through internationally acceptable procedures.

Developing EFL Writing Materials

The ELT research staff has been planning a new writing series intended for EFL learners at the elementary and intermediate levels in Taiwan. Market research and textbook analysis are being carried out to collect information for the design of the syllabus, contents and methodology. To meet the needs of today's teachers and learners, online teaching and learning resources will be developed along with the textbooks, and studies will be conducted to explore suitable e-learning models in which textbook materials, online resources, and computer-mediated communication (CMC) technologies can be integrated in a coordinated way.

Developing Online Teaching and Learning Resources

Developed by the Japanese teaching/research team, *Japanese GoGoGo* is a four-level series designed specifically for elementary-level learners of Japanese in Taiwan. Since its publication, the series has been well received by both teachers and learners of Japanese. To provide further support to the users of the series, the Japanese teaching/research team has been creating various online teaching and learning resources, including lesson plans, teaching tips, supplementary worksheets, online exercises, and cultural notes. These online resources are intended to help teachers optimize classroom instruction and to help learners develop autonomous learning skills.

Developing Foreign Language Courses for Specific Purposes

From the perspective of training program development, the primary goal in 2007 is to design and trial new foreign language courses for specific purposes, particularly in the academic and business areas. Studies will be conducted on teaching materials, assessment methods, and pedagogical approaches, and the research findings derived will be applied to curriculum planning and instructional design for the new courses. According to Ms Rose Hung, Head of the Department of Teaching and Training:

> With the changing needs of today's teachers and learners in mind, our teaching/ research teams will explore different ways in which textbook materials, online resources, assessment systems and computer-mediated communication technologies can be integrated and coordinated to facilitate effective learning. It is hoped that in the near future, the LTTC will be able to provide learning solutions to a wider range of foreign language learners in Taiwan and to empirically examine the learning outcomes of various instructional designs on the basis of valid evaluation parameters.

Conclusion

In this chapter, we have presented a descriptive account of the activities and programs performed by the LTTC. It is obvious that the LTTC has maintained a strong reputation in the areas of language training and testing in Taiwan. In line with the social and economic development of Taiwan society, the LTTC dedicates itself to continue to extend its services to meet the emerging needs of teachers, learners, test-takers, and other stakeholders by developing new teaching and testing programs and materials, sponsoring academic activities and research, and engaging itself in international partnerships to provide the public with more up-to-date information and resources.

Regarding the future vision of the LTTC, Professor Tien-en Kao, Executive Director of the LTTC, states:

> Since its establishment fifty-five years ago, the LTTC has been dedicated to providing a wide range of foreign language teaching and testing services to meet the needs of language education in Taiwan. Particularly, due to the wide recognition of the GEPT in recent years, the LTTC has assumed a more influential role in EFL education in Taiwan. Therefore, the LTTC will in the coming years take on more social and professional responsibilities. We will enhance the quality of both our teaching and our testing programs by applying the highest international standards and adopting advanced technologies and original concepts. Also, we will increase our effort to reinforce research and development through a variety of publications, and active participation at academic conferences both at home and abroad.

Like any large-scale language training and testing organization, the LTTC faces the twenty-first century with some unknowns. However, with its strategic long-term plan, it is confident of facing the future by providing language training and testing programs that are beneficial to the Taiwanese community.

Acknowledgments

We would like to acknowledge our appreciation to the LTTC Executive Director Professor Tien-en Kao for giving us permission to work on this chapter; Ya-lin Olivia Tsai for assistance in editing the chapter, and Rose Hung, Echo Wei, Rachel Wu, and Joyce Chin for providing information about various aspects of the testing and training programs. We would also like to thank other LTTC staff for help in providing documents, materials, and technical support.

Notes

1. While different names of the organization are used in this section, the current name (LTTC) is used in the rest of the chapter.
2. For the most recent composition and members of the Board of Directors, please refer to the LTTC website: http://www.lttc.ntu.edu.tw/history3.htm
3. The term "language training" used in this chapter refers to "language teaching" and "language learning".
4. The GEPT discussed in this chapter refers to the test developed by the LTTC, which is known formally as the LTTC GEPT.
5. For details regarding the structure of the skill components, item types, and sample items, please refer to the GEPT website: http://www.gept.org.tw
6. A criterion-referenced test "examining the level of the knowledge of, or performance on, a specific domain of target behaviors (i.e., the criterion) which the candidate is required to have mastered" (Davies et al., 1999, p. 38).
7. The chapter includes quotes from LTTC staff including Jessica Wu, Rose Hung, and Tien-en Kao when they commented on aspects of the LTTC.
8. For details regarding the structure of the skill components, item types, and sample items, please refer to the FLPT website: http://www.lttc.ntu.edu.tw/flpt/FLPTe.htm
9. In a norm-referenced test, a test-taker's score is compared with a norm, or the scores of a large group of individuals similar to the targeted test-takers. Thus, the test scores provide information about a given test-taker's ranking in a group of people with respect to his/her English ability.
10. For details regarding the structure of the skill components, item types, and sample items, please refer to the CSEPT websites: http://www.lttc.ntu.edu.tw/CSEPT1.htm (Level 1) and http://www.lttc.ntu.edu.tw/CSEPT2.htm (Level 2)
11. For brief information regarding these tests in Chinese, please refer to: http://www.lttc.ntu.edu. tw/TST.htm. For the English version, please refer to: http://www.lttc.ntu.edu.tw/E_LTTC/languagetesting.htm
12. Thirteen of these reports are available at: http://www.lttc.ntu.edu.tw/academics/geptreport. htm
13. The word lists are available at: http://www.lttc.ntu.edu.tw/academics/wordlist.htm
14. This information for test-takers is also available online for all tests. For the GEPT, please refer to: http://www.lttc.ntu.edu.tw/GEPT.htm; for the FLPT: http://www.lttc.ntu.edu.tw/FLPT. htm; for the CSEPT: http://www.lttc.ntu.edu.tw/CSEPT1.htm

References

Alderson, J. C., Figueras, N., Kuijper, H., Nold, G., Takala, S. & Tardieu, C. (2006). Analysing tests of reading and listening in relation to the Common European Framework of Reference: The experience of the Dutch CEFR Construct Project. *Language Assessment Quarterly*, 3(1), 3–30.

American Psychological Association, American Educational Research Association, & National Council for Measurement in Education (APA/AERA/NCME). (1999). *Standards for educational and psychological testing.* Washington, DC: APA/AERA/NCME.

Bachman, L. (2005). Building and supporting a case for test use. *Language Assessment Quarterly,* 2(1), 1–34.

Davies, A., Brown, A., Elder, C., Hill, K., Lumley, T. & McNamara, T. (1999). *Dictionary of language testing: Studies in language testing 7.* Cambridge, UK: Cambridge University Press.

Educational Testing Service (ETS). (2002). *ETS standards for quality and fairness.* Princeton, NJ: ETS.

Educational Testing Service (ETS). (2003). *ETS standards for quality and fairness.* Princeton, NJ: ETS.

Joint Committee on Testing Practices (JCTP). (2004). *Code of fair testing practices in education.* Washington, DC: JCTP.

Kunnan, A. J. (Ed.). (2000). *Fairness and validation in language assessment.* Cambridge, UK: Cambridge University Press.

Kunnan, A. J. (2004). Test fairness. In M. Milanovic & C. Weir (Eds.), *European language testing in a global context* (pp. 27–48). Cambridge, UK: Cambridge University Press.

Kunnan, A. J. (2008). Towards a model of test evaluation: Using the test fairness and wider context frameworks. In L. Taylor & C. Weir (Eds.), *Multilingualism and assessment: Achieving transparency, assuring quality, sustaining diversity* (pp. 229–251). Papers from the ALTE Conference, Berlin, Germany. Cambridge, UK: Cambridge University Press.

Kuo, G. (2005). A preliminary corpus study on EFL test-takers' writing proficiency. Proceedings of the Eighth Academic Forum on English Language Testing in Asia, Hong Kong, SAR, China, 27–35. Hong Kong: Hong Kong Examinations and Assessment Authority.

Language Training and Testing Center (LTTC). (1968–69). *Language Center administrative report.* Taipei, Taiwan: LTTC.

Language Training and Testing Center (LTTC). (1971–72). *Language Center annual report.* Taipei, Taiwan: LTTC.

Language Training and Testing Center (LTTC). (1973–74). *Language Center annual report.* Taipei, Taiwan: LTTC.

Language Training and Testing Center (LTTC). (2003). *Concurrent validity studies of the GEPT Intermediate Level, GEPT High-Intermediate Level, CBT TOEFL, CET-6, and the English Test of the R.O.C. College Entrance Examination.* Taipei, Taiwan: LTTC.

Language Training and Testing Center (LTTC). (2004). *Investigating the English proficiency of students in vocational schools and technical colleges and their learning outcome.* Taipei, Taiwan: LTTC.

Language Training and Testing Center (LTTC). (2005). *Mapping the GEPT to the Common English Yardstick for English Education in Taiwan (CEY).* Taipei, Taiwan: LTTC.

Language Training and Testing Center (LTTC). (2006) *College Student English Proficiency Test.* [Brochure]. Taipei, Taiwan: LTTC, http://www.lttc.ntu.edu.tw/CSEPT1.htm (Level 1) and http://www.lttc.ntu.edu.tw/CSEPT2.htm (Level 2)

Language Training and Testing Center (LTTC). (2007). *General English Proficiency Test.* [Brochure]. Taipei, Taiwan: LTTC, http://www.gept.org.tw

Language Training and Testing Center (LTTC). (2008). *Foreign Language Proficiency Test.* [Brochure]. Taipei, Taiwan: LTTC, http://www.lttc.ntu.edu.tw/flpt/FLPTe.htm

Weir, C. J. & Wu, J. (2002). Parallel-form reliability—a case study of the GEPT Spoken Performance Test. *Proceedings of the Fifth International Conference on English Language Testing in Asia,* Tokyo, Japan (29–58). Japan: The Society for Testing English Proficiency, Inc.

Weir, C. J. & Wu, J. (2006). Establishing test form and individual task comparability: a case study of semi-direct speaking test. *Language Testing,* 23(2), 167–197.

Wu, J. (in press). *Some Taiwanese students' and teachers' views on language testing and assessment.* Taipei, Taiwan: Language Training and Testing Center.

Wu, J. and Wu, R. (2007). Using the CEFR in Taiwan: the perspective of a local examination board. Paper presented at The Fourth Annual EALTA Conference, Sitges, Spain.

Wu, R. & Chin, J. (2006). An impact study of the Intermediate Level GEPT. *Proceedings of the Ninth International Conference on English Testing in Asia,* Taipei, Taiwan (41–65). Taipei, Taiwan: College Entrance Examination Center.

Part III

Test Use and Consequences: Views from Test-Users

Test Quality: Theoretical/Conceptual Points of View

7 From TOEFL pBT to TOEFL iBT

Recent Trends, Research Landscape, and Chinese Learners

David D. Qian, *The Hong Kong Polytechnic University*

The Test of English as a Foreign Language (TOEFL) is designed to measure the English proficiency of non-native speakers of English in using and understanding English as it is spoken, written, and heard in college and university settings. In the last few decades, the TOEFL has been an important international test for Chinese learners of English, especially for those who plan to pursue their university or graduate degrees in the USA or Canada. This chapter examines three aspects of the TOEFL test that are closely connected to Chinese learners: (1) the trend relating to the volume of Chinese TOEFL candidates over a period of 10 test years from 1995 to 2005, as compared with the global TOEFL population; (2) the trend relating to the mean TOEFL scores obtained by Chinese candidates in the period of 1995–2007, as compared with those obtained by the global TOEFL population, and (3) the areas and foci of internationally published research on all aspects of the TOEFL from 1995 to 2007. Based on this study of trends and research reports, there is a clear indication that both the TOEFL test and Chinese learners may benefit from further research focused on Chinese TOEFL candidates. The chapter concludes by proposing 12 topic areas for future TOEFL research concerning Chinese learners, who at present account for approximately 20 percent of the global TOEFL population.

Introduction

The Test of English as a Foreign Language (TOEFL) is developed and administered by the Educational Testing Service (ETS), a non-profit organization located in New Jersey, USA. The TOEFL test is designed to measure "the ability of nonnative speakers of English to use and understand English as it is spoken, written, and heard in college and university settings" (TOEFL, n.d.). For decades, the TOEFL has been a major English proficiency test for international students intending to study in North American universities. In addition to American and Canadian colleges and universities which require TOEFL test scores from their international applicants, many government agencies, scholarship programs, and licensing and certification agencies also make use of TOEFL scores in selecting their candidates (Banerjee & Clapham, 2003). Furthermore, numerous academic institutions in other countries and regions, such as Argentina, Australia, Austria, Belgium, Brazil, Denmark, France, Georgia, Germany, Hong Kong, Iceland, India, Israel, Italy, Japan, Korea, Morocco, the Netherlands, Norway, Spain, Switzerland, Taiwan and the UK, also refer to TOEFL scores in making selection decisions (ETS, 2007a). For these reasons, many international job applicants are required to take the TOEFL test in order to acquire good jobs in companies or organizations where English communication is essential. In fact, more than 6,000 institutions and agencies in 110 countries rely on TOEFL scores for recruitment (TOEFL, n.d.). Therefore, the influence of the TOEFL test has been enormous in many regions of the world over the past several decades. For many learners of English as a foreign language (EFL) throughout the world, the TOEFL is a high-stakes test because their admission to a university of their choice or their success in securing an attractive job often hinges upon a satisfactory TOEFL score.

The TOEFL was first administered to 592 test candidates on February 17, 1964 at 55 testing centers in 34 countries and regions (Qian, 2008a; Spolsky, 1995), which included Hong Kong and Taiwan but not the Chinese Mainland for historical reasons. The second administration was held in November of the same year. By the time of its third administration in January 1965, the test was already delivered in 63 countries and regions.

Research into and development of the TOEFL test have been ongoing ever since the inception of the test in 1963. In 2008, the TOEFL test celebrated its 45th anniversary of existence. Over the past 45 years, the test has experienced a number of changes in its structure, format, and delivery mode. While some of the changes have been relatively minor, others have been significant. In terms of structure and format, the test has evolved from a test composed almost entirely of discrete-point items and multiple-choice (MC) questions in the early years to a complex measure which is more communication-oriented and includes significant portions of performance-based and direct testing tasks. In terms of delivery mode, the test has gone through three main stages: paper-based testing (pBT) introduced in 1964, computer-based testing (cBT) introduced in 1998, and Internet-based testing (iBT) introduced in 2005.

Unlike its predecessors, namely, the TOEFL pBT and cBT, which purported to test only listening, reading and writing skills, the TOEFL iBT also assesses speaking proficiency in addition to the other three skills. This new version of the test emphasizes the measurement of integrated skills and is therefore expected to provide better information to institutions about students' communicative ability for academic purposes in an English-speaking setting. The TOEFL iBT was first administered in China in September 2006.

The TOEFL iBT, which is delivered entirely on the Internet, is approximately 4 hours long and consists of four sections: Reading, Listening, Speaking, and Writing. Most tasks of the test require the test-taker to combine more than one language skill in completing the task (ETS, 2006).

Over the past decades, there has been a great volume of research on various aspects of this high-stakes test. How learner variables affect individual performances on the test has been one of the main topics studied by researchers. Within the area of learner variables and characteristics, one variable is particularly relevant to the present study, namely, the learner's first language (L1) background. When a high-stakes test such as the TOEFL is administered to an international population composed of speakers of over 140 languages, one tends to ask whether, and if so how, test-takers' L1 backgrounds will affect their performance on the test.

ETS was clearly aware of this issue when they conducted a study to determine whether prompts in the TOEFL cBT (computer-based testing) writing caused significant differences in the performances of candidates from three Asian and three European language backgrounds (Lee, Breland, & Muraki, 2004). The language groups involved in the comparisons were Chinese, Japanese, and Korean on the Asian side and Spanish, German, and French on the European side. The study indicated that about one-third of the writing prompts were flagged with significant differences during the comparisons of the group means, but because of the small effect sizes derived based on those significant differences, the study waved aside the suggestion that the differences should matter and concluded that the raw score differences detected "might be largely ascribable to the difference in mean ELA (English language ability) scores between the two groups" (p. 20). However, the study stopped short of directly comparing individual L1 groups and no conclusion could thus be drawn about whether L1 background is a critical variable that can influence a candidate's test performance significantly. This study appears to be one of very few ETS studies comparing in some way performances of test candidates from different L1 groups.

While the TOEFL is taken by EFL learners from more than 140 L1 backgrounds (143 in the 2003–04 test year), Chinese TOEFL candidates often account for about 20 percent, and even more than 20 percent in many years, of the total number of TOEFL candidates globally, constituting the largest L1 candidate group. EFL learners who speak Chinese as L1 share, although to varying extents, one thing in common: knowledge of their L1 and influence of their L1 on the TOEFL score, assuming that there is L1 influence on their TOEFL scores. There is strong belief that the L1 variable plays an important role in the learning of an L2. The hypothesis that the distance of a learner's L1 to the target language will influence the learning outcome of, as well as the test score on, the target L2 has already been supported by empirical research (Liceras, 1986; Lett & O'Mara, 1990; Snow, 1998). Snow's (1998) investigation was particularly noteworthy because of its comprehensiveness and rigorous design. With statistical evidence based on data derived from 26 countries, Snow concluded that the historical relatedness of a native language to English significantly affects test candidates' performance on the TOEFL.

The TOEFL test has been a major international English proficiency test for Chinese learners since 1981 when the test was first administered in China. Furthermore, Hong Kong and Taiwan were among the first regions witnessing the earliest implementation of the test when it was made available to the world in 1964. Because of its influential status in China, Hong Kong, and Taiwan; because of the assumption that L1 background will most likely affect the performance on an EFL test such as the TOEFL; and because of the fact that Chinese learners of English form the largest TOEFL candidate group, a need is keenly felt to take a very careful look at a number of issues and aspects of the TOEFL that traditional research studies on TOEFL have not covered. Therefore, the present study was conducted to examine three of those aspects in the context of the implementation of the TOEFL test for Chinese learners over the past decade or so. The three aspects are: recent trends with respect to the Chinese TOEFL population in terms of annual test-taker volumes; recent trends in TOEFL scores attained by Chinese learners; and areas and foci of recent internationally published research on the TOEFL test.

Research Questions for the Present Study

In the ever-evolving global testing market where competition is fierce, and in an increasingly open economic market where university graduates in China are facing more options than ever before when it comes to career choice, the present study was conducted with a view to understanding how Chinese learners fare on the TOEFL test. In particular, the study aimed to examine the volume of TOEFL candidates over the years and how candidates have performed on the TOEFL test, as reflected by test scores. Specific research questions covering a period of up to 13 years from 1995 to 2007 are as follows:

1   What is the trend in the annual volume of Chinese TOEFL candidates from different regions during the period of 1995–2005 in relation to the annual volumes of global TOEFL candidates during the same period?
2   How does the trend of the global candidate volume compare with those of all Chinese TOEFL candidates from different regions during the period of 1995–2005?
3   What is the trend in TOEFL annual mean scores obtained by Chinese TOEFL candidates from different regions during the period of 1995–2007 in relation to the global TOEFL candidates during the same period?
4   How does the trend in global mean scores compare with that of all Chinese TOEFL candidates during the period of 1995–2007?
5   What have been the main foci of internationally published TOEFL research from 1995 to 2007?
6   What are the discernable research gaps in the internationally published TOEFL research concerning Chinese learners?

Method

The six research questions can be categorized into three groups: (1) Questions 1 and 2 are focused on the trend of annual, relative numbers of test candidates; (2) Questions 3 and 4 compare TOEFL scores; and (3) Questions 5 and 6 examine the foci of recent, internationally accessible TOEFL research in order to determine what is still needed for future research on TOEFL candidates who speak Chinese as their first language.

Timeframe

For the trends in TOEFL candidate volumes and scores, the present study spans a period of 10 test years,[1] from July 1995 to June 2005. This particular period was chosen because 1995 saw the implementation of the restructured TOEFL test (see the earlier discussion on the development of the TOEFL test in this chapter). Therefore, 1995 could be seen as a strategic point for the TOEFL test, when it took an important step toward becoming more focused on testing communicative language skills than its previous version. The end-point for the study of the trends was 2005 because relevant data on TOEFL candidates were not available beyond this point: ETS seems to have stopped releasing information on test candidate volumes after 2005.

   The timeframe for research questions on the comparisons of TOEFL scores spans a period of over 12 years starting from July 1995 and ending in December 2007. Again,

July 1995 was chosen because it was the time the TOEFL cBT was first released. I was able to extend the period under investigation to December 2007 due to the recent availability of TOEFL iBT score summaries for 2006 and 2007 (ETS, 2007c, 2008).

The timeframe for the survey of TOEFL research was slightly longer. The starting point was January 1995, and the end point was extended to December 2007. The ending year was extended from 2005 to 2007 because studies published after 2005 are already available in various journals and on the ETS research website. For this part of the study, the calendar year system, rather than the test year system, was adopted because TOEFL research reports and journals papers are published according to the calendar year system.

Types and Sources of Data

The data for Questions 1–4 concerning TOEFL mean scores and annual volumes of test-takers were mainly collected from the TOEFL annual data summaries published by ETS (1995, 1996, 1997, 1998, 1999, 2000, 2001, 2003, 2004, 2005a, 2007b, 2007c, 2008).

Questions 5–6 were addressed based on analytical results from a collection of international research publications on the TOEFL test made available during the period from January 1995 to December 2007. The survey was composed of two phases. In Phase 1, three series of ETS research publications on TOEFL, namely, *TOEFL Research Reports*, *TOEFL Monographs*, and *TOEFL iBT Research Series*, were examined issue by issue. The series of *TOEFL Research Reports* covers general TOEFL research, whereas the series of *TOEFL Monographs* are devoted exclusively to TOEFL 2000 research, which eventually led to the successful implementation of the TOEFL iBT: The Next Generation TOEFL Test. The *TOEFL iBT Research Series* specifically deals with issues related to the construction, implementation, scoring, administration, and use of the TOEFL iBT. In total, 34 TOEFL Research Reports, 34 TOEFL Monographs and two studies in the new *TOEFL iBT Research Series* were identified and collected for analysis.

The series of *TOEFL Research Reports* has a long tradition, and the first report in this series (Clark, 1977) was published in 1977. Launched in 1996 with the publication of its first monograph (Ginther & Grant, 1996), *TOEFL Monographs* was designed to publish exclusively monographs on the research and development of the Next Generation TOEFL Test. The series serves as a main outlet for the research output from TOEFL 2000, which has laid the theoretical, empirical, and technological ground for the TOEFL iBT. *TOEFL iBT Research Series* is the youngest among the three series. To date, two reports have been published in this series, the first of which (Xi & Molaun, 2006) appeared in 2006.

In Phase 2 of this part of the present survey, research papers on the TOEFL test which were published in various internationally-refereed academic journals from 1995 to 2007 were collected and examined. Care was taken to ensure that all selected papers were expressly about TOEFL research, not about using the TOEFL test as an instrument for research on other foci. During this phase of the data collection, an enormous number of journal issues were searched through either electronic databases or hard copies. In addition to some general electronic searches through Google Scholar and a highly comprehensive collection of international electronic databases accessible via the main library at the Hong Kong Polytechnic University, at least 22 international language research journals were also searched individually, covering a period of 13 years from 1995 to 2007. In total, 29 relevant studies were identified. It must be pointed out that, however, while the searches were conducted on a fairly large scale, they were by no means exhaustive. For example, there might be missing studies due to the possibility that they are either not registered in any public or commercial database or that the keywords or keyword phrases used for the searches did not match any words or phrases in the article. Also, due to technical limitations, the searches were not extended to edited books, which might contain some relevant and valuable articles. However, the 100 or so research papers collected in this manner should sufficiently represent internationally published TOEFL research, especially research on TOEFL iBT, over the past 13 years.

Results

Recent Trends in the Volumes of Global and Chinese-Speaking TOEFL Candidates

This section addresses Research Questions 1 and 2. Table 7.1 was compiled based on the data collected from the TOEFL data summary reports covering the period of 1995–2005 (ETS, 1995, 1996, 1997, 1998, 1999, 2000, 2001, 2003, 2004, 2005a). It can be seen from the table that the data for 2002–03 are missing because they are somehow not provided in any ETS publication. The comparisons end in June 2005 because, as explained earlier, information on test candidate volumes is not available beyond June 2005. In Table 7.1, the candidate numbers for TOEFL cBT and pBT are combined for easier comparisons. Unfortunately, as the TOEFL iBT was first implemented in September 2005, the current study is unable to report on the volumes of TOEFL iBT candidates.

Table 7.1 shows that both the global and Chinese TOEFL populations were on the rise during the 3-year period of 1995–98. However, a blip occurred during 1998–99. Then from 1999 to 2002, the size of both types of candidates leveled off. After that, however, a clear drop appeared again in 2003–04, in both types of populations. What seems noteworthy then is the candidate volumes for the 2004–05 test year, when the global size appeared to pick up slightly, but the volume of Chinese candidates seem to continue a gradual, but obvious, sliding downward. For most of those years under study, the total Chinese candidate population accounted for over 20 percent of the global TOEFL candidate population. It reached as high as 24 percent in the test year of 2001–02. But during two test years, 1995–96 and 2004–05, the proportion of Chinese candidates only accounted for 18 percent of the worldwide TOEFL population, which were the two lowest points during the 10-year period.

Table 7.1 also reveals the trends of candidate volumes on the Chinese Mainland, in Hong Kong, and in Taiwan. It can be seen that the Mainland candidate group was expanding steadily from 1995–2002, but after that year, a sharp drop suddenly occurred. In Hong Kong, the decline of the TOEFL volume was steady year by year during the whole 10-year period. In 1995–96, the TOEFL population in Hong Kong was recorded to be 33,051 candidates; however, in 2004–05, this figure dropped to 7,526, an alarming and unprecedented reduction of 67 percent. This significant decline has also been pointed out in a recent survey (Qian, 2008b) of policies and practices of English language testing in Hong Kong. Coincidentally, in the summer of 2002, the International English Language Testing System (IELTS), which is jointly owned, developed, and delivered by the British Council, IDP: IELTS Australia, and the University of Cambridge ESOL Examinations, was adopted by the Hong Kong government as the test for its Common English Proficiency Assessment

Table 7.1 Comparisons of TOEFL Candidate Volumes (cBT and pBT): Chinese Compared with the Rest of the World (1995–2005)

	95–96	96–97	97–98	98–99	99–00	00–01	01–02	03–04	04–05
Mainland	58,240	73,206	79,964	81,721	107,038	110,364	127,815	97,407	85,048
Hong Kong	33,051	29,184	22,343	14,979	14,501	11,932	9,344	7,687	7,526
Macau	1,267	1,097	1,070	1,297	709	483	429	466	492
Taiwan	46,785	49,737	52,826	43,038	44,213	40,057	25,559	21,917	26,560
Other Chinese	7,780	493	4,919	1,138	2,056	1,533	1,119	989	1,125
All Chinese	131,563	152,731	161,122	142,173	168,497	164,141	163,928	128,388	120,751
Global TOEL population	731,297	794,989	786,345	616,633	728,811	703,021	688,904	632,761	663,750
Chinese in global TOEFL population (%)	18%	19%	20%	23%	23%	23%	24%	20%	18%

Note
The data for the 2002–03 test year are not available.

Scheme (CEPAS), which measures the English language proficiency of graduating students from all government-funded universities in Hong Kong. In the 2002–03 academic year, 8,500 graduating university students in Hong Kong sat for the CEPAS-IELTS, and in the 2006–07 academic year, the number of CEPAS-IELTS candidates increased to 9,850. It is not clear whether this adoption has indeed been a factor in the recent significant drop in the TOEFL candidates volume in Hong Kong but it is certainly a possible cause.

In Taiwan, the candidate volume increased from 1995 to 1998. However, the volume started to fall after 1998. The decline was gentle at first, but became sharp after 2000. The largest annual candidate volume of 52,826 was recorded for Taiwan in the 1997–98 test year, and the smallest candidate volume was reported in 2003–04, when only 21,917 candidates took the TOEFL test, showing a decrease of 59 percent from 1997–98. Clearly, the phenomenon of volume reduction in all three main regions of Chinese candidates is worthy of the attention of TOEFL stakeholders, and in particular ETS.

Recent Trends in TOEFL Scores Obtained by Chinese-speaking Candidates

This section addresses Research Questions 3–4. Table 7.2 indicates that the general Chinese TOEFL population, in particular the candidates from the Chinese Mainland, clearly and consistently outperformed the overall world TOEFL population in the first 10 years under study. However, the performance of the Chinese Mainland group, which forms the majority of the Chinese candidate population, appears to have weakened during the 2005–07 period based on the test results of the TOEFL iBT administrations. On the other hand, the mean scores of Hong Kong and Taiwan candidates rose steadily in the first half of the 12-year period. In the second half of the period, their mean scores seemed to be rather stable around 550 for the Hong Kong group and just over 530 for the Taiwan group. Although in the early years of the 12-year period, the Mainland group clearly outperformed the other two groups by a considerable margin, the trend now appears to be changing since the introduction of the TOEFL iBT: Not only are the gaps becoming narrower among the three groups of test candidates but in the case of the Mainland group and Hong Kong group the situation has been reversed. In the 2005–06 test year, the Hong Kong candidates scored 550 points on average while the mean score of the Mainland group dropped sharply to 543 from a mean of 559 in the previous year. From January to December 2007, the Hong Kong group maintained the same performance level but the Mainland group improved only very slightly by a mere 4 points, therefore still being outperformed by the Hong Kong group. At the same time, the mean scores of the Taiwan group basically leveled off.

Another noteworthy point indicated by Table 7.2 is that during the 12-year period, the world TOEFL population's mean score improved quite substantially. In 2001–02, their mean score reached 560 but it declined somewhat to the 550–552 range in the following years. To compare their own attained mean scores at the beginning (1995–96) and the end (2007) of the period, the global test population improved by 23 points. In comparison, the mean score level of the combined Chinese TOEFL population improved by only 15 points during the same period, from 532 in 1995–96 to 547 in 2007, although in 2001–02 their mean was as high as 563. This considerable drop in the mean score is likely affected by the decline of the mean score of the Chinese Mainland group, which constitutes the overwhelming majority of the Chinese TOEFL candidate population.

Table 7.2 Comparisons of pBT and iBT Mean Scores Obtained by Chinese and Global TOEFL Candidates (1995–2007)

	95–96	96–97	97–98	98–99	99–00	00–01	01–02	03–04	04–05	05–06[1]	2007[2]
Mainland	556	555	560	562	559	560	563	555	559	543 (76)	547 (78)
Hong Kong	518	520	523	524	524	531	527	542	542	550 (80)	550 (80)
Macau	498	506	512	506	505	514	NA	525	518	530 (71)	517 (66)
Taiwan	509	507	508	510	515	519	523	532	533	530 (71)	533 (72)
All Chinese	532	532	537	543	546	551	563	555	558	537 (75)	547 (77)
Global	527	526	532	531	535	540	560	552	552	550 (80)	550 (80)

Notes

In this table, only TOEFL pBT and iBT mean scores are used because the majority of Chinese candidates, who account for the major portion of the Chinese TOEFL population, had access to only the pBT version until September 2006, when the iBT version entered China.

The data for the 2002–03 test year are not available.

1 The numbers in brackets in this column are the iBT mean scores, used as the basis for the converted pBT mean scores in the same cell.

2 The mean scores for 2007 are based on all iBT scores occurring from January to December of that year.

Recent TOEFL Research and Chinese Learners

This section addresses Questions 5 and 6. As mentioned in the Method section, altogether about 100 published reports, papers and monographs were collected for analysis in this study. There were two foci of the analysis for each study inspected: (1) classification of research areas, and (2) if the study used data directly from test-takers or language learners, whether Chinese EFL learners were involved in the research. Table 7.3 summarizes the results of the analysis. The categories used in the tables were adapted from those used in the latest issue of an ETS research newsletter, *The Researcher* (ETS, 2005b), for categorizing ETS research publications on the TOEFL.

The following comments are made based on the information provided in Table 7.3. First, for TOEFL research studies that directly involve EFL learners and where learners' L1 background information is discernable, a large proportion of the studies have involved Chinese learners. In fact, in studies belonging to this category, only a very few studies do not involve Chinese learners. Therefore, it would be fair to say that sufficient attention has been accorded to Chinese learners in TOEFL research, in comparison with other EFL learner groups. On the other hand, the content analysis of the data also shows that almost none of the studies that have involved Chinese learners cover Chinese learners exclusively. Generally speaking, in TOEFL research Chinese learners only form part of the TOEFL population sample. Therefore, in that sense, it would also be fair to say that Chinese learners, as an EFL learner group with a unique L1 background, have not really been on the priority list of the TOEFL research agenda. This situation calls for serious attention.

Discussion and Conclusion

Now the above analyses to address individually the six research questions stated earlier in the paper are summarized.

> RQ1 *What is the trend in the annual volumes of Chinese TOEFL candidates from different regions during the period of 1995–2005 in relation to the annual volumes of global TOEFL candidates during the same period?*

The global TOEFL candidate volume was on the rise during the 3-year period of 1995–98. From 1998 to 1999, however, the volume decreased slightly. Then from 1999 to 2002, the volume was fairly steady. In the 2003–04 test year, the global volume dropped slightly. However, the number seems to have picked up after that. A comparison of the beginning and end of the 10-year period shows that there was an annual net loss of 67,547, or 9 percent, of candidates toward the end of the period.

Collectively, the Chinese TOEFL candidate volume was increasing during the same period (1995–98), but then dropped during the 1998–99 test year. From 1999 to 2002, the Chinese candidate volume leveled off. However, from 2003 to 2005, the volume appears to drop gradually to the lowest point of the 10-year period under study. Nevertheless, if different regions are examined separately, their trends appear to be different. It seems that the trend of the Chinese Mainland candidate volume has basically reflected that of the global candidate volume. The trend of the Taiwan candidate volume was quite similar to that of the Mainland candidate volume from 1995 to 1998. However, after that, the

Table 7.3 A Summary of ETS Research Reports and International Journal Articles on TOEFL Published from 1995 to 2007

Research Area	No. of TOEFL Research Reports	No. of TOEFL Monographs	No. of TOEFL iBT Research Reports	Total no. of Reports[1] (No. of reports covering Chinese Learners)	No. of Journal Articles (No. of reports covering Chinese Learners)
Test validation	9	13	0	22 (2)	10 (5)
Test reliability	1	2	0	3 (1)	5 (4)
Test information	4	1	1	6 (3)	1 (0)
Examinee performance	5	5	0	10 (6)	7 (6)
Test use	4	3	0	7 (4)	0 (0)
Test construction	1	6	0	7 (0)	1 (0)
Test implementation	8	3	1	12 (5)	2 (1)
Applied technology	4	3	0	7 (1)	3 (0)
Total	36	36	2	74 (22)	29 (16)

Note
[1] The total numbers in this column are slightly larger than the actual number of the research reports, which is 70, because one of the reports covers three categories and two other reports cover two categories each and were counted as an independent study in each category.

Taiwan volume started to drop. The decline was slow at first but it has been quite sharp since 2000. Comparing the two candidate volumes at the lowest point (2003–04) and highest point (1996–97) during the 10-year period, there is a decrease of 59 percent in candidate volume from its peak in 1996–97. Hong Kong has also witnessed a continuous decline in TOEFL candidate volume during the whole 10-year period. Compared with the volume of 1995–96, the first test year under study, the total number of candidates in 2004–05 was only 7,526, or a mere 23 percent of the 1995–96 volume of 33,051.

> RQ2 How does the trend in the global candidate volume compare with those of all Chinese TOEFL candidates from different regions during the period of 1995–2005?

The trend of the Chinese TOEFL candidate volume has largely conformed to that of the volume of global candidates. However, a difference can be observed in the 2004–05 test year. As the cut-off year of the present study was 2005, there is insufficient data on which to base a firm conclusion because of this slight difference. However, there is a need to monitor the trend after 2005 if possible. In any case, Chinese learners have always been the largest L1 group of the global TOEFL candidate population. During the 10-year period under study, the proportion of Chinese TOEFL candidates accounted for, in most years, more than 20 percent of the global TOEFL candidate volume. Therefore, it is extremely important for ETS to take notice of Chinese learners as a collective TOEFL candidate community.

> RQ3 What is the trend in the annual mean scores obtained by Chinese TOEFL candidates from different regions during the period of 1995–2007 in relation to the TOEFL annual mean scores for the global TOEFL candidates during the same period?

In general, the mean score of the global TOEFL population experienced a steady and continuous increase from the 1995–96 test year to the 2001–02 test year. During that period, there was an increase of 33 points from 527 to 560, an increase of more than 6 percent. After that, a mild decrease of 8 points was observed for the period of 2002–05. This slight drop was likely caused by the mean score decrease of the candidates from the Chinese Mainland, which is further explained in the next question.

Among the three main Chinese candidate groups, the Chinese Mainland group posted the highest mean TOEFL scores in most of the test years during the 12-year period under study. Most notably in the 1995–96 test year, the gaps between the Mainland group and the Hong Kong and Taiwan groups were as wide as 38 and 47 points, respectively. However, the gaps seem to have narrowed in recent years. Surprisingly, toward the end of the 12-year period, the gap between the mean scores of the Mainland group and the Taiwan group was only 14 points and the Hong Kong group actually surpassed the Mainland group by 3 points in the mean score. That appears to be a substantial change. In other words, the test performance of Hong Kong and Taiwan candidates has improved greatly while that of the Mainland group has actually slightly weakened since the TOEFL iBT was implemented.

> RQ4 How does the trend in global mean scores compare with that of all Chinese TOEFL candidates during the period of 1995–2007?

The overall test performance of both the global and Chinese TOEFL populations improved considerably during the 12-year period. However, the extent of their improvements vary: The worldwide TOEFL population made an improvement of 23 points during the 12-year period, while the mean scores of the Chinese TOEFL population increased by just 15 points during the same period. However, it must be pointed out that this comparison cannot be considered scientifically accurate because the worldwide TOEFL population also includes the Chinese TOEFL population, which accounts for between 18–24 percent of the world TOEFL population in any given test year. It is not clear, however, whether the increase of the scores of both the global and Chinese TOEFL populations suggests an improvement of the general English proficiency level of the candidates or a possible decrease of the difficulty level of the test. Further investigation into this question is clearly desirable.

RQ5   What have been the main foci of internationally published TOEFL research from 1995 to 2007?

In the past 13 calendar years, TOEFL research studies have been conducted in a variety of areas. However, in terms of main categories, test validation, examinee performance, and test implementation appear to be the three focal areas of ETS internal research. For articles published in internationally refereed academic and professional journals, the research foci appear to be, again, on test validation and examinee performance. This situation is understandable since test validation and examinee performance are two extremely important areas for language testing both for test-developers and test-users. Test implementation, on the other hand, is of vital importance to test-developers at ETS.

RQ6   What are the discernible research gaps in the internationally published TOEFL research concerning Chinese learners?

Although most published TOEFL studies directly involving EFL learners have covered Chinese learners reasonably well, two dimensions still seem to be missing. First, few studies in ETS publications or internationally refereed journals have focused their attention exclusively on characteristics of Chinese TOEFL candidates. Second, when they were included in a large number of TOEFL studies that appear in international outlets, Chinese learners were often used only to form part of an international test candidate sample. In fact, except for a study by Snow (1998), which looks into how the historical relatedness of second and native languages affects second language performance, few of those studies were designed to expressly compare L1 groups in order to determine whether and how differences in their test performance and other related aspects may have been caused by their different L1 backgrounds. This situation calls for attention from research planners and more effort should be made to determine in what way and to what extent learners' native language background serves as a variable in their test performance. This issue not only concerns the Chinese TOEFL population but also the other 140+ native language groups constituting the worldwide TOEFL population. As the distance between Chinese and English is considerably larger than that between English and most other European languages, the case for Chinese learners is more urgent and is thus worthy of the immediate attention of TOEFL researchers.

Identifying a Research Agenda for the TOEFL iBT

Recently, the TOEFL Committee of Examiners (2007) announced its 2008 research program on TOEFL iBT, which includes the following components:

1. Teaching, Learning, and Assessment of English for Academic Purposes
    1.1. Design, administer, and evaluate innovative, theoretically principled tasks for language learning (e.g., integrated tasks, multi-stage tasks) to inform the development of teaching and assessment materials. Proposals should include an explicit plan that directly addresses how the effectiveness of the tasks will be determined.
    1.2. Investigate the ways in which TOEFL test results are used to inform language teaching and learning goals and objectives.
    1.3. Determine threshold levels of language proficiency required for effective performance on TOEFL iBT integrated tasks and identify instructional supports to enable learners to achieve these levels.

2. Test Use
    2.1. Document current practices for using TOEFL iBT scores in academic or other contexts for (a) policy (admissions, financial support, licensing accountability), (b) program (placement and promotion), or (c) pedagogical purposes.
    2.2. Investigate the interpretation and use of TOEFL iBT score reports by individual test-takers.
    2.3. Investigate users' (ESL teachers, faculty, administrators, and test-takers) perceptions, beliefs, and attitudes towards TOEFL iBT as a measure of academic language ability in different contexts (e.g., country, program).

3. Validation
    3.1. Compare performance on TOEFL iBT speaking with performance on direct measures (interview, peer/group interactions) of speaking.
    3.2. Investigate the effect of test-taker characteristics (e.g., anxiety, attitudes, and beliefs) on the performance of TOEFL iBT speaking and/or writing tasks.
    3.3. Compare English language performance on actual academic tasks and on TOEFL iBT tasks.

The proposed research program includes test-takers' perceptions, beliefs, and attitudes toward TOEFL iBT and the effect of test-taker characteristics, suggesting that ETS continues to pay attention to research relating to test-takers. However, the research program also stops short of pinpointing L1 background as an important characteristic of the test-taker, which implies that research on the effect of L1 influence on test performance will likely continue to be missed from ETS-sponsored research in the next few years. In this regard, what research is urgently needed about Chinese learners? The following questions all appear to be urgent, relevant, and necessary:

1   How do Chinese learners perceive the TOEFL iBT, especially its new delivery mode and multi-stage, integrated-skills task format?

2 What are Chinese EFL teachers' and learners' beliefs about the new TOEFL iBT test as a measure of their English language proficiency?

3 Since the constructs of the TOEFL iBT, which feature a considerable number of multi-stage, integrated-skills tasks, are different from that of the TOEFL pBT and TOEFL cBT, to what extent and in what ways do Chinese EFL learners believe that the iBT version is an improved version and will measure their language proficiency more accurately and fairly than the pBT and cBT versions?

4 How will Chinese learners react affectively to the new structure, task format, and delivery mode of the TOEFL iBT?

5 How will Chinese learners' test-taking strategies and psychological processes change due to the change of the test structure, format, and delivery mode?

6 How will Chinese learners' test preparation methods and approaches change due to the change of the test structure, format, and delivery mode?

7 How will the change in test mode from pBT to iBT affect Chinese learners' test performance?

8 How will the introduction of multi-stage, integrated tasks and the change in test structure and task format affect Chinese learners' test performance, given that a large number of learners have already been familiar with the single-skill measures featured in the old paper-and-pencil mode?

9 Will the new TOEFL iBT test produce some beneficial washback effects on EFL teaching and learning on the Chinese Mainland, in Taiwan, and in Hong Kong? If so, where and how can the beneficial effects be evidenced?

10 Will the trends of the current TOEFL candidate volumes continue in the Chinese Mainland, Hong Kong, and Taiwan, especially with the increasing competition from other English language proficiency tests of international status, such as IETLS, as well as with pressure from the job market in the Chinese Mainland which now offers greater opportunities for university graduates?

11 What will the score trends look like after the TOEFL iBT is fully implemented on the Chinese Mainland, in Hong Kong, and in Taiwan? Will the current trends continue or will the trends change to a different pattern?

12 Why are the TOEFL markets in Hong Kong and Taiwan declining so significantly in recent years? Will the decline continue after the implementation of the TOEFL iBT?

Hopefully, future research based on these topics will provide valuable insights into various important but under-researched aspects of Chinese EFL learners *vis-à-vis* the implementation of the new TOEFL iBT on the Chinese Mainland, in Hong Kong, and in Taiwan.

Acknowledgments

A special thankyou goes to Sathena Chan for her valuable assistance in collecting a large volume of relevant information on TOEFL research publications, which has greatly facilitated the completion of this chapter. I am also highly appreciative of the constructive comments from Liying Cheng and Andy Curtis on an earlier draft.

Notes

1. The TOEFL test year typically runs from July 1 to June 30 for the following period: from July 1995 to June 2005.

References

Banerjee, J. & Clapham, C. (2003). Test of English as a Foreign Language computer-based test (TOEFL cBT). In C. Coombe & N. Hubley (Eds.), *Assessment Practices* (pp. 95–99). Waldorf, MD: TESOL Publications.

Clark, J. L. D. (1977). *The performance of native speakers of English on the Test of English as a Foreign Language.* TOEFL Research Reports No. 1. Princeton, NJ: Educational Testing Service.

Educational Testing Service. (1995). *TOEFL: Test and score data summary: 1995–96 edition.* Princeton, NJ: ETS.

Educational Testing Service. (1996). *TOEFL: Test and score data summary: 1996–97 edition.* Princeton, NJ: ETS.

Educational Testing Service. (1997). *TOEFL: Test and score data summary: 1997–98 edition.* Princeton, NJ: ETS.

Educational Testing Service. (1998). *TOEFL: Test and score data summary: 1998–99 edition.* Princeton, NJ: ETS.

Educational Testing Service. (1999). *TOEFL: Test and score data summary: 1999–2000 edition.* Princeton, NJ: ETS.

Educational Testing Service. (2000). *TOEFL: Test and score data summary: 2000–2001 edition.* Princeton, NJ: ETS.

Educational Testing Service. (2001). *TOEFL: Test and score data summary: 2001–2002 edition.* Princeton, NJ: ETS.

Educational Testing Service. (2003). *TOEFL: Test and score data summary: 2002–2003 edition.* Princeton, NJ: ETS.

Educational Testing Service. (2004). *TOEFL: Test and score data summary: 2003–04 test year data.* Princeton, NJ: ETS.

Educational Testing Service. (2005a). *TOEFL: Test and score data summary: 2004–05 test year data.* Princeton, NJ: ETS.

Educational Testing Service. (2005b). *The researcher.* Princeton, NJ: ETS.

Educational Testing Service. (2006). *Information and registration bulletin for Internet-based testing (iBT). TOEFL iBT: The Next Generation TOEFL Test.* Princeton, NJ: ETS.

Educational Testing Service. (2007a). 2006–07 TOEFL/TSE institution codes. Retrieved May 22, http://www.ets.org/media/tests/toefl/

Educational Testing Service. (2007b). *TOEFL: Test and score data summary for TOEFL computer-based and paper-based tests: 2005–06 test year data.* Princeton, NJ: ETS.

Educational Testing Service. (2007c). *TOEFL: Test and score data summary for TOEFL Internet-based test: September 2005–December 2006 test data.* Princeton, NJ: The Author.

Educational Testing Service. (2008). *TOEFL: Test and score data summary for TOEFL Internet-based and paper-based tests: January 2007–December 2007 test data.* Princeton, NJ: ETS.

Ginther, A. & Grant, L. (1996). *A review of the academic needs of native English-speaking college students in the United States.* TOEFL Monograph Series MS 1. Princeton, NJ: ETS.

Lee, Y., Breland, H. & Muraki, E. (2004). *Comparability of TOEFL CBT writing prompts for different native language groups.* TOEFL Research Reports No. 77. Princeton, NJ: ETS.

Lett, J. A., Jr. & O'Mara, F. E. (1990). Predictors of success in an intensive foreign language learning context. In T. S. Parry & C. W. Stansfield (Eds.), *Language aptitude reconsidered* (pp. 222–260). Englewood Cliffs, NJ: Prentice Hall.

Liceras, J. M. (1986). *Linguistic theory and second language acquisition: A Spanish normative grammar of English speakers.* Tübingen, Germany: Gunter Narr Verlag.

Qian, D. D. (2008a). From single words to passages: Contextual effects on predictive power of vocabulary measures for assessing reading performance. *Language Assessment Quarterly: An International Journal,* 5, 1–19.

Qian, D. D. (2008b). English language assessment in Hong Kong: A survey of practices, developments and issues. *Language Testing,* 25, 85–110.

Snow, M. S. (1998). Economic, statistical, and linguistic factors affecting success on the test of English as a foreign language (TOEFL). *Information Economics and Policy,* 10, 159–172.

Spolsky, B. (1995). *Measured words.* Oxford: Oxford University Press.

TOEFL Committee of Examiners (2007). *TOEFL Committee of Examiners (COE) 2008 research program.* Retrieved April 30, http://www.ets.org/research

TOEFL. (n.d.). http://www.ets.org/toefl/

Xi, X. & Molaun, P. (2006). *Investigating the utility of analytic scoring for the TOEFL® Academic Speaking Test (TAST).* TOEFL ibT Research Report No. 1. Princeton, NJ: ETS.

8   IELTS
International English Language Testing System

Janna Fox, Carleton University
Andy Curtis, The Chinese University of Hong Kong

An increasing number of Chinese learners are taking the IELTS test for admission to English-medium universities abroad, but how much is known about the relationship between this test and Chinese test-takers? This chapter examines the properties of the test, reviews literature regarding IELTS and Chinese learners, and summarizes the views of 15 Chinese international students, who took the test and were studying in a Canadian university.

Introduction

Although the Test of English as a Foreign Language (TOEFL) has traditionally been the preferred test of internationally-bound Chinese learners, an increasingly popular alternative is the International English Language Testing System (IELTS). IELTS has flourished under the joint management of the British Council, the University of Cambridge Local Examinations Syndicate (UCLES) (renamed more recently as Cambridge ESOL, English for Speakers of Other Languages), and the Australian International Development Programme (IDP). According to the official IELTS website (www.ielts.org), since 1989 "more than 6,000 education institutions, faculties, government agencies and professional organizations around the world recognize IELTS scores" and more than 940,000 people a year are now using IELTS in 120 countries. Facts and figures which highlight IELTS' rapid growth over a relatively short time span of 20 years.

IELTS and Chinese Learners

In the past decade, the number of IELTS test locations worldwide has increased to over 300, with more than 30 official test locations in the People's Republic of China (PRC). Although the estimated number of candidates has grown from approximately 80,000 in 1999 to close to 1 million in 2007 (Davies, 2008), the precise number of Chinese learners taking IELTS is unclear, as this information is not reported by the test-developer. Interpretation of actual numbers of test-takers is made more difficult because there are two versions of IELTS, one for academic/study purposes (known as the Academic module) and one for migration or employment purposes (known as the General Training module). It is the Academic module that is the focus here. What the test-developer does publish is information regarding the mean performance by sub-test and overall scores of test-takers taking the academic version of the test. Further, the Academic module test-takers are identified by most frequent first languages (L1) and countries of origin. Thus, it is possible to compare, for example, the average relative strength of test-takers taking IELTS from mainland China with test-takers taking the test worldwide.[1] Based on 2007 test data, IELTS test-takers from mainland China received somewhat lower scores compared with test-takers worldwide. They were strongest in academic reading, with an average reported band score of 5.76 (the average for test-takers worldwide was 5.88) but weakest in writing with an average band score of 5.12 (the average for test-takers worldwide was 5.47). Speaking scores for test-takers from mainland China were also lower on average at 5.26 (test-takers worldwide score 5.81 on average). Further, test-takers from mainland China were also well behind IELTS test-takers worldwide in listening, scoring on average 5.45 (test-takers worldwide scored 5.94).

Further, L1 Chinese test-takers were listed among the most frequent first language groups, and test-takers from mainland China, Hong Kong and Taiwan were listed among the most frequent countries or regions of origin. It is interesting to find Hong Kong among the most frequent "countries of origin" listed by the test-developer, given the relatively small population of Hong Kong (approximately 7 million). Other countries or regions on this list include mainland China (1.3 billion), India (1.13 billion), Indonesia (235 million), and Taiwan (23 million). Although no data were provided by the test-developer, the number of test-takers *per capita* in Hong Kong must be exceptionally high for it to be included in the most frequent list. The increase in IELTS test-taking in Hong Kong is no doubt related to the 2002 decision by the Hong Kong Government's University Grants Council (UGC) to make IELTS the basis of their Common English Proficiency Assessment Scheme (CEPAS). In this scheme, all UGC-funded university students in Hong Kong are encouraged to take the IELTS exam before the end of their 3-year, first degree (see also Qian, Chapter 7).

There are a number of other reasons for the increased use of IELTS in high stakes university admission contexts by Chinese learners. First, some countries have actively promoted the use of IELTS for students applying from abroad. Australia has gone further, stating that although other English language tests are available, IELTS is required for Chinese students who wish to obtain a student visa (Feast, 2002). Second, with the shift by the Educational Testing Service to computer delivery for the TOEFL iBT, wait times for students have increased. IELTS is an attractive alternative. It is widely available and widely accepted for university admission. Finally, because IELTS tested speaking and writing (along with reading and listening) long before the advent of TOEFL iBT, IELTS was considered more in keeping with models of communicative language teaching, which have been popular in recent years.

IELTS Test Structure

There are four sub-test modules in the IELTS, which take 2 hours, 45 min to complete.

1   *Listening Module*: 40 items in four sections (30 min). Test-takers listen *once* to a recording and answer questions. Time is provided at the end of the test for test-takers to transfer answers to the answer sheet.

2   *Reading Module*: 40 items in three sections (60 min). Texts from 2,000 to 2,750 words in length reflect a range of academic genres, including book passages, journal, or newspaper articles. A wide variety of question types are used (e.g., multiple choice, short answer, flow chart completion, etc.). Answers must be recorded in the reading answer sheet before the end of the hour.

3   *Writing module*: two tasks of 150 and 250 words, respectively (60 min). Task 1 requires test-takers to describe a chart, table or graph (at times there is a combination of these input forms). Task 2 requires test-takers to write an essay on a general academic topic.

4   *Speaking Module*: one-on-one interview between examiners and test-takers (15 min). The interview is divided into three sections: (1) general introductory questions related to personal information and two topics of general interest; (2) a prepared monologue on a pre-selected topic with questions; and (3) more demanding questions about the topic of the monologue. All responses are recorded.

Trained raters mark IELTS speaking and writing modules. Raw scores are converted to band scores from 1 to 9. Although test-users are advised to use sub-test scores and some universities do include requirements for each sub-test, typically only a minimum overall score is listed by universities as their admission requirement. Most institutions require a 6–6.5 overall band score on IELTS for admission.

What Does the Research Say: IELTS and Chinese Learners?

International Publications

Increasing numbers of Chinese learners in English-medium universities have prompted more research dedicated to their experiences with testing, teaching and learning. There appears to be a surprising lack of research, however, regarding the impact of IELTS (or TOEFL) on Chinese learners within their home countries. For example, the 2008 special issue of *Language Testing* focused on language testing in Asia. Although Ross (2008) notes in the introduction that, "Issues of equal access and fairness are most acute when language testing takes on a gate-keeping function as it does in admissions testing" (p. 8), there was only one article related to high-stakes external test impact on learners in Korea (Choi, 2008). Cheng's (2008) article in the same issue highlighted test development within China but did not consider the impact of externally developed tests such as IELTS. There is, however, considerable research relating scores on high-stakes tests like IELTS to academic outcomes (e.g., course completion, withdrawal, or GPA). On the one hand, some researchers (Ciccarelli, cited in Feast, 2002) have reported that IELTS scores accurately predict academic performance and "a student's ability to cope with academic English" (Ciccarelli, 2001, p. 3). Others (Feast, 2002) have taken a more conservative position, reporting significant, positive, but weak relationships between IELTS scores at admission and academic performance. On the other hand, Moore and Morton (2005), find important disconnects between the types of writing elicited by the test and those required for university study—a finding that is reinforced by Durkin's (2004) study of Chinese graduate students in the UK.

Indeed, there is an increasing amount of research that reports concerns over the inadequacy of such tests in identifying students with acceptable levels of written English. For example, Edwards, Ran and Li (2007) report on what they refer to as "an uneven playing field" for Chinese students entering postgraduate study in British universities. In their study, interview and focus group data highlighted the limitations of current tests of English used for university admission. In particular, university teachers expressed concern that the levels of written English currently accepted for admission of Chinese students, who fall far short of the writing capabilities of first language (L1) students, may have resulted in an ill-advised lowering of standards. Mayor (2006) also raises concern over Chinese candidates' performance on the IELTS test, finding that Chinese students who have performed well within the Chinese educational system "may import into their English writing a range of hitherto valued practices from their Chinese writing and/ or their English language classes" (p. 104). She argues that Chinese students' lack of awareness of academic/cultural differences may negatively impact both their language proficiency test scores and/or their ultimate academic achievement as international students. Hamp-Lyons and Zhang (2001) take a more critical perspective, questioning the cultural bias of tests like IELTS as "gate-keepers for universities in western countries" which reflect "a mono-cultural" view (pp. 111–112).

Sun and Chen (1997) express concern over the disparity between high test scores and Chinese students' difficulty adapting to academic and social challenges they face while studying in the USA. In a Canadian study of international student adaptability, Myles and Cheng (2003) explored the social and cultural adaptation processes of five Chinese graduate students (out of a sample of 12). They found that "although difficulty with adjustment varied, most successful students developed key understandings of Canadian academic culture by networking with international students with similar cultural and/or linguistic backgrounds" (p. 259). This strategic approach limited the potential for cross-cultural communication between the Chinese and Canadian students, a phenomenon that is also reported in a recent study by Cheng and Fox (2009).

Since Cortazzi and Jin's (1996) seminal work, contrasting Chinese educational culture and students' experience within it with expectations of performance in English-medium/ Western academic cultures, there have been many studies focusing on the unique experience of Chinese international students studying abroad. For example, Skyrme (2007) provided an interesting view of two Chinese international students enrolled in the same course in a New Zealand university in her longitudinal case study. Neither student passed the course, but one of the students developed reading skills over the period that led him to a deeper understanding of the course and increased competency as a university student, while the other experienced failure without understanding what he needed to do, how to do it or why. Similarly, Durkin's (2004) study identified the need for greater awareness of differences in academic expectations as well as cultural influences on classroom behavior of Chinese students in British universities.

With the increased use of IELTS in the high stakes context of university admission, there has been a concomitant increase in the amount of research regarding test preparation courses and their relationship to English for Academic Purposes (EAP) courses and test performance. Green (2007) examined whether dedicated IELTS preparation classes offered to international students in the UK gave learners an advantage in improving their writing test scores and found that there was no significant difference in score gains between those studying in pre-sessional EAP courses and those engaging in dedicated IELTS preparation courses. Green suggests that more research is needed regarding test preparation in other countries.

IELTS Research Reports

Having reviewed internationally published research regarding Chinese test-takers, their performance on IELTS, and implications for their learning, we next examine the research reports that are produced annually by the test-developer. Of particular interest, given the extraordinarily high numbers of Chinese test-takers, was the emphasis placed by the test-developer on research regarding their test performance.

The IELTS website provides information about research that has been commissioned and/or published by the test-developer in two sites:

1   A list of 'rounds' of research with article titles:[2] http://ielts.org/teachers_and_researchers/research.aspx
2   A list of 'volumes' of published research articles that can be ordered with abstracts: http://ielts.org/teachers_and_researchers/research/volumes.aspx

At time of publication, the test-developer had commissioned 74 studies, but only 41 studies from the research rounds had been published in eight volumes, with round one released in 1998. Interestingly, three of the commissioned studies specifically examined issues related to Chinese test-takers, but they have not yet been published. One study involved a comparison of scripts produced by Chinese and Greek test-takers in response to the IELTS writing tasks; the second examined memorized scripts produced in response to IELTS writing tasks by Chinese test-takers; the third investigated the tactics and strategies used by Chinese test-takers in response to the listening sub-test. Hopefully, the test-developer will publish these studies in the near future.

Interviews with Chinese International Students

We asked 15 Chinese international students, who took the IELTS and were studying in a Canadian university, about taking IELTS and the relationship between the test and their first year of undergraduate study. The findings summarized here were part of a longitudinal study (Fox, 2009) that involved a total of 292 undergraduate students. Only the interview data elicited from 15 Chinese students are reported here. Semi-structured interviews with the students were recorded and analyzed at intervals from September 2007 to May 2008. Three key issues emerged: performance gaps between the test and their undergraduate courses; test experiences; and test preparation processes.

First, participants were asked to compare what they were doing for their university courses (both EAP and degree-related courses) with what they were required to do in taking the IELTS for admission. Interestingly, none of the 15 Chinese students immediately or automatically connected their language performance on IELTS with how they were using language in their university courses. In the first set of interviews with the participants, five of the students responded that there was "no connection". One explained, "I take math . . . so no relationship".

One of the Chinese students compared the writing elicited by the IELTS and the TOEFL iBT and the writing she needed to do for her academic courses in political science:

> On IELTS the writing is sort of general so I just think about my opinion and I write. It's familiar like. On TOEFL iBT it's more difficult. I have to read and write and I can't just say what I think. The TOEFL is harder for me, but I think it is much more like what I'm doing now in my courses . . . both my EAP and the political science courses.

Her comments reflect issues that have been raised in the research literature regarding the adequacy of IELTS writing tasks in representing writing that is required for university study.

The potential gap between IELTS test-writing and university-writing was mentioned by three of the students from China, who identified "writing essays" as the task they felt most under prepared for in their first year courses. They pointed out gaps between what IELTS asked them to do and what they were expected to do in their courses. For example, one student noted:

> Most surprising thing for me to write an essay because this was totally new for me. In China I write essays in English but they are like 120 words! Here [in Canada] they ask for like 8 pages of writing. I would never put up 8 pages in my life!

Another student drew a comparison between the IELTS test preparation course she had taken and what she did in her university courses:

> In IELTS preparation course I write for practice, but 2 pages only. But in my courses now I write after reading a whole lot of articles and trying to find ideas . . . It's not enough for you to just put in information from the articles. You need to express your own ideas in the essays. This was new to me.

Ten of the 15 students reported a disparity between their IELTS sub-scores and their perceived abilities in English. For example, one of the Hong Kong participants compared his high test score in speaking with his actual ability to communicate with his Canadian university classmates: "here . . . I don't say anything. They can't understand me or when I try, I have to speak slowly and they lose interest. I guess it makes me a little unhappy." Another student felt that the test consistently underestimated his ability to use written English: "It surprises me, you know, how bad my writing is on IELTS, when I always get good marks for writing in my university classes."

Students who repeatedly took IELTS without showing improvement on their overall scores reported negative washback from the test:

> After so many times [taking the test], I feel so nervous when I'm writing because I'm afraid I lost all my confidence. I'm kind of a loser in the test situation . . . I can't show my real skill. Now I fear test in regular class too . . . just nervous about it.

The Chinese students considered here also commented on the difference between working under pressure of time on the IELTS, and the ways in which they managed their time when working on assignments for their courses. As one student put it: "Too much pressure. Everything so fast and I can't think on the test. In my class, I can take time to think. When I think . . . I just do much better with it."

The third recurring issue was the role that test preparation played in the test performance of the 15 Chinese students. Eight of them had attended IELTS test preparation courses before taking the test. One Hong Kong student remarked:

> My IELTS prep course did not focus on the whole thing. I mean my English is not better because I go to the prep course. They gave me whole lot of tests, hundreds of tests, and they give me every topic in IELTS, and if you prepare every one, you can pass. Even I don't understand the reading, I get the question right.

Another student commented on similar approaches in her test preparation course in mainland China: "Only about the test . . . 6 to 8 tests every day for three months . . . just focus on pass the test." This comment was similar to another student's:

> Because IELTS has fixed number of both oral and essay questions, they [the test preparation course] give you every one and you just go back to prepare. So I did well on the test because of practice. If you go beyond, this is not really your ability in English . . . or maybe I think it is just ability to pass the test. I got what I wanted . . . my score was good enough to get into university here.

One of the students from mainland China took another approach to preparing for the test:

> My mother sent me to one of those schools. I only stay one day though. I didn't like the boring way they prepare you for the test. Every day you take tests and talk about tests and take more tests. I couldn't do it. So I came to Canada and stay with my uncle and I study ESL for 6-months and also take some courses about IELTS here, and I think my English is much better for that. I also pass the test first time.

Ross (2008) comments on the phenomenon of test preparation courses, pointing out that admission to universities is sometimes less a matter of high-stakes standardized tests of language or language proficiency itself, and more the indirect result of parents' capacity to pay for test preparation. Ross notes "test preparation in some Asian nations has become a massive enterprise which can exert considerable influence" (p. 7). Certainly, the increasing number of test preparation schools in China is evidence of this influence.

Conclusion

This chapter examined the IELTS and its use by Chinese learners applying for study abroad. Although there are increasing numbers of studies focusing on Chinese learners that examine issues of test impact on teaching and learning, these studies have for the most part been conducted in "inner-circle" countries that have received Chinese international students—Australia, New Zealand, UK, USA, and Canada. In contrast, there is a notable lack of research regarding the impact of high-stakes tests such as IELTS on Chinese learners in their home countries. Clearly, this is a research focus that needs additional attention within mainland China, Hong Kong, Taiwan and other broader Chinese contexts. As evidenced in the interviews with the 15 Chinese students considered above, the importance of the impact of high-stakes proficiency tests like IELTS on Chinese learners should not be underestimated.

Notes

1. The data regarding test-takers worldwide was derived from the mean band scores for female and male test-takers, which also included Chinese test-takers (see http://www.ielts.org).
2. Rounds correspond to years. In other words, 14 years of research, 1995–2008, are summarized on this site.

References

Cheng, L. (2008). The key to success: English language testing in China. *Language Testing*, 25, 15–37.

Cheng, L. & Fox, J. (2009). Towards a better understanding of academic acculturation: Second language students in Canadian universities. *Canadian Modern Language Review*, 65(2), 307–333.

Choi, I. (2008). The impact of EFL testing on EFL education in Korea. *Language Testing*, 25, 39–62.

Ciccarelli, A. (2001). *IELTS issues for UniSA: Internal report.* Adelaide: University of South Australia.

Cortazzi, M. & Jin, L.X. (1996). Cultures of learning: Language classrooms in China. In H. Coleman (Ed.). *Society and the Language Classroom* (pp. 169–206). Cambridge, UK: Cambridge University Press.

Davies, A. (2008). Assessing Academic English: Testing English proficiency, 1950–1989—the IELTS solution. In M. Milanovic & C. Weir (Eds.), *Studies in Language Testing.* Cambridge, UK: Cambridge University Press.

Durkin, K. (2004). *Challenges Chinese students face in adapting to academic expectations and teaching/learning styles of U.K. Masters' courses, and how cross cultural understanding and adequate support might aid them to adapt.* Retrieved July 7, 2008, http://www.britishcouncil. org/zh/china-education-scholarships-china-studies-grant-awardlist-kathydurkin.pdf

Edwards, V., Ran, A. & Li, D. (2007). Uneven playing field or falling standards?: Chinese students' competence in English. *Race, Ethnicity and Education*, 10, 387–400.

ESOL. (2003). *International English Language Testing System (IELTS): Annual Review 2003.* Cambridge, UK: British Council, IELTS Australia, and University of Cambridge ESOL Examinations.

Feast, V. (2002). The impact of IELTS scores on performance at university. *International Education Journal*, 3(4), 70–85.

Fox, J. (2009). Moderating top-down policy impact and supporting EAP curricular renewal: Exploring the potential of diagnostic assessment. *Journal of English for Academic Purposes*, 8(1), 26–42.

Green, A. (2007). Washback to learning outcomes: A comparative study of IELTS preparation and university pre-sessional language courses. *Assessment in Education*, 14(1), 75–97.

Hamp-Lyons, L. & Zhang, B. (2001). World Englishes: Issues in and from academic writing assessment. In J. Flowerdew & M. Peacock (Eds.), *Research Perspectives on English for Academic Purposes* (pp. 101–116). Cambridge, UK: Cambridge University Press.

Mayor, B. (2006). Dialogic and hortatory features in the writing of Chinese candidates for the IELTS test. *Language, Culture, and Curriculum*, 19, 104–121.

Moore, T. & Morton, J. (2005). Dimensions of difference: A comparison of university writing and IELTS writing. *Journal of English for Academic Purposes*, 4, 43–66.

Myles, J. & Cheng, L. (2003). The social and cultural life of non-native English speaking international graduate students at a Canadian university. *Journal of English for Academic Purposes*, 2, 247–263.

Ross, S. (2008). Language testing in Asia: Evolution, innovation, and policy challenges. Special issue: Language testing in Asia. *Language Testing*, 25, 5–13.

Skyrme, G. (2007). Entering the university: The differentiated experience of two Chinese international students in a New Zealand university. *Studies in Higher Education*, 32, 357–372.

Sun, W. & Chen, G. (1997). Dimensions of difficulties: Mainland Chinese students encounter in the United States. ERIC Document Reproduction Service No. ED408635.

9 Chinese Test-takers' Performance and Characteristics on the Michigan English Language Assessment Battery

Xiaomei Song, Queen's University

The Michigan English Language Assessment Battery (MELAB) is designed to measure the advanced-level English proficiency of learners who use English as a second or foreign language. The MELAB results are recognized worldwide among universities, colleges, and educational organizations. This chapter starts with an introduction of the test structure, scoring procedures, and important test qualities, including validity and reliability of the MELAB, as well as strengths and limitations of the test. The chapter then analyzes performance and characteristics of the 2004[1] MELAB Chinese test-takers, including those from mainland China, Hong Kong, and Taiwan. This part of the chapter first describes the overall test score distribution compared with the whole 2004 MELAB population, then explores group differences by age, gender, purpose(s) for taking the MELAB, and geographical location. Finally, the chapter summarizes the findings, discusses the implications, and addresses the limitations of the study.

As universities and community colleges in the USA and Canada are engaged in aggressive programs of internationalization, and North American immigration has increasingly drawn from language groups other than English, there has been a steady increase in the number of professionals and learners using English and taking standardized English tests. Within this global population, Chinese learners are among the largest groups of international and immigrant students studying at English medium universities (Shi, 2006), and according to Canada census statistics (Chui, Trun, & Flanders, 2005), professionals and skilled workers from China are two of the largest immigrant groups in Canada. In order to be enrolled in various academic programs and to be recognized by professional societies, a large number of Chinese professionals and learners take English language proficiency tests such as the Test of English as a Foreign Language (TOFEL) and the International English Language Testing System (IELTS) annually. In addition to these tests, the Michigan English Language Assessment Battery (MELAB) is one of the English language proficiency tests designed to measure the advanced-level English proficiency of learners who use English as a second or foreign language. This chapter reviews the MELAB and investigates the performance and characteristics of MELAB Chinese test-takers.

There are a number of reasons for targeting this group of test-takers for this study. First, Chinese test-takers constitute one of the largest groups who take English language proficiency tests such as the TOFEL, IELTS, and MELAB annually. There are several research projects investigating the impact of candidate-related variables on test performance, for example, first languages on TOEFL essays (Lee, Breland, & Muraki, 2004), gender of IELTS oral test-takers (O'Loughlin, 2002), and students' majors in the reading section of the TOEFL (Hale, 1988). There are also MELAB annual research reports discussing descriptive statistics including first language groups, however, no specific information is revealed about the performance and characteristics of Chinese test-takers. Therefore, empirical research needs to be conducted with MELAB Chinese test-takers.

Second, as China is in transition, having opened itself to the world starting in the late 1970s after decades of isolation, it is now experiencing rapid developments in social, economic, and educational exchanges with other countries. These changes have given rise to a pressing demand for studying and using English as the desire to learn English is sweeping the country (Jiang, 2003). Also, the educational system in China is changing. English as a compulsory subject in the primary school curriculum was introduced in 2001, with more than 130 million children having been given formal classroom English education (Shi, 2006). These political, social, economic, and educational factors have had a great impact on English language teaching and learning in China (Gan, Humphreys, & Hamp-Lyons, 2004). Therefore, it is crucial for professionals and practitioners inside China and outside China to better understand contemporary Chinese learners.

Test Review

The MELAB has been developed by the English Language Institute at the University of Michigan (ELI-UM), which has a long history of English language proficiency testing and administration since 1956. The test used to be administered worldwide but is now limited to certain designated cities within the USA and Canada. The test is given on scheduled dates and times every year. Many educational institutions in the USA, Canada, Britain, and elsewhere accept the MELAB as an alternative to the TOEFL and IELTS.

Test Formats and Scoring

The current MELAB consists of three parts: a written composition, a listening comprehension test, and a written test containing grammar, cloze, vocabulary, and reading comprehension problems (referred to as GCVR). An optional speaking test is also available. Part 1, Composition—is a 30-min, impromptu essay response to one of two topics or prompts. Test-takers may be asked to give an opinion on something and to support their position, to describe something from their experience, or to explain a problem and offer possible solutions. Most MELAB compositions are one or two pages long (about 200–300 words). Part 2, Listening—is a 30-min, audio-recorded segment containing 50 questions. The listening part includes short sentences and longer discourse segments, such as a mini-lecture or a radio interview. All listening items are multiple-choice with three options. The third part of the MELAB usually contains 100 items: 30 grammar; 20 cloze; 30 vocabulary; and 20 reading comprehension questions (GCVR). Test-takers have 75 min to complete the GCVR four-choice, multiple-choice questions. The optional speaking part requires test-takers to engage in a 10–15 min individual conversation with local examiners. Examiners ask test-takers questions about their backgrounds, future plans, and opinions on certain issues and topics; they might also ask test-takers to explain or describe something in detail within their fields of specialization.

A MELAB score consists of scores for three different parts of the test (composition, listening, and GCVR) as well as a final MELAB score, which is the average of three scores. Scores on the optional speaking part are not included in the average. Regarding Part 1: Composition—each essay is scored by at least two trained raters who read independently on the basis of a clearly developed 10-step holistic scale (see *MELAB Technical Manual*, 2003, pp. 59–60). A third rater is employed in cases where there is a large discrepancy between the scores of the first two raters (the *MELAB Technical Manual* does not explain what constitutes a "large" discrepancy), or between a composition score and scores on other parts of the MELAB. The scale descriptors concentrate on clarity and overall effectiveness, topic development, organization, and range, accuracy and appropriateness of grammar and vocabulary. All listening and GCVR items are multiple-choice; therefore, test answer sheets for Parts 2 and 3 can be scanned by computer. As for the optional speaking part, examiners comment on fluency/intelligibility, grammar/vocabulary, and interactional skills. Functional language use or sociolinguistic proficiency is also considered. A full description of requirements in speaking scores which range from the lowest (1) to the highest (4) is given, with levels in between given plus or minus, for example, 2+, or 3–.

Reliability

MELAB test questions and forms are extensively tested for optimum reliability. Studies have shown the MELAB is reliable and fair in general. For example, Homburg's (1984) research showed that intra-rater reliability estimates, a measure of the consistency of a single rater's scoring, was between .87 and .94. In the 2004 and 2005 Research Reports (Johnson, 2005, 2006), reliability estimates for two ratings (by two raters) in 2004 and 2005 were .84 and .88, and .89 and .92 for three ratings (by three raters), respectively. In Spaan's (1993) study, 88 participants wrote two MELAB compositions during the same test administration. The correlation between scores on the two compositions was .89. As for the listening and GCVR parts of the MELAB, reliability coefficients ranged from .82 to .95 (*MELAB Technical Manual*, 2003). In the years 2004 and 2005, the average Cronbach's alpha estimates for the listening part were .87 and .89, respectively; for the GCVR part, these estimates were .94 and .96. To estimate the reliability of the speaking part, 34 test-takers were chosen randomly between November 2005 and February 2006 to be rated by local examiners and a MELAB senior rater. The correlation between the scores was .42. In 1991, a scale test/re-test study was conducted with 63 MELAB test participants who spoke 19 different languages (*MELAB Technical Manual*, 2003). The test/re-test reliability coefficients over the two versions of the test were .54, .82, and .92 for the writing, listening, and GCVR, respectively. The final score of the reliability coefficient was .91, which indicates a high degree of consistency. Because the MELAB test formats have not changed since 1985, the 1991 study results are still relevant to the current MELAB.

Validity

Kunnan (2004) described a test fairness framework, which discussed important qualities of validity such as content representativeness, construct- or theory-based validity, and criterion-related validity. The MELAB shows evidence of content-related validity, construct-related validity, and criterion-related validity. Regarding content-related validity, the *Manual* (2003) provides content-related evidence of validity, as it describes the process of test development for each part, the nature of the skills that the test is designed to measure, and a description of the prompts and item types. Tight control of current and retired test forms helps to ensure accurate scores that are undistorted by cram classes or prior knowledge of test questions. As a result, the MELAB can help institutions become effective recruiters by providing a generally fair estimate of test-takers' English language proficiency levels.

Three types of construct-related evidence of the MELAB are discussed in the *Manual* (2003). First is the general construct that the MELAB is designed to measure is English language proficiency for academic study. According to Bachman's (1990) model, language knowledge consists of organizational knowledge (grammatical and textual knowledge) and pragmatic knowledge (lexical, functional, and sociolinguistic knowledge). Clearly, the MELAB targets both organizational and pragmatic knowledge and measures English proficiency focusing on both the forms and the functions of language use. Second, the *Manual* (2003) reports on factor analysis with Parts 2 and 3 of the MELAB with two types of analysis: item factor analysis of the individual items, and principal component analysis of variables representing testlet scores. Two constructs were thus clearly presented: listening comprehension and grammar/vocabulary/reading comprehension. The third type of construct-related evidence about the MELAB focuses on the performance of native speakers of English on the MELAB. Between 1996 and 1998, 218 test-takers who claimed English as their native language performed markedly higher than 7,555 non-native English speakers on both part scores and final scores. About 78 percent of the self-identified native speakers scored 90 or above while only 10 percent of non-native speakers scored 90 or above (*MELAB Technical Manual*, 2003).

The *Manual* (2003) uses two ways to provide criterion-related information on the validity of the MELAB: TOEFL scores and teachers' assessments of students' English proficiency. Studies were conducted to measure the relationship between the MELAB and TOEFL scores. For example, a MELAB/TOEFL study in 2001 was involved 110 volunteer participants. The correlation between the two sets of scores was .89. In 1991, a validity study was conducted to compare the MELAB scores and teachers' assessments of students' English proficiencies. Moderately strong relationships (.54 and .67, respectively) were found in this study, suggesting similarities in the ways that the MELAB and teachers assess their students with stronger relationship with ESL undergraduate/graduate students.

Strengths and Limitations

In general, the MELAB had provided evidence of effective test design, development, and administration processes. Test security and validation are maintained at high levels to ensure that MELAB results are valid reflections of test-takers' English proficiency.

All completed test papers are sent to the ELI-UM for scoring, with score reports sent to test-takers (unofficial score reports) and to institutions (official score reports) after the papers are scored. In addition, the ELI-UM provides various information and documents about the test design, administration, scoring, and interpretation of scores. Since 2005, the ELI-UM has published annual reports discussing descriptive statistics and reliability estimates, and as this information is available to the general public, it attracts an audience with expertise and an interest in language testing.

The MELAB appears to be a thoughtfully constructed, reliable, and well-documented test with good fairness (Weigle, 2000). Potential test users are given ample information on MELAB to look through and assess their own strengths and weaknesses in language learning and use. However, the MELAB has its limitations. One weakness is its lack of accessibility. According to Kunnan (2004), a fair test must provide equal educational, financial, geographical, and personal access. While the MELAB has been maintained with high security, there exists a limit in accessibility, since the MELAB is only administered in certain designated cities in the USA and Canada. Furthermore, concerns with reliability and validity of the MELAB often result in a discrete-item testing format, a format which lacks authenticity, interactiveness, and practicality (Bachman & Palmer, 1996). Therefore, test-takers tend to focus more on micro-level accuracy than macro-level appropriateness, and there is an imbalance between linguistics knowledge and pragmatic knowledge (Weigle, 2000). Up to now, studies have been conducted to investigate the test qualities and examinee-related variables of the MELAB (e.g., Gao, 2007; Song, 2005; Wagner, 2004), but very little empirical research has been carried out to investigate the impact and washback of the MELAB.

Method

This study was conducted with the purpose of better understanding the performance and characteristics of Chinese test-takers on the MELAB. In order to investigate Chinese test-takers' performance and characteristics in the MELAB, the 2004 MELAB part scores and final scores of Chinese test-takers from across North America were obtained from the ELI-UM and used in this study. As stated earlier, the ELI-UM has published annual reports discussing descriptive statistics of the whole population and first language groups, including Chinese. The 2004 Research Report (Johnson, 2005) reported there were 174 Chinese test-takers[2] among 2,013 MELAB test-takers who came from more than 30 countries and regions. For this study, specific information about those 174 Chinese test-takers was analyzed in terms of their age, gender, purpose(s) for taking the MELAB, geographical location, part scores, and final scores. Among the 174 Chinese test-takers, 140 came from mainland China, 20 from Hong Kong, and 14 from Taiwan. The age of the test-takers ranged from 18 to 56, with a mean of 25.43 for the 173 test-takers who responded to the question regarding age. The majority of test-takers took the MELAB in order to go to college or university programs (112, 64 percent). Other reasons included: professional certificate (45, 25.7 percent); going onto a graduate program (12, 6.9 percent); and other reasons (2, 1.1 percent). The speaking part is optional for test-takers, and 83 Chinese test-takers took the speaking test, out of 1,049 speaking-test-takers in total.

Descriptive statistics were first calculated to determine the overall score distribution of the Chinese test-takers on composition, listening, GCVR, and speaking (the optional part) as well as their final scores. Next, the Chinese test-takers' performance was compared with the total population of the MELAB test-takers. Descriptive statistics were then also calculated according to gender, purpose(s) for taking the MELAB, geographical location, and age, to see how the sub-groups performed relative to each other. One-way analysis of variance (ANOVA) was used to show whether there was statistical significance between/among different groups by age, gender, purpose, and geographical location. The significance level was set at .05.

Results

Descriptive Statistics

For a total of 174 Chinese MELAB test-takers in 2004, the means of composition, listening, GCVR, and final scores were 75.89, 77.27, 71.91, and 75.05, respectively. Of 174 Chinese test-takers, 83 took the speaking test. There are 10 scores for speaking: 1, 1+, 2–, 2, 2+, 3–, 3, 3+, 4–, and 4. These scores were converted into a 0–9 scale for analytic purposes: 1=0, 1+ = 1, ... 4 = 9. The minimum and maximum scores were 4 and 9, respectively, which equal actual scores of 2+ and 4 on the speaking scoring range. The mean was 7.58, which is between actual scores of 3+ and 4–. Compared with the whole population of the MELAB 2004 test-takers based on the 2004 Research Report (Johnson, 2005), the means of part scores and final scores among Chinese test-takers were higher than the means of the whole population, except for the speaking test, in which they had the same mean score. The mean for listening (77.27) was higher than the average score (76.32) of the whole population, and the means for GCVR (71.91) and writing (75.89) were slightly higher than for the whole population (71.23, 75.39, respectively). As a result, the mean of final scores for Chinese test-takers was .72 higher than for the average of the whole population, and the mean for the optional part, speaking, was the same for Chinese test-takers as for the whole population (7.58). Since part scores and final scores for the whole population were not accessible to the researcher, ANOVA could not be conducted to compare the differences in means between MELAB Chinese test-takers and the whole population.

Group Differences by Gender, Purpose, Geographical Location, and Age

Table 9.1 gives a complete description of group differences. Male Chinese test-takers outperformed female Chinese test-takers in all four part scores and final scores, which was consistent with the score distribution of the whole population of the MELAB test-takers (Johnson, 2005). While male test-takers performed better than female test-takers on average, female test-takers obtained the highest and lowest scores for the four part scores and the final scores, except that male test-takers received the highest score in the listening part. It seems that female test-takers tended to show a larger variation than males did. However, one-way ANOVA showed no significant difference between female and male test-takers in part scores and final scores.

The majority of Chinese test-takers wrote the MELAB for the purpose of attending college or university programs (112, 64 percent). Test-takers who planned to go to colleges or universities outperformed those who planned to go for graduate programs or looked for professional certificates in all parts and final scores. While test-takers who intended to go to graduate programs performed better than those who wanted to obtain professional certificates for listening, GCVR, and final scores, test-takers wanting to obtain professional certificates outperformed in composition and oral. There was no statistically significant difference found among groups according to purposes for which the MELAB was taken.

Test-takers from Hong Kong outperformed test-takers from mainland China and Taiwan in all four part scores and final scores. The mainland test-takers performed better than Taiwan test-takers in composition and speaking, while Taiwan test-takers performed better in listening, GCVR and final scores. There was no statistical difference found among test-takers from mainland China, Hong Kong, and Taiwan.

Table 9.1 shows the descriptive statistics by age group for composition, listening, GCVR, final scores, and speaking. Four age groups were distinguished: below 20; 20–29; 30–39; and above 39. This followed the 2004 Research Report (Johnson, 2005),

Table 9.1 Descriptive Statistics of Gender, Geographical Locations, Purposes and Age

Part	Group	n	Mean	SD	Group	n	Mean	SD
Composition	Male	62	75.94	5.10	Mainland	140	75.69	6.43
	Female	112	75.87	6.94	HK	20	77.90	6.26
					Taiwan	14	75.00	5.10
Listening	Male	62	77.65	10.07	Mainland	140	76.84	10.60
	Female	112	77.06	10.32	HK	20	80.05	7.38
					Taiwan	14	77.64	9.58
GCVR	Male	62	71.98	11.55	Mainland	140	71.36	13.08
	Female	112	71.88	13.40	HK	20	75.40	10.77
					Taiwan	14	72.43	11.87
Total	Male	62	75.19	7.77	Mainland	140	74.63	8.69
	Female	112	74.96	8.85	HK	20	77.90	7.28
					Taiwan	14	75.14	7.32
Speaking	Male	27	7.74	.81	Mainland	61	7.57	1.08
	Female	56	7.50	1.19	HK	14	7.61	.94
					Taiwan	8	7.38	1.41
Composition	Coll/Uni.	112	76.40	6.25	<20	35	76.80	5.45
	Graduate	12	73.67	3.26	20–29	97	76.25	6.70
	Profession	45	75.22	7.33	30–39	26	73.15	4.08
	Other	2	76.00	1.41	>39	15	76.80	7.94
Listening	Coll/Uni.	112	78.80	8.53	<20	35	79.74	6.31
	Graduate	12	76.75	10.56	20–29	97	77.61	10.36
	Profession	45	73.93	13.04	30–39	26	72.23	13.98
	Other	2	75.50	3.54	>39	15	78.00	6.45
GCVR	Coll/Uni.	112	73.36	12.01	<20	35	74.66	11.01
	Graduate	12	70.58	12.19	20–29	97	71.66	12.64
	Profession	45	68.76	14.65	30–39	26	69.42	15.17
	Other	2	76.50	2.12	>39	15	72.40	12.63
Total	Coll/Uni.	112	76.18	7.80	<20	35	77.03	6.65
	Graduate	12	73.75	7.12	20–29	97	75.19	8.63
	Profession	45	72.73	10.15	30–39	26	71.65	9.65
	Other	2	76.00	1.41	>39	15	75.09	8.47
Speaking	Coll/Uni.	52	7.66	1.00	<20	16	7.38	.81
	Graduate	3	6.33	1.53	20–29	46	7.54	1.22
	Profession	24	7.49	1.18	30–39	12	7.42	.90
	Other	2	8.00	.000	>39	9	7.89	1.05

but combinations of some age groups were used to fit the context. For instance, age groups 30–34 and 35–39 in the 2004 Research Report (Johnson, 2005) were combined as 30–39 in this study. The test-takers ranged in age from 18 to 56, with one test-taker not reporting his/her age. In general, test-takers below 20 years of age outperformed all other groups in all part scores and final scores, except speaking, in which the mean score was lower than the mean scores of all the other groups. Test-takers between 30 and 39 years of age performed the lowest or near lowest in all four part scores and final scores. However, ANOVA results again showed no significant difference among age groups.

Discussion

This chapter reviewed the MELAB and analyzed the characteristics and performance of the 2004 cohort of MELAB Chinese test-takers. In spite of its shortcomings, the MELAB is a reliable and well-documented test (Weigle, 2000). The ELI-UM testing center not only provides annual descriptive statistical analysis of test performance, but also presents evidence of its content-related validity, construct-related validity, and criterion-related validity. In contrast, many national and regional exams in China are lacking continuous and systematic research regarding test qualities (Cheng & Qi, 2006). However, as discussed earlier, the MELAB format of discrete-items leads to a lack of authenticity, interactiveness, and practicality. This feature has impacted on Chinese test-takers who have a great deal of experience with multiple choice examinations and have received much input in linguistics knowledge but less pragmatic knowledge (Cheng & Qi, 2006). Consequently, Chinese MELAB test-takers have done well on its discrete-item format compared with formats such as blank-filling or matching.

The overall performance of this group of Chinese test-takers was average or above average compared with the whole population of 2004 MELAB test-takers. Compared with their performance in composition, listening, and reading (GCVR) parts, in which their scores were higher than for the whole population, Chinese test-takers performed in a similar fashion to the whole population in speaking. This result may be partly due to the fact that the English curriculum, textbooks, and testing systems in China attach importance to linguistic knowledge rather than to communicative competence (Cheng & Qi, 2006; Li, 1990). Chinese learners of English are often infused with input on phonological, morphological, semantic, lexical, and syntactic knowledge from teachers and textbooks. However, they do not generally establish a solid foundation in initiating and maintaining communication. Moreover, since speaking requires constant two-way interaction, an understanding of sociocultural norms and practices, and an awareness of non-verbal language meanings, these learners may encounter social challenges such as isolation and a lack of social skills in communication, which inevitably impede their progress in oral communication when they study in an English medium university (Fox, Cheng, Berman, Song, & Myles, 2006).

In relation to gender and test performance, the Chinese 2004 MELAB male test-takers performed better than the female test-takers, but there was no statistically significant difference between two groups. In contrast, female test-takers tended to obtain the highest and lowest scores in part scores and final scores. This result does not support the findings of the study conducted by Wen and Johnson (1997), in which female learners performed significantly better than male learners on the National Matriculation English

Test (NMET) and the Test for English Majors—Band 4 (TEM-4). In this present study, the mean difference favored males while female scores varied more widely than male scores did. The reason for this result is not clear and a more in-depth investigation is warranted.

Further, most test-takers wrote the MELAB for the purpose of going to college or university programs and they generally performed better than groups who planned to go to graduate programs or looked for professional certificates. Two reasons might account for this result. First, test-takers who took the MELAB for the purpose of going to universities generally ranged in age from 18 to 25. This group of test-takers was born in the 1980s, and has been provided with better learning conditions and more opportunities for learning English in the Chinese educational system (Lam, 2002) compared with Chinese test-takers who were born earlier. Second, this group of test-takers might show more rapid social, cultural, and academic adaptation and acculturation in English-speaking countries due to their comparatively young age and high motivation to learn. They might, then, more easily develop learning and coping strategies to achieve their social and academic goals in the midst of their intercultural adaptation process. An in-depth investigation is, however, needed in order to better understand the reasons behind this result.

Geographically, test-takers from Hong Kong outperformed test-takers from mainland China and Taiwan in all four part scores and final scores. This might be explained by Hong Kong's longer history of English education and longer exposure to English as a result of being a British territory for more than a century. Settlers from western countries integrated a modern western-style education system into the Hong Kong school system in which English was given a more prominent place than that in mainland China and Taiwan (Lin, 1997). Many schools and universities in Hong Kong used English as the medium of instruction, whereas Chinese was not even considered an official language until 1974 (Evans, 2000). Currently, English is one of the official languages in Hong Kong, and is commonly used in places such as universities and courts. Students start to learn English as early as in Grade One (Choi, Kam, & Ramsey, 2003). Although most people in Hong Kong have limited access to English in their daily life, English is still as equally valid as Chinese in many areas of language use and communication (Lin, 1997). All of these factors could contribute to Hong Kong test-takers having performed better than other groups.

Teenage test-takers outperformed all other groups in composition, listening, reading (GCVR), and on the final scores, but performed the lowest in oral communication. Their outperforming in composition, listening, and reading (GCVR) might be due to a situation in which the young generation of Chinese learners is experiencing rapid social and economic changes in China, and with China's entry into the World Trade Organization (WTO) and Beijing's hosting of the 2008 Olympics, China is in the midst of an English fever (Jiang, 2003). The Chinese government made English a compulsory subject nationwide starting from Grade Three in 2001 (Jiang, 2003), while at the same time, bilingual and immersion programs have been in increasing demand especially in economically more advanced cities such as Beijing and Shanghai.

In contrast to the implicit or explicit claims made by classroom teachers and educators that Chinese learners are passive in class, lacking in critical thinking, and are obedient to authority, the new generation is critical of their teachers, learning materials/

environment and themselves (Shi, 2006, p. 137). These rapid educational, social, and economic changes might all contribute to better performance of Chinese teenage test-takers in composition, listening, and reading compared with test-takers of other age groups. However, these reasons cannot explain why this teenage group, below 20 years of age, received the lowest scores in oral communication compared with other age groups, and although test-takers between 30 and 39 years of age received the lowest or nearly lowest scores in all four part scores and final scores, this group received most of their education in the 1980s, when China had just started opening its doors to the world and socioeconomic and educational reforms had just begun. Therefore, this group has not been provided with the learning opportunities available to younger learners.

Conclusion

Given that China is at a stage of rapid changes in terms of its social, economic, and educational systems, it is crucial for educational professionals and practitioners both within and outside China to understand test performance of Chinese learners, including their cultural backgrounds, motivations, attitudes, beliefs and values, expectations, learning styles, learning strategies, and learning behaviors. For technical reasons and because of time constraints, this study focused on a relatively small group of Chinese test-takers, so data from more than a 1-year administration are needed to cross-validate the findings of this study for further research. If item-level data can be obtained in the future, a more all-inclusive picture may be achieved to describe the impact of examinee-related variables of the MELAB on Chinese test-takers.

Notes

1. There is a time lag in collecting and filing annual test data for MELAB, since there are dozens of MELAB administrations conducted every year. When the chapter was drafted in early 2006, 2004 data was the latest data which could be accessed from the English Language Institute at the University of Michigan.
2. The number of Chinese test-takers has increased since then. For the years 2005, 2006, and the latest 2007, the numbers of Chinese/total test-takers were 345/2,351, 1,183/4,794, and 1,243/4,510, respectively (Johnson, 2006, 2007; Johnson & Song, 2008).

References

Bachman, L. (1990). *Fundamental considerations in language testing.* Oxford: Oxford University Press.

Bachman, L. & Palmer, A. (1996). *Language testing in practice: Designing and developing useful language test.* Oxford: Oxford University Press.

Cheng, L. & Qi, L. (2006). Description and examination of the National Matriculation English Test. *Language Assessment Quarterly, 2,* 53–70.

Choi, B., Kam, M. & Ramsey, D. (2003). Education and schooling in Hong Kong: Under one country, two systems. *Childhood Education, 79*(3), 137–144

Chui, T., Trun, K. & Flanders, J. (2005, spring). Chinese Canadians: Enriching the cultural mosaic. *Canadian Social Trends, 76.* Retrieved May 25, 2008, http://dsp-psd.pwgsc.gc.ca/Collection-R/Statcan/11–008-XIE/0040411–008-XIE.pdf

Evans, S. (2000). Hong Kong's new English language policy in education. *World Englishes, 19,* 185–204.

Fox, J., Cheng, L., Berman, R., Song, X. & Myles, J. (2006). *Costs and benefits: English for Academic Purposes instruction in Canadian Universities.* Carleton Papers on Applied Language Studies (CPALS) Volume XXIII: A monograph on English for Academic Purposes in Canadian universities. Ottawa, Canada: Carlton University.

Gan, Z., Humphreys, G. & Hamp-Lyons, L. (2004). Understanding successful and unsuccessful EFL students in Chinese universities. *The Modern Language Journal,* 88, 229–244.

Gao, L. (2007). *Cognitive-psychometric modeling of the MELAB reading items.* Unpublished PhD dissertation, University of Alberta, Edmonton, Alberta, Canada.

Hale, G. A. (1988). *The interaction of student major-field group and text content in TOEFL reading comprehension.* (TOEFL Research Report No. 25). Princeton, NJ: Educational Testing Service.

Homburg, T. J. (1984). Holistic evaluation of ESL compositions: Can it be validated objectively? *TESOL Quarterly,* 18, 87–107.

Jiang, Y. (2003). English as a Chinese language. *English Today,* 74(19), 3–8.

Johnson, J. & Song, T. (2008). *Research reports: MELAB 2007 descriptive statistics and reliability estimates.* Ann Arbor, MI: University of Michigan Press.

Johnson, J. (2005). *Research reports: MELAB 2004 descriptive statistics and reliability estimates.* Ann Arbor, MI: University of Michigan Press.

Johnson, J. (2006). *Research reports: MELAB 2005 descriptive statistics and reliability estimates.* Ann Arbor, MI: University of Michigan Press.

Johnson, J. (2007). *Research reports: MELAB 2006 descriptive statistics and reliability estimates.* Ann Arbor, MI: University of Michigan Press.

Kunnan, A. J. (2004). Test fairness. In M. Milanovic, C. Weir, & S. Bolter (Eds.), *Europe language testing in a global context: Selected papers from the ALTE conference in Barcelona* (pp. 27–48). Cambridge, UK: Cambridge University Press.

Lam, A. (2002). *Language education in China: Policy changes and learners' experiences.* Oxford: Blackwell.

Lee, Y., Breland, H. & Muraki, E. (2004). *Comparability of TOEFL CBT writing prompts for different native language groups* (TOEFL Research Report No. RR-77). Princeton, NJ: Educational Testing Service.

Li, X. (1990). How powerful can a language test be? The MET in China. *Journal of Multilingual Multicultural Development,* 11, 393–404.

Lin, A. (1997). Bilingual education in Hong Kong. In J. Cummins & D. Corson (Eds.), *Encyclopedia of Language and Education Volume 5: Bilingual education* (pp. 281–290). Dordrecht, Holland: Kluwer Academic.

MELAB (2003) *MELAB technical manual.* Ann Arbor, MI: University of Michigan Press.

O'Loughlin, K. (2002). The impact of gender in oral proficiency testing. *Language Testing,* 19, 169–192.

Shi, L. (2006). The success to Confucianism or a new generation? A questionnaire study on Chinese students' culture of learning English. *Language, Culture and Curriculum,* 19, 122–147.

Song, X. (2005). Language learner strategy use and English proficiency on the MELAB. *Spann Fellow Working Papers in Second or Foreign Language Assessment,* 3, 1–26.

Spaan, M. (1993). The effect of prompt in essay examinations. In D. Douglas & C. Chapelle (Eds.), *A new decade of language testing research: Selected papers from the 1990 Language Testing Research Colloquium* (pp. 98–122). Alexandria, VA: TESOL.

Wagner, E. (2004). A construct validation study of the extended listening sections of the ECPE and MELAB. *Spann Fellow Working Papers in Second or Foreign Language Assessment,* 2, 1–25.

Weigle, S. C. (2000). The Michigan English language assessment battery (MELAB). *Language Testing,* 17, 449–455.

Wen, Q. & Johnson, R. (1997). L2 learner variables and English achievement: A study of tertiary-level English majors in China. *Applied Linguistics,* 18, 27–48.

10 The Public English Test System

Jianda Liu, Guangdong University of
Foreign Studies

*The Public English Test System (PETS;「全国公共英语等级考试」) was established
by the National Education Examinations Authority (NEEA) in the People's
Republic of China to provide assessment and certification of the communicative
English language skills of the general public at a variety of levels of competence.
This chapter describes the background, objectives and development principles, level
criteria, formats, weighting, administration and assessment criteria of the PETS
tests, and then discusses the reliability and validity of the test system. The chapter
concludes with an exploration of the problems and challenges facing the PETS tests.*

Test Description

Background

Since the introduction of Reform and the Open Door Policy in China in the 1980s, there
has been an increasing need for a large number of professionals and highly qualified
personnel from different fields to be able to communicate directly with foreigners in
English (see Chapter 1). However, the historical situation of English language teaching
in China could hardly meet these new social demands, and since the beginning of the
1990s, the Chinese authorities have expressed concerns over the quality of communicative
English language teaching and learning in China. The authorities were also worried by the
absence of any uniform and well-established standards against which to measure English
language competence in China, as well as by the lack of a national system of English
language examinations available to the general public (Liang, Milanovic, & Taylor,
1999). One of the authorities concerned was the National Education Examinations
Authority (NEEA).

As indicated in Chapter 3, the NEEA is responsible for all national tests, including
tests for university entrance and for adult learners, and it administers more than 10
public English examinations which are individually designed for special purposes as a
result of different policy demands under special historical conditions after the Cultural
Revolution.[1] These exams were not placed on a common scale and there was a lack of
consistency in standards, with different standards being used at the same school grade or
the same standard being applied to different levels of testing (NEEA, 1999). Moreover,
not all language skills (listening, speaking, reading, and writing) were measured in all

of the examinations, and there was a general emphasis on grammar and reading and a relative neglect of listening and speaking skills. Examinations reflected a mixture of norm-referenced and criterion-referenced standards and no uniform system of administration and management existed before the mid-1990s (Liang et al., 1999). Foreign language examination reform thus became an urgent and important matter.

After the NEEA had realized the importance and urgency of the reform, in 1996 the Ministry of Education (MoE) promulgated a new syllabus for English courses in junior and senior secondary schools with specified requirements for listening and speaking skills; certain other modifications were also made.[2] Following the new syllabus, students' listening abilities were tested in the National Matriculation Test in 1999, as an experiment. In light of this, it became feasible and necessary for public English examinations to include listening and speaking as new language skills to be tested (NEEA, 1999). Consequently, the establishment of PETS (The Public English Test System) in China by the NEEA was initiated.

The nationwide College English Test[3] was started in 1987 by the MoE, but only college and university students were eligible for this test. During the early 1990s, the MoE authorities pointed out that research into and reform of English examinations should be carried out. The NEEA also came to realize the importance and urgent need to establish a framework for measuring the competence of English language learners outside the college and university system (NEEA, 1999). In 1996, with technical and professional support from the University of Cambridge Local Examinations Syndicate (UCLES), the PETS tests were designed to provide assessment and certification of the communicative English language skills of the general public at a variety of competence levels.

Objectives and Development Principles

The PETS project sought to reform existing tests and to develop new tests as appropriate, adopting a more criterion-referenced approach and placing greater emphasis on communicative skills in English rather than on a traditional grammar-based knowledge of the language. A major objective, therefore, was to give priority to listening and speaking (Liang et al., 1999). According the NEEA, the PETS aims to:

1 rationalize publicly available, criterion-referenced English language tests within a 5-level framework ranging from the level of English equivalent to that of Junior Secondary School level to the level required by graduates studying/working overseas
2 be available to all learners of the English language, with no restriction on age, profession, or academic background, so as to promote English learning nationwide and promote social development
3 increase the validity of tests by improving testing methods so as to enable candidates to develop their communicative competence, especially their listening and speaking skills
4 identify general and specific objectives of public English tests at different levels on one common ability scale so as to differentiate between the various tests and rationalize standards for the five levels

5   ensure the same interpretation of the scores of different tests of PETS at the same level and improve the reliability of tests, so that PETS can be related to tests for matriculation, tests for going abroad, tests for self-taught learners and thus make possible the diversification of the use of PETS test scores. (NEEA, 1999, pp. 3–4)

During the development of different levels of the PETS tests, features of the test use context were carefully considered. The development was based on the following core principles (Liang et al., 1999; NEEA, 1999, p. 4).

1   The PETS tests should provide an adequate focus on communicative language ability. Given that the aim of most English learners in China is to use English to communicate, PETS materials and assessment criteria focus on communicative competence. It is assumed that this will encourage more communicative language teaching and learning.

2   The PETS tests should provide a coherent system of levels clearly linked to one another. This means that competence at higher levels subsumes that of lower levels. Structural knowledge should be emphasized less at the higher levels than at the lower levels. Accuracy, while important, should not dominate to the detriment of fluency. Knowledge of vocabulary remains important but should be assessed in a meaningful way.

3   The PETS tests should take account of the current language teaching and testing situation in China. While reform of the testing system is considered of great importance, reform which does not build on the current situation and move it forward in a generally acceptable manner and at an appropriate pace is likely to fail. This implies the need to acknowledge the current value placed upon the learning of grammar and vocabulary, while at the same time seeking to place greater emphasis on speaking and listening, as well as taking into account the practical implications of large-scale speaking and writing assessment in the Chinese context. The PETS is designed to reform the existing testing system, but it is anticipated that the PETS and the matriculation test system will co-exist for a transitional period of 5–7 years. During this period, it will be up to the MoE, the NEEA, and the demands from schools to decide whether the PETS will replace the present matriculation tests in China. In other words, it will be adopted by choice on the part of the provincial governments and educational bodies rather than through any compulsory switch.

4   The PETS tests should take account of current technological developments in testing and of possible technological advances in the future. This means that, as far as possible, computer and other technology currently available should be used in the management of item writing, testing, and scoring and that consideration should be given to potential developments in testing technology, such as the establishment of multi-media banking and computerized tests.

Level Criteria

The framework of the PETS incorporates five distinct but coherent levels of assessed proficiency, ranging approximately from the level of English expected at Junior Secondary School (after 3 years of English study) to the level of English required by graduates planning to study and/or work abroad.[4] PETS-1 is designed for the elementary level. PETS-2 is for the lower-intermediate level, corresponding to the key level for university entrance; it is anticipated that this test may ultimately replace the National Matriculation English Test (NMET) currently used as a requirement for secondary school students wishing to go on to tertiary study (also see Chapters 16 and 17; Cheng & Qi, 2006 for a review of the NMET). PETS-3 is for the intermediate level, and it corresponds approximately to the standard of English required of a non-English major after 2 years of English study at college or university in China. PETS-4 is at the upper-intermediate level, approximately equivalent to the standard of English required of a non-English major after 3 years of English study at college or university in China. Candidates who meet the standards of this level should have a standard of English which is adequate for them to undertake postgraduate study or research within China. This standard of English should also be adequate for them to work as personal assistants, managers, or researchers. PETS-5 is at the advanced level, approximately equivalent to the standard of English required of an English major after 2 years of study. Candidates at this level are expected to have a standard of English which is adequate for them to undertake postgraduate study or academic research work abroad in an English-medium country. This standard of English should also be adequate for them to work at a professional or managerial level in China or abroad (Liang et al., 1999; NEEA, 1999).

The 7th edition of *Level Criteria, Test Specifications and Sample Materials* was produced in 1999, specifying the PETS level criteria which describe an overall proficiency scale that is both performance and linguistically oriented. Each of the four skills—listening, reading, writing and speaking—is also described at each scale level.

The five PETS levels outline in detail a level description, formal language knowledge, and language use. The level description defines the likely candidature for each PETS level in terms of age, and educational and/or occupational background. This description takes into account what is known of both the actual and the potential populations. The formal language knowledge definition describes the grammatical and vocabulary knowledge expected of candidates at each PETS level, taking into account features of the grammatical syllabuses and vocabulary lists[5] which are currently in use at each level. The language use definition, based in part on the model of communicative language activities developed within the European context of language learning and teaching (Council of Europe, 1996), describes what materials candidates should be able to handle and what they are expected to be able to do.

In terms of communicative language activities to be assessed at all the levels of PETS; a distinction is drawn between productive, receptive, and interactive activities at all five levels. Productive activities include both oral production (speaking) and written production (writing). Receptive activities include aural reception (listening), visual reception (reading), and audio-visual reception (for example, watching a film or video). Many communicative activities, however, such as conversation and correspondence, are interactive. Participants alternate as producer(s) and receiver(s), constructing discourse together through the negotiation of meaning according to co-operative learning principles. Interaction, therefore, involves the participants in both productive and receptive activity (NEEA, 1999, p. 7).

The PETS system includes elements which test the candidates' abilities to engage in productive, receptive, and interactive activities at all five levels. Detailed information for the PETS level description, formal language knowledge, and language use can be found in National Education Examinations Authority (1999, pp. 8–10). The PETS level criteria also include a specification of grammatical content as part of the overall test specification. A detailed specification of grammatical structures in English has been drawn up for PETS Levels 1, 2, and 3. This draws not only on the content of English language teaching syllabuses currently used in China, but also on work done by the Council of Europe for the Waystage, Threshold, and Vantage specifications of language (van Ek & Trim, 1991a; 1991b; 1997). Such a grammar specification has not been developed for PETS Levels 4 and 5, where it is expected that the teaching of grammar should cease to be explicit. At these higher levels of proficiency in universities in China, grammar should instead be contextualized within the ongoing development of reading and writing skills. The grammar specification is intended to be of practical use to those who have an interest in the content of the PETS tests, particularly test-writers, coursebook designers, teachers, and the test candidates themselves (NEEA, 1999, p. 11).

The teaching and learning of vocabulary has always played an important role in foreign language development in China and the tradition of vocabulary lists, largely based upon frequency counts, is well-established throughout the educational curriculum.[6] For this reason, a vocabulary list has been compiled for each level, drawing upon existing wordlists at the relevant levels and adapting these to include additional vocabulary items related to specific activities or work situations. Five vocabulary lists containing 1,000, 2,000, 4,000, 5,500, and 7,500 words have been drawn-up for Levels 1, 2, 3, 4, and 5, respectively, with higher level lists including the content of the lower level lists.

Topic and functional/notional specifications have been developed in a similar way. For PETS Levels 1, 2, and 3, detailed topic lists have been drawn up based on the National Curriculum for English Language Teaching as well as textbooks used in secondary schools and universities in China and the Council of Europe's *Threshold Level 1990* (van Ek & Trim, 1991b). Functional/notional specification derives from the current teaching syllabus for College English in China and for equivalent levels and *Waystage* 1990 (van Ek & Rim, 1991a) and *Threshold Level 1990* (van Ek & Trim, 1991b). However, for PETS Levels 4 and 5, no such topic and functional/notional specifications are provided on the grounds that learners at these levels of proficiency are able to operate in contexts involving a wide variety of topic areas, functions, and notions beyond those specified for PETS Level 3.

The level criteria also include a breakdown of the specific listening, reading, writing, and speaking skills which are considered particularly relevant at each PETS level and which are likely to form the testing focus of individual test items/tasks within the PETS tests. This categorization is compatible with the model of communicative language activities which draws a distinction between receptive activities (listening, reading), productive activities (writing, speaking), and interactive activities (listening and speaking) (Council of Europe, 1996). In addition, a short translation task is included in the Level 4 test as a means of assessing candidates' detailed and accurate comprehension of complex ideas and sentence structures in English.

Test Formats

The formats of the tests at all five PETS levels were designed according to a standard template composed of two separate test components. One is referred to as the Written

Test which consists of sections assessing listening comprehension, use of English, reading comprehension, and writing. The other component is an Oral Test designed to assess candidates' speaking abilities.

For PETS Levels 1 and 2, the instructions for the Oral Test, for the listening comprehension, use of English, reading comprehension, and writing tasks in the Written Tests are given in Chinese in order to encourage successful performance of the candidates at these lower levels of proficiency. For PETS 3, 4, and 5, the language used in both the Written Test and Oral Test is English, although task input for the writing tasks in Levels 3 and 4 may involve the use of a small amount of reading materials in Chinese.

The test profiles for PETS Levels 1–5 contain an overview of the complete test followed by a description of each test section covering listening comprehension, use of English, reading comprehension, and writing in the Written Test (see http://www.neea.edu.cn/zsks/ggyydj/show_sort_ggyydj.jsp?class_id=07_08 for more details). A description of the Oral Test is also given: the different parts of this test focus on candidates' abilities to interact in English. In addition, the test profiles specify the number of parts, the focus for each part, the item or task type, the number of items/tasks, the timing for each section, the weighting of each section, and the format of the answer sheet on which the candidates write their responses. The Oral Test description gives the number of examiners and their roles, the number of candidates, the nature of the spoken interaction, and the timing for each part.

Weighting of Test Sections

Since the number of test items is not the same for all five levels, the relative weighting of test sections should be considered across all five levels. Each test section contains different numbers of items and its raw score does not necessarily correspond to the importance of the language skill tested; therefore, each test section of the PETS within the Written Test is allocated a weighting reflecting the percentage contributed by each particular section to the total score. For example, in PETS Level 3, Listening Comprehension, Use of English, Reading Comprehension, and Writing in the Written Test account for 30 percent, 15 percent, 30 percent, and 25 percent of the total score, respectively. Variations in the weighting of the same test section across different levels reflects the evolving and shifting role of different language skill components as proficiency increases (NEEA, 1999). The number of items and their relative weightings (in brackets) in the Written Test are shown in Table 10.1.

Administration

The PETS tests were conducted first in some provinces and municipalities in 1999, but with only 28,577 participants (Anonymous, 2006a). Since 2003, the PETS tests have been open to people throughout the country and the tests are conducted twice a year in March and September for Levels 1, 2, 3; in June and December for Level 5; and once a year (March) for Levels 1B and 4. Candidates can choose to take the written tests and the oral tests together or separately. The test duration for the written test is 90 min for Level 1; 120 min for Levels 2 and 3; and 140 min for Levels 4 and 5. The test duration

Table 10.1 The Number of Items and their Relative Weightings (in brackets) and Test Timing Allocation (min) in PETS Written and Oral Test Levels 1–5

		Level 1	*Level 2*	*Level 3*	*Level 4*	*Level 5*
Listening	Items/weighting	25 (30%)	20 (30%)	25 (30%)	20 (30%)	30 (30%)
Comprehension	Timing	20	20	25	30	35
Use of English	Items/weighting	25 (25%)	35 (20%)	20 (15%)	20 (10%)	20 (10%)
	Timing	20	25	15	15	20
Reading	Items/weighting	20 (30%)	20 (30%)	20 (30%)	25 (35%)	30 (35%)
Comprehension	Timing	30	35	40	60	50
Writing	Items/weighting	3+1 (15%)	10+1 (20%)	1+1 (25%)	1 (25%)	1 (25%)
	Timing	20	40	40	35	35
Total	Items/weighting	74 (100%)	86 (100%)	67 (100%)	66 (100%)	81 (100%)
	Timing	90	120	120	140	140
Oral Test	Timing	8	10	10	12	15

for the oral test is 8 min for Level 1; 10 min for Levels 2 and 3; 12 min for Level 4; and 15 min for Level 5.

Table 10.1 displays the time allocations for test components across all five levels. The number of participants has been increasing rapidly since the PETS tests were made available to people throughout China in 2003. The number rose from about 320,000 in 2002 to 697,000 in 2004 and over 850,000 in 2005 (Anonymous, 2006b).

Assessment Criteria

For the writing assessment, a set of criteria for use at each level has been developed. A general marking scheme, together with a task-specific marking scheme, has been developed for each individual task. For the oral assessment, a candidate's performance is assessed by two examiners, one of whom acts as the assessor and provides an analytical assessment of a candidate's performance, while the interlocutor provides a global assessment. The marks given by the assessor are double-weighted to produce the overall score (NEEA, 1999). The total possible score for the written test is 100, while that for the oral test is 5, with the cut-off score set at 60 for the written test and 3 for the oral test.

Test Quality

To investigate the quality of a test, its reliability and validity are usually evaluated. Traditionally, the means of accumulating validity have been grouped into three categories: content-related validity, criterion-related validity, and construct-related validity (Guion, 1980). Kunnan's (2004, 2006) test fairness framework also specifies that validity should include important qualities such as content validity, construct validity, and criterion-related validity. Messick (1989, 1996), however, proposed a unified theory of validity which integrates test use, values and consequences. He identified six aspects of validity: (1) judgmental/logical analyses which concern content relevance and representativeness, as well as technical quality; (2) correlational or covariance analyses, which include mainly internal consistency reliability, multitrait-multimethod matrix, and factor analysis; (3) analyses of test-taking processes, which are predominantly realized through protocol analysis wherein respondents are asked to think aloud during task performance or to describe retrospectively the procedural steps they employed; (4) analyses of group differences and changes over time, which include cross-sectional comparisons of the performance of different criterion groups and longitudinal comparisons of performance for the same group at two or more points in time; (5) responsiveness of scores to experimental treatment and manipulation of conditions which attempt to alter test scores in theoretically predicted ways; (6) and testing consequences which include evidence and rationale for evaluating the intended and unintended consequences of score interpretation and use (Liu, 2006). Messick's unified theory has become the most cited, authoritative reference on validity. The following discusses the quality of the PETS tests based on Messick's validity theory.

Reliability

One major problem that exists in the estimation of test reliability is test length (Albus, Bielinski, Thurlow, & Liu, 2001; Lee, 1981). A long test, other things being equal, has a higher reliability coefficient than a short one. Objectivity, including test length, test format, and scoring method, is one of the indexes of reliability (Cheng & Qi, 2006). Therefore, to achieve better reliability, the PETS developers have taken a range of measures from those identified above. First, a sufficient number of items were included (see Table 10.1) for large sampling and reliability enhancement. Second, for the PETS Levels 1–3, the majority of their items (nearly 90 percent) were in an MC format to increase objectivity. In addition, inter-rater reliability, another important aspect of reliability considerations in a test (Bachman & Palmer, 1996; Kunnan, 2006), was also considered.

In the Written Test and the Oral Test of the PETS, measures such as carefully developed marking criteria, marker training, item weighting, and double marking were taken to ensure good inter-rater and intra-rater reliability. Meanwhile, the NEEA is trying to increase its reliability by means of modern technology. To that end, a computer-aided oral testing system has been developed for lower levels of the PETS and will be put to use in 2008 (Anonymous, 2008).

Validity

Before the PETS was developed, not all of the public English examinations in China measured all language skills (listening, speaking, reading, and writing), and there was a general emphasis on grammar and reading with a relative neglect of listening and speaking skills (NEEA, 1999; Wang, 2000). The inclusion of listening and speaking into the PETS as new language skills to be tested was thus a great step towards better content validity, which refers to the extent to which the test questions represent the skills in the specified subject area (Brualdi, 1999). Regarding content representativeness, the construct to be measured by the PETS was defined by the NEEA as the formal language knowledge component of grammar and vocabulary, plus the language use component of listening, reading, speaking, and writing tested through receptive (listening and reading), productive (writing and speaking), and interactive activities (listening and speaking). The language knowledge component and the language use component at all five levels are tested through five parts: listening comprehension, use of English, reading comprehension, writing, and the oral test (NEEA, 1999). Content validity appears to have been well realized in the PETS, however, other aspects of validity as proposed by Messick (1989, 1996) remain unknown, as few studies have yet been conducted to investigate the validity of the PETS (NEEA, 1999).

Impact and Washback

Thus far, although only a few studies have been conducted to investigate the consequences of the PETS, the test has had an impact on Chinese society. As stated in the *Level Criteria, Test Specifications, and Sample Materials* (NEEA, 1999), the different levels of the PETS tests are primarily administered as national proficiency tests to meet various new and emerging social needs. The PETS tests at some levels will gradually replace the current English (as a general subject) tests for self-taught learners. The Higher Education Self-taught Examination Offices of the Shanghai Municipality, Shaanxi Province and Sichuan Province issued documents in 2003 specifying that the PETS tests at Levels 2 and 3 could be used to replace the Public English Tests I and II,[7] respectively—compulsory tests of English for earning a diploma for the National Self-Taught Examinations. Those who passed PETS Levels 2 and 3 could be exempted from the Public English Tests I and II, respectively (Higher Education Self-Taught Examination Office of Shanghai Municipality, 2003).

Some levels of PETS tests are also used for matriculation purposes. For example, the Hunan Provincial Education Examination Board, the organization responsible for different education tests in Hunan Province, specified that from 2007 those test-takers who passed the Oral Test of PETS Level 2 could be exempted from the Oral Test portion of the Matriculation English Test, the university entrance test of English in Hunan Province (Anonymous, 2007b). It was also stipulated that the test results for the PETS Level 5 were valid for 2 years for those candidates seeking government sponsorship for overseas academic development. The impact of the PETS tests on society was also shown by the various coaching schools set up to help candidates prepare for the tests, which is not necessary positive washback.

The NEEA took into account relevant teaching situations in designing evaluation standards for tests at different levels in the PETS. However, the PETS tests will not be a substitution or replacement for school-based English tests. As a public English test system, the PETS tests are not intended to evaluate the English teaching of any particular school, as the tests aim not to interfere with the regular teaching of English language at any academic institution. Students in secondary schools, colleges, and universities (not including vocational schools) are not allowed to take the PETS tests, except in cases where they take the tests for matriculation (NEEA, 1999). Therefore, no evidence so far has shown that the PETS tests have had a washback effect on classroom teaching and learning in schools and universities. However, as more and more tests, especially some matriculation tests, are to be gradually replaced by PETS tests, it is not unreasonable to anticipate that the PETS tests will have a washback effect on the teaching and learning of English by Chinese students in the near future.

Problems and Challenges

The first live administration of all five levels of the PETS tests took place in September 1999, with over 33,000 candidates sitting for these tests. The number of candidates is changing with an annual increase of 40 percent to 60 percent (Anonymous, 2006c). In 2005, more than 30 provincial testing agencies administered the PETS tests, and the total number of candidates reached over 850,000. It was estimated that by the end 2005, more than 2.75 million candidates had sat the tests in China (Yu, 2006). In 2007 alone, the number of test-takers reached over 1 million (Anonymous, 2008).

With the dramatic increase in the number of candidates taking the tests, the PETS tests are increasingly accepted by the Chinese public as authoritative proof of one's English proficiency. However, to date, few empirical studies have been conducted to validate the PETS tests, and because of the lack of research literature on the PETS, no data about the reliability and validity of the PETS tests are currently available. Therefore, there is an urgent need for empirical studies to be conducted into the validity, reliability, fairness, and impact of these tests, as well as into possible washback and other components outlined in Messick's (1989, 1996) unified validity framework, Bachman and Palmer's (1996) test usefulness framework, and Kunnan's (2004) test fairness framework.

A systemic and comprehensive program of research is therefore needed to validate the PETS tests at all levels. Unlike the National Matriculation English Test (NMET) (see Chapters 16 and 17) and other tests such as the College English Test (Chapters 14 and 15) and the Test for English Majors, the PETS test papers are not released to the public after the tests are administered. Consequently, researchers have no way of obtaining authentic test papers; therefore, it will be the responsibility of the PETS organizing committees and the NEEA to sponsor and organize such research studies, in the way that the Educational Testing Service (ETS) and the University of Cambridge ESOL Examinations (UCLES) have been doing.

The PETS tests consist of speaking tests and writing tests (although reading and listening skills are also tested) and a critical issue in the large-scale assessment of writing and speaking is the development of appropriate marking schemes and systems for the management of item writing and oral examiners. This is particularly true in the Chinese context where candidate numbers for the PETS tests could total more than 1 million annually across all five levels by 2007 (Liang et al., 1999). Therefore, the training of examiners and raters has become extremely important to ensure inter-rater and intra-rater reliability. Though efforts have been made to address issues relating to the recruitment, instruction, training, co-ordination, monitoring, and evaluation of examiners for the writing and speaking assessments, more studies need to be carried out to ensure the reliability of these tests. It was intended that certain levels of the PETS would replace a number of existing tests, including some matriculation tests. In this case, comparability between different tests becomes very important. Therefore, research is also needed to investigate the comparability between the PETS tests and the other tests they are intended to replace.

The success of the shift of the Test of English as a Foreign Language (TOEFL) from a paper-and-pencil test to a computerized and Internet-based test also indicates a developmental direction for the PETS. With computerization, the PETS tests will be available to more and more people. Notwithstanding the nearly 1 million candidates who have taken the PETS tests at all levels, the influence of the PETS tests is still not large compared with that of other English tests in China, such as the College English Test. Comparably, many people still do not know the PETS tests well, and the results of the PETS tests are still not widely accepted by the public, neither in China nor outside China. All these factors indicate that the NEEA and the PETS organizing committees should make an effort to make the tests more widely known to more people in China and around the world. Meanwhile, many more systematic and comprehensive research studies should be conducted to validate the PETS tests, as without such support from reliable and valid academic research, the PETS tests will lack the credibility necessary for people to accept the test results. Given the scarcity of such academic research, there are some great challenges ahead for the PETS test-developer.

Notes

1. The Cultural Revolution (1966–76) involved a mass mobilization of urban Chinese youth. Schools were closed and students were encouraged to join units which denounced and persecuted Chinese teachers and intellectuals. There were also widespread book burnings and mass relocations. The Cultural Revolution also caused economic disruption. After 10 years, the movement was brought to a close in 1976.
2. The Ministry of Education issued a new syllabus for English courses at the senior secondary level in 2003 which divided English language teaching and learning into nine levels with each level containing several modules. These modules include all language skills, listening, speaking, reading, and writing (Ministry of Education, 2003). The new syllabus embodies the shift from examination-oriented to essential-qualities-oriented schooling which highlights the cultivation of independent thinking, a creative spirit, and practical ability.
3. The College English Test (CET) is an examination under the supervision of the Ministry of Education with the intention of objectively and accurately measuring the communicative English ability of college students and to provide positive washback on English language learning and teaching in colleges and universities in China. The CET is a large-scale standardized test. It claims to be a "criterion-related norm-referenced test" (Anonymous, 2007a). The test is divided into two levels, Band 4 and Band 6, and is administered twice a year (see Chapter 4 for a detailed review of the CET).
4. At an earlier stage, PETS Level 1B (which is not a formal part of the PETS system) was developed in response to the desire for a graded national English test at a level lower than PETS Level 1. The test is intended mainly for people working as government officials, work unit managerial staff, or technical workers who, for historical reasons, had little formal foreign language education (NEEA, 1999).
5. The PETS system includes a specification of vocabulary content as part of the overall test specification. A vocabulary list of words and short phrases is thus used for each PETS level. These lists are intended to be of practical use to those who have an interest in the content of the PETS tests, particularly item-writers for the tests, course book designers, teachers, and the test candidates (NEEA, 1999).
6. Such vocabulary lists exist in most language curriculums and large-scale language testing syllabuses in China.
7. Public English I and II are two compulsory courses for students (non-English majors) engaged in the National Self-taught Programs. The candidates must pass the corresponding tests (Public English Test I and II) in order to receive their college education diplomas (see also Chapter 3).

References

Albus, D., Bielinski, J., Thurlow, M. & Liu, K. (2001). *The effect of a simplified English language dictionary on a reading test (LEP Projects Report 1)*. Minneapolis, MN: University of Minnesota,

National Center on Educational Outcomes. Retrieved March 1, 2007, http://education.umn. edu/NCEO/ OnlinePubs/LEP1.html

Anonymous. (2006a). How's the PETS? Retrieved March 2, 2007, http://www.neea.org.cn/zsks/ ggyydj/infor.jsp?infoid=3309&class_id=07_04_01

Anonymous. (2006b). Development of PETS. Retrieved March 8, 2007, http://www.eduexam.cn/ webootr/Article/ShowArticle.asp?ArticleID=144

Anonymous. (2006c). Specialists talking about PETS. Retrieved February 22, 2007, http://learning. sohu.com/20060114/n241421001.shtml

Anonymous. (2007a). College English Test Band 4 and Band 6. Retrieved April 20, http://www. cet.edu.cn/cet_concept1.htm

Anonymous. (2007b). PETS Oral Test will replace MET Oral Test from 2007 in Hunan. Retrieved March 2, http://www.qq-soft.net/200611/1908/ m2m147990. shtml

Anonymous. (2008). Number of PETS candidates reached over one million in 2007. Retrieved March 20, http://news.edulife.com.cn/200801/ 09135029842.shtml

Bachman, L. F., & Palmer, A. S. (1996). *Language testing in practice.* Oxford: Oxford University Press.

Brualdi, A. (1999). Traditional and modern concepts of validity. *ERIC/AE Digest Series, EDO-TM-99-10.*

Cheng, L. & Qi, L. (2006). Description and examination of the National Matriculation English Test. *Language Assessment Quarterly: An International Journal,* 3, 53–70.

Council of Europe. (1996). *Modern Languages: Learning, Teaching, assessment. A Common European Framework of Reference.* Strasbourg, France: Council of Europe Press.

Guion, R. M. (1980). On trinitarian doctrines of validity. *Professional Psychology,* 11, 385–398.

Higher Education Self-taught Examination Office of Shanghai Municipality. (2003). Notice on the replacement of Self-taught Public English Tests with PETS. Retrieved March 1, 2007, http:// www.yuloo.com/wyks/pets/ dongtai/20030528104317438.html

Kunnan, A. J. (2004). Test fairness. In M. Milanovic & C. Weir (Eds.), *European Year of Languages Conference Papers, Barcelona, Spain* (pp. 27–48). Cambridge, UK: Cambridge University Press.

Kunnan, A. J. (December, 2006). *Towards a model of test evaluation: Using the Test Fairness and the Test Context Frameworks.* Paper presented at the International Conference on Language Testing, Guangzhou, Guangdong, China.

Lee, Y. P. (1981). Some notes on internal consistency reliability estimation for tests of language use. *Working Papers in Linguistics and Language Teaching,* 4, 19–27.

Liang, Y., Milanovic, M. & Taylor, L. (1999). Setting up a dynamic language testing system in national language test reform: the Public English Test System (PETS) in China. *Foreign Languages,* 3, 7–13.

Liu, J. 2006. *Measuring interlanguage pragmatic knowledge of Chinese EFL learners.* Frankfurt, Germany: Peter Lang.

Messick, S. (1989). Validity. In R. Linn (Ed.), *Educational measurement* (pp. 13–103). New York: Macmillan.

Messick, S. (1996). Validity and washback in language testing. *Language Testing,* 13, 241–256.

Ministry of Education, P. R. C. (2003). *Syllabus for English Courses (Trial).* Beijing, China: People's Educational Press.

NEEA National Education Examinations Authority, P. R. C. (1999). *China Public English Test System (PETS): Level criteria, test specifications, and sample materials.* Beijing, China: National Education Examinations Authority.

van Ek, J. A. & Trim, J. L. M. (1991a). *Waystage 1990.* Cambridge, UK: Cambridge University Press.

van Ek, J. A. & Trim, J. L. M. (1991b). *Threshold Level 1990.* Cambridge, UK: Cambridge University Press.

van Ek, J. A. & Trim, J. L. M. (1997). *Vantage Level.* Strasbourg: Council of Europe.

Wang, X. (2000). Reform of English tests: The establishment of PETS. *Journal of Zhengzhou University of Technology (Social Science)*, 18(8), 19–21.

Yu, J. (2006). Computerized Test for PETS. *China Education Press*, Retrieved October 18, 2007, http://edu.people.com.cn/GB/4932651.html

11 The Graduate School Entrance English Examination

Lianzhen He, Zhejiang University

As one of the two compulsory sub-tests in the National Graduate School Entrance Test battery, the Graduate School Entrance English Examination (GSEEE; 「研究生英语入学考试」) is one of the two main high-stakes English tests in the People's Republic of China, the other being the National Matriculation English Test (NMET;「高考英语」). Following the increase in the number of students enrolled in colleges and universities, a trend that started in 1999, the number of test-takers of the GSEEE has been on the rise, reaching a record high of 1,282,000 in 2007. This chapter, starting with an introduction to the test, discusses the role and extent of the test, addressing such issues as the use of the test, the impact of the test, and the role of coaching programs and schools.

Introduction to the GSEEE

The Graduate School Entrance English Examination (GSEEE; 「研究生英语入学考试」) is one of the four sub-tests for non-English majors in the National Graduate School Entrance Test battery. The four sub-tests are: the foreign language test (over 90 percent of the test-takers sit for the GSEEE); the politics test; and two sub-tests related to the subject areas the test-takers choose to study. The first two sub-tests are designed and administered by the National Education Examinations Authority (NEEA) of the Ministry of Education in the People's Republic of China (PRC) and the last two sub-tests are designed by individual educational or research institutions. With a full score of 500, 100 marks each for the foreign language test and the politics test and 150 marks for each of the two subject-related tests, the Graduate School Entrance Test consists of a preliminary written test of 3 hours for each sub-test, and a final test, usually an interview administered by each educational or research institution. Depending on the number of candidates that can be accepted into Master's programs[1] across the country each year and the performance of all test-takers, the Ministry of Education decides on two cut-off scores for preliminary selection, one being the total score and the other being the score from each of the subject tests. The ratio of test-takers entering the final test to those that can be accepted into Master's programs is between 1.2:1 and 1.5:1.

The GSEEE is a norm-referenced English language proficiency test. Over the past years, the GSEEE syllabus has been revised several times for various reasons, some to do with administration and some to do with the changes in the demands on graduate students in terms of their English language ability. Up to the year 2001, the GSEEE included five sections: Structure and Vocabulary (20 percent), Cloze (10 percent), Reading Comprehension (40 percent), English-Chinese Translation (15 percent), and Writing (15 percent) (National Education Examinations Authority [NEEA], 2001). In 2002, a listening section was introduced, and the GSEEE became a test made up of four sections: Listening Comprehension (20 percent), Cloze (10 percent), Reading Comprehension including English-Chinese Translation (50 percent) and Writing (20 percent) (NEEA, 2002). The listening section was dropped in 2005 for administrative reasons. Problems arose in some areas where test-takers complained about the poor quality of sound of the listening materials, and a decision was made to drop the listening section in the preliminary selection process. The format of the GSEEE from 2005 onward is shown in Table 11.1 (NEEA, 2005).

As is shown in Table 11.1, the GSEEE from 2005 onward comprises three sections. Section I is a Cloze test of vocabulary and grammar with 20 blanks. In Section II, Reading Comprehension, there are three parts. Part A includes reading comprehension items based on four passages, each on a different topic. Part B takes one of the following three item types: (1) A text with five gaps where sentences or paragraphs are removed. The sentences or paragraphs that are removed from the text are put together with one or two extra sentences or paragraphs and test-takers are required to choose the most suitable one that fits into each numbered gap; (2) A text with five numbered parts and a list of headings. Test-takers are required to choose a heading from the list that best fits or summarizes the meaning of each numbered part of the text. The first and last paragraphs of the text are not numbered and there are two extra headings; (3) A passage with jumbled sentences or paragraphs which test-takers are required to put into correct order. Part C of the Reading Comprehension section is a text with five sentences underlined; test-takers are required to translate the sentences into Chinese. Section III—Writing, includes two parts, Part A being a practical writing task and Part B an essay writing task. The Ministry of Education requires that listening comprehension be included in the final test.

Test-takers of the GSEEE generally fall into the following two groups. One group is made up of undergraduates who want to continue their studies after obtaining their bachelor's degree, while the other consists of those who, after graduation from colleges or universities, have worked for a few years, and want to do a Master's degree. Following the increase in the number of students enrolled in colleges and universities—a trend that started in 1999—the number of test-takers of the National Graduate School Entrance Test has also been on the rise. The total number of test-takers of the GSEEE since 2001 (statistics provided by the NEEA) has reached 7,540,108; the number from 2001 to 2008, respectively is 460,000, 600,612, 701,094, 915,269, 1,135,319, 1,244,714, 1,282,000, and 1,201,100. The increase is a direct result of economic growth and the improvement of people's living standard in China in recent years. With the expansion of undergraduate education, more and more college graduates wish to pursue graduate education. The Ministry of Education, in responding to this need, decided to increase enrollment. The number of test-takers has been increasing year by year, with the largest increases occurring in 2004 and 2005—an increase of more than 200,000 each over the previous year. This increase accords with the increase in the number of undergraduates enrolled in colleges and universities from 1999 onward.

Table 11.1 Format of the GSEEE from 2005 Onward

Section	Part	Input	Testing Areas	Item Type	Number of Items	Score
I Cloze		1 text (240–280 words)	Vocabulary & Structure	MC cloze (4 options)	20	10
II Reading Comprehension	A	4 texts (1,600 words in total)	Reading skills	MC (4 options)	20	40
	B	1 text (500–600 words)	Understanding the structure of a text	Multiple matching	5	10
	C	1 text (400 words with 5 sentences underlined)	Understanding complex sentences	Translation from English into Chinese	5	10
III Writing	A	Question or prompt	Written expression	Practical writing (about 100 words)	1	10
	B	Question or prompt	Written expression	Essay writing (160–200 words)	1	20
Total					50+2	100

The GSEEE is a high-stakes test in that the decision on the cut-off scores is a life-changing one for the test-takers. It also has an impact on other stakeholders, such as the parents of the test-takers, the colleges and the universities that the test-takers are from, the educational or research institutions accepting the candidates into their Master's programs, educational policy-makers, employers, and society at large. For college or university students, doing a higher degree, in many cases, means the chance of better job opportunities or better chances for professional development. In addition, for many colleges and universities, the number of students admitted into various Master's programs is often used as a yardstick against which the quality of their undergraduate programs is gauged.

Test Design, Development and Analysis

The GSEEE which is currently in use was developed in 1989. Over the years, testing professionals have worked closely with the NEEA in designing and revising the GSEEE test specification and syllabus based on needs analysis and changes in the social and economic demands on graduate students. Alderson, Clapham, and Wall (1995) point out that the development and publication of test specifications and syllabuses is a central and crucial part of the test construction and evaluation process therefore both test developers and test-users need test specifications and syllabuses. The GSEEE syllabus, updated and published each year, contains such information as the purpose of the test, the sections in the test and the number of items in each section, the weight of each section, the types of texts chosen, the language skills tested, the item types, and a vocabulary list.[2] A complete test administered in the previous year including all the instructions is also provided, together with the key for objective items and rating criteria for constructed-response ones (NEEA, 2004).

Item writers of the GSEEE are all professors of English from major universities in China with experience in teaching students whose English language proficiency is similar to those taking the test. These professors have also received training in item writing and test development. In writing the items, great efforts are made to follow the test specification and syllabus, and strict quality control is exercised in terms of the choice of materials, content coverage, vocabulary control, the proportion of word knowledge items to syntactic structure items being tested, and coverage of the reading skills listed in the syllabus. The process of writing items involves careful editing and moderation. After the test, objective items are machine-scored and rating criteria for constructed-response items are provided for raters across the country to refer to. The results of item analyses are released each year. Tables 11.2 and 11.3 provide some of the data released (NEEA, 2006b).

Table 11.2 Comparison of Difficulty of Each Part in the GSEEE 2003, 2004, and 2005

Part	Reading Comprehension				Writing	
Year	Cloze	Multiple Choice Reading	English-Chinese Translation	Multiple Matching	Part A	Part B
2003	.45	.49	.52	NA	NA	.48
2004	.56	.50	.53	NA	NA	.48
2005	.50	.47	.52	.42	.58	.54

Table 11.3 Distribution of Item Difficulty in the GSEEE 2005

Item Difficulty			0–0.3	>0.3–0.7	>0.7–1
Item number	Cloze		1, 5, 7, 8	3, 4, 6, 9, 10, 11, 12, 13, 14, 15, 19	2, 16, 17, 18, 20
	Reading Comprehension	A	21, 26	22, 23, 25, 28, 30, 31, 32, 33, 34, 35, 36, 37, 38, 39, 40	24, 27, 29
		B	43, 44	41, 45	42
		C		46, 47, 48, 49, 50	
	Writing				
Number of items			8	33	9
Percentage			16%	66%	18%

The mean of the test total score from 2003 to 2005 was between 45 and 50; test difficulty between .45 and .5; and test reliability between .75 and .85. Similar statistics are found for the GSEEE administered before 2003 and after 2005. Table 11.2 shows that the newly introduced Multiple Matching in Reading Comprehension was the most difficult, probably because test-takers were not familiar with this new format and there were not many coaching materials available. From Table 11.3, we can see that most of the items, 66 percent, were of medium difficulty (between .3 and .7), 16 percent of the items were difficult (between 0 and .3) and 18 percent of the items were easy (between .7 and 1). The two tables together show that the GSEEE is a rather difficult test with high reliability.

The Test Use of the GSEEE

Two of the major uses of language tests are: (1) as sources of information for making decisions within the context of educational programs, and (2) as indicators of abilities or attributes that are of interest in research on language, language acquisition, and language teaching (Bachman, 1990). The purpose of the GSEEE, according to the NEEA, is also two-fold: to measure test-takers' knowledge of English and their ability to use the language for a degree program or for research; and to provide information for educational or research institutions in selecting candidates for their Master's programs.

The GSEEE as a Measure of Test-takers' Knowledge of English and their Ability to Use the Language for a Degree Program or for Research

The GSEEE, as specified in the syllabus (NEEA, 2005, 2006a, 2007), is a test of the test-takers' English language ability, including their knowledge of the language (grammatical competence, textual competence, and sociolinguistic competence) and language skills (reading and writing). The four skills: listening, speaking, reading, and writing are all required of the candidates for Master's programs. Listening and speaking are tested in the final test, so the syllabus only includes reading and writing skills tested in the preliminary test administered at the national level.

Under the heading of Reading, the syllabus specifies that test-takers should be able to understand materials from books, journals, newspapers, and magazines. They should also be able to understand materials, technical manuals, and product introductions related to the subject area of their study or work. The reading skills tested include: understanding the main idea of a text and detailed information; making inferences and judgments; guessing the meaning of unknown words from the context; understanding the structure of a text; understanding the writer's intention, attitude, and opinions; and distinguishing between argument and supporting evidence. For writing, test-takers are required to produce practical writings, including letters for personal and business use, memos, abstracts, reports, and so on. They should also be able to write descriptive, narrative, expository, and argumentative essays. In addition, test-takers are also tested on their: (1) grammatical competence including those competencies involved in language usage (Widdowson, 1978) such as knowledge of vocabulary (choice of words) and syntax; (2) textual competence (cohesion and coherence); and (3) sociolinguistic competence (sensitivity to register).

Both the knowledge and skills tested in the GSEEE are within the target language use domain discussed in Bachman and Palmer (1996). In other words, the language use tasks included in the GSEEE are a set of specific language use tasks that the test-takers are likely to encounter outside the test itself in their future studies or research. The test-users, particularly the educational and research institutions accepting the candidates, want to generalize the inferences made about test-takers' language ability based on their performance on the test. The GSEEE is thus generally used as a baseline in English course(s) for non-English major graduate students, since the candidates accepted into the Master's programs are considered to have reached a certain level of English proficiency.

The GSEEE for Selection Purpose

One basic purpose of tests in educational programs is to provide information for making decisions which may be of two types: decisions about individuals and decisions about the program (Bachman, 1990). For individuals, tests may be used for selection, placement, diagnosis, and progress and grading. One of the most common uses of language tests for making decisions regarding selection is in conjunction with measures of other abilities such as academic aptitude and achievement (Bachman, 1990).

The major use of the GSEEE is for selection. Because the number of test-takers is far beyond the number of candidates that can be accepted into various Master's programs, a decision has to be made yearly about the criteria for acceptance. For preliminary selection, in addition to a cut-off total score, the Ministry of Education decides on a cut-off score for the sub-tests.

Given the differences in educational resources available across a vast country like China, the country is divided into three broad categories of areas with different cut-off scores. Class A areas include 18 more economically developed provinces and municipalities; Class B areas include three provinces and municipalities in north-western and south-western China; and Class C areas include five less developed provinces and all of the five autonomous regions. Different cut-off scores are also set for different disciplines.

Table 11.4 shows the cut-off total score for the National Graduate School Entrance Test and the cut-off score for the GSEEE in 2007 (Ministry of Education, 2007). As

Table 11.4 Cut-off Score on Total and that on the GSEEE in 2007

Discipline	Class A areas		Class B areas		Class C areas	
	Total	English	Total	English	Total	English
Philosophy	305	46	300	44	295	41
Economics	325	53	320	51	315	48
Law	335	53	330	51	325	48
Education (Physical Education Excluded)	305	50	300	48	295	45
Literature (Art Excluded)	350	55	345	53	340	50
History	290	41	290	41	280	36
Science	305	49	300	47	295	44
Engineering	290	41	285	39	280	36
Agronomy	285	40	280	38	275	35
Medical Science (Chinese Traditional Medicine Excluded)	295	44	290	42	285	39
Military Science	300	46	295	44	290	41
Management	330	54	325	52	320	49
Physical Education	305	45	300	43	295	40
Art	325	45	320	43	315	40
Chinese Traditional Medicine	285	43	280	41	275	38
Average		**47**		**45**		**42**

Table 11.4 shows, the average cut-off score of the GSEEE for the preliminary test in 2007 in Areas A, B, and C is 47, 45, and 42, respectively, with the score for Literature (Art excluded) the highest (55, 53, and 50, respectively) and that for Agronomy the lowest (40, 38, and 35, respectively).

Impact of the GSEEE

As a high-stakes test, the impact of the GSEEE is multi-faceted. High-stakes tests are those whose results are used to make important decisions that immediately and directly affect test-takers and other stakeholders (Madaus, 1988). Bachman and Palmer (1996) also consider impact as one of the six qualities of test usefulness. "The impact of test use operates at two levels: a micro level, in terms of the individuals who are affected by the particular test use, and a macro level, in terms of the educational system or society" (Bachman & Palmer, 1996, pp. 29–30). A variety of individuals will be affected by the use of a given test in any particular situation. GSEEE stakeholders include test-takers, educational policy-makers, educational or research institutions, employers, and society at large.

To better understand the impact of the GSEEE, a study was conducted by the author. The questionnaire survey was designed and administered to 386 trainees participating in a coaching program in Hangzhou in December 2006, 1 month before they took the GSEEE 2007. A total of 356 valid responses were collected (a 92 percent response rate). The questionnaire included questions concerning the purpose of their taking the GSEEE, the reason they attended the coaching program and their expectations of it. Informal interviews were also conducted with 10 English teachers of non-English major graduate students. The results are reported below.

Impact on Test-takers

Test-takers can be affected by three aspects of the testing procedure: (1) the experience of taking the test and, in some cases, of preparing for the test; (2) the feedback they receive regarding their performance on the test; and (3) the decisions that may be made about them on the basis of their test scores (Bachman & Palmer, 1996). Most relevant to the context of this study are test-takers' preparations for the GSEEE and decisions made regarding their acceptance or non-acceptance into various Master's programs.

In most Chinese colleges and universities, non-English major students take College English courses during their first and second undergraduate years. By the time they take the GSEEE in their last undergraduate year, they no longer have College English courses and they usually need to spend several weeks or months preparing for the GSEEE. For those test-takers who take the test after they have worked for some years, the time for preparation may be even longer, which may mean a long period of absence from their jobs as well as a big investment of money and time. In my study, more than half of the trainees (58.4 percent) involved in the survey spent 3–6 months preparing for the GSEEE and the average expense was about 800 yuan (Chinese RMB), with the largest share spent on test-oriented instruction in coaching programs/schools.

The decisions made on the basis of their test scores affects test-takers directly in a number of ways. Results of the survey show that the majority of trainees, 78.4 percent, took the GSEEE in order to seek better job opportunities. Because of the increase in undergraduate enrolment and the ensuing ever-competitive job market, college or university graduates with only a Bachelor's degree will have comparably fewer job opportunities than those with graduate degrees: the trainees therefore felt that a Master's degree might give them an edge in employment opportunities. Thus acceptance or non-acceptance into a Master's program had serious consequences for these test-takers. For those who were already employed, the consequences were also potentially serious. Some trainees, in responding to the question regarding their reasons for taking the GSEEE, wrote that they were facing the threat of losing their jobs if they did not get a Master's degree within a couple of years.

Impact on Society and the Educational System

Test developers and users should consider the societal and educational value systems that inform the use of their tests. Also of concern is the consequence of the use of a language test for the educational system and for society. For high-stakes tests, which are used to make major decisions about large numbers of individuals, the potential impact of the test must be considered. Bachman and Palmer (1996) suggest ways of assessing the potential consequences of a test, both positive and negative. As was mentioned in the previous section, test-takers take the GSEEE at a time when they no longer attend College English classes or when they are already at work, so they have to spend time and money preparing for the test. In responding to the survey question, "What do you think is the best way to prepare for the GSEEE?", among the 356 trainees surveyed, more than 80 percent of them (295) chose the option, "To go to a coaching school". This need for instruction/coaching and this preference for coaching programs/schools has given rise to "professional"[3] test instructors/coaches as well as to a great volume of coaching materials and a large number of coaching schools, thus creating sizeable business opportunities for those involved. Among all the major tests administered in the People's Republic of China, including the National Matriculation English Test (NMET), the College English Test (CET) and the Public English Test System (PETS), the GSEEE has the largest market share. An estimate by China Kaoyan (中国考研) shows that the annual market value of coaching materials and programs for the National Graduate School Entrance Test is approximately 3 billion yuan, of which GSEEE-related coaching materials and programs take the biggest share.

When asked to rank the different parts in the GSEEE in terms of difficulty, 67.4 percent of the trainees put Writing Part B at the top, followed by Writing Part A. In answering the question regarding their expectations from the coaching programs/schools, over 95 percent of the trainees chose B ("By teaching us some test-taking strategies"), C ("By familiarizing us with the test format and ultimately helping us automatize test performance") or D ("By trying to make predictions about the content/topic area of the forthcoming test and providing us with some samples for the writing tasks"), with D topping the list (52.2 percent). It is obvious that the trainees' immediate goal is to get a high score in the GSEEE in order to pass the preliminary test. Consequently, to cater for the trainees' needs to achieve this short-term goal, teaching to the test has become a common practice in these coaching programs/schools: in effect, this involves operationalizing the test construct in training classes (Qi, 2005). The instructors/coaches employ teaching activities such as teaching to the test content, teaching to the test formats, and automatizing test performance.

Role of the Coaching Programs/Schools and Its Impact on Teaching

As was mentioned in the previous section, the test-takers' need for instruction/coaching and their preference for coaching programs/schools have given rise to some "professional" test instructors/coaches. To cater for the desires of the test-takers, the coaching programs/schools try to familiarize them with the format of the GSEEE and teach to the format rather than trying to help improve the trainees' English language proficiency. Instructors/coaches also put a lot of time and effort into analyzing the GSEEE papers of the previous years and, based on the analyses, trying to make predictions about the content/topic areas of the forthcoming GSEEE and equipping the trainees with some strategies to cope with the test.

One typical example is the various writing samples provided for the trainees in these coaching programs/schools. For several years, the writing task in the GSEEE was about a certain social problem or phenomenon (e.g., respecting the old, considering international football stars as role models). A picture is used as a prompt and instructions are given. Trainees tend to spend a great deal of time preparing for the writing section of the test because they know that the writing section is weighted heavily in the GSEEE (10 points for Writing Part A and 20 points for Writing Part B). The trainees also recognize that when they are no longer taking College English courses, or when they are working, they lack practice in writing tasks: they therefore expect the coaching programs/schools to help them with writing practice.

To prepare the trainees for the writing tasks, the coaching programs/schools provide several samples of essays for them to use no matter what social problem or phenomenon is being discussed. The following are two sample versions for Writing Part B taken from the marking center in China's Zhejiang province in February 2007.

Sample 1

It goes without saying that <u>the symbolic meaning conveyed</u> should be given deep consideration. What on earth can be derived from <u>*these* interesting and instructive drawings</u>? There is no doubt that <u>what *the* painter virtually aims to convey is deep and profound</u>. <u>Primarily</u>, we can learn that <u>such case is far from being rare and upsetting parallels can be found</u> anywhere from our neighborhood and around the world. <u>What's more</u>, there has been a growing concern nowadays over <u>the worsening phenomenon</u>. It is hard to imagine what our society would be like years later if <u>such pervasive trend</u> goes unchallenged . . .

Sample 2

Simple as <u>*the* image</u> is, <u>*the* implications</u> mirrored are apparently far-reaching. <u>Initially</u>, nowhere in history has <u>*the* issue</u> been talked about so much as in our society today. <u>In the second place</u>, <u>*the* painting</u> reveals an upsetting story and an increasing number of similar events happened and happening are heard or repeated in nearly all aspects of our life. <u>Additionally</u>, <u>*the* painter</u> intends to convince us that a package of programs should be initiated to handle <u>*the* grim situation</u>.

We can see that in both samples, the social problem or phenomenon under discussion is not specified. The vagueness of the issue under discussion renders the samples suitable for whatever social problem or phenomenon is involved. The use of definite articles, determiners, and pronouns seems to be pointing at a particular social problem or phenomenon, but in fact it is like an all-purpose adhesive that can be applied in any context to a problem or phenomenon that needs to be addressed. In addition, the use of such cohesive devices as "primarily", "initially", "additionally", "what's more", "in the second place", helps to make the articles better organized.

Among the 27,248 essays marked at the center in Zhejiang province in February 2007, essays including the above two samples make up more than 10 percent, some with slight changes here and there. Together with other samples of a similar nature, essays following such sample versions make up more than 20 percent of the essays marked at the center. This phenomenon shows that the coaching programs/schools are indeed feeding the trainees with what they need and the trainees' expectations from the coaching programs/ schools are largely met.

But various problems arise with the above-mentioned phenomenon. One problem is that it creates difficulties for raters. The NEEA provides rating criteria which specify requirements for content and language. The criteria include: (1) coverage of the main points; (2) the use of a variety of syntactic structures and vocabulary; (3) the smoothness/ naturalness of the language used; (4) the use of cohesive devices and the coherence of the article; and (5) appropriateness of the register. What should raters do with essays containing such paragraph(s) shown in the two samples? The author of this chapter, as a member of the quality control group during the marking process, has had the experience of finding different scores given to such essays. Some raters gave a score as high as 18–19 out of a total of 20 for this part, while some gave a score between 5 and 8. Some even went to the extreme by giving a score as low as 2–3. Apart from the inter-rater differences, intra-rater differences in rating were detected. The author discussed the rating criteria with some of the raters concerned and learned the reason behind these differences. Some raters, when they first came across essays of this kind, tended to give high scores because they were impressed by the richness of vocabulary, the well-organized paragraph(s), and the use of discourse markers. But as they read more and more of such essays, they got bored and once they realized what had happened, they decided to punish the test-takers following such samples by giving them a low score. This kind of rater response and behavior raises some very serious questions about the training of raters and how well they are prepared for the task of rating large numbers of test papers. It is therefore suggested that larger samples be collected before the actual marking process and more detailed criteria be given for rater training.

The other problem relates to curriculum design of the English course(s) at educational or research institutions. The aim of the GSEEE is, in part, to measure the test-takers' knowledge of English and their ability to use the language for a degree program or for research. Candidates who are accepted into Master's programs are considered to have reached a certain level of English language proficiency. But are the scores they have obtained reliable indicators of their target language ability despite the high reliability that test designers have maintained? This is the major concern of the author and was thus the focus of the informal interviews with 10 English teachers of non-English major graduate students. The interviews, unstructured and informal ones, were carried out during the period of the marking of essays and the interviewees were raters. Among the 10 interviewees, seven were female and three were male.

The participants all had been teaching non-English major graduate students for more than 5 years, and some over 10 years, and they were all familiar with the GSEEE, practices in coaching programs/schools, and the Master's candidates who were accepted into various programs. They had all been involved in the marking of the constructed-response items in the GSEEE. The results of the interviews point to two related problems. First, the reliability of the constructed-response items is problematic as the large number of essays following sample versions creates difficulties for raters in applying the rating criteria accurately. If the reliability is problematic, the interpretations made from test scores will also be problematic. Second, curriculum for the English course(s) at the graduate level is difficult to design and implement. The educational or research institutions accepting the candidates want to generalize the inferences made about the test-takers' language ability based on their performance on the test. But when it is difficult to make these kinds of generalizations, as a result of the test-oriented coaching programs/schools, it is difficult for educational or research institutions to decide on the total number of teaching hours for the English courses and the kind of English courses to be included in Master's programs.

Conclusion

This chapter, following an introduction to the GSEEE, discussed the use and impact of the GSEEE test in China. Since its first administration in 1989, the GSEEE, as an important measuring instrument, has played a significant role in promoting educational reform and in upgrading the quality of graduate education. But like any other high-stakes tests whose results are used to make important decisions that immediately and directly affect test-takers and other stakeholders, the impact of the GSEEE has been great, both on test-takers themselves and on many other parties, stakeholders, and organizations. The selection function of the GSEEE compels the instructors/coaches and test-takers to work for the immediate goal of raising test scores. Teaching to the content and format of the test and automatizing test-takers' test performance through mock tests have rendered the validity of the GSEEE problematic. This author, therefore, believes that future efforts should be made in the following areas.

First, validation studies of the GSEEE should be conducted. Wood (1993) thinks that validity is ultimately more important than reliability. Messick (1989) pointed out that the key issues of test validity are the interpretability, relevance and utility of scores, the importance of value implications of scores as a basis for action, and the functional worth of scores in terms of social consequences of their use. As a high-stakes test that has been in use for nearly 20 years, validation studies like the one carried out for the CET (Yang & Weir, 1998) will prove a worthwhile effort. As long as test administrators and educational authorities make claims that they are assessing this or that ability or skill, they should be able to provide evidence of validity.

Second, in item design and test development, efforts should be made with regard to test methods. According to Bachman (1990), in addition to the abilities to be measured, the test methods that are used have an important effect on test performance. Of particular relevance here is the input for the writing task. Instead of giving a visual prompt, other forms of input, verbal input for example, may be used. Input should also vary from year to year, so the problem of instructors'/coaches' predicting the writing task and test-takers' memorizing a sample and including the sample in their essays can be addressed and perhaps partly solved.

Third, some statistical tools might be applied to the process of marking constructed-response items for better quality control. One way is to monitor inter-rater and intra-rater consistency. Inter-rater inconsistency may occur when different raters are looking at different aspects of language while intra-rater inconsistency may occur when the same rater applies the same set of criteria inconsistently in rating the language performance of different individuals. Also, since the essays and other constructed-response items are marked in each individual province, municipality, or autonomous region, with the cut-off scores for three areas set by the Ministry of Education; inter-center consistency should also be monitored if possible. Another way would be to monitor the correlation between test-takers' scores on objective items and their scores on constructed-response items. This, to some extent, would help to identify raters who are inconsistent in applying the set of criteria. Given the considerable impact of the GSEEE on the individuals and the society at large, the author would strongly argue for more relevant research into the test from a variety of perspectives.

Notes

1. The GSEEE is for entrance into Master's programs only. Exams for entrance into PhD programs are developed and administered by individual educational or research institutions and the difficulty level varies greatly.

2. The GSEEE syllabus includes a list of approximately 5,500 required words.
3. These people do this as a profession (job), but they are not professional.

References

Alderson, J. C., Clapham, C. & Wall, D. (1995). *Language test construction and evaluation.* Cambridge, UK: Cambridge University Press.
Bachman, L. F. (1990). *Fundamental considerations in language testing.* Oxford: Oxford University Press.
Bachman, L. F. & Palmer, A. (1996). *Language testing in practice.* Oxford: Oxford University Press.
Madaus, G. F. (1988). The influence of testing on the curriculum. In L. N. Tanner (Ed.), *Critical issues in curriculum: Eighty-seventh yearbook of the National Society for the Study of Education* (pp. 83–121). Chicago: University of Chicago Press.
Messick, S. (1989). Validity. In R. L. Linn (Ed.), *Educational measurement* (3rd ed.). New York: Macmillan.
Ministry of Education (2007). GSEEE cut-off score in 2007 [2007年全国招收硕士研究生进入复试最低分数线确定]. Beijing, P.R.C.: Ministry of Education.
National Education Examinations Authority (2001). *GSEEE Syllabus.* Beijing, China: Higher Education Press.
National Education Examinations Authority (2002). *GSEEE Syllabus.* Beijing, China: Higher Education Press.
National Education Examinations Authority (2004). *GSEEE Syllabus.* Beijing, China: Higher Education Press.
National Education Examinations Authority (2005). *GSEEE Syllabus.* Beijing, China: Higher Education Press.
National Education Examinations Authority (2006a). *GSEEE Syllabus.* Beijing, China: Higher Education Press.
National Education Examinations Authority (2006b). *The GSEEE Item Analysis.* Beijing, China: Higher Education Press.
National Education Examinations Authority (2007). *GSEEE Syllabus.* Beijing, China: Higher Education Press.
Qi, L. X. (2005). Stakeholders' conflicting aims undermine the washback function of a high-stakes test. *Language Testing, 22,* 142–173.
Widdowson, H. G. (1978). *Teaching language as communication.* Oxford: Oxford University Press.
Wood, R. (1993). *Assessment and testing: A survey of research.* Cambridge, UK: Cambridge University Press.
Yang, H. Z. & Weir, C. (1998). *Validation study of the National College English Test.* Shanghai, China: Shanghai Foreign Language Education Press.

12　The General English Proficiency Test

Viphavee Vongpumivitch, National Tsing Hua University

This chapter aims to review research studies that have been conducted on the General English Proficiency Test (GEPT;「全民英檢」) and evaluate the findings using Bachman and Palmer's (in press) assessment use argument framework. By treating the research results as supports to the assessment use claims, areas that need further investigation are highlighted throughout the chapter.[1]

Background of the GEPT

The General English Proficiency Test (GEPT) is a suite of five-level standardized tests of English as a Foreign Language (EFL) developed by the Language Training and Testing Center (LTTC) in Taiwan (see Chapter 6). It was stated both on the test's official websites[2] and in many of the LTTC published research reports that the GEPT was created "in order to implement the educational ideal of 'lifelong learning' and effectively promote the environment in which everyone [in Taiwan] studies English" as well as to "create an assessment system that will be suitable for each level of learners in Taiwan" (Language Training and Testing Center [LTTC], 2000a, p. iv). There is no statement, however, that specifically explains the types of decisions that may be made based on the GEPT test scores. Thus, in reality, the GEPT scores are used for a variety of decisions in various settings; from job/scholarship applications to university admission, placement, and graduation (see Chapter 6). A website hosted by the LTTC (http://www.lttc.ntu. edu.tw/p1.htm) contains lists of places that are using the GEPT scores, which include at least 39 government offices and private sectors, 126 universities and colleges, and 315 junior and senior high schools. While some of the listed institutions state specific levels of the GEPT that they require, for the majority of the institutions, it is unclear which level of the GEPT is required and why.

The five levels of the GEPT targets different levels of EFL proficiency. The GEPT elementary and intermediate test contents have a clear focus on the MOE[3] curricula for junior and senior high schools, respectively. The GEPT high-intermediate test, on the other hand, targets Taiwanese university graduates whose major was not English. This is potentially problematic in terms of test content coverage since the MOE does not have a specific curriculum for university EFL programs and thus, university-level English curricula and textbooks vary a great deal across Taiwan. The same problem persists in the advanced level of the GEPT, which targets either Taiwanese university graduates who majored in English or someone who has received a degree from a university or graduate school in an English-speaking country. The fact is that English-major curricula and textbooks are not the same across universities in Taiwan. Moreover, the distinction of the English vs. non-English majors at the undergraduate level suggests a controversial assumption that English major graduates would have a higher level of EFL proficiency than those who majored in other subjects. Meanwhile, the reference to universities or graduate schools in English-speaking countries is the first time that the GEPT mentions a non-Taiwanese educational system. The equivalence of the different types of EFL learners targeted by the advanced level GEPT is not yet proven. Finally, content coverage of the highest level of the GEPT (Superior) is also problematic because it purports to cover the very broad domain of language use of a well-educated native speaker.

Although it is not yet clear whether the GEPT tests have indeed promoted lifelong learning as the LTTC has hoped, what is clear is that for most Taiwanese learners, English is regarded as the most important foreign language. As of May 2007, at least 2.6 million people have registered for the GEPT tests (see Chapter 6). Vongpumivitch (2006) found that from the test-takers' point of view, having a GEPT certificate means having a tangible evidence of one's English proficiency. The facts that the LTTC is associated with National Taiwan University, the most prestigious university in Taiwan, and that the GEPT project was partially funded by the MOE strengthen the credibility of the tests in the public's opinion.

GEPT-related Studies and the Assessment Use Argument Framework

Since 2001, many research studies have been conducted both by researchers who are affiliated with the LTTC and by those who are not, such as university professors and graduate students. For every level of the GEPT, the LTTC provides a research report of its pilot study results (LTTC, 1999, 2000a, 2000b, 2002a, 2002b[4]). These pilot study research reports contain rich information, including the general level description, skill-area descriptions, test formats and structures, analysis of content coverage, performance data, and questionnaire data. Furthermore, LTTC researchers have conducted many research studies, such as analyses of GEPT test performance data and test-takers' feedback (Wei & Kuo, 2003; J. Wu, 2002a, 2002b; R. Wu, 2003), a corpus analysis of written performance (Kuo, 2005), an analysis of parallel form reliability (Weir & Wu, 2006), validation studies (Chin & Kuo, 2004), comparisons of GEPT test scores with other tests (Chin & Wu, 2001; LTTC, 2003), and a GEPT test impact study (Wu & Chin, 2006).[5] In addition, non-LTTC researchers have investigated aspects of the GEPT, such as test impact (Shih, 2006; Teng, Kuo, Wang, & Chang, 2006; Vongpumivitch, 2006), item analysis (Tung, Bai, & Shi, 2005), and a comparison of GEPT test scores with another test (the PETS in China) (Gong, 2002).

These studies can be regarded as a collection of evidence that support the use of the different levels of the GEPT. To make sense of all the evidence that has been collected so far on the GEPT, this chapter applies a recent framework proposed by Bachman and Palmer (in press) to the research findings that are available. The goal is to evaluate whether enough evidence has been gathered to support the uses of the GEPT tests for different purposes in Taiwan. Below is an explanation of Bachman and Palmer's framework, together with a rationale for adopting this framework in this chapter.

The Assessment Use Argument (AUA) Framework and a Rationale for its Adoption

Bachman and Palmer (in press) propose that an assessment use argument (AUA) can be used as an overarching inferential framework to guide the design and development of language assessment as well as the interpretation and use of language assessment results. The process of justifying the use of a particular test in the AUA includes two parts: (1) articulating the *claims, warrants and rebuttals* (highlighted by Bachman & Palmer, in press) for that specific test, and (2) providing *backing* to support the claims by supporting the warrants and weakening the rebuttals. The term *claim* refers to "the interpretation that we want to make, on the basis of the data, about what a test-taker knows or can do" (Bachman, 2005, p. 9). A claim should be based on data, which, in language testing, refers to test-takers' responses to assessment tasks. The term *warrant* refers to "propositions that we use to justify the inference from data to claim" (Bachman, 2005, p. 10). Warrants need to be supported by *backing*, which refers to "theory, prior research or experience or evidence collected specifically as part of the validation process" (Bachman, 2005, p.10). *Rebuttals* refer to alternative explanations or counterclaims, i.e., statements that would weaken or refute the claim that was made about the interpretation of the test scores. Rebuttals may be supported, weakened or rejected by additional data that are collected.

To articulate an assessment use argument (AUA), Bachman and Palmer (in press) suggest four claims that need to be articulated and supported in a test development project.

Claim 1: The consequences of using an assessment and of the decisions that are made are *beneficial* to all stakeholders.

Claim 2: The decisions that are made are *equitable* to all stakeholders.

Claim 3: The interpretations about the ability to be assessed are *meaningful, impartial, generalizable, relevant,* and *sufficient.*

Claim 4: Assessment reports (scores, descriptions) are *consistent* across different assessment tasks, different aspects of the assessment procedure, and across different groups of test-takers.

Bachman and Palmer (in press) illustrate how these claims can be made through some common kinds of warrants and rebuttals and provide examples of ways to provide backing for the warrants. It is important to note that Bachman and Palmer clearly state that not all of the warrants and backings that they suggest will necessarily be required in every assessment situation. In fact, each assessment situation is unique and different types of warrants and backing will be required for different assessments. Since the GEPT is unique to Taiwan, undoubtedly not all of the warrants and backing that Bachman and Palmer describe will be applicable. Despite the fact that the GEPT tests were not designed and developed based on Bachman and Palmer's framework, the assessment use argument (AUA) can provide an important perspective on the GEPT. A benefit of treating research findings regarding the GEPT as backing for the warrants in the AUA framework is that this approach can highlight the fact that several warrants that Bachman and Palmer suggest have already been strongly supported by the research studies on the GEPT. However, more backing is still needed to justify many of the warrants. It is hoped that the application of the AUA framework in this chapter will stimulate more discussion that will lead to the improvement of the GEPT and provide a direction for current and future test development projects in Taiwan.[6]

The four claims suggested by Bachman and Palmer (in press) address the issue of test use in a top-down manner, as it would be addressed in the process of designing and developing a test. In other words, one would first convince the test-users of the positive consequences of the use of the assessment and the decisions that will be made on test design and use (the first claim). Then, one would consider the equitability of those decisions (the second claim.) Next, one needs to make sure that the interpretations made from the assessment performance about the ability to be assessed are meaningful, impartial, generalizable, relevant and sufficient (the third claim.) Finally, one needs to have consistent assessment reports (scores and descriptions) (the fourth claim). However, since there are many uses of the GEPT in Taiwan, this chapter will discuss the four claims in reverse order, i.e., from bottom-up, as it would be in the case of a test-user who wants to evaluate the overall usefulness of the test. The first consideration is the consistency of assessment reports (the fourth claim) and the final consideration is the benefits of the uses of the GEPT (the first claim).

Claim 4: Assessment reports (scores, descriptions) are consistent across different assessment tasks, different aspects of the assessment procedure, and across different groups of test-takers.

The first warrants for this claim are that task characteristics are consistent across assessment tasks, and administrative procedures are followed consistently across different occasions and for all test-taker groups. Society at large assumes that the LTTC has for its internal use the design statement, blueprints, and task specifications that would enable their test task/item writers to create tasks that have consistent characteristics across forms (Shih, 2006). As the GEPT is a standardized testing system, it is also assumed that the LTTC has created a test administration manual that can be strictly followed by test administrators, and that every test administration is monitored or supervised. However, these assumptions are not necessarily based on published materials. While details of task/item types, their performance requirements, and time allocation are all written very clearly on both the official GEPT website[7] and pilot study research results (LTTC 1999, 2000a, 2000b, 2002a, 2002b), no details relating to the consistency of actual administrative procedures are available. This lack of evidence could be a rebuttal to the warrant related to consistency of administrative procedures.

Other warrants to support consistency claims involve scoring criteria, scoring procedures, rater training, and the nature of the ratings (fairness, severity, inter/intra-rater consistency). Bachman and Palmer (in press) suggest that scoring criteria and procedures should be specified, that raters must undergo training and be certified, and that raters must be trained to avoid bias for or against different groups of test-takers. A review of GEPT research findings shows strong evidence regarding these aspects for the GEPT. For all levels of the GEPT, details about the rationale, creation, and revision of the scoring criteria are provided in the pilot study research reports; rater reliability indices are found to be higher than .8 (LTTC 1999, 2000a, 2000b, 2002a, 2002b). The interpretations that raters made of each of the rating classifications are investigated, taken into consideration, and applied to the revision of the rating scales and to rater training (Chin & Kuo, 2004; R. Wu, 2003).

Despite this strong evidence regarding scoring consistency, some questions remain. While the GEPT test registration manual (LTTC, 2006) indicates clearly that ratings of the writing and speaking sections of the intermediate, high-intermediate, advanced, and superior GEPT are the averages of two raters, the manual does not give clear information about the number of raters who are involved with the ratings of the writing and speaking sections of the elementary GEPT. A crucial piece of information is also missing, namely the background and characteristics of the raters who are recruited. The pilot study research reports (LTTC, 1999, 2000a, 2000b, 2002a, 2002b) are very clear about the rating procedures that took place during the pilot stage, but the actual rater training and rating procedures that have taken place in the actual test administrations are not reported in subsequent studies. Interviews with test-takers show that the general public did not think to question the background and characteristics of the GEPT raters until prompted, and when prompted, become curious about the issue (Vongpumivitch, 2006). This lack of information may be a rebuttal to the rater-related warrants.

Finally, the last sets of warrants to support the consistency claim involve internal consistency of tasks/items, equivalence of scores across different forms, stability of scores across different administrations, and whether or not assessment reports are of comparable consistency across different groups of test-takers. Review of GEPT research studies shows that the LTTC has presented strong evidence regarding these aspects (LTTC, 1999, 2000a, 2000b, 2002a, 2000b; Wei & Kuo, 2003; Weir & Wu, 2006; J. Wu, 2002a; R. Wu, 2003). For example, Weir and Wu (2006) argued for the reliability of the speaking section of the intermediate GEPT in terms of the parallel forms which were used. Ratings on the scale of one to five were analyzed with correlation analysis, factor analysis, ANOVA, and multi-faceted Rasch analysis. In addition to this quantitative analysis, for each task type a checklist of task difficulty was created by the authors and given to the raters for their judgments on the degree to which the forms were parallel in terms of code complexity (lexical and syntactical features), cognitive complexity (content familiarity and information processing), and communicative demand (time pressure). Finally, checklists of linguistic functions were distributed to raters to enable them to identify the functions they expected each item of the tests to elicit as well as equality of the difficulty of the pictures used. Results showed that the forms could generally be considered as parallel. Still, more evidence could be gathered on stability of scores across different administrations, especially for the writing and speaking sections, and other types of studies that Bachman and Palmer (in press) listed could be conducted, such as a FACETS study that uses groups as a facet, comparison of consistency estimates for different groups, and studies using generalizability theory.

Claim 3:   The interpretations about the ability to be assessed are meaningful, impartial, generalizable, relevant, and sufficient.

Five concepts are involved in this claim. First, interpretations about the ability to be assessed are *meaningful* if they are made with respect to a general theory of language ability, a particular learning syllabus, or needs analysis. For all levels of the GEPT test, the skill area descriptions are stated as can-do statements; in other words, they are written as: "An examinee who passes this level [of the GEPT] can . . ." For example, the speaking skill description for the high-intermediate level of the GEPT states the following:

An examinee who passes this level can fluently express his/her opinion about issues he/she is interested in. At work, he/she can socialize with native English speakers; explain the contents of a task or project; conduct business transactions and participate in discussions; give brief reports or express his/her opinions in a meeting.[8]

Based on the evidence gathered from the GEPT research reports, it seems that for the elementary and intermediate levels of the GEPT, the ability statements are made based on consultation with the guidelines for junior and senior high school English education written by Taiwan's Ministry of Education (LTTC, 1999, 2000a). The high–intermediate level ability statements, on the other hand, are written based on consultations with some university-level EFL textbooks and instructors (LTTC, 2000b). The extent to which those selected EFL textbooks are representative of all EFL textbooks that are used in universities across Taiwan is not clear. As stated earlier in this chapter, unlike at the junior and senior high school levels, the Ministry of Education does not have a nationwide university-level EFL curriculum. As a result, no reference to a specific syllabus or a particular theory of language ability is mentioned in the research reports of the GEPT advanced and superior levels (LTTC, 2002a, 2002b).

Justifications of the constructs of the GEPT tests are made through multitrait-multimethod (MTMM) analysis and exploratory factor analysis. Test comparison studies conducted by the LTTC researchers include Chin and Wu's (2001) comparison of the GEPT intermediate level with Japan's Society of Testing English Proficiency (STEP) test, the LTTC's (2003) comparison of the GEPT intermediate and high-intermediate levels with the Taiwanese University Entrance English Exam, the College English Test-Band 6 (see Chapter 4), and TOEFL CBT, and the LTTC's (2005) attempt to compare multiple levels of the GEPT with the Ministry of Education's *The Common English Yardstick for English Education in Taiwan (CEY)*. In all of these studies, strong correlations were found and claims related to criterion-related validity were supported. Exploratory factor analysis typically showed that measures of reading and writing in the GEPT tests load to the same factor as other tests' measures of reading, writing, grammar, and vocabulary (LTTC, 2003; Weir & Wu, 2006; J. Wu, 2002a). Test comparison studies by non-LTTC researchers have also found strong correlations, such as Gong's (2002) comparison of the GEPT intermediate level with the Public English Test System (PETS) in China (see Chapter 10), and Sim's (2006) comparison of the GEPT high–intermediate level with his university's language proficiency exam. Tung et al. (2005) provided additional evidence on the match between the GEPT test content (number of words used and topics of the listening and reading passages) and junior and senior high school textbooks. Although this evidence is strong, more qualitative evidence could be collected. For example, to date, no verbal protocol analysis has been conducted to examine whether the GEPT test items/tasks engage the ability defined in the construct definition.

The second warrant for the third claim is that interpretations about the ability to be assessed are *impartial* if they are made without bias against any groups of test-takers. Bachman and Palmer (in press) argue that individuals should be treated impartially during all aspects of the administration of the assessment, whether at the registration stage or the test-taking stage. It is clear from the evidence at hand that the LTTC has taken very good care of this requirement. The content, procedures, and passing criteria are listed very clearly on both the GEPT website and test registration manual. Preparation for the test can be completed either through self-presentation or through attending a course, or one can prepare for the test for free by visiting the GEPT study guide website which contains sample item types (http://www.gept.org.tw/). However, interviews with test-takers reveal that some test-takers have concerns regarding cost and familiarity with testing conditions and equipment (Vongpumivitch, 2006). For example, one test-taker shared her negative experience with taking the tape-mediated speaking section of the high-intermediate GEPT in a large language lab where she could hear other test-takers talking while she was trying to perform on the test. These concerns can be treated as rebuttals to the impartiality warrant.

An aspect that is more important to the impartiality warrant is that assessment items/tasks must not include content that is topically/culturally/linguistically inappropriate, that response formats or content do not favor or disfavor some test-takers, and that individuals have equal opportunity to demonstrate the ability to be assessed. Furthermore, assessment-based interpretations should be comparable across different groups of test-takers. To respond to this, the LTTC has conducted many studies on the speaking section of the intermediate test levels to ensure that there is no bias in cognitive complexity, code complexity, or the communicative demands of the test tasks (J. Wu, 2001, 2002b, 2003, 2005). However, several examples of backing suggested by Bachman and Palmer (in press) are not yet available from the GEPT. While positive answers have already been obtained from EFL teachers and students that the content of the GEPT reflect EFL teaching at junior and senior high schools (LTTC, 1999, 2000a), bias review panels are not mentioned. Moreover, we still need empirical studies that use differential item functioning (DIF), multi-group confirmatory factor analysis (CFA) or hierarchical linear modeling (HLM) methodologies to analyze test results.

Furthermore, to date, we still have no empirical studies to investigate whether the interpretations made based on the GEPT scores provide equally good predictions of performance on target language use (TLU) tasks for different groups of test-takers (e.g., gender groups, groups of learners with different amounts of English exposure, students versus working adults). There is not yet an empirical study to see whether test scores provide significant and equivalent predictors of performance on tasks in the TLU domain for different groups of test-takers (e.g., junior high school students' performance in high schools, high school students' performance in universities, or university graduates' performance after graduation). Despite the fact that many agencies and universities are requiring GEPT scores for different purposes, no follow-up study has been conducted to investigate the predictability of test scores. This lack of such information is a rebuttal to the impartiality warrant.

The third warrant is the *generalizability* warrant, which states that the interpretations about the ability to be assessed are *generalizable* if they generalize to the TLU domain. Bachman and Palmer (in press) explain that this means the characteristics (e.g., input, expected response, type of interaction) of the assessment tasks correspond closely to those of the TLU tasks. The expectation is that the assessment tasks would then engage the same abilities as required to perform the TLU tasks. In addition, the criteria and procedures for evaluating the responses to the assessment tasks should correspond closely to those that stakeholders have identified as important for assessing performance in the TLU tasks. Finally, the assessment-based interpretations should generalize to performance on tasks in the TLU domain.

In the case of the GEPT, the backing for the generalizability warrant is a potential problem. While the general level descriptions and skill area descriptions of the GEPT tests mention many target language use tasks that an examinee who passes each level of the test can do, it is never explicitly stated that the characteristics of the GEPT test item types and tasks directly correspond to specific TLU tasks. In practice, it would be very difficult to design tasks to correspond to all of the TLU tasks that are listed in the general level descriptions and skill area descriptions. To support the generalizability warrant, the LTTC has provided user questionnaire data showing that junior and senior high school EFL teachers and students think that the content of the GEPT corresponds to the content of the textbooks and EFL teaching at schools (LTTC 1999, 2000a). This can be considered a strong support for the generalizability warrant since it shows the stakeholders' perceptions of the authenticity of the assessment tasks. However, this evidence is only available for the lower levels of the GEPT (the elementary and intermediate levels), which focus on the junior and senior high school curriculum. In the higher levels of the GEPT, where the MOE's curriculum is no longer applicable, the LTTC phrased the questions on their user questionnaires more broadly, asking whether test-takers think that their language skills can be measured by the tests (LTTC, 2000b, 2002a, 2002b). Thus, it can be said that there was not an independent expert judgment about the degree of correspondence between assessment tasks and TLU tasks, nor was there a linguistic analysis of such a correspondence. In the same manner, it is not clear whether the criteria used to evaluate responses to the GEPT test tasks correspond to the criteria used to evaluate responses to the TLU tasks. Finally, since there is no data on test-takers' real world language performance, empirical studies investigating whether test scores provide significant predictors of performance on tasks in the TLU domain have not been carried out.

Perhaps one of the most controversial aspects of the GEPT general ability description is the fact that in each level of the GEPT tests, many occupations are listed as "professions that should possess each ability level" (see LTTC 1999, 2000a, 2000b, 2002a, 2002b, and the GEPT websites). For example, for the advanced level, it is stated that "in Taiwan, [the GEPT advanced] level of English proficiency is required for high-level business professionals; negotiators in business and government; English language teachers; researchers; translators; foreign affairs officials; international news personnel" (J. Wu, 2002a, p. 94). Such a recommendation or requirement could be a source of some controversy, as all together, a great many occupations are listed among the five levels of the GEPT. These range from administrative assistants, maintenance personnel, taxi drivers, and service personnel in department stores, restaurants, hotels, and tourist facilities to marketing and sales personnel, technicians, nurses, switchboard operators, police officers, business professionals, secretaries, engineers, research assistants, airline flight attendants, airline pilots, air traffic controllers, customs officials, tour guides, news media personnel, and information management personnel. The basis on which these associations are made is not clear, and although the LTTC may have already conducted need analysis studies, evidence from these studies is not available.

A large number of needs analyses would have to be conducted to support the claim that the LTTC has made about the language ability levels that are required from people in these different occupations. In other words, there is a need for empirical studies to substantiate the association between the real-world target language use situations of these occupations and the ability descriptions that the LTTC has provided. Test-takers who were university students and had passed the high-intermediate GEPT test expressed their doubts about their own ability to engage in work-related tasks that are listed in the GEPT skill area descriptions, especially the writing and speaking descriptions (Vongpumivitch, 2006). Specifically, they did not see how the characteristics of the GEPT speaking test tasks corresponded to some of the work-related tasks that are listed in the speaking description, such as, ". . . can socialize with native English speakers [at work]; explain the contents of a task or project; conduct business transactions . . .; give brief report . . ." (see more details at: http://www.lttc.ntu.edu.tw/E_LTTC/gept_eng_hi.htm). They also did not see how GEPT high-intermediate writing tasks tested their ability to "write general work-related reports and messages." Therefore, despite the fact that they had passed the high-intermediate GEPT test, they were not certain whether they could perform these work-related tasks in real life. It seems that many more studies need to be conducted on language use in work-related situations. This lack of information is currently a rebuttal to the generalizability warrant.

The fourth warrant is the *relevance* warrant supporting that the interpretations about the ability to be assessed are relevant to the decision to be made. In other words, a case should be made that the assessment-based interpretations are helpful to the stakeholders who make the decisions and, further, that these interpretations are good predictors of the decisions that are made. Bachman and Palmer (in press) suggest that opinions can be collected from assessment users and other stakeholders, and empirical studies can be conducted to see whether the test scores provide significant and equivalent predictors of the decisions that are made. Given the various types of decisions that the test scores from the different levels of the GEPT are used for, the backing for this warrant could be very difficult to collect. Different decisions such as university admission, the granting of scholarships, recruitment, and promotion require different evidence of the predictive power of the GEPT. The list of GEPT users on the GEPT website mentioned earlier in this chapter is a growing list, and it is unknown whether scientific methods have been applied to collect opinions from all of the decision-makers in these institutions regarding the usefulness of the GEPT test scores. This lack of information is a rebuttal to the relevance warrant.

Finally, the fifth warrant is that the interpretations about the ability to be assessed are *sufficient* for the decision to be made. Again, in the case of the GEPT, the backing for this warrant is difficult to form because of the variety of the purposes for which the GEPT tests are being used. A review of the GEPT research studies shows that the LTTC has conducted standard-setting procedures to ensure the appropriateness of cut scores (LTTC 1999, 2000a, 2000b, 2002a, 2002b). Research results also show that performance by test-takers at higher levels of proficiency is of better quality than that of test-takers at lower levels of proficiency (Chin & Kuo, 2004; Kuo, 2005; Wei & Kuo, 2003). However, despite the strong evidence that has been collected, it seems that cut scores are decided based on considerations of appropriate passing rates and test difficulty levels instead of on considerations of the decisions to be made based on the test scores. It is crucial that follow-up studies with test-takers and prediction studies are conducted to investigate the sufficiency of information for making decisions. To date, such studies have not yet been conducted.

Claim 2: The decisions that are made are equitable *to all stakeholders.*

Bachman and Palmer (in press) explain that equitably-made decisions are those that (a) reflect relevant legal requirements and existing community *values,* and (b) the decisions are *equitable* for those stakeholders who are affected by the decision. An examination of laws, regulations, and policy would provide backing for the value warrant, while an examination of rules in assessment specifications, standard setting procedures for setting cut scores, and studies of the relationship between assessment performance and classification decisions would provide backing for the equitability warrant.

Evidence that is available from GEPT-related studies provides strong backing for the equitability warrant. The LTTC has been very careful with test fairness considerations, making sure that test performance data in the piloting stages are collected to eliminate potential false positives (i.e., individuals passing the test when they should not have) and false negatives (i.e., individuals failing the test when they should not have) (LTTC 1999, 2000a, 2000b, 2002a, 2002b). As for the value warrant, it is clear that the development of the GEPT reflects the prominence of tests in all walks of life in Taiwan.

Claim 1: The consequences of using an assessment and of the decisions that are made are beneficial *to all stakeholders.*

The stakeholders of the different levels of the GEPT tests are Taiwanese learners of EFL who are 12 years old and above (i.e., every learner who is eligible for test registration), their parents, EFL teachers across Taiwan, and everyone in Taiwanese society who plans to use or is using the results of the GEPT to make various academic and professional decisions. To support this claim, a case has to be made that the use of the GEPT tests and the decisions that are made based on the GEPT test scores are *beneficial* to all stakeholders.

Bachman and Palmer (in press) list several warrants regarding the nature of assessment reports. First, they suggest that assessment reports for individual test-takers are treated confidentially. This warrant is easily supported, as assessment reports for of individual test-takers are treated professionally and confidentially by the LTTC. Moreover, the assessment reports are distributed to stakeholders in a timely manner. However, whether the assessment reports are presented in ways that are *clear* and *understandable* to all stakeholder groups remains to be investigated.

To back this warrant, one would have to clarify the meaning of *clear* and *understandable* and collect stakeholders' opinions about this aspect of the GEPT score reports. Currently, the score reports of the GEPT tests are a sheet of paper on which four scores are indicated, one for each of the four language skills tested (listening, speaking, writing, and speaking) (see Figure 12.1). When looking at the numbers on the score card, test-takers know whether they have scored higher or lower than the passing criteria. However, these numbers do not shed light on test-takers' strengths and weaknesses in performance. For example, in her conversation with the author of this chapter, the recipient of the GEPT score report card in Figure 12.1 stated that she still does not know why she only received

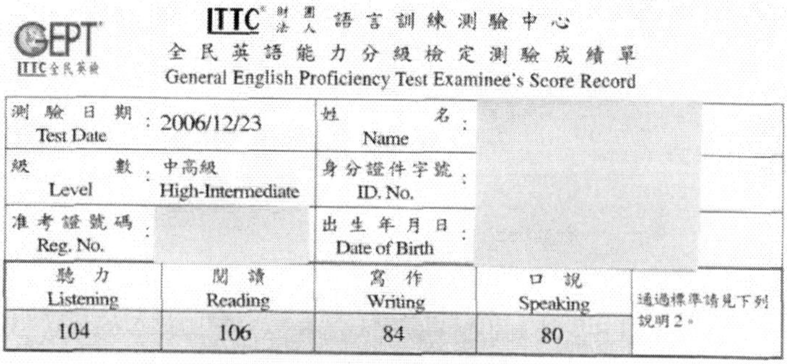
GEPT
LTTC 全民英檢
LTTC 財團法人 語言訓練測驗中心
全民英語能力分級檢定測驗成績單
General English Proficiency Test Examinee's Score Record

測驗日期 Test Date :	2006/12/23	姓名 Name :	
級數 Level :	中高級 High-Intermediate	身分證件字號 ID. No. :	
准考證號碼 Reg. No. :		出生年月日 Date of Birth :	

聽力 Listening	閱讀 Reading	寫作 Writing	口說 Speaking	通過標準請見下列說明 2。
104	106	84	80	

Figure 12.1 A Partial Image of an Actual GEPT Report Card

borderline passing scores for the writing and speaking sections of the test she took. The passing score was 80 in each section; she received a score of 84 for writing and 80 for speaking. Supposing that this student had scored less than 80 points in the writing or speaking section, she would still not know how she could change her status from failing to passing in her next attempt at the GEPT. In other words, by only providing numerical data, the score report leaves test-takers with only a relatively vague understanding of their English language ability, for example, that he/she is "good" or "not good" enough to pass this level of GEPT (Vongpumivitch, 2006). It does not let them know anything else about their language ability.

The GEPT test registration manual (LTTC, 2006) clearly indicates that the GEPT tests are proficiency tests and do not aim to produce any diagnostic information. While this explanation is understandable, a brief and general overview of performance in paragraph format would be appreciated by the test-takers, especially those who took the test for self-assessment purposes. In fact, some test-takers view this lack of information as a failure on the part of the GEPT to truly promote life-long learning of English (Vongpumivitch, 2006). From the teachers' perspectives, Wu and Chin (2006) found that teachers hope to have more information about the GEPT rating scales as well as sample test responses so that they can better understand the GEPT standards and, in turn, better help their students.

Recently, there has been a significant effort by the LTTC (Wu & Chin, 2006) as well as other researchers such as Shih (2006), Teng et al. (2006) and Vongpumivitch (2006) to collect evidence on the impact that the different levels of the GEPT have on instructional settings. This evidence supports the warrant that the assessment helps promote good instructional practice and effective learning. Based on the results of these recent studies, it seems that while the impact that the GEPT has on teaching is mixed, there is a positive trend. Traditional Taiwanese EFL classrooms emphasized grammar and vocabulary while communication was often neglected because the English test paper in the university entrance examination only covered reading and writing. Wu and Chin (2006) found that, partly because the GEPT tests oral language performance, listening and speaking have started to receive attention in the classroom. However, the more influential factors that shape the impact of the GEPT are teachers' teaching philosophies and real world constraints. Shih (2006) found that the GEPT had an observable washback effect at one university which requires students to pass the first stage of the GEPT intermediate level or the mock GEPT exam that the foreign language department created. On the other hand, the GEPT had little washback effect on teachers' practices at another university which did not have a policy on the GEPT.

Both Vongpumivitch (2006) and Shih (2006) found that the GEPT had no long-term impact on most students' learning. For example, one small group of students did study English for up to 2 months mainly to prepare for the tests, but then the urge to study decreased. Wu and Chin (2006) found that students' own proficiency level influenced their perceived effects of the test. The majority of teachers acknowledged that while the test may have increased students' motivation to improve their listening and speaking skills, such effects are more salient in students who have higher levels of English ability. On the other hand, the teachers believed that the test created anxiety among students who have lower levels of ability. This indicates that the impact of the GEPT is different on different learners (see Alderson & Wall, 1993).

Finally, to support the beneficial consequences of the decisions that are made based on the GEPT test scores, Bachman and Palmer (in press) indicate that input from stakeholders could be collected to support the warrant that all stakeholders benefit from the decisions that they made based on GEPT results, such as hiring, promoting, certifying, granting scholarships, and making decisions about university graduation. In addition, data could be collected to show that the consequences of decision classification errors, that is, false positives and false negatives, have detrimental consequences for the stakeholders who are affected. Unfortunately, these warrants are not yet well supported because of the broad range of uses made in Taiwan of GEPT results.

Conclusion

While much research has been done on the different levels of the GEPT, this chapter is an attempt to review all available studies on the tests in light of Bachman and Palmer's (in press) assessment use argument framework. This review of the GEPT research studies finds strong support for the argument that GEPT assessment reports are consistent. Mixed support, however, is provided for the argument for test interpretations. One of the problems is the broad range of test uses and the different decisions that are being made based on GEPT test scores. More research studies will need to be conducted, either by the LTTC or scholars outside the institution, to ensure the meaningfulness, impartiality, generalizability, relevance, and sufficiency of the interpretations about the abilities being assessed. Finally, while there have been several interesting research studies on the impact of the GEPT in recent years, more data should be collected to support the argument for the beneficial consequences of the test use. It is hoped that this chapter will spark an interest in searching for more evidence that could strengthen the claims that are being made about the GEPT. A strong assessment system is beneficial to an educational system as well as to society at large, and further research on the GEPT could be the vehicle through which better EFL education and assessment in Taiwan can be achieved.

Acknowledgments

The author would like to thank Dr Jessica Wu of the LTTC for her kind provision of the LTTC research reports. Heartfelt thanks also go to Dr Lyle F. Bachman who gave the author the idea to use the assessment use argument framework in this chapter and for his encouragement; to Dr Antony Kunnan for his very helpful comments on earlier drafts of this chapter; and to Dr Liying Cheng, the co-editor of this book. Finally, the author would like to thank Miss Anne Yu-Ying Lai for her indispensable translation work and clear explanation of the necessary Chinese documents. Any faults that remain in this chapter are the author's own responsibility.

Notes

1. This review only includes research that was conducted prior to March 2007, which was the cut-off time for gathering materials for the present chapter.
2. The official English website of the GEPT test is: http://www.lttc.ntu.edu.tw/E_LTTC/gept_eng_main.htm
3. Taiwan's Ministry of Education.
4. All pilot study reports are available in Chinese at: http://www.lttc.ntu.edu.tw/academics/thesis.htm
5. See a complete list of LTTC publications in Chapter 6.
6. The application of the AUA framework in this chapter is the author's personal interpretation of the model and unavoidably reflects this author's own biases in interpreting the available research data.
7. The official GEPT website (http://www.lttc.ntu.edu.tw/E_LTTC/gept_eng_main.htm) provides links to facts regarding the GEPT and relevant research resources.
8. Readers can find the complete listing of the GEPT general level description and skill-area descriptions when they click on the link for each of the five levels of the GEPT on the official GEPT English website at: http://www.lttc.ntu.edu.tw/E_LTTC/gept_eng_main.htm.

References

Alderson, J. C. & Wall, D. (1993). Does washback exist? *Applied Linguistics*, 14, 115–129.

Bachman, L. F. (2005). Building and supporting a case for test use. *Language Assessment Quarterly: An International Journal*, 2, 1–34.

Bachman, L. F. & Palmer, A. S. (in press). *Language Assessment in the Real World*. Oxford University Press.

Chin, J. & Kuo, G. (2004). "全民英檢" 九十三年優級測驗 [A validation report on the superior level GEPT] (Technical Report No. 7). Taipei, Taiwan: Language Training and Testing Center [LTTC].

Chin, J. & Wu, J. (2001). STEP and GEPT: A concurrent study of Taiwanese EFL learners' performance on two tests. *Proceedings of the Fourth International Conference on English Language Testing in Asia*, Taipei, Taiwan.

Gong, B. (2002). Comparative studies of GEPT and PETS in Taiwan and China. *Selected Papers from the special International Symposium on English Teaching / Fourth Pan Asian Conference*. Taipei, Taiwan.

Kuo, G. (2005). A preliminary corpus study on EFL test-takers' writing proficiency. *Proceedings of the Eighth International Conference on English Language Testing in Asia* (pp. 27–35), Hong Kong.

Language Training and Testing Center [LTTC]. (1999, August). 全民英語能力分級檢定測驗: 中級測驗研究報告 [GEPT Intermediate Level Research Report]. Taipei, Taiwan: LTTC.

Language Training and Testing Center [LTTC]. (2000a, September). 全民英語能力分級檢定測驗: 初級測驗研究報告 [GEPT Elementary Level Research Report]. Taipei, Taiwan: LTTC.

Language Training and Testing Center [LTTC]. (2000b, September). 全民英語能力分級檢定測驗: 中高級測驗研究報告 [GEPT High-Intermediate Level Research Report]. Taipei, Taiwan: LTTC.

Language Training and Testing Center [LTTC]. (2002a, January). 全民英語能力分級檢定測驗: 高級測驗研究報告 [GEPT Advanced Level Research Report]. Taipei, Taiwan: LTTC.

Language Training and Testing Center [LTTC]. (2002b, July). 全民英語能力分級檢定測驗: 優級測驗研究報告 [GEPT Superior Level Research Report]. Taipei, Taiwan: LTTC.

Language Training and Testing Center [LTTC]. (2003, July). 全民英檢同期效度研究報告 [Concurrent Validity Studies of the GEPT Intermediate Level, GEPT High-Intermediate Level, CBT TOEFL, CET-6, and the English Test of the R.O.C. College Entrance Examination]. Taipei, Taiwan: LTTC.

Language Training and Testing Center [LTTC]. (2005, March). 共同英語能力指標與全民英檢級數參照第一階段研 究 [Mapping the GEPT to the Common English Yardstick for English Education in Taiwan (CEY)]. Taiwan: LTTC.

Language Training and Testing Center [LTTC]. (2006). 九十五年初級 中級 中高級測驗報名手冊 [GEPT test registration manual for elementary, intermediate, and high-intermediate levels, year 2006]. Taipei, Taiwan: LTTC.

Shih, C. M. (2006). Perceptions of the *General English Proficiency Test* and its washback: A case study at two Taiwan technological institutes. Unpublished doctoral dissertation, University of Toronto, Canada.

Sims, J. (2006). A model for creating a reliable and valid university proficiency exam. *Proceedings of the Twenty-third Conference on English Teaching and Learning in the Republic of China* (pp. 978–988). Taipei, Taiwan: Kuan Tung International Publications.

Teng, S. C., Kuo, C. Y., Wang, C. H. & Chang, M. C. (2006). Teachers' perceptions of the GEPT and its impact. *Proceedings of 2006 International Conference and Workshop on TEFL & Applied Linguistics*, (pp. 339–346). Department of Applied English, Ming Chuan University.

Tung, H. C., Bai, C. F. & Shi, Y. T. (2005). The item analysis of the elementary and intermediate level of GEPT listening and reading practice tests by LTTC. *Proceedings of the 2005 International Conference and Workshop on TEFL & Applied Linguistics*, Ming Chuan University.

Vongpumivitch, V. (2006). An impact study of Taiwan's General Proficiency English Test (GEPT). Paper presented at annual Language Testing Research Colloquium, Melbourne, Australia.

Wei, S. H. & Kuo, S. L. (2003). "全民英檢" 九十一年高級複試測驗 [Report of the 2002 administration of the second stage of the advanced GEPT test (writing and speaking)]. *Selected Papers from the Twelfth International Symposium on English Teaching* (pp. 599–616). Taipei, Taiwan.

Weir, C. J., & Wu, J. (2006). Establishing test form and individual task comparability: a case study of semi-direct speaking test. *Language Testing*, 23, 167–197.

Wu, J. (2001). Investigation of test-takers' views on difficulty at task level: a case study of GEPT-Intermediate spoken performance. *Proceedings of the Eighteenth International Conference on English Teaching and Learning in the Republic of China, Department of Applied English, Ming Chuan University* (pp. 362–377). Taipei: Crane Publishing.

Wu, J. (2002a). Assessing English proficiency at advanced level: The case of the GEPT. *Proceedings of the International Conference on Language Testing and Language Teaching* (pp. 93–100). Shanghai, China.

Wu, J. (2002b). Investigation of test-takers' views on difficulty at task level: A case study of GEPT-intermediate spoken performance. *English Teaching & Learning* (英語教學), 26(4), 107–124.

Wu, J. (2003). Task difficulty in semi-direct speaking tests—code complexity. *English Teaching & Learning* (英語教學), 27(4), 79–98.

Wu, J. (2005). Effect of familiarity on spoken performance in a picture description task. *Proceedings of the 22nd International Conference on English Teaching and Learning in the Republic of China*,

Department of English, National Taiwan Normal University (pp. 330–341). Taipei: Crane Publishing.

Wu, R. (2003). Assessing advanced-level English writing: A report on the case of the GEPT. *Proceedings of the Sixth International Conference on English Language Testing in Asia.* Seoul, Korea.

Wu, R. & Chin, J. (2006). An impact study of the intermediate level GEPT. *Proceedings of the Ninth International Conference on English Testing in Asia* (pp. 41–65), Taipei, Taiwan.

Part IV

Test Use and Consequences: Views from Test-Users

Test Quality: Empirical Studies

13 Chinese EFL Learners' Discoursal Performance in the Cambridge ESOL FCE Speaking Test

Culture-Specific or Test-Driven?

Yang Lu, University of Nottingham

Tasks in oral assessment have been used to elicit ample amounts of test-taker oral production for examiners to judge the speaking abilities assessed. However, research has suggested that test-takers' discoursal performance in oral assessment could be culture-specific rather than test-driven due to the sociolinguistic variations caused both by the candidates' interlanguage pragmatics and the conversational styles in their first languages. To investigate if this is the case with Chinese test-takers, this study used a discourse framework based on a hybrid of functional and systemic approaches to examine the initiation, elaboration, cohesion and coherence produced by 22 Chinese test-takers in the speaking test of the First Certificate in English (FCE) examination. Comparisons were made between their discoursal performance and that of a group of Italian test-takers and a bilingual group in which the test-takers' first languages were different. Discourse analysis and statistical data indicated that sociolinguistic variation in the Chinese test-takers' discoursal performance might not be the only factor that significantly influenced their overall performance on the speaking test. Types of tasks and interlocutors may also affect the discourse structures produced and the sociolinguistic variation. A complex picture of test-driven and culture-specific performance by Chinese test-takers is presented in this chapter.

Introduction

The discourse domain of language learners' proficiency has been known for its complex nature because of the sociolinguistic factors involved in the ability to create coherent spoken and written texts (Bachman, 1990; Canale, 1983; Canale & Swain, 1980). In oral assessment, specifically, it has been widely recognized that sociolinguistic variations in English as a foreign language (EFL) in test-takers' discoursal performance can be attributed to learners' cultural backgrounds and their interlanguage pragmatics (Ross, 1998; Young, 1995; Young & Halleck, 1998). Therefore, attempts have been made by testing organizations to control the discourse structures and language functions produced by candidates, so that their spoken output can be in line with the intended output to allow examiners to assess the test-takers' oral proficiency as accurately as possible.

Tasks in Oral Assessment and Factors Affecting Test-takers' Discourse Performance

Different types of tasks have been used to elicit oral production for examiners to judge the level of test-takers' oral proficiency, based on the assumption that those purposefully designed tasks can generate the expected language output. Test designers, as has been assumed, can manipulate what the test-takers say by specifying the context of specific tasks such as goal, location, audience, or interlocutor. However, Douglas (1998) showed that tasks cannot guarantee what test-takers will actually say in reality because EFL learners are influenced by features of the context which are salient to them, and these features can vary in speaking tests from test-taker to test-taker.

Luoma (2004) also argued that, although some features of task context can be controlled and their effects on spoken discourse can be predicted, the actual spoken output by candidates can often prove that the control is not as successful and the prediction is not as accurate as it is anticipated. To maximize control and accuracy, Luoma suggested, it is important that tasks used to assess competence in spoken language be valid in construct and format so as to increase the reliability of a speaking test. In practice, therefore, examination boards have been vigorously (re)designing and refining various types of tasks to limit test-taker variables reflecting cultural and linguistic backgrounds. For example, interview tasks with carefully designed questions for examinees to provide information and decision-making tasks with carefully selected goals to facilitate discussions and negotiations among candidates.

The format of tasks has also been an important factor in operating speaking tests to assure the control of test-takers' oral output. Tasks involving individual speech, pair or group interaction, role play, or simulation are designed to generate different discourse patterns, so that examiners can assess candidates' competence for managing their discourse. However, when task types request the participation of the examiner, another concern arises, namely the interlocutor effect, which could affect the performance of the test-takers due to the position and authority of the examiner. Studies have suggested that examiners' discourse styles may change the level of difficulty of a speaking test (Brown & Hill, 1998) or accommodate with an examinee's level of oral proficiency (Ross & Berwick, 1992). To minimize the effect of examiners' discourse styles, test developers have relied on vigorous training and standardizing examiners or implemented interlocutor frames or scripts to keep examiners' discourse styles in line with the designed constructs and purpose of an oral exam (Lazaraton, 1996a, 1996b). However, as O'Sullivan and Lu (2004) found, examiners' deviation from such scripts do not necessarily and significantly affect test-takers' performances.

Sociolinguistic Variations in Test-takers' Discoursal Performance and Characteristics of Chinese EFL Test-takers' Spoken Discourse

Agar (1994, p. 102) proposed a concept called 'rich point' to define the contrasting language use often experienced by second or foreign language speakers in communication with native speakers (NS) of the target language. One of the rich points noted in discourse-based studies in EFL speaking tests is topic elaboration, which EFL test-takers from certain cultures may find difficult to perform in oral assessment (Young, 1995; Young & Halleck, 1998). Young (1995) investigated the topic organization of EFL test-takers' dyadic discourse in the speaking test of FCE examination. Eleven of the subjects were at the intermediate proficiency level, and spoke Arabic, Cantonese, Japanese, Mandarin,[1] Spanish, or Thai as their first language. The rest were at the advanced level, and their first languages were Danish, French, German, or Italian. The results of discourse analysis using a modified social-psychological model (Young & Milanovic, 1992) revealed that the advanced group produced a larger quantity of talk, sustained on topics longer and elaborated on their answers to questions more than the intermediate group did.

Young and Halleck (1998) argued that these differences could have been caused by the test-takers' different cultural and linguistic backgrounds, as the intermediate group were mostly from an East Asian background and the advanced group were from a Western background. Their native conversational styles are different, which may have affected their competence to elaborate on topics of conversation. Therefore, elaborating in spoken discourse may be a rich point difficult for EFL learners from certain cultures whose native discourse styles are considerably different from those found in English conversations.

To see if this is the case, Young and Halleck compared the spoken discourse of another three Japanese/Mexican pairs at superior, advanced, and intermediate levels with the expectation that the Mexican learners should perform better than the Japanese learners, since they supposedly come from a talkative culture, while the latter from a taciturn culture. Results of discourse analysis confirmed this, showing that the Mexican test-takers developed and expanded more on the topics raised and they were also judged by examiners as the one with higher level in speaking. Hence, Young and Hallack proposed that, since the examiners are from the Western culture and regarded elaboration on topics as a norm in conversation in English, the Japanese test-takers may have been disadvantaged or under-evaluated because of their non-Western taciturn styles in spoken discourse.

Ross's investigation (1998) into the Japanese test-takers' minimalist approach to interviews in EFL oral assessment seems to support Young and Halleck's (1998) argument. He discovered that the minimalist approach led to unelaborated responses which could have given the impression that Japanese test-takers were uncooperative or passive in interview discourse. Ross suggested that this minimalist approach could have been caused by the negative transfer of pragmatics in Japanese learners' interlanguage, since elaborating on ideas and information provided in the test contradicts Japanese conversational norms, which do not favour verbosity.

Studies on acquisition of pragmatics and discourse strategies in Chinese (Tao & Thompson, 1991) and Chinese formulaic opposition markers in oral interaction (Kuo, 1992) have shown sociolinguistic differences between the learners' first language and Chinese are important factors for interlanguage development. In addition, empirical studies of spoken language investigating features in the interlanguage pragmatics of learners of Chinese have found that requests in Chinese are indirect and accompanied by supportive moves to soften the situation (Zhang, 1995a, 1995b); complaints are made in Chinese with suggestions, while disagreement is expressed with the offering of opinions (Du, 1995).

To date, however, there have been few empirical investigations with sufficient data on the characteristics of Chinese EFL learner's spoken discourse and the influence of these characteristics on learners' performances in speaking tests. Similarly, in discourse-based validation studies in oral assessment, there has also been comparatively little research exploring the features of Chinese test-takers' spoken discourse and their impact on the candidates' discoursal performance.

Characteristics of EFL Learners' Spoken Discourse and their Relationship to Overall Oral Proficiency Levels

A substantial amount of studies have been done on the characteristics of EFL learners' spoken discourse and the relationship between their discoursal performance and their levels of oral proficiency. The former has applied the functional approach for analysing spoken discourse in English in order to differentiate NS and EFL learners' spoken discourse. This approach has taken advantage of a well-defined hierarchical structure with explicit criteria for analysis as well as the flexibility for modification (Burton, 1981; Coulthard & Brazil, 1981; Francis & Hunston, 1987; Sinclair & Coulthard, 1975; Stubbs, 1981). This approach describes not only the language functions in use but also the cohesive relationships and prepositional development between or among utterances in learners' discourse (Hatch & Long, 1980; Lu, 2006).

Hoey (1991) applied this approach to a conversation by three Brazilian EFL learners, and observed that their spoken discourse did not show much "sophistication in conversation skills in English" (p. 66). In specific, compared with the exchange structures and the types of moves in natural conversation in English by NS, there were much more adjacency pairs and fewer "dispreferred responses", bound-opening, follow-up, and challenging moves in the discourse. The consequences were that the three Brazilian learners seldom sustained and disrupted in the conversation. They seemed overly co-operative, rarely rejecting, confronting or disagreeing with each other. In addition, Hoey observed that the learners' discourse hasty, staccato and transactional in nature that dealt with topics briefly without much extension or elaboration.

McCarthy and Carter (1994) also employed the functional approach to investigate the differences between the interview discourse produced by EFL learners at different proficiency levels and a NS of English. A modified Sinclair and Coulthard (1975) model using IRF1/F2 (Initiation-Response-Follow-up1-Follow-up2) was applied with *Acts* created to suit the interview discourse. The analysis revealed that it was at the level of *Move* that the characteristics in the spoken discourse produced by the NS and the learners were substantially different. The NS interviewer tended to expand her questions to get more details as well as commenting more frequently on a response. In contrast, the advanced learner never elaborated on questions and gave only minimal verbal or vocal acknowledgements to a response, while the lower-intermediate learner did the same with his questions and made no comments on the interviewee's responses.

McCarthy and Carter (1994) and Hoey (1991) have seemed to observe a similar tendency in learners' discourse, i.e., transactional rather than interactional discourse. Such spoken discourse lacks the interpersonally-oriented language functions and elaborated configurations of speech acts which are expected in English conversation. Thus, McCarthy and Carter cautioned that the lack of such discourse features in EFL learners' spoken discourse can be due to both the sociolinguistic variables existing in learners' cultural backgrounds and to the NS perception of NNS discourse styles.

Research on EFL learner's spoken discourse and its relationship with levels of their oral proficiency has been discourse-based validation studies in oral assessment. They investigate if certain kinds of discourse features produced by EFL test-takers' positively relate to their levels of oral proficiency, which have shown that in interactive discourse, test-takers with high level initiate and sustain substantially more than lower-level candidates (Chalboub-Deville, 1996; Hasselgren, 1997; Lazaraton, 1998; Lazaraton & Wagner, 1996; Lu, 2006; Young & Halleck, 1998). In monologic discourse, the indicators for higher levels seem to be coherent and extended individual speech with lexical cohesive ties used (Lazaraton & Riggenbach, 1990; Lazaraton, 1993, 1998; Lu, 2006). This means that the EFL test-takers who tended to give more information, ask more questions, develop topics, elaborate ideas, and speak coherently in monologues would be judged as more competent in spoken English, whereas those who did not may be judged as less competent.

To conclude, sociolinguistic variations in EFL test-takers' discoursal performance has been found crucial for judging their oral proficiency levels in oral assessment. Tasks have been designed with great care to ensure that the expected oral output is elicited from test-takers of diverse cultural and linguistic backgrounds. However, such tasks can not completely control the influence of the test-takers' cultures and first languages and NS examiners sometimes can be the cause of under-evaluation of candidates' spoken language due to their linguistic background and expectations. Though there have been a number of discourse studies on the characteristics of EFL learners' spoken discourse, there has been insufficient empirical studies on the sociolinguistic variations in Chinese EFL test-takers' spoken discourse performance and the potential effects of those variations on their levels of oral proficiency judged by high-stake oral exams. Since the population of Chinese EFL test-takers is considerably large for the high-profile EFL language tests globally (see Chapters 7–9), it is important to explore issues relating to the impact of the sociolinguistic variation in their discourse performance and for testing organizations to know if Chinese test-takers' oral production is driven by their culture or the test itself.

Methodology

Cambridge FCE Speaking Test

The data for this research were collected through an agreement between the University of Cambridge Local Examinations Syndicate (UCLES) EFL Division (now Cambridge ESOL) and the researcher. The data relate to the First Certificate in English (FCE) Speaking Test which in Cambridge ESOL's suite of General English examination is at Level B2 of the Common European Framework of Reference (CEFR). Successful candidates are recognized as 'Independent User' and learners at post-intermediate level.

The FCE Speaking Test adopts a traditional face-to-face approach and a paired format consisting of two candidates and two examiners. One of the examiners takes the role of an interlocutor examiner, interacting with the test-takers and assessing them using a Global Rating Scale. The other examiner takes the role of an observing assessor who uses an Analytic Rating Scale.

There are four tasks in the FCE Speaking Test: Interview, Individual Long-turn, Two-way Collaborative Task, and Three-way Discussion, which are designed to elicit expected output by the candidates of certain language and discourse features (see UCLES, 2008, p. 52). According to the FCE Handbook (UCLES, 1997, p. 59), the two rating scales, the Global Rating Scale and the Analytic Rating Scale, are used for different purposes. The former is intended to reflect the interlocutor examiner's first-hand judgment and is a less detailed version of the latter. The Analytic Rating Scale is based on the assessor's systematic examination of the candidates' performance in four criteria: Grammar and Vocabulary; Discourse Management; Pronunciation and interactive Communication.

Data

A total of 30 audio-taped FCE Speaking Tests were provided by Cambridge ESOL with the subjects' four analytical sub-scores, global score, overall score and their bio-data such as age, gender, and first languages. The data were divided into three groups for the purposes of the present research: Chinese Data, Italian Data and Mixed First Language (MFL) Data. In total, 62 subjects were involved.

The 22 Chinese EFL test-takers all spoke Chinese, 10 of whom were from Taiwan and 12 from mainland China. In the MFL group, there were two Japanese, one Filipino, Thai, Arabic, and Korean test-takers. The rest of the group spoke French, Spanish, German, Italian and Slovene. The Italian group consisted of 22 NS of Italian. The rationale for dividing the data into two monolingual groups and one bilingual group were:

1   The Chinese test-takers' discoursal performance should be compared with a group of test-takers whose first language is different and ideally represents a Western culture in order to see the impact on the tasks and judgement of the examiners;
2   The Chinese test-takers' discoursal performance should also be compared with a group of candidates in a bilingual mode where candidates do not share a first language in order to see if the same impact would occur when they may have to conform to the norms and conventions in English spoken discourse.

The taped speaking tests were transcribed with a focus on reflecting the language functions and the relationship between and among those functions in spoken interaction. Phonetic or paralinguistic features were transcribed only when they made a difference to the interaction. The first draft of the transcriptions was proofread by three Chinese EFL professionals, while randomly selected extracts of the second draft were proofread by 11 native speakers of English who are either teachers of English for Academic Purposes or EFL specialists. Further corrections were made when discourse analysis (DA) was conducted or whenever listening to the audiotape was called for.

Based on the initial task-specific DA models for analysing interactive and monologic discourse (Lu, 2006), DA was conducted on the transcriptions in order to identify the targeted discourse features (TDFs) which may indicate levels of oral proficiency. Modifications to the initial models were then made which guided the final analysis. The TDFs produced by each subject were counted and averaged for the Interview and Three-way Discussion tasks because of likely unequal opportunities for the candidates to speak. Two sample *t*-tests using Minitab Statistic Software was applied to see the significance of differences in the discoursal performance between the Chinese Data and the Italian Data, and between the Chinese Data and the MFL Data. Finally, Pearson product-movement correlations were calculated to see the correlation between the test-takers' discoursal performance and their overall performance as judged by the FCE assessment.

Discourse Analysis

A hybrid of the functional (Sinclair & Coulthard, 1975) and systemic (Eggins & Slade, 1997) approach was applied for analyzing the interactive discourse elicited by the Interview, Two-way Collaborative, and Three-way Discussion tasks. Generic structure analysis (Eggins & Slade, 1997) and the rhetoric template used in discourse-based studies in oral assessment (Lazaraton & Riggenbach, 1990; Lazaraton, 1993) were incorporated to analyze the monologic discourse elicited by the Individual Long-turn Task.

Since the initial models for the DA were developed with reference to the theoretical backgrounds and findings of previous empirical studies, the task-specific modules (Lu, 2006) used to analyze the spoken discourse were finalized through vigorous modifications of the DA model. The key principle for modification was that the TDFs implemented in the models should be as distinctive and frequent in the test-takers' discourse as possible in order to increase the reliability of the analysis and describe truthfully the sociolinguistic variation in their discoursal performance. Table 13.1 presents the TDFs finalized at Level 1, 2 and 3 of the discourse for analysing the interactive and monologic discourse.

Hypotheses

I   The Chinese test-takers' overall discoursal performance is significantly different ($p<.05$ for sample t-tests) from those of the Italian and MFL groups because of different cultural and linguistic backgrounds, as shown by the numbers of TDFs produced at Levels 1, 2, and 3 of the spoken discourse.

Table 13.1 TDFs Included in Task-Specific DA Models at Level 1, 2 and 3 of the Discourse

Task	Level 1	Level 2	Level 3
Interview	Sustaining	Prolonging Appending	Elaborating Extending Enhancing
Individual Long Turn	Coherence Continuing	Describing Comparing Informing Opinion Extended Describing Extended Comparing Justifying Opinion	Prolonged Describing Prolonged Comparing Prolonged Justifying
Two-way Collaborative	Initiating Sustaining	Informing Eliciting Prolonging Developing Appending	Elaborating Extending Enhancing Extended Supporting Extended Confronting
Three-way Discussion	Initiating Sustaining	Informing Prolonging Appending Extended Supporting	Elaborating Extending Enhancing

II   The Chinese test-takers' discoursal performance on the FCE tasks is significantly different (p<.05 for sample t-tests) from those of the Italian and MFL groups because of different cultural and linguistic backgrounds, as shown by the numbers of TDFs produced at Levels 1, 2, and 3 of the spoken discourse.

III   The Chinese test-takers discoursal performance positively and significantly (p<.05 for Pearson product-movement correlation) relate to their overall performance as assessed by FCE speaking test, as shown by the correlation coefficients between the FCE overall scores (FCEOS) and the total numbers of TDFs produced, and those at Levels 1, 2, and 3 of the spoken discourse.

Results and Interpretation

Differences between Chinese Test-takers' Overall Discoursal Performance and those of the Italian and MFL Groups

Figure 13.1 shows that, in general, greater amounts of *Sustaining* were produced by all three groups. This may have been a *Move* in the discourse which was highly demanded for performance on the three interactive tasks, or it may have been a preferred or more accessible TDF to the test-takers' interlanguage.

Nonetheless, t-test results showed that most of the significant differences exist between the Chinese and the Italian subjects, although the MFL subjects, as the Italian subjects did, sustained more in Level 1 of the spoken discourse than the Chinese test-takers. This indicates that the Chinese learners did not remain on the topics raised by themselves, the examiner, or the other candidates as long as the Italian test-takers and those in the bilingual mode for the speaking test.

At Level 2 of the discourse, the Chinese subjects produced fewer *Informing* moves than the Italian test-takers, which suggest that they were less likely to provide information related to topics initiated. At Level 3, the Chinese subjects elaborated and enhanced less on their responses to the examiners or on the topics initiated by themselves. As a result, Hypothesis I is partially supported, indicating that cultural background and the influence of the Chinese subjects' first language could have caused some differences in

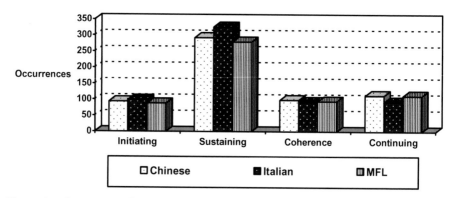

Figure 13.1 Occurrences of TDFs at Level 1 of the Discourse Produced by the Three Groups

their discoursal performance. In specifics, the Chinese subjects' and the Italian subjects' cultural backgrounds and their first languages seem to affect significantly and to a greater extent the types of discourse features that they tended to use.

The MFL group, on the other hand, produced a greater amount of *Elaborating* at Level 3 of the discourse, which is considered more native-like in English conversations due to their interpersonally-oriented nature through clarifying, restating, or exemplifying in order to involve interlocutors (McCarthy & Carter, 1994). This suggests that the spoken discourse produced by the MFL group is more interactional rather than transactional. Operating in a bilingual mode could have promoted this type of discoursal performance.

Differences in Discourse between Chinese Test-takers' Task Performance and those of the Italian and MFL Groups

T-test results show that more significant differences in the discourse on the tasks by the three groups occurred during the interview task (see Table 13.2). At Level 1 and 2 of the spoken discourse the Chinese subjects did not stay on their answers to the examiners' questions as long as the Italian subjects. At Level 3, details of the non-elaborative style of Chinese learners' speech revealed that they consistently elaborated and extended less than subjects in the other two groups. This means that their answers to the examiners' questions were shorter and lacked the expansion produced by their Italian and MFL counterparts who more often restated, clarified and offered examples or additional information to their initial answers to the examiners' questions.

Interestingly, much fewer significant differences exist in the discoursal performance on the Two-way Collaborative task by the three groups. *T*-tests showed that the Chinese subjects in the decision-making process were less likely to inform and enhance, providing less information and justifying their proposals, agreements and disagreement less frequently than the other two groups. This could have resulted in a rather hasty spoken discourse which has a transactional nature as they were working toward a decision or solution. Similarly, there are also fewer significant differences in the

Table 13.2 T-test on Differences in Discoursal Performance between Chinese and Italian and MFL Groups on the Interview Task

Level of Discourse/TDF	Groups with Difference	Means	Estimated Difference	p value
Level 1: Sustaining	Chinese	1.604		
	Italian	2.43	−.829	.033
Level 2: Prolonging	Chinese	1.526		
	Italian	2.33	−.805	.027
Level 3: Elaborating	Chinese	.322		
	MFL	.590	−.268	.007
Level 3: Elaborating	Chinese	.322		
	Italian	.584	−.262	.016
Level 3: Extending	Chinese	.747		
	MFL	1.211	−.464	.043
Level 3: Extending	Chinese	.747		
	Italian	1.287	−.540	.027

discoursal performance on the Three-way Discussion task than those for the interview task. Intriguingly, however, the Chinese group substantially produced more *Appending* moves than the MFL group. This means that they would not abandon the topics as willingly as the MFL subjects and would retrieve turns by elaborating, extending, or enhancing. Another significant difference is that the Chinese subjects were less likely to elaborate on the information they provided and their answers to the questions asked by the interlocutors' examiners. This shows again that the MFL subjects tend to clarify, restate, or exemplify their previous moves, demonstrating more interactive nature in their discoursal performance. Consequently, Hypothesis II is also partially supported because there is no significant difference between the Chinese test-takers' discoursal performance on the Individual Long-turn task and that by the other two groups.

The Effect of Sociolinguistic Variation on Chinese Test-takers' Overall Discoursal Performance

The significant correlation coefficients in Table 13.3 show that the Chinese test-takers' FCE overall scores (FCEOS) in the speaking test positively correlated with the total numbers of TDFs that they used in discoursal performance. More specifically, if they made more initiations by giving information or asking questions in the interactive discourse, the scores awarded to them by the FCE speaking test would be higher. In the monologic discourse, if they produced greater amounts of extended speech, the FCE overall scores would also be higher.

However, the significant but rather low positive correlation coefficients indicate the FCE assessment of the Chinese test-takers' overall performance was not affected substantially in the present study. In other words, the Chinese EFL test-takers were not disadvantaged to a greater extent by the sociolinguistic variations in their spoken discourse. As a result, Hypothesis III is also partially supported by five significant and positive correlation coefficients out of 23 correlations tested.

Discussion and Conclusion

This study explored the sociolinguistic variation in the Chinese EFL test-takers' discoursal performance in the FCE speaking test and its impact on their overall performance in Cambridge ESOL's FCE Speaking Test. The findings have led to the following discussion and some tentative conclusions.

Table 13.3 Significant Correlation of Chinese FCEOS versus TDF Total and versus TDFs at Different Levels of Discourse

Correlation	Discourse Level	Coefficient	p value
FCEOS vs. TDF Total		.548	.008
FCEOS vs. Initiating	1	.612	.002
FCEOS vs. Continuing	1	.678	.001
FCEOS vs. Informing	2	.567	.006
FCEOS vs. Eliciting	2	.469	.028

Chinese EFL Test-takers Belonging to a Taciturn Culture

The present research has supported the studies (Young, 1995; Young & Halleck, 1998) that suggested that the Chinese test-takers from Eastern Asian backgrounds may find elaborating on topics or their answers to examiner questions more difficult than would test-takers from Western cultural backgrounds. DA results revealed that the Chinese subjects produced smaller amounts of topic elaboration than the Italian test-takers. Further, they were not as native-like in their spoken discourse as the subjects in the bilingual mode, who may have had to conform more to an English discourse style to enable their partners to understand them better. Those have resulted that the Chinese test-takers may have seemed passive, unenthusiastic, and task-oriented, producing a spoken discourse regarded as transactional in nature as Hoey (1991) and McCarthy and Carter (1994) observed in their studies.

Such a discourse pattern which lacks interactiveness and topic elaboration implies that the Chinese test-takers belong to a taciturn culture and their discoursal performance may have been influenced by their upbringing in the culture which encourages brief and concise responses to questions raised by elders or people in authority in order to show respect.

In contrast, sustaining on topics may come naturally to the Italian test-takers, as it could be a conversational style familiar to them or appreciated in their culture. On the other hand, the MFL group's tendency to use more native-like spoken discourse indicates that pairing up candidates from different cultural and linguistic backgrounds may create a task condition that elicits greater amounts of native-like discourse features in candidate output and reduces the impact of sociolinguistic variation.

However, although the DA and statistical analysis have shown that among the three groups of subjects, the Chinese test-takers are the least "talkative", the MFL group more 'talkative' and the Italians the most "talkative", the Chinese subjects were only slightly disadvantaged or under-evaluated for being the least 'talkative' test-takers by the FCE speaking test. Nonetheless, questions can be asked what would have happened if the Chinese test-takers had taken the test in the bilingual mode with the Italian candidates or someone from a "talkative" culture. Would the examiners' judgment have been influenced to a greater extent by differences in topic elaboration? Further studies are needed to answer such questions to know more about the effect of the Chinese test-takers' taciturn culture.

Task Control on Sociolinguistic Variation in Chinese Test-takers' Spoken Discourse

Of the four tasks for the FCE speaking test, the Individual Long-turn has seemed a more controlling task type on the discoursal performance by the three groups, as there is no significant difference in the amount of the TDFs produced. Subjects in all three groups used similar amount of *Moves* and *Acts* in the monologic discourse when describing, comparing and giving their opinions on the pictures. In contrast, the interactive tasks, especially the interview task, created more variation between the Chinese test-takers' discourse and those by the Italian and MFL groups. The variation involves four out of six TDFs analyzed for the interview discourse, indicating that interviews may not be an efficient type of task to control sociolinguistic variation caused by cultural and linguistic backgrounds.

In the Two-way Collaborative and Three-way Discussion tasks, however, the number of significant differences reduced greatly, with only two TDFs involved for each task. This was unexpected, since the task types which either involves only candidates or examiners as interlocutors are supposed to generate more language functions or types of exchanges which could trigger sociolinguistic variation. Possible answer to this unexpected outcome may be the Chinese culture's concerns for their own or others' face in performing speech acts as suggested by previous studies on Chinese pragmatics (Du, 1995; Zhang 1995a, 1995b). They have shown that native-speakers of Chinese are more conscious of power relative to social status and age when faced with a range of linguistic options. Thus, the Chinese EFL test-takers involved in the study may have chosen to speak less in the interview discourse in order to protect the interlocutor examiners' face rather than to say more which might challenge their authority.

When the presence of the examiner was removed in the two-way task or made less threatening in the three-way task, the Chinese subjects may have felt freer and spoke more, resulting in fewer significant differences between the numbers of TDFs produced by them and the Italian and MFL test-takers. As a result, less sociolinguistic variation in the Chinese test-takers' discoursal performance was observed, which seems to imply that their discoursal performance in the two tasks became test-driven rather than cultural-specific. This also seems to suggest that in reality task manipulation does not necessarily guarantee the candidate oral output expected by test designers. What test-takers will actually say could be uncertain, depending either their cultural and linguistic backgrounds or the demands of the oral examination.

This study also shows that formats of tasks in oral assessment can be intangible and complicated, changing from situation to situation. For example, it may be true that the interlocutor examiner's presence in the interview task could have been the reason for the smaller amount of *Sustaining* produced by the Chinese test-takers. But it is difficult to explain why in the three-way task when the interlocutor's presence was restored in the interaction the Chinese subjects were surprisingly daring, producing a significantly larger amount of *Appending* than that used by the other two groups. To regain a lost turn by ignoring new topics initiated by others in an oral interaction could be considered imposing or even impolite in both Western and Eastern cultures, as it interrupts other speakers and disrupts the flow of discourse. Why were the Chinese test-takers in this case not worried that they would offend the interlocutors' and the other candidates' face? In contrary to the fact that cultural and linguistic backgrounds could have affected the Chinese test-takers' discoursal performance, they could also have been affected by other test-specific factors, such as an intention to out-perform other candidates or the effort to realize the advice given by teachers on the preparatory classes they attended before the exam, which is often "Speak as much as you can in the speaking test."

In conclusion, Chinese EFL test-takers' cultural and linguistic backgrounds could lead to sociolinguistic variation in their spoken discourse as they complete different tasks in speaking tests. However, the variation depends on the types of tasks undertaken and on the types of discourse features indicative of EFL learners' levels of oral proficiency. Monologue tasks seem to control such variations more effectively, while interactive tasks may be less controlling of the variation due to factors such as the status or power of interlocutors involved. Most of the differences between the Chinese test-takers' overall discoursal performance and that of the test-takers from a Western culture can be seen in the amount of sustaining on topics and the interactiveness in spoken discourse as compared to test-takers who are in a bilingual mode where they do not speak the same first language as their partners. However, discoursal performance on different types of tasks cannot be as predictable as test-developers would like to because test-takers' cultural and linguistic backgrounds do not always affect their discoursal performance on any tasks. Therefore, this research suggests that Chinese test-takers' discoursal performance can be both culture-specific and test-driven. Moreover, though it seems that sociolinguistic variation does not affect Chinese test-takers' overall performance greatly as judged by oral examiners, if they ask more questions and elaborate more in interactive and monologic discourse, their overall performance could be judged as better.

Note

1. Mandarin, Standard Spoken Chinese, is called *Putonghua* in mainland China, and *Guoyu* in Taiwan.

References

Agar, M. H. (1994). *Language shock: Understanding the culture of conversation.* New York: Morrow.

Bachman, L. F. (1990). *Fundamental considerations in language testing.* Oxford: Oxford University Press.

Brown, A. & Hill, K. (1998). Interviewer style and candidate performance in the IELTS oral interview (IELTS Research Reports Volume 1, pp. 1–19). Sydney, Australia: IELTS Australia.

Burton, D. (1981). Analyzing spoken discourse. In M. Coulthard & M. Montgomery (Eds.), *Studies in discourse analysis* (pp. 61–81). London: Routledge and Kegan Paul.

Canale, M. (1983). From communicative competence to language pedagogy. In J. C. Richards & R. W. Schmidt (Eds.), *Language and communication* (pp. 2–27). London: Longman.

Canale, M. & Swain, M. (1980). Theoretical bases of communicative approaches to second language teaching and testing. *Applied Linguistics*, I(1), 1–47.

Chalboub-Deville, M. (1996). Performance assessment and the components of the oral construct across different tests and rater groups. In M. Milanoric & N. Saville (Eds.), *Studies in language testing*, Volume 3 (pp. 57–61). Cambridge, UK: Cambridge University Press.

Coulthard, J. & Brazil, D. (1981). Exchange structure. In M. Coulthard & M. Montgomery (Eds.), *Studies in discourse analysis* (pp. 82–106). London: Routledge and Kegan Paul.

Douglas, D. (1998). Testing methods in context-based second language research. In L. F. Bachman & A. D. Cohen (Eds.), *Interface between second language acquisition and language testing research* (pp. 141–155). Cambridge, UK: Cambridge University Press.

Du, J. S. (1995). Performance of face-threatening acts in Chinese: Complaining, giving bad news, and disagreeing. In G. Kasper (Ed.), *Pragmatics of Chinese as native and target language* (pp. 165–206). Haiwaii: Second Language Teaching & Curriculum Center, University of Hawai'i at Manoa.

Eggins, S. & Slade, D. (1997). *Analysing casual conversation.* London: Cassell.

Francis, G. & Hunston, S. (1987). Analysing everyday conversation. In M. Coulthard (Ed.), *Discussing discourse* (pp.121–161). Birmingham, UK: English Language Research.

Hasselgren, A. (1997). Oral test subskill scores: What they tell us about raters and pupils. In A. Huhta, V. Kohonen, L. Kurki-Suonio & S. Luoma (Eds.), *Current Developments and Alternatives in Language Assessment. Proceedings of LTRC 96, Second Language Acquisition: A book of readings* (pp. 241–256). Rowley, MA: Newbury House.

Hatch, E. & Long, M. (1980). Discourse analysis, what's that? In D. Larsen-Freeman (Ed.), *Discourse analysis in second language research* (pp. 1–40). Rowley, MA: Newbury House.

Hoey, M. (1991). Some properties of spoken discourse. In R. Bowers & D. Brumfit (Eds.), *Applied linguistics and English language teaching* (pp. 66–84). Basingstoke: Macmillan.

Kuo, S. H. (1992). Formulaic opposition markers in Chinese conflict talk. Paper presented at Georgetown University Round Table on Languages and Linguistics, Georgetown, Washington DC.

Lazaraton, A. (1993). *The development of a quality control template based on the analysis of CASE transcriptions.* Report prepared for the EFL Division, University of Cambridge Local Examinations Syndicate, Cambridge, UK.

Lazaraton, A. (1996a). Interlocutor support in oral proficiency interviews: the case of CASE. *Language Testing*, 13, 151–172.

Lazaraton, A. (1996b). A qualitative approach to monitoring examiner conduct in the Cambridge assessment of spoken English (CASE). In M. Milanovic & N. Saville (Eds.), *Performance testing, cognition, and assessment: Selected papers from the 15th Language Testing Research Colloquium* (pp. 18–33). Cambridge, UK: Cambridge University Press.

Lazaraton, A. (1998). *An analysis of differences in linguistic features of candidates at different levels of the IELTS speaking test.* Report prepared for the EFL Division, University of Cambridge Local Examinations Syndicate, Cambridge, UK

Lazaraton, A. & Riggenbach, H. (1990). Oral skills testing: A rhetorical task approach. *Issues in Applied Linguistics*, 1, 196–217.

Lazaraton, A. & Wagner, S. (1996). *The revised Test of Spoken English (TSE): Analysis of native speaker and nonnative speaker data* (TOEFL Monograph Series MS-7). Princeton, NJ: Educational Testing Service.

Lu, Y. (2006). *A discourse analytic study of EFL test-takers' spoken discourse competence and its impact on their oral proficiency and spoken grammatical competence.* Unpublished PhD thesis, University of Reading, Reading, UK.

Luoma, S. (2004). *Assessing speaking.* Cambridge: Cambridge University Press.

McCarthy, M. & Carter, R. (1994). *Language as discourse: Perspectives for language teaching,* London: Longman.

O'Sullivan, B., & Lu, Y, (2004). *The impact on candidate language of examiner deviation from a set interlocutor frame in the IELTS Speaking Test (IELTS Research Reports, Volume 6, 2006).* Cambridge: IELTS Australia and British Council.

Ross, S. (1998). Divergent frame interpretations in language proficiency interview interaction. In R. Young & W. He (Eds.), *Talking and testing: Discourse approaches to assessment of oral proficiency* (pp. 333–353). Amsterdam and Philadelphia: Benjamins.

Ross, S. & Berwick, R. (1992). The discourse of accommodation in oral proficiency examinations. *Studies in second language acquisition*, 14, 159–176.

Sinclair, J. & Coulthard, M. (1975). *Toward an analysis of discourse.* Oxford: Oxford University Press.

Stubbs, M. (1981). Motivating analysis of exchange structure. In M. Coulthard & M. Montgomery (Eds.), *Studies in discourse analysis,* London: Routledge, pp. 107–119.

Tao, H. Y. & Thompson, S. (1991). English backchannels in Mandarin conversations: A case study of superstratum pragmatic "Interference". *Journal of Pragmatics*, 16, 61–75.

UCLES. (2008). FCE Information for candidates. Retrieved June, 12, http://www.candidates.cambridgeesol.org/exams/cae.htm

UCLES. (1997). *First Certificate English: Handbook.* Cambridge: UCLES.

Young, R. (1995). Conversational Styles in Language Proficiency Interviews. *Language Learning*, 45, 3–42.

Young, R. & Halleck, G. B. (1998). 'Let them eat cake!': Or how to avoid losing your head in cross-cultural conversations. In R. Young & A. W. He (Eds.), *Talking and testing: Discourse approaches to the assessment of oral proficiency* (pp. 359–388). Philadelphia: Benjamins.

Young, R. & Milanovic, M. (1992). Discourse variation in oral proficiency interviews. *Studies in Second Language Acquisition*, 14, 403–24.

Zhang, Y. Y. (1995a). Strategies in Chinese requesting. In G. Kasper (Ed.), *Pragmatics of Chinese as native and target language* (pp. 23–68). Hawaii: Second Language Teaching & Center, University of Hawai'i at Manoa.

Zhang, Y. Y. (1995b). Indirectness in Chinese requesting. In G. Kasper (ed.), *Pragmatics of Chinese as native and target language* (pp. 69–118). Hawaii: Second Language Teaching & Center, University of Hawai'i at Manoa.

14 Exploring the Relationship between Chinese University Students' Attitudes towards the College English Test and their Test Performance

Jing Zhao, The Ohio State University
Liying Cheng, Queen's University

This study explored the relationship between Chinese university students' attitudes towards the College English Test Band 4 (the CET-4) and their test performance. Students' attitudes were explored through a questionnaire, which consisted of five theoretically-driven constructs. Students' total scores on the CET-4 were utilized to indicate their test performance. A total of 212 students from two universities in a southern city in China participated in this study. The results of the study showed that students held strong yet mixed feelings towards the CET-4. Two factors, test-taking motivation and test-taking anxiety/lack of concentration, were the best predictors of students' test performance on the CET-4. Student's attitudes towards the CET-4 accounted for about 15.4 percent of the variance in their test performance. The factor test-taking anxiety/lack of concentration differentiated female from male students. Three factors: test-taking anxiety/lack of concentration; test-taking motivation; and belief differentiated high-achieving students from low-achieving students in their CET-4 performance.

Introduction

Studies have been conducted measuring students' attitudes towards high-stakes language testing (e.g., Cheng, 1998; Hughes & Bailey, 2002; Kellaghan, Madaus, & Airasian, 1982; Paris, Lawton, Turner, & Roth, 2000; Shohamy, Donitsa-Schmidt, & Ferman, 1996). However, fewer studies have been conducted on the relationship between students' attitudes towards testing and their actual test performance. In fact, most of the existing literature has examined students' attitudes towards testing without linking attitudes to the exploration of students' performance. As several researchers (e.g., Bachman & Palmer, 1996; Bloom, 1982; Ryan, 2001) have suggested, there seems to exist a relationship between the two. The present study, therefore, investigated the relationship between students' attitudes and their test performance. The study focused on one of China's largest language proficiency tests—the College English Test Band 4 (CET-4). The CET-4 is also one of the most important high-stakes tests in China, as a pass on the CET is a graduation requirement for many Chinese university students (see Chapter 4 for more details about the CET). In addition, many studies conducted in China over the past 20 years in relation to the CET have shown the impact of the test on the teachers and learners of English (Chen & Zhang, 1998; Li, 1995; Lu & Wang, 1998; Pan, 1998; Zhang, 2003). However, none of these studies discussed students' attitudes towards the CET-4 in conjunction with their actual test performance, which is the focus of this study.

Students' Attitudes and their Test Performance

Several studies (Cheng, 1998; Kellaghan et al., 1982; Paris et al., 2000) have been carried out to measure students' attitudes towards high-stakes testing. The study by Kellaghan et al. was carried out in the Republic of Ireland, which did not have a tradition of using standardized tests. The participants were 2,147 sixth-Grade pupils who were divided into two treatment groups. For one treatment group (no-information group), teachers had no access to students' test scores. For the other treatment group (test-information group), teachers were informed of students' test scores. The findings revealed that the majority of pupils in both treatment groups clearly held positive attitudes towards the tests. In general, only less than one-quarter of the students showed negative feelings or reactions to the test-taking experience.

Cheng's study (1998) used a survey questionnaire to investigate whether the changes made to the Hong Kong Certificate of Education Examination in English (HKCEE) changed students' perceptions and attitudes towards their English learning. Participants were 844 Hong Kong secondary students taking the old HKCEE in 1994 and 443 students who were to take the new HKCEE in 1996. Part of the questionnaire used in the study explored students' attitudes towards public examinations. The purpose was to see whether the changes to HKCEE were associated with changes in students' attitudes between the 2 years. The results showed that students' attitudes towards public examinations were not changed by the introduction of the new test. The students' attitudes towards most of the statements in the survey did not show significant differences over the 2 years.

Paris et al. (2000) carried out a large-scale study in which they surveyed a wide range of students in the USA. Students' views of tests were investigated in three studies. In Study 1, 40-item questionnaires were issued to 974 students from Grades 2–11 in four different states. The findings showed that students held generally positive views about achievement tests but that increasing age was accompanied by more negative attitudes. Study 2 investigated the students' attitudes towards the Michigan Educational Assessment Program (MEAP). The participants were 240 students in Grades 4, 7, and 10. Many items showed significant negative changes with age. The results also showed that high achievers (above the 85 percent percentile) and low-achievers (below the 40 percent percentile) answered many items significantly differently. In Study 3, 61 5th-Grade and 65 8th-Grade students were asked to report their views about the California Achievement Test (CAT) compared to their views of classroom tests. The results showed that fifth graders reported more positive views than did eighth graders. In addition, fifth graders reported equally positive views of CAT and classroom tests. Eighth graders reported significantly more positive perceptions of classroom tests than of the CAT. Overall, the results of all three studies showed a pattern of increasingly negative perceptions of tests as students grew older. Paris et al. (2000) attributed the older students' negative attitudes to repeated exposure to high-stakes tests.

However, Kellaghan et al. (1982) showed different results as their participants in general held positive attitudes towards the test. In accounting for this difference, Paris et al. (2000) stated that the different history of testing experiences and expectations of teachers, parents, and students in the two countries were contributing factors. Another more recent study (Hungerland, 2004) might offer some explanations for the different results of the studies. She stated that attitudes towards a test might be shaped by what she called test-specific factors and contextual factors. Test-specific factors included test properties (e.g., test format), test practice and material, test-specific attitudes, and practice-test mismatch. Contextual factors included attitudes towards English and the language learning environment, the role of English in achieving goals, test practice in and outside the classroom, teacher role in test preparation, parental expectations as well as test result consequences and perceptions of fairness. These factors appeared to be specific to certain high-stakes tests, which implied that students might react differently to different types of high-stakes tests.

Therefore, it seems worthwhile to listen to students' voices on different types of tests in different countries. It will be enlightening to investigate the phenomenon in a country such as China, which has a long tradition of examinations (see Chapter 2) and where there is an increasing emphasis on English testing such as the CET-4. As an important high-stakes test in China, the CET-4 has captured the attention of many researchers (Chen & Zhang, 1998; Li, 1995; Lu & Wang, 1998; Pan, 1998; Zhang, 2003), although most of the published articles have been based on self reports rather than on empirical data. In Chen and He's study (2003), 240 questionnaires were issued to students to investigate the influence of the CET-4 on students' attitudes towards learning. They concluded that the CET-4 provided motivation for the students' English learning. However, the disadvantages of the CET-4 far outweighed its advantages. Some students devoted most of their time to reading and grammar which are weighted more in the CET-4 examination and gave up practicing speaking skills, which is an optional requirement. As a result, in spite of being engaged in English for many years, they still could not speak English fluently. However, as mentioned earlier, Chen and He's study did not discuss students' attitudes towards the CET-4 in conjunction with their test performance. The following three studies, reviewed below, linked students' attitudes with their test scores. Although they were not conducted in language education contexts, they offered direct guidance to this study.

Arvey, Strickland, Drauden, & Martin's (1990) study was carried out in the job selection context in which the Test Attitude Survey (TAS) was developed to measure job applicants' attitudes towards the Armed Services Vocational Aptitude Battery (ASVAB). The results showed that a small but significant relationship existed between the TAS factor scores and the test performance.

Karmos and Karmos' (1984) study aimed at exploring the relationship between students' attitudes towards the SAT (Stanford Achievement Test) and their test performance. A total of 360 students in Grades 6–9 from three schools participated in the study. The results showed that the students held moderately positive attitudes towards the SAT. The attitudes of students in the study accounted for 14 percent of the variance in scores on their SAT. The total attitudinal score for females was significantly higher than the score for males. The results also showed that for total attitudinal scores, high achievers scored significantly higher than low achievers. It is worth pointing out that the correlation in this study between the total attitudinal mean and test performance was significant but very small (.37). In addition, the results did not indicate whether or not there was a causal relationship between students' attitudes and their test performance. In Karmos and Karmos' study, the survey focused on students in the middle grades and concentrated on their affective evaluations, whereas the present study focused on students at the tertiary level within the Chinese English learning context and the survey encompassed constructs of attitudes.

To sum up, as shown in previous studies (e.g., Karmos & Karmos, 1984; Paris et al., 2000), not only high achievers and low achievers, but also males and females hold different attitudes towards testing. Therefore, four research questions were put forward for the present study:

1 What are Chinese university students' attitudes towards the CET-4?
2 What relationships exist between attitudinal factors and students' performance on the CET-4?
3 What attitudes differentiate high achievers (above 80th percentile) from low achievers (below 20th percentile) on the CET-4?
4 Do sex differences exist in attitudes and their relation to test performance?

Methodology

Questionnaire

For this study, an attitudinal questionnaire (see Zhao, 2006) was designed and used in the study to survey students' attitudes specifically towards the CET-4. The questionnaire consisted of 39 items concerning students' attitudes towards the CET-4 on a 5-point scale: 1 = Strongly disagree, 2 = Disagree, 3 = Undecided, 4 = Agree, 5 = Strongly agree.

The questionnaire was designed based on the Test Attitude Survey developed by Arvey et al. in 1990. Five of the nine scales from the questionnaire were used in the present study: motivation; belief in tests; comparative anxiety (test-taking anxiety in the present study); lack of concentration; and test ease, as these were the attitudinal constructs most frequently referred to in the literature and most suitable for the context of this study.

The items in the five scales were, however, modified specifically to relate to the CET-4. The final version of the questionnaire consisted of 39 items.

Test Performance

Both the questionnaire and participants' test scores on the CET-4, which was held in June, 2005, were used to explore the relationship between students' attitudes towards the CET-4 and their test performance. Students' test performance was indicated by their CET-4 total scores.

Participants

Approximately 300 non-English major undergraduates were invited to participate in the present study. The students came from two comprehensive universities in Guangzhou, China. Each of the two participating universities offers more than 20 programs, such as law, computer science, chemical engineering, biology, and communication. Students in these two universities come from different provinces of China, including Hong Kong and Macao. The participants in this study were in their third year of university, and were aged from 19 to 23.

As in many other Chinese universities, most of the non-English major students in the two universities are required to sit the CET-4 and the two participating universities relate students' CET-4 scores to their graduation diplomas. Participants who do not pass the CET-4 do not receive their diplomas. In addition, as one of the most prosperous cities in China, Guangzhou is a place full of job opportunities, and many companies in Guangzhou deem a high level of English proficiency as indispensable for university graduates. Therefore, a high CET-4 score is an asset for graduates when they seek jobs. As a result, the CET-4 is a high-stakes test for the students who participated in the study.

Data Collection Procedures

Before the study was carried out, official approval was obtained from the two participating universities. As it usually takes 2 months to obtain CET-4 scores (the participants' scores on the CET-4 administered in June 2005 were available in August 2005), attitudinal questionnaires were issued in September, 2005, approximately 2 months after the participants took the CET-4 at the end of June 2005. After the questionnaires were collected, students' test scores were obtained from the universities.

Data Analysis

Several quantitative methods were employed to address the four research questions. Although the test attitude survey was already divided into five subscales, exploratory factor analysis was conducted to see whether the results were in accordance with the hypothesized theoretical structures assumed to underlie the test attitude survey within the context of the study. Exploratory factor analysis was conducted because the study was carried out in an EFL academic situation rather than in a job selection context as indicated by Arvey et al.'s study (1990). Principal component factoring with direct oblimin rotation was used in the factor analysis to classify students' attitudes towards the CET-4.

To address the first research question—to investigate Chinese university students' attitudes towards the CET-4, descriptive statistics (i.e., means, standard deviations) were analyzed to illustrate students' attitudes towards the CET-4 at both the item and the scale levels. To address the second research question—to explore the relationships between attitudinal factors and students' performance on the CET-4, correlations and multiple stepwise regression were conducted. To address the third and fourth questions, *t*-tests, correlations, and stepwise multiple regressions were employed.

Results

Participants

Approximately 300 participants from two universities in Guangzhou were invited to participate in this study. Among the 213 returned questionnaires, only one had missing values exceeding 10 percent, which was four items of the total questionnaire numbers. This case was removed from the dataset, making a total of 212 valid responses, including 145 females and 63 males (four participants did not indicate their gender). SPSS 12.0 was used to conduct the data analysis. An alpha level of .05 was used for all tests of significance.

Exploratory Principal Component Analyses

A Scree Plot was used to determine the appropriate number of factors to extract. The Scree Plot indicated that a four-factor model was the most appropriate fit with the data. All four of these factors had eigenvalues greater than one. Therefore, the four-factor solution was adopted in the present study. The four-factor solution produced interpretable results, accounting for about 41 percent of the variance. Seven items were discarded from further analysis as they had double loadings on two factors and each of the two loadings was higher than .3. The remaining 32 items were classified into four factors.

The first factor contained items measuring test-taking anxiety and lack of concentration. The items with high pattern coefficients on factor 1 generally fitted into the predetermined subscales of test-taking anxiety and lack of concentration in the attitudinal questionnaire. As the two subscales of lack of test-taking anxiety and concentration measured affective dimension of attitudes (part of the tripartite model of attitude structure mentioned above), it is acceptable that the items in the two subscales were classified into factor 1. Two items from the subscale of test ease also had high loadings on factor 1.[1] Therefore, the appropriate label for factor 1 was defined as "Test-taking anxiety/lack of concentration," which was mainly a combination of items from two subscales of the original questionnaire.

The second factor generally measured students' motivation for taking the CET-4. Therefore, factor 2 retained its original name "Test-taking motivation". The third factor measured students' belief in the CET-4. Two items from the scale of Test-taking Motivation, "I didn't put much effort into CET-4" and "I tried my best on CET-4" had high loadings on factor 3. However, this result was understandable and interpretable. Therefore, the original name in the questionnaire, "Belief in CET-4" was kept for factor 3. The fourth factor measured test ease, so it also retained the original name. Thus, factor 1 "Test-taking anxiety/lack of concentration" was composed of 17 items; factor 2 "Test-taking motivation" consisted of five items; factor 3 "Belief in CET-4" consisted of seven items and the last factor "Test ease" was composed of three items. The eigenvalues for the four factors were 6.30, 5.40, 2.30, and 1.97, respectively. The variance explained by the four factors was 16.1 percent, 13.9 percent, 5.9 percent, and 5.0 percent, respectively.

Descriptive Statistics at the Scale Level

Descriptive statistics were conducted at the factor scale level, which displays students' attitudes towards the CET-4 at the scale level. Factor 2, Test-taking motivation, received the strongest agreement (mean = 3.87 on a 5-point Likert Scale) among the students, followed by factor 1, Test-taking anxiety/lack of concentration (mean = 2.79), factor 3 (mean = 2.43), and factor 4 (mean = 2.35). These results show that on one hand, the students

Table 14.1 Descriptive Statistics and Independent Sample *t*-test of Females ($n = 145$) and Males ($n = 63$); of Higher Achievers' ($n = 42$) and Low Achievers' ($n = 42$) Attitudes toward the CET-4

Factor	Gender	Mean	p	Performance	Mean	p
1 Test-taking Anxiety/	Female	2.84	.03	High	2.60	<.001
Lack of Concentration	Male	2.65		Low	3.05	
2 Test-taking Motivation	Female	3.94	.07	High	4.05	.02
	Male	3.73		Low	3.65	
3 Belief in CET-4	Female	2.41	.19	High	2.55	.03
	Male	2.53		Low	2.27	
4 Test Ease	Female	2.30	.14	High	2.49	.18
	Male	2.48		Low	2.26	

were strongly motivated to try to do well on the CET-4; on the other hand, however, they were not confident or they were anxious about whether they could do well on it.

Attitudinal scale scores were computed and compared for the 145 female students and 63 male students. As reported in Table 14.1, female students' ratings for two of the attitudinal factors, Test-taking anxiety/lack of concentration and Test-taking motivation, were slightly higher than those of male students. As for factor 3, Belief in CET-4, and factor 4, Test ease, female students' ratings were a little lower. The results of independent sample *t*-tests ($p<.05$, $df = 206$) show that only factor 1, Test-taking anxiety/lack of concentration, differentiated female from male students. Female students were less confident or more anxious about their test-taking abilities with the CET-4 than male students. The other three factors, Test-taking motivation, Belief in CET-4 and Test ease, did not produce significant differences between the two groups.

Attitudinal factor scores were also compared for the 42 students with high CET-4 performance (who scored above the 80th percentile) and the 42 students with low performance (who scored below the 20th percentile). The results of the *t*-test ($p<.05$, $df = 82$) are also presented in Table 14.1. The strongest difference was for factor 1, Test-taking anxiety/lack of concentration, with low-achieving students agreeing more strongly that they were more worried about taking the test. For factor 2, Test-taking motivation, high-achieving students also scored significantly higher than low-achieving students. High achievers were more motivated to do well on the CET-4. Factor 3, Belief in the CET-4, differentiated high achievers from low achievers as well. High achievers were more likely to believe that the CET-4 reflected their true abilities in comparison with low achievers. The results of the *t*-test also show that there was no significant difference between high- and low-achieving students' ratings for factor 4, Test ease.

Stepwise Regression Analysis

Stepwise multiple regression analysis was conducted to examine the relationship between students' attitudes towards the CET-4 and their test performance. Several stepwise regression analyses were performed to examine which of the four attitudinal factor(s) could best predict all students' performance, females' and males' performance, and high achievers' and low achievers' performance on the CET-4. These stepwise regression analyses were performed with the CET-4 total scores as the dependent variable and the

Table 14.2 Multiple Regression: Students' Attitudes toward the CET-4 and their Test Performance ($n = 212$)

Model	Factor	$ß$	t	p	R^2
1	Test-taking Anxiety/Lack of Concentration	−.26	−4.05	<.001	.068
2	Test-taking Anxiety/Lack of Concentration	−.25	−3.86	<.001	.124
	Test-taking Motivation	.25	3.80	<.001	
3	Test-taking Anxiety/Lack of Concentration	−.23	−3.63	<.001	.154
	Test-taking Motivation	.21	3.18	.002	
	Belief in CET-4	.19	2.91	.004	

four attitudinal factors as the independent variables. Table 14.2 presents the results of regression analysis examining which attitudinal factor(s) could best predict the students' test performance on the CET-4.

As shown in Table 14.2, students' attitudes had a significant effect on the prediction of their performance on the CET-4. Three attitudinal factors, Test-taking motivation, Belief in CET-4, and Test-taking anxiety/lack of concentration, best predicted students' performance on the CET-4. Students who reported that they were more motivated to do well tended to have higher test scores. Students who believed more strongly that the CET-4 reflected their true abilities tended to get higher scores. Students who reported that they were more confident/less anxious about taking the CET-4 tended to obtain higher scores. The linear regression model presented in Table 14.2 was able to explain 15.4 percent of the variance in the students' CET-4 test scores. The results were in accordance with the findings of Karmos and Karmos' study (1984), in which students' overall attitudes accounted for about 14 percent of the variance in their test performance.

Two attitudinal factors, Test-taking motivation and Test-taking anxiety/lack of concentration, best predicted female students' performance on the CET-4. Those female students who were more motivated to do well on the test got higher scores. Those who reported having more confidence/less anxiety in taking the CET-4 tended to obtain higher scores. Together these two attitudinal factors could explain 10.4 percent of the variance in female students' performance on the CET-4. Factor 3, Belief in CET-4, was the best predictor of male students' performance on the CET-4. Those male students who reported believing in the CET-4 more tended to obtain higher scores. This factor was able to explain 19.7 percent of the variance in male students' CET-4 scores.

Factor 2, Test-taking motivation, was the best predictor of high-achieving students' performance on the CET-4. Those students who reported that they had higher motivation to do well tended to obtain higher scores. This factor explained 33.8 percent of the variance in high achievers' scores on the CET-4. Factor 2, Test-taking motivation, was also the best predictor of low-achieving students' performance on the CET-4. The low achievers who reported being more motivated to do well on the CET-4 tended to have higher scores. Test-taking motivation accounted for 32.2 percent of the variance in low achievers' scores on the CET-4.

Discussion

Several findings emerged from the present study. As indicated by the results obtained from the scale level, students generally held strong yet mixed feelings towards the

CET-4. Most students reported having strong motivation to do well on the CET-4 as shown by the mean for the factor Test-taking motivation, which was 3.87 (on a 5-point Likert scale). This is understandable as the CET-4 does have a certain importance, which can not be ignored by the students. The two universities in the study set their own pass rate for the CET-4. If students could not pass the test, they would most likely not receive their undergraduate diplomas. However, at the same time, students were not sure of their abilities to perform well on the CET-4, so they were anxious about taking the test and could not concentrate on it well. This point can be shown by their ratings for the factor Test-taking anxiety/lack of concentration, which had a moderately high mean of 2.7.

Moreover, gender differences were found in the present study. Females rated the factor Test-taking anxiety/lack of concentration significantly higher than males. *T*-test results showed that compared with males, females stated they were less confident of their abilities to do well on the CET-4, i.e., they were more anxious about taking the CET-4 and could not concentrate on it well. Considerable research has already been carried out into the differences in attitudes and performance between boys and girls and similar findings were reported in these studies. For example, in the study of Cole, Martin, Peeke, Seroczynski, and Fier (1999), the third- and sixth-Grade students reported on their feelings of depression, symptoms of anxiety, and their perceived academic competence in a questionnaire which was then compared to the objective measures of their academic competence as provided by their teachers. Gender differences were found in the study with girls reporting higher levels of anxiety and depression while also underestimating their academic competence. Boys, however, showed a lower level of anxiety and overestimated their competence. Similarly, gender differences were evident in the study of Locker and Cropley (2004) in which 520 secondary school students participated. The results showed that females consistently reported greater levels of anxiety and negative affect, especially immediately before important school examinations. Males, however, displayed higher positive affect and self-esteem and lower levels of depression and anxiety before and after testing. Hodge, McCormick, and Elliot (1997) also examined the levels of test anxiety in a large group of adolescents who prepared for and completed examinations. Their results showed that a large number of students, particularly females, were experiencing high levels of anxiety and depression during this period. Clark and Trafford (1996) ascribed the differences between females and males to the fact that female students tended to be more likely to report openly their feelings of anxiety.

In addition, the results of the present study show that test-taking motivation was an important factor which differentiated high achievers from low achievers. High-achieving students reported being more motivated to do well on the CET-4 than low-achieving students. This finding coincides again with that of Clark and Trafford (1996) who observed a lack of motivation in lower-achieving students. Low achievers' unwillingness to make more of an effort to do well on the CET-4 may also be due to their past repeated poor test performance (Paris et al., 2000), making them lose confidence and interest in the CET-4. This view is similar to that of Oller and Perkins (1978) who held that attainment in language learning generated positive attitudes and failure led to demotivation: "high achievers tend to develop positive attitudes as they go along and low achievers become increasingly disenchanted (p. 94)." Similar views were also shared by Clark and Trafford who suggested that early success was likely to lead to a more positive desire to continue with the subject. One suggestion to improve students' interest, especially low-achieving students, is to help them develop some test-taking skills. Mastery of such test-taking skills might increase students' interest in the test and focus students on the task of responding well to test items, thus increasing their willingness to exert more effort on the test (Karmos & Karmos, 1984).

Another finding arising from the present study is that the factor Test-taking anxiety/ lack of concentration had a negative correlation with students' test performance. The results are in accordance with those of the previous research (e.g., Hembree, 1988; Birenbaum & Nasser, 1994) conducted on investigating the relationship between test-taking anxiety and test performance, which supported the assertion that high test-taking anxiety led to underachievement. It is noteworthy that Test-taking anxiety/lack of concentration is also a factor that significantly differentiated high-achieving students from low-achieving students. Low-achieving students tended to be more anxious about taking the CET-4. Regarding this point, Zeidner and Schleyer's (1998) study offered an explanation, describing how individuals who feel less academically confident might have lower expectations of success, which might in turn lead to increased test- or exam-related anxiety and result in a poorer performance.

The literature also offers some suggestions about how to reduce students' test-taking anxiety. Karmos and Karmos (1984) suggested that one way to relieve students' test-taking anxiety was to engage them in test-anxiety reduction activities. Greenberg et al. (1992) found that self-esteem served an anxiety-buffering function and that raising self-esteem would reduce anxiety. In addition, King, Ollendick, and Molloy (1998) described the utility of relaxation programs in schools, which could provide benefits for problems such as headaches and test anxiety.

It should also be pointed out that in the present study only 15.4 percent of the variance in students' CET-4 scores was accounted for by students' attitudes. This finding is consistent with the results from Karmos and Karmos' (1984) study in which students' attitudes towards the standardized test accounted for 14 percent of the variance in their test performance. Such results are attributable to the fact that many factors other than taker-takers' attitudes might influence their test performance. Many studies have focused on this field of investigation. For example, Bachman (1990) proposed a general model to explain these factors which might influence test performance. In this model, four categories were considered to influence test scores: (1) test-takers' communicative language abilities, which were made up of language competencies, strategic competence, and psychophysiological mechanisms; (2) test method facets, including environment, rubric, input, expected response, and relationships between input and response; (3) personal characteristics consisting of cultural background, background knowledge, cognitive abilities, sex, and age, which related to the present study; (4) random factors including interactions among components of communicative language ability.

Considering that there are many factors which may influence test performance, it is not surprising that in this study, test-takers' attitudes predicted only a small portion of the variance in their test performance.

Conclusion

The present study investigated the relationship between Chinese university students' attitudes towards the CET-4 and their test performance. The study is a washback study, i.e., it is a study investigating the influence of language testing on students. As pointed out earlier, much research has been done on the influence of testing on teaching and learning, yet few have investigated students' attitudes towards testing, especially in second/foreign language education (Wall, 2000). Also, studies investigating students' attitudes towards testing have had disparate results because of different histories of test-taking experiences in different countries (Paris et al., 2000). This present study was conducted within the Chinese EFL context, where a long tradition of examinations existed. This study also echoed Wall's call for more research into the impact of testing on students' learning. Therefore, this study is a washback study that focused on the "washback to the learners" (Bailey, 1996). The study explored students' attitudes towards the CET-4 in conjunction with their test performance. However, it is different from previous washback research conducted on the CET-4 (e.g., Li, 1995; Chen & Zhang, 1998; Zhang, 2003) which did not investigate the relationship between students' attitudes towards the CET-4 and their test performance. In this way, this study sheds some light on washback studies investigating various aspects of teaching and learning, especially in the field of second/foreign language education.

In a practical sense, understanding students' attitudes towards the CET-4 can provide CET-4 stakeholders with information which can be used in planning for efforts to improve students' learning and consequently their CET-4 scores. The present study shows that when researchers or CET-4 stakeholders consider variables that influence students' language test scores, students' attitudes should be taken into consideration as they accounted for more than 15 percent of the variance in students' test performance.

Note

1. This result was expected, as in the pilot study of the questionnaire, the pilot participants disagreed on the two items in terms of the subscales into which they should be classified into.

References

Arvey, R. D., Strickland, W., Drauden, G. & Martin, C. (1990). Motivational components of test taking. *Personnel Psychology*, 43, 695–717.

Bachman, L. F. (1990). *Fundamental considerations in language testing.* New York: Oxford University Press.

Bachman, L. F. & Palmer, A. S. (1996). *Language testing in practice.* Oxford: Oxford University Press.

Bailey, K. M. (1996). Working for washback: A review of the washback concept in language testing. *Language Testing*, 13, 257–279.

Birenbaum, M. & Nasser, F. (1994). On the relationship between test anxiety and test performance. *Measurement and Evaluation in Counseling and Development*, 27, 293–301.

Bloom, B. S. (1982). *Human characteristics and school learning.* New York: McGraw-Hill.

Chen, C. & Zhang, Y. (1998). A perspective on the College English Teaching syllabus in China. *TESL Canada Journal*, 15, 69–74.

Chen, Z. & He, Y. (2003). Influence of CET-4 on college students and some suggestions. *Journal of Technology College Education*, 22(6), 40–41.

Cheng, L. (1998). Impact of a public English examination change on students' perceptions and attitudes towards their English learning. *Studies in Educational Evaluation*, 24, 279–301.

Clark, A. & Trafford, J. (1996). Return to gender: Boys' and girls' attitudes and achievements. *Language Learning Journal*, 14, 40–49.

Cole, D. A., Martin, J. M., Peeke, L. A., Seroczynski, A. D. & Fier, J. (1999). Children's over and underestimation of academic competence: A longitudinal study of gender differences, depression, and anxiety. *Child Development*, 70, 459–473.

Greenberg, J., Soloman, S., Pyszczynski, T., Rosenblatt, A., Burling, J., Lyon, D., et al. (1992). Why do people need self-esteem? Converging evidence that self-esteem serves an anxiety-buffering function. *Journal of Personality and Social Psychology*, 63, 913–922.

Hembree, R. (1988). Correlates, causes, effects, and treatment of test anxiety. *Review of Educational Research*, 58, 47–77.

Hodge, G. M., McCormick, J. & Elliot, R. (1997). Examination-induced distress in a public examination at the completion of secondary schooling. *British Journal of Educational Psychology*, 67, 185–197.

Hughes, S. & Bailey, J (2002). What students think about high-stakes testing. *Educational Leadership*, 59, 74–76.

Hungerland, R. (2004). *The role of contextual factors in mediating the washback of high-stakes language assessment*. Unpublished master's thesis, Carleton University, Ottawa, Ontario, Canada.

Karmos, A. H. & Karmos, J. S. (1984). Attitudes towards standardized achievement tests and their relation to achievement test performance. *Measurement and Evaluation in Counseling and Development*, 17, 56–66.

Kellaghan, T., Madaus, G. F. & Airasian, P. W. (1982). *The effects of standardized testing*. Boston: Klumer Nijhoff.

King, N. J., Ollendick, T. H. & Molloy, G. N. (1998). Utility of relaxation of training with children in school settings: A plea for realistic goal setting and evaluation. *British Journal of Educational Psychology*, 68, 53–66.

Li, X. (1995). Comments on CET-4. *Liaoning Higher Education Research*, 4, 94–95.

Locker, G. & Cropley, M. (2004). Anxiety, depression and self-esteem in secondary school children, *School Psychology International*, 25, 333–345.

Lu, L., & Wang, Z. (1998). On reforms of CET-4. *Heilongjiang Higher Education Research*, 4, 85–86.

Oller, J. W. & Perkins, K. (1978). Intelligence and language proficiency as sources of Variance in self-reported affective variables. *Language Learning*, 28, 85–97.

Pan, J. (1998). Several suggestions for College English testing and teaching. *Journal of Tianjin University of Commerce*, 2, 63–68.

Paris, S. G., Lawton, T. A., Turner, J. C. & Roth, J. L. (2000). Developing disillusionment: Students' perceptions of academic achievement tests. *Issues in Education*, 1/2, 17–46.

Ryan, A. M. (2001). Explaining the Black-White test score gap: The role of test perceptions. *Human Performance*, 14, 45–75.

Shohamy, E., Donitsa-Schmidt, S. & Ferman, I. (1996). Test impact revisited: Washback effect over time. *Language Testing*, 13, 298–317.

Wall, D. (2000). The impact of high-stakes testing on teaching and learning: Can this be predicted or controlled? *System*, 28, 499–509.

Zeidner, M. & Schleyer, E. J. (1998). The big-fish-little-pond for academic Self-concept, test anxiety and school Grades in gifted children, *Contemporary Educational Psychology*, 24, 305–329.

Zhang, X. (2003). On the negative effects of CET-4. *Education Science*, 19, 38–40.

Zhao, J. (2006). *Exploring the relationship between Chinese university students' attitudes towards College English Test and their test performance*. Unpublished master's thesis, Queen's University, Kingston, Ontario, Canada.

15 Chinese EFL Students' Perceptions of the Classroom Assessment Environment and their Goal Orientations

Xiaoying Wang, Beijing Foreign Studies University
Liying Cheng, Queen's University

This study explored the relationship between Chinese EFL students' perceptions of the classroom assessment environment and their goal orientations. A questionnaire survey was conducted with 503 first-year undergraduates enrolled in the College English course from one university in China. Data were analyzed using exploratory factor analyses and multiple regression analyses. The results indicated that Chinese EFL students perceived their classroom assessment environment to be three-dimensional: learning-oriented, test-oriented, and praise-oriented. Four types of goal orientations emerged for this sample: performance approach goals, performance avoidance goals, mastery external goals, and mastery in-class goals. The learning-oriented dimension positively predicted mastery in-class goals, mastery external goals, and performance approach goals. The test-oriented dimension positively predicted performance avoidance goals and negatively predicted mastery external goals. The praise-oriented dimension only positively predicted performance approach goals. This study not only tested the generalizability of goal orientation theory in a different subject area and cultural context from previous studies, but also discovered a link between goal orientation theory and L2 motivational orientations.

Introduction

Over the last decade, the relationship between classroom assessment and student motivation has received more and more attention (Archer & Scevak, 1998; Black & Wiliam, 1998; Brookhart, 1997; Brookhart & DeVoge, 1999, 2000; Crooks, 1988; Maslovaty & Kuzi, 2002; Stiggins, 2002). Traditionally, the role of classroom assessment in motivating students was typically to provide a basis for the use of rewards or punishments so as to entice or intimidate students to put more effort into learning (Stiggins, 2002). However, research in the field of academic motivation in schools has demonstrated that external contextual factors such as rewards or punishments do not influence motivation directly. Rather, such contextual factors affect one's cognitions, self-perceptions, beliefs, and expectations for success, and these in turn influence motivation (e.g., Bandura, 1997; Brookhart, 1997; Dweck, 1986; Weiner, 1986). Therefore, in order to arrive at a better understanding of the relationship between classroom assessment and student motivation, this study used goal orientation theory, and investigated the relationship between students' perceptions of their classroom assessment environment and their goal orientations in the English as a foreign language (EFL) context in China (see Chapter 4 for more context information).

In the field of L2 motivation (motivation for students learning a second or foreign language), the integrative versus instrumental motivation theory (Gardner & Lambert, 1972) has been the major theoretical framework for many studies over the years (e.g., Belmechri & Hummel, 1998; Gardner & MacIntyre, 1991). In recent years, several influential cognitive motivation theories proposed in educational psychology have entered the L2 motivation field (for a review, see Dornyei, 2003). Although goal orientation theory has also emerged as a prominent theory for its explanatory power in a variety of subject areas and with subjects of different age groups and ethnicities (e.g., Dweck, 1986; Middleton & Midgley, 1997; Pintrich, 2000), there have been almost no attempts to adopt this theory in L2 motivation studies (Dornyei, 2003, p. 9). Therefore, this study applied goal orientation theory to this EFL learning context and examined how Chinese EFL learners' perceptions of their classroom assessment environment were associated with their goal orientations.

This study focused on students' perceptions of their classroom assessment environment, because research indicates that teachers and students may have differing perceptions of classroom assessment (Shohamy, 1998), and students' perceptions are the filter that mediates the influence of classroom assessment environment on student efforts and achievement (Brookhart, 1997, p. 170). It is students' perceptions of their psychological environment that are presumed to play the more important role in the goal adoption process than the objective environment itself (Ames, 1992; Maehr & Midgley, 1991).

This study was situated in a Chinese EFL learning context. More specifically, it was situated in the College English course offered to first-year non-English major university students (see Chapter 4). The reasons for deciding on this context are as follows: first, so far, most of the research findings on classroom assessment environment and on student goal orientation are specific to Western students and in the school context. Fewer studies have been conducted with Chinese learners in an EFL context. While Chinese learners live in their own cultural learning context, this study expanded the current understanding to see if previous research findings are universal or culturally specific. Second, recent advances relating to goal orientation have centered on whether goal orientation is a two-factor construct or a three-factor construct, which will be presented in detail in the literature review. It is hoped that this study will help in the debate by identifying the structure of goal orientations Chinese EFL learners have and examining which framework is more warranted given this particular sample and its learning context. Finally, our own experience as university EFL teachers informed us that classroom assessments did not always bring about the effects we as teachers expected. Some students would work hard whether there were assessments or not. Some students would only work hard when they were going to be assessed and they invested different amounts of effort depending on the importance of the assessments. Still other students would not even try to work hard despite the upcoming assessments. Therefore, by uncovering Chinese EFL learners' perceptions of classroom assessment environment, their goal orientations, and the relationship between the two, this study has helped EFL teachers in China and/or those in similar teaching contexts deepen their understanding of their classroom assessment practices, reflect on their classroom assessment environment, and try to create the kinds of environments that will promote optimal goal orientations among their students.

Theoretical Framework

Classroom Assessment Environment

First put forward by Stiggins and Conklin (1992) who identified and tested eight key factors of the classroom assessment environment through a series of studies conducted in the 1980s, the concept of a classroom assessment environment was further enhanced in Brookhart's (1997) theoretical framework. Based on a synthesis of the classroom assessment environment and social-cognitive theories of learning and motivation, Brookhart (1997) argued that, in classroom settings, teachers create the classroom assessment environment through administering classroom assessment tasks and providing feedback to students. The assessment tasks may transmit a sense of expectations to students and the feedback may allow students to figure out how well they have met those expectations. As a result, the classroom assessment environment may motivate students to put more effort into their studies, and achieve more.

Brookhart (1997) proposed five dimensions of the classroom assessment environment: teacher attitudes toward subject matter and students, use of different forms of assessment, teacher preparation in assessment principles, integration of assessment with instruction, and communication of assessment results. She acknowledged that external contexts such as institutional policies also played an important role in influencing teachers' actual classroom assessment practices. This study, conducted from students' perspectives, mainly focused on two dimensions: students' perceptions of their teacher's use of different forms of assessment methods and students' perceptions of their teacher's feedback (communication of assessment results), since the other dimensions had to be examined from teachers' perspectives.

Goal Orientations

Goal orientation refers to integrated patterns of beliefs that represent both the reasons for pursuing an achievement task and the criteria for evaluating success on the task (Ames, 1992; Pintrich, 2000). Two qualitatively different goal constructs—mastery goals and performance goals—have received most attention in this research area.[1] Mastery goals emphasize that one pursues a task in order to develop one's skills, understand one's work, improve one's competence, or achieve a sense of mastery based on self-referenced standards. In contrast, performance goals emphasize that one pursues a task in order to demonstrate one's competence, outperform others, or achieve a sense of superiority based on norm-referenced standards (Ames, 1992; Dweck, 1986; Maehr & Meyer, 1997).

While a large body of research suggests a number of positive outcomes associated with mastery goals (e.g., Dweck, 1986; Pintrich & Schunk, 1996), the effects of pursuing performance goals are less clear. Recent research that has divided performance goals into two subtypes, performance approach goals and performance avoidance goals, has contributed to the clarification of the relationship among performance goals, motivation, and performance (e.g., Elliot & Harackiewicz, 1996; Middleton & Midgley, 1997).

Performance approach goals emphasize working hard in order to outperform others, while performance avoidance goals emphasize doing the minimum work to avoid looking incompetent or stupid. Performance avoidance goals have been linked to a host of negative motivational processes and learning behaviors (for a review, see Elliot, 1999); however, findings concerning performance approach goals are still inconsistent. Some studies showed a positive relation between performance approach goals, better performance, and greater achievement (e.g., Elliot & Church, 1997), while some other studies found a positive relation between performance approach goals and test anxiety, shallow processing of information, and unwillingness to seek help with schoolwork (e.g., Middleton & Midgley, 1997; Midgley, Kaplan, & Middleton, 2001). Considering this disagreement, an ancillary purpose of this study was to find out whether the two-construct or the three-construct framework of goal orientations was warranted given this particular sample in the Chinese EFL context.

Classroom Assessment Environment and Students' Goal Orientations

A small number of studies have empirically examined variables that are within the two dimensions of the classroom assessment environment in relation to goal orientations (Archer & Scevak, 1998; Butler, 1987; Church, Elliot, & Gable, 2001; Lackey, Miller, & Flanigan, 1997; Maslovaty & Kuzi, 2002).

When teachers' assessment feedback was examined in relation to students' goal orientations (Butler, 1987; Lackey et al., 1997), feedback was operationalized based on the nature of feedback: whether it focused students' attention on the tasks (task-involving) or on the self (ego-involving). These two studies all adopted the two-construct framework of goal orientation theory to study its relationship to assessment feedback. Both studies (Butler, 1987; Lackey et al., 1997) indicated that assessment feedback is an important aspect influencing students' goal orientations. Task-involving feedback tended to enhance mastery goals, but the influence of ego-involving feedback such as praise or grades was less clear. These types of teacher feedback were incorporated into the design of the present study.

When teachers' assessment methods were examined in relation to students' goal orientations (Archer & Scevak, 1998; Church et al., 2001; Maslovaty & Kuzi, 2002), assessment methods were understood in a broad sense including types of assessment methods, grading, task difficulty, and task frequency. More specifically, the variables examined in these studies included process-oriented assessment, alternative assessment, traditional assessment, evaluation focus,[2] grading harshness,[3] and evaluation type.[4] Except for Church et al.'s study in which the three-construct framework was applied, all the other studies adopted the two-construct framework of goal orientation theory. The results of these studies showed that process-oriented assessment, alternative assessment, and criterion-referenced evaluation tended to enhance mastery goals, while traditional assessment, evaluation focus, grading harshness, and norm-referenced evaluation tended to enhance performance goals.

Overall, the literature indicated that the above variables within the classroom assessment environment played an important role in influencing students' goal orientations. However, no empirical studies have been found that examined such relationships in an EFL context in China. Therefore, the present study incorporated the variables emerging from the above studies to examine Chinese EFL students' perceptions of their classroom assessment environment in relation to their goal orientations. This study, therefore, addressed the following three research questions: (1) What are the dimensions of students' perceptions of their classroom assessment environment in the College English course? (2) What are the dimensions of students' goal orientations in the College English course? (3) What are the relationships between students' perceptions of their classroom assessment environment and their goal orientations in the College English course?

Methodology

Participants

The participants in this study were 503 non-English-major university students (56.5 percent female) enrolled in the College English course in one university in southern China. First-year undergraduate students were approached to minimize the washback effects of the CET-4 on teachers' classroom assessment practices and consequently on students' perceptions of their classroom assessment environment (see Cheng, Rogers, & Wang, 2008). They were around 18 and 19 years of age. They had studied English for at least 6 years in their secondary school and had all passed the national university entrance examination in English before they entered the university. They were from 12 College English classes, taught by six teachers. They were students with 15 different undergraduate majors, including electronic science and technology, applied mathematics, advertising, Japanese language, economics, Chinese language and literature, arts design, information management, financing, accounting, public management, business management, international economics and trade, law, and applied chemistry. Students in this university were grouped into different College English classes based on their majors.

Instrument

A questionnaire was used, as it is an efficient and effective way to obtain the information needed in this study. The questionnaire consisted of three parts. Items in the first part, perceptions of classroom assessment environment, were mainly designed based on the variables emerging from the literature review and aspects perceived to be salient in the Chinese context, or adapted from Church et al.'s (2001) questionnaire. Items in the second part, goal orientations, were adapted from two questionnaires used in previous studies (Elliot & Church, 1997; Midgley et al., 1998) when these researchers explored goal orientations within the contexts of general education. Adaptations were made only at the word level to make the sentences more appropriate for the Chinese context, except for one item (G15) which was an attempt to integrate the theoretical constructs of goal orientation theory and the salient characteristics of Chinese EFL learners' motivation to learn English. The information from the last part of the questionnaire (students' gender and major) was used for describing the participants.

Since this study was situated in a Chinese EFL context, the questionnaire was translated into Chinese to ensure accurate understanding. Because of the uniqueness of this questionnaire and this study context and to ensure validity of the instrument, a pilot study was conducted among 103 first-year undergraduates enrolled in the College English course at a northern university in China during the first week of June 2003 with permission from that university and with student written consent. The questionnaire was further revised based on the pilot study results. In the end, the final questionnaire consisted of 24 items measuring perceived classroom assessment environment and 15 items measuring goal orientations (see Wang, 2004 for details about the questionnaire).

The first part of the questionnaire measured the following aspects of assessment feedback: personal relevance and meaningfulness (1, 4, 11, 13, 15, 24) (task-involving), public evaluation (3, 6, 9, 12), and evaluation focus (7, 23) (ego-involving); and the following aspects of assessment methods: process-/product-oriented (2, 5, 8, 14, 20), grading harshness (10, 16), task variety (17), task difficulty (18, 22), and assessment frequency (19, 21). The second part measured three types of goal orientations—mastery goals (1, 4, 7, 10, 13), performance-approach goals (2, 5, 8, 11, 14), and performance-avoidance goals (3, 6, 9, 12, 15). For both parts, students were asked to indicate the degree to which they agreed with each item on a five-point Likert scale (1 = strongly disagree, 5 = strongly agree).

Data Collection Procedures

The study was conducted in a university in southern China[5] during the last 2 weeks of June 2003. Written permission from the university was obtained to administer the questionnaire during College English classes. A total of 503 students volunteered to participate in this study. After written consent was obtained from the participating students, the questionnaire was administered in students' own classrooms in their normal College English course. One teacher helped administer the questionnaire to ensure consistency across classes. It took around 15–20 min to complete the questionnaire.

Data Analysis

After the data were collected, exploratory factor analyses were performed on the first two parts of the questionnaire separately to address the first two research questions. The mean and standard deviation of each factor scale were calculated to show the general patterns of students' perceptions, and zero-order correlations among the factors were calculated to show the relationships among the factors. To address the third research question, standard multiple regression analyses were performed on the sample as a whole. Because the participants were from 12 different classes, class membership was entered as an independent variable using dummy coding to examine if they made a difference in the relationships.

Results

Data Screening

Both factor analysis and multiple regression analysis assume normal distribution of the data and linear relationship among the variables. Outlier cases, outlier variables, multicollinearity, and singularity may distort such statistical analyses. Therefore, in order to enhance the analyses involved in this study, students' responses to the two measures of classroom assessment evaluation and their goal orientation were examined through various SPSS procedures for accuracy of input, missing data, and the fit between the distributions of the variables and the assumptions of factor analysis: normality, linearity, outliers among cases, multicollinearity, and singularity (Tabachnick & Fidell, 1996).

In this sample of 503, none of the variables had missing values above 5 percent of the total respondents, and 38 cases had one or two or three random missing values. However, one participant had three missing values for the first part of the questionnaire (10.7 percent of the total number of the variables for this part). Because factor analyses were conducted separately for the two measures, this case was removed, making the total sample 502. Further SPSS analysis (normality, linearity, outliers among cases, multicollinearity, and singularity) revealed five other cases to be potential outliers. An examination of these cases showed that for the five cases, the respondents either selected one choice through almost all of the variables or selected choices in a certain pattern causing their responses to be self-contradictory. Therefore, these five cases were deleted from the sample as outliers, leaving 497 cases for analyses. This dataset was used for all subsequent analyses.

Descriptive Statistics

Descriptive statistics of all the variables were performed for this sample of 497 including mean, median, mode, standard deviation, kurtosis, skewness, and frequency. The results revealed that students' opinions on most of the questionnaire items were spread among the five choices, except for four items (A4, A12, A23, G13), where students' opinions clustered together. Specifically, most students agreed or strongly agreed (A4, altogether 78.3 percent) that their classroom assessments were informative to them in the sense that they helped them find out their weaknesses in English. However, most students disagreed or strongly disagreed that their classroom assessment environment was focused on evaluation (A12, altogether 93.4 percent) or emphasized negative public evaluation (A23, altogether 78.1 percent). Regarding their goal orientations, the majority of students agreed or strongly agreed (G13, altogether 84.5 percent) that they preferred course material to be interesting even if it is difficult to learn.

Perceived Classroom Assessment Environment

Principal axis factoring with oblimin rotation was performed on the 24 items on students' perceived classroom assessment environment. Oblimin rotation was used to enhance the interpretability of the factor solutions because this measure was basically measuring one overriding construct, perceived classroom assessment environment, and its dimensions should be correlated theoretically. Before the analyses were performed, all the missing values were replaced by the medians[6] of the corresponding items to make full use of the available data. The analyses revealed that the three-factor solution was the best solution in terms of fewer items with fewer low loadings or cross loadings and easier interpretation. The three factors explained 27.31 percent of the common variance. The loadings below .32 were deleted.

The 12 items loaded onto factor one focused on regarding assessment features and assessment feedback as a way to enhance students' learning and, therefore, this factor was named learning-oriented environment. The five items loaded on to factor two focused on regarding assessment as a way to examine the final products of students' learning and, therefore, this factor was named test-oriented environment. The two items loaded onto factor three focused on the positive side of teachers' evaluation and, and therefore, this factor was named praise-oriented environment. Four items (A5, A6, A12, A19) did not load onto any factor, and item 23 had cross-loadings, so they were not included in the creation of each factor scale. The clustered responses and/or the heterogeneity of the items might have contributed to such low loadings or cross loadings.

To understand the tendency of students' perceptions on each dimension of the classroom assessment environment as well as the relationships among the dimensions, descriptive statistics were conducted on the three dimensions (see Table 15.1). It was found that the three dimensions were basically orthogonal. Students in general thought their classroom assessment environment was more learning-oriented (mean = 3.30) and praise-oriented (mean = 3.16) than test-oriented (mean = 2.87).

Goal Orientations

For this part of the questionnaire, students' responses were subjected to both principal component analyses (PCA) with varimax rotation and principal axis factoring (PAF) analyses with oblimin rotation for comparability to the analyses conducted by other researchers (Elliot & Church, 1997; Middleton & Midgley, 1997). For both types of analyses, the four-factor solution produced a simple structure compared with the two-factor or three-factor solution. Under PCA, only one item (G15) had cross loadings and the four factors explained 54.04 percent of the total variance. Under PAF, only one item (G13) had low loadings on all the factors, and the four factors explained 38.47 percent of the common variance.

Items intended to measure performance approach goals (G2, G5, G8, G11, G14) were all loaded onto factor one. Items intended to measure performance avoidance goals (G3, G6, G9, G12) were loaded mainly onto factor two (except G15). G15 was specifically designed for this EFL context, but this result showed that it did not match the goal orientation theory. Items intended to measure mastery goals were separated into two groups. An examination of these items indicated that what distinguished the two groups seemed to be whether the goals of learning English were specifically concerned with grasping the materials in this College English course (G1, G10, G13), or for a purpose not restricted to this course (G4, G7). Under PCA, G13 was mainly loaded with G1 and G10, confirming the above assumption. However, under PAF, G13 did not load onto any

Table 15.1 Descriptive Statistics, Reliabilities, and Zero-Order Correlations for Perceived Classroom Assessment Environment Factors

Factor	No. of Variables	Scale Mean	Scale SD	Item Mean	Reliability	Correlation		
						F1	F2	F3
F1	12	39.67	6.09	3.30	.82			
F2	5	21.00	3.12	2.87	.65	−.048		
F3	2	6.31	1.77	3.16	.57	.230**	.089*	

$n = 497$. F1, Learning-oriented environment; F2, Test-oriented environment; F3, Praise-oriented environment.
* $p<.05$ (2-tailed), ** $p<.01$ (2-tailed).

Table 15.2 Descriptive Statistics, Reliabilities, and Zero-Order Correlations for Goal Orientations

Factor	No. of	Scale	Scale	Item	Reliability	Correlations			
	Variable	Mean	SD	Mean		F1	F2	F3	F4
F1	5	16.40	3.53	3.28	.75				
F2	4	11.95	3.08	2.99	.69	.17*			
F3	2	7.10	1.64	3.55	.60	.21*	−.18*		
F4	2	7.67	1.45	3.84	.52	.31*	.12*	.22*	

$n = 497$. F1, Performance approach goals; F2, Performance avoidance goals; F3, Mastery external goals; F4, Mastery in-class goals. *$p<.01$ (2-tailed).

factor, indicating that it was not quite tapping the same factor as G1 and G10. Descriptive statistics of G13 showed that 84.5 percent of the respondents agreed or strongly agreed with this statement. Such clustered responses probably explained the fact that it did not load well with G1 and G10 under PAF. Therefore, factor three, with G4 and G7 mainly loaded onto this factor, was named mastery external goals; factor four, with G10 and G1 mainly loaded onto this factor, was named mastery in-class goals.

To understand the general tendency of students' adoption of each type of goal orientations and the relationships among different types of goal orientations, descriptive statistics were conducted on the four types of goal orientations (see Table 15.2). It can be seen that students' goal orientations were highest on mastery in-class goals (mean = 3.84), followed by mastery external goals (mean = 3.55) and performance approach goals (mean = 3.28).[7] Their performance avoidance goals were the lowest (mean = 2.99). The four types of goal orientations were not highly correlated.

Relationships between Perceived Classroom Assessment Environment and Goal Orientations

Four multiple regression analyses were performed with each of the four types of goal orientations as dependent variables and the three factors from classroom assessment environment and class membership as independent variables. Table 15.3 presents the standardized beta coefficients for the four regression analyses when the sample was considered as a whole.

In terms of overall contribution, perceived classroom assessment environment was more highly associated with performance avoidance goals and mastery external goals than with performance approach goals and mastery in-class goals. In terms of the contributions of individual independent variables, learning-oriented environment moderately and positively predicted mastery in-class goals (standardized beta = .25), slightly predicted mastery external goals (standardized beta = .16) and performance approach goals (standardized beta = .11), but did not predict performance avoidance goals. Test-oriented environment strongly and positively predicted performance avoidance goals (standardized beta = .42), negatively predicted mastery external goals (standardized beta = −.22), but did not predict performance approach goals or mastery in-class goals. The least predictive independent variable was praise-oriented environment. It only slightly predicted performance approach goals (standardized beta = .15), but did not predict any other types of goal orientations. Regarding class

Table 15.3 Standardized Beta Coefficients for Regression Equations with Goal Orientations as Dependent Variables

	Performance Approach Goals	Performance Avoidance Goals	Mastery External Goals	Mastery In-class Goals
Learning-oriented	.11*		.16***	.25***
Test-oriented		.42***	−.22***	
Praise-oriented	.15**			
Class Three			.17**	
R	.22*	.44***	.35***	.26**
R²	.05*	.20***	.13***	.07**

*p<.05, **p<.01, ***p<.001.

differences, only Class Three significantly predicted students' mastery external goals (standardized beta = .17).

Discussion

This study investigated the relationship between Chinese EFL students' perceptions of classroom assessment environment and their goal orientations in the College English course. In general, students in this sample perceived mainly three types of classroom assessment environments—learning-oriented, test-oriented, and praise-oriented. They also revealed four types of goal orientations—performance approach goals, performance avoidance goals, mastery external goals, and mastery in-class goals. Multiple regression analyses indicated that both learning-oriented environment and test-oriented environment were predictive in influencing students' goal orientations, but the praise-oriented dimension was not predictive. Situated in this Chinese EFL context, some of the results of this study corroborated the results from previous studies, while some other results seemed to stand out for this particular learning context.

With regard to the perceived classroom assessment environment, the learning-oriented and test-oriented dimensions from this study matched the mastery-goal-enhancing and performance-goal-enhancing dimensions emerging from previous studies when the two-construct goal orientation framework was used to describe students' perceptions of classroom or school level practices (e.g., Ames & Archer, 1988; Anderman & Midgley, 1997; Roeser, Midgley, & Urdan, 1996). In those studies, original goal orientation theory was applied to describe classroom environment, and two dimensions of classroom environment emerged: a mastery-goal-enhancing dimension that emphasized improvement, progress, learning, taking challenges, and criterion-referenced evaluation; and a performance-goal-enhancing dimension that emphasized normatively high ability, social comparison, and high grades (Ames & Archer, 1988). In this study, when the emphasis was laid on students' perceptions of teachers' classroom assessment practices only, two similar dimensions also emerged. First, the learning-oriented dimension focused on classroom assessments that have personal relevance and meaningfulness to students and serve as a means for students to grow. They were conducted in a variety of ways and followed by timely feedback. This dimension emphasized classroom assessment for student learning. Therefore, this dimension was similar to the mastery-goal-enhancing dimension. Second, the test-oriented dimension of classroom assessment environment focused on task difficulty, grading harshness, and evaluation focus. This dimension emphasized the importance of tests and students' performances on the tests. Therefore, this dimension was similar to the performance-goal-enhancing dimension.

What is unexpected is the praise-oriented dimension. Praise was previously considered to be performance-goal-enhancing (Ames, 1992; Butler, 1987). However, in this study, this dimension was not correlated with the test-oriented dimension (see Table 15.1). Instead, this dimension was weakly correlated with the learning-oriented dimension. Studies on feedback offer some explanation for such results (Ryan, Connell, & Deci, 1985; Tunstall & Gipps, 1996). The fact that the learning-oriented dimension and the praise-oriented dimension were correlated was probably because both dimensions were related to assessment feedback. However, this correlation was weak, probably because the two dimensions were of a different nature. According to Tunstall and Gipps' typology, the learning-oriented dimension involved feedback which was informational in nature, while the praise-oriented dimension involved feedback of a positive evaluative nature.

In this EFL learning context, students' responses to the first part of the questionnaire revealed that their perceived classroom assessment environment was more learning-oriented (mean = 3.30) and praise-oriented (mean = 3.16) than test-oriented (mean = 2.87). Such results contradict most people's assumptions about the learning context in China. China is known for its evaluation-driven educational system and examination-oriented learning context (Qi, 2004; Wang, 1996). However, in this study, Chinese EFL learners did not feel their classroom assessment environment was primarily test-oriented. Instead, they felt their classroom assessment environment was both learning enhancing and evaluative in a positive way. One possible explanation for such results is that, when the study was conducted, students were near the end of their first year of their College English course and were still 1 year away from the external standardized test, the College English Test. In an interview study investigating ESL/EFL teachers' classroom assessment practices at the tertiary level (Cheng & Wang, 2007), the researchers found that Chinese EFL teachers' instruction and assessment practices were not very much influenced by external standardized testing when the test was still far away, but were greatly influenced when the test was approaching. Since teachers' assessment practices were the major sources for creating the classroom assessment environment, how teachers' assessment practices were influenced by external standardized testing would indirectly influence students' perceived classroom assessment environment.

With regard to goal orientations, the results from this study partially supported the three-construct framework of goal orientation theory. The debate about the number of constructs in goal orientation theory was centered on whether the performance approach–avoidance distinction was influential. Previous discussion on this issue was based on the correlation between performance approach goals and performance avoidance goals (Elliot & Church, 1997; Middleton & Midgley, 1997). In the present study, this correlation was .17 ($p<.01$) (see Table 15.2), which showed that performance approach goals were distinct from performance avoidance goals. In this sense, the results from this study supported the three-construct framework of goal orientation theory.

However, this study did not fully support either the three-construct or the two-construct framework regarding the mastery goals scale. Mastery goals were a very consistent scale in previous studies (Elliot & Church, 1997; Middleton & Midgley, 1997;

for a review, see Midgley et al., 1998). However, in this study, the mastery goals scale was split into two groups: mastery external goals and mastery in-class goals with a low correlation ($r = .22$, $p<.01$). The fact that they were distinct from each other may indicate a discrepancy between what students were learning in this course and what they were interested in. The traditional integrative versus instrumental orientations for learning a second/foreign language (Gardner & Lambert, 1972) could offer some explanation. An integrative orientation emphasizes the interest in the language and "the notion of identification with the community," while an instrumental orientation emphasizes "practical reasons without implying any interest in getting closer socially with the language community" (Masgoret & Gardner, 2003, p. 129). In this study, mastery external goals were more like integrative orientation in the sense that both emphasize personal interest in the English language and culture. Mastery in-class goals were more like instrumental orientation in the sense that students work hard to grasp the content of this course mainly for some practical reason such as gaining good scores or passing the CET, rather than out of personal interest.

In this EFL learning context, students' goal orientations were highest on mastery in-class goals, followed by mastery external goals and performance approach goals. Their performance avoidance goals were the lowest (see Table 15.2). Such results are inconsistent with Salili, Chiu and Lai's (2001) study in which Chinese students' goal orientations were examined in Hong Kong. In their study, the researchers found that both Hong Kong Chinese and Canadian Chinese students had higher performance goals than mastery goals. The results from this study are just the opposite. One possible explanation probably lies in the characteristics of the participants. In Salili et al.'s study, the participants were Grade 12 or 13 students who were going to enter universities. Therefore, perhaps students from all three groups (Hong Kong Chinese, Canadian Chinese, and European Chinese) had higher performance goals than mastery goals, due to the strong competition involved in entering a university. However, in the present study, the participants were near the end of their first year in their university study, and the national standardized testing was still 1 year away. Therefore, the students were not under very much pressure, and they valued mastery goals more than performance goals in this College English course.

Regarding the relationships between students' perceptions of their classroom assessment environment and their goal orientations, the patterns of the results were somewhat expected in light of the previous literature.

The patterns regarding the learning-oriented dimension were similar to those of the mastery-goal-enhancing dimension from previous studies (Church et al., 2001; Maslovaty & Kuzi, 2002; Roeser et al., 1996), in the sense that both had a positive association with mastery goals. However, while this mastery-goal-enhancing dimension had little relationship with performance goals in previous studies, this learning-oriented dimension had a positive relationship with performance approach goals. This may indicate that this learning-oriented dimension probably contained some cues that promoted performance approach goals in this context.

The patterns regarding the test-oriented dimension were similar to those of Church et al.'s (2001) study, but had some discrepancies with the results of studies that were based on the two-construct framework of goal orientations (Maslovaty & Kuzi, 2002; Roeser et al., 1996). In these studies, the researchers found that the perceived performance-goal-enhancing dimension of the classroom/school environment was only positively related with performance goals. In the present study, the test-oriented dimension positively predicted only performance avoidance goals and negatively predicted mastery external goals. Such discrepancies probably resulted from the different ways of categorizing goal orientations. When goal orientations were examined in a more detailed way, as in the present study, the significant influence on individual goal orientations could be seen.

Differing from the results of Butler's (1987) study in which praise was found to influence performance goals, the patterns of the praise-oriented dimension in this study showed that this dimension was positively associated with performance approach goals only. This might be further evidence showing the distinction between the two types of performance goals. Furthermore, this result should be reasonable, for as a kind of positive evaluative feedback (Tunstall & Gipps, 1996), praise should encourage the notion of competing against each other and trying to outperform others.

Only Class Three significantly predicted students' mastery external goals. Such a result probably showed that the classroom assessment environment was more learning-oriented in this class. However, further data are needed to prove such a claim.

For university-level students, a number of studies have found positive associations between mastery goals, adaptive learning behaviors, and learning outcomes as well as negative associations between performance avoidance goals, maladaptive learning behaviors, and learning outcomes (e.g., Elliot & Church, 1997; Harackiewicz, Barron, & Elliot, 1998). In addition, as classroom situations often engender some competition and social comparison, students often adopt both mastery goals and performance-approach goals, especially at the university level (Harackiewicz et al., 1998; Midgley et al., 2001). Consequently, the results from the present study may imply that in classroom teaching, teachers should try to create a learning-oriented classroom assessment environment by focusing more on the process of learning and helping students see the relevance and meaningfulness of classroom assessment to their learning. When praise is used, it should be connected with learning, rather than with a good score only. Further studies should be conducted to quantify and qualify these elements so as to offer more applicable suggestions to classroom teachers.

Conclusion

This study investigated Chinese EFL learners' perceptions of their classroom assessment environment, their goal orientations, and the relationships between the two through a questionnaire survey. This study is significant in the following two aspects. First, this study applied goal orientation theory from educational psychology to the examination of L2 motivation in a Chinese EFL learning context. By doing this, it not only tested the generalizability of goal orientation theory in a different subject area and a different cultural context from previous studies, but also discovered a link between goal orientation theory and L2 motivational orientations. The research results not only supported the three-construct framework of goal orientation theory in the sense that performance approach goals were distinct from performance avoidance goals, but also evidenced the value of traditional L2 motivation theory. Second, this study linked classroom assessment with student motivation and contributed to an understanding of how the classroom assessment environment might influence students' goal orientations in this EFL learning context in China. The study results may stimulate EFL teachers at the tertiary level in China and similar EFL contexts to reflect on their classroom assessment practices and to think of ways to enhance the optimal goals for their students so as to enhance student learning.

However, this study is limited in the following ways. First, this study only examined one linear relationship among the complex and multi-level relationships between classroom assessment, student motivation, and student learning. Because of the constraints of our research design, we focused only on students' perceptions, while data on teachers' actual classroom assessment practices and students' achievement scores were not collected. Other variables that may also influence students' adoption of goal orientations, such as variables in the home (Gonzalez, Doan Holbein, & Quilter, 2002) and self-attributed motives and competence expectancies (Elliot & Church, 1997), were not taken into consideration in this study. Therefore, the pedagogical implications of this study are greatly limited. Future research should be expanded to include teachers' actual classroom assessment practices, students' learning variables, and students' learning outcomes so as to bring about a more comprehensive understanding of the relationship between classroom assessment, student motivation, and student learning. Second, the instrument used in this study is new in the sense that the questionnaire items were adapted and translated, and some items were designed by the authors. Such changes made to the original questionnaire in terms of rephrasing and translation restricts the interpretation of the present study results. Furthermore, the convenience sample of students from one university in this study limits the generalizability of the results. Therefore, future research should use stratified random sampling to ensure proportional representation of the population subgroups in the sample.

Notes

1. Different researchers have used different terms to label these two constructs: a task/learning/ mastery goal, and an ability/ego/performance goal (Ames, 1992; Dweck, 1986; Maehr & Meyer, 1997). In this study, the terms mastery goals and performance goals are used, as we feel they best fit the Chinese EFL context.
2. Evaluation focus is defined as "the degree to which students perceive that the professor emphasizes the importance of grades and performance evaluation in the course" (Church et al., 2001, p. 44).
3. Grading harshness is defined as "the extent to which students view the grading structure as so difficult that it minimizes the likelihood of successful performance" (Church et al., 2001, p. 44).
4. Evaluation type is defined as "either criterion-referenced or norm-referenced evaluation" (Church et al., 2001, p. 44).
5. We did not use the same university for the pilot and main study due to the SARS crisis in China during the time of the research. However, both universities are medium-sized comprehensive universities, with around 2000 first-year undergraduate students enrolled in the College English course.
6. Similar results were obtained when the missing values were replaced by the means of the corresponding items. The same processes were conducted with the second part of the questionnaire.
7. Paired sample *t*-tests among the four types of goal orientations indicated that the mean differences among the four goal orientations were significant at the $p<.001$ level (please refer to Table 15.2).

References

Ames, C. (1992). Classrooms: Goals, structures, and student motivation. *Journal of Educational Psychology*, 84(3), 261–271.

Ames, C. & Archer, J. (1988). Achievement goals in the classroom: Students' learning strategies and motivation processes. *Journal of Educational Psychology*, 80(3), 260–267.

Anderman, E. M. & Midgley, C. (1997). Changes in achievement goal orientations, perceived academic competence, and grades across the transition to middle-level schools. *Contemporary Educational Psychology*, 22(3), 269–298.

Archer, J. & Scevak, J. J. (1998). Enhancing students' motivation to learn: Achievement goals in university classrooms. *Educational Psychology*, 18(2), 205–223.

Bandura, A. (1997). *Self-efficacy: The exercise of control*. New York: Freeman.

Belmechri, F. & Hummel, K. (1998). Orientations and motivation in the acquisition of English as a second language among high school students in Quebec City. *Language Learning*, 48(2), 219–244.

Black, P. & Wiliam, D. (1998). Inside the black box: Raising standards through classroom assessment. *Phi Delta Kappan*, 80(2), 139–148.

Brookhart, S. M. (1997). A theoretical framework for the role of classroom assessment in motivating student effort and achievement. *Applied Measurement in Education*, 10(2), 161–180.

Brookhart, S. M. & DeVoge, J. G. (1999). Testing a theory about the role of classroom assessment in student motivation and achievement. *Applied Measurement in Education*, 12(3), 409–425.

Brookhart, S. M. & DeVoge, J. G. (2000). *Classroom assessment, student motivation, and achievement in elementary and middle school*. Paper presented at the Annual Meeting of the American Educational Research Association, New Orleans, LA.

Butler, R. (1987). Task-involving and ego-involving properties of evaluation: Effects of different feedback conditions on motivational perceptions, interest, and performance. *Journal of Educational Psychology*, 79(4), 474–482.

Cheng, L., Rogers, T. & Wang, X. (2008). Assessment purposes and procedures in ESL/EFL classrooms. *Assessment and Evaluation in Higher Education*, 33(1), 9–32.

Cheng, L. & Wang, X. (2007). Grading, feedback, and reporting in ESL/EFL classrooms. *Language Assessment Quarterly*, 4(1), 85–107. Special Issue: International Perspectives on Classroom Assessment.

Church, M. A., Elliot, A. J. & Gable, S. L. (2001). Perceptions of classroom environment, achievement goals, and achievement outcomes. *Journal of Educational Psychology*, 93(1), 43–54.

Crooks, T. J. (1988). The impact of classroom evaluation practices on students. *Review of Educational Research*, 58(4), 438–481.

Dornyei, Z. (2003). Attitudes, orientations, and motivations in language learning: Advances in theory, research, and applications. *Language Learning*, 53(Suppl. 1), 3–32.

Dweck, C. S. (1986). Motivational processes affecting learning. *American Psychologist*, 41(10), 1040–1048.

Elliot, A. J. (1999). Approach and avoidance motivation and achievement goals. *Educational Psychologist*, 34(3), 169–189.

Elliot, A. J. & Church, M. (1997). A hierarchical model of approach and avoidance achievement motivation. *Journal of Personality and Social Psychology*, 72(1), 218–232.

Elliot, A. J. & Harackiewicz, J. M. (1996). Approach and avoidance achievement goals and intrinsic motivation: A mediational analysis. *Journal of Personality and Social Psychology*, 70(3), 461–475.

Gardner, R. C. & Lambert, W. E. (1972). *Attitudes and motivation in second language learning*. Rowley, MA: Newbury House Publishers.

Gardner, R. C. & MacIntyre, P. D. (1991). An instrumental motivation in language study: Who says it isn't effective? *Studies in Second Language Acquisition,* 13(1), 57–72.

Gonzalez, A. R., Doan Holbein, M. F. & Quilter, S. (2002). High school students' goal orientations and their relationship to perceived parenting styles. *Contemporary Educational Psychology,* 27(3), 450–470.

Harackiewicz, J. M., Barron, K. E. & Elliot, A. J. (1998). Rethinking achievement goals: When are they adaptive for college students and why? *Educational Psychologist,* 33(1), 1–21.

Lackey, J. R., Miller, R. B. & Flanigan, C. (1997). *The effects of written feedback on motivation and changes in written performance.* Paper presented at the Annual Meeting of the American Educational Research Association, Chicago, IL.

Maehr, M. L. & Meyer, H. A. (1997). Understanding motivation and schooling: Where we've been, where we are, and where we need to go. *Educational Psychology Review,* 9(4), 371–409.

Maehr, M. L. & Midgley, C. (1991). Enhancing student motivation: A school-wide approach. *Educational Psychologist,* 26(3&4), 399–427.

Masgoret, A. M. & Gardner, R. C. (2003). Attitudes, motivation, and second language learning: A meta-analysis of studies conducted by Gardner and associates. *Language Learning,* 53, supplementary issue 1, 167–210.

Maslovaty, N. & Kuzi, E. (2002). Promoting motivational goals through alternative or traditional assessment. *Studies in Educational Evaluation,* 28(3), 199–222.

Middleton, M. & Midgley, C. (1997). Avoiding the demonstration of lack of ability: An underexplored aspect of goal theory. *Journal of Educational Psychology,* 89(4), 710–718.

Midgley, C., Kaplan, A. & Middleton, M. (2001). Performance-approach goals: Good for what, for whom, under what circumstances, and at what cost? *Journal of Educational Psychology,* 93(1), 77–86.

Midgley, C., Kaplan, A., Middleton, M., Maehr, M. L., Urdan, T., Anderman, L. H. et al. (1998). The development and validation of scales assessing students' achievement goal orientations. *Contemporary Educational Psychology,* 23(2), 113–131.

Pintrich, P. R. (2000). An achievement goal theory perspective on issues in motivation terminology, theory, and research. *Contemporary Educational Psychology,* 25(1), 92–104.

Pintrich, P. R. & Schunk, D. H. (1996). *Motivation in education: Theory, research and applications.* Englewood Cliffs, NJ: Prentice Hall.

Qi, L. (2004). Has a high-stakes test produced the intended changes? In L. Cheng and Y. Watanabe, with A. Curtis (Eds.), *Washback in language testing: Research contexts and methods* (pp. 171–190). New York: Lawrence Erlbaum Associates, Inc.

Roeser, R. W., Midgley, C. & Urdan, T. (1996). Perceptions of the school psychological environment and early adolescents' psychological and behavioral functioning in school: The mediating role of goals and belonging. *Journal of Educational Psychology,* 88(3), 408–422.

Ryan, R. M., Connell, J. P. & Deci, E. L. (1985). A motivational analysis of self-determination and self-regulation in the classroom. In C. Ames & R. Ames (Eds.), *Research on motivation in education: Volume 2. The classroom milieu* (pp. 13–51). Orlando, FL: Academic.

Salili, F., Chiu, C. & Lai, S. (2001). The influence of culture and context on students' motivational orientation and performance. In F. Salili, C. Chiu & Y. Hong (Eds.), *Student motivation: The culture and context of learning* (pp. 221–247). New York: Kluwer Academic/Plenum Publishers.

Shohamy, E. (1998). Inside the "black box" of classroom language tests. *Studia Anglica Posnaniensia,* 33, 343–352.

Stiggins, R. J. (2002). Assessment crisis: The absence of assessment for learning. *Phi Delta Kappan,* 83(10), 758–765.

Stiggins, R. J. & Conklin, N. F. (1992). *In teachers' hands: Investigating the practices of classroom assessment.* Albany, NY: SUNY Press.

Tabachnick, B. G. & Fidell, L. S. (1996). *Using multivariate statistics* (3rd ed.). Boston: Allyn & Bacon.

Tunstall, P. & Gipps, C. (1996). Teacher feedback to young children in formative assessment: A typology. *British Educational Research Journal, 22*(4), 389–404.

Wang, G. (1996). Profiles of educational assessment systems world-wide: Educational assessment in China. *Assessment in Education: Principles, Policy & Practice, 3*(1), 75–88.

Wang, X. (2004). *Chinese EFL students' perceptions of classroom assessment environment and their goal orientations in the College English course.* Unpublished master's thesis, Queen's University, Kingston, Ontario, Canada.

Weiner, B. (1986). *An attributional theory of motivation and emotion.* New York: Springer-Verlag.

16 Should Proofreading Go?

Examining the Selection Function and Washback of the Proofreading Sub-test in the National Matriculation English Test[1]

Luxia Qi, Guangdong University of Foreign Studies

This chapter reports on an empirical study of the functions of the proofreading sub-test of the National Matriculation English Test (NMET) in the People's Republic of China. The study was motivated by an urgent need for empirical studies to inform decisions about test reform. In addition, it was hoped that the study would provide further evidence that there is a tension between the two goals of the NMET, i.e. to accurately select secondary school graduates for the limited places at universities and colleges in China, and to direct English teaching and learning in the way intended by the test constructors and policy-makers. To provide background information on the study, this chapter begins with a description of current test reforms in China and the functions of the NMET. The research focus and purpose, methodology, and results of the study are then discussed, followed by conclusions and implications for policy of further reforms of the NMET in China.

Background to the Study

A new round of reforms of the National Matriculation English Test (NMET) in China is underway. The NMET, the National University Entrance Examination on the subject of English (see Chapter 3), brings about intense washback on school teaching and learning. This round of reforms was triggered by a top-down change in test paper development policy proposed by the Ministry of Education in 2004. It was decided that the NMET test paper, which had been developed by the National Education Examinations Authority (NEEA) annually for the whole country, should be developed locally in seven provinces and four municipalities[2] following strictly the NMET testing syllabus. The NEEA should continue to develop the unified paper for use in the rest of the country (see Chapter 3; Mo, 2004). From then to 2008, however, some changes have been made to the composition of the locally developed NMET papers and the Ministry of Education has tacitly consented to the changes. Some provinces have removed the listening sub-test, others have revised the writing test, and still others have replaced the proofreading sub-test with a reading-and-form-filling item.

Good as the opportunity is for decentralized local reforms of the test which might reflect regional difference in a huge country like China, it is worrying that most of these changes appear to have been made in haste and it is doubtful that they are based on validation studies or other relevant research of the NMET. Few reports of such studies are seen in the literature and rationale for the changes is rarely made public in China. What impact these changes will have on the function of the NMET as a selection tool, on the candidates, and on the relevant curricula is unknown and unpredictable. What is almost certain, however, is that more provinces will jump on the bandwagon and make changes to the NMET developed locally in their own provinces. It appears to be urgent and desirable to carry out empirical studies on the NMET as a whole and on the role of its components in particular to inform decisions about further reforms, which will have tremendous impact on its test-takers and other stakeholders in China.

Focus and Purpose of the Study

The present study aims at an understanding of the contributions made by the proofreading sub-test to the NMET as a selection tool and as a washback agent. From the day of its inception, the NMET was intended to serve dual purposes: to select secondary school graduates for universities and colleges in China, and to induce positive washback on English language teaching in secondary schools (Gui, Li & Li, 1988). It was found, however, that the tension between the two purposes of the same test had prevented much of the intended positive washback effect from actually occurring (Qi, 2005). Such tension corresponds to the tension between validity and reliability discussed by testing specialists (Heaton, 1988; Li, 1997). Thus, it was hoped that the results of this study would not only inform decisions on reforming the test content and format, but also provide fresh evidence for the argument that it is extremely difficult, if not impossible, to make a high-stakes test serve these two purposes well.

The proofreading sub-test was chosen as the focus of the study because it was the most controversial sub-test in the NMET when the present study was initiated in 2005. One province that was given the right to produce its own NMET paper had removed the proofreading and more were considering following suit, based on the assumptions about its negative washback (Chen Hong, personal communication, February 2006).

The proofreading sub-test provides a short text of about 10 lines, with some lines being correct and the other lines containing errors, of which there are three types. A Type One Error is an incomplete sentence where one word needs to be added to make it complete. A Type Two Error is a sentence with an extra word, which makes it incorrect: the word should therefore be deleted. A Type Three Error is a sentence with a grammatically incorrect word, which needs to be changed (for an example of this sub-test, see Cheng & Qi, 2006, p. 68). Marking of the proofreading is to a great extent objective. One mark is awarded to a right correction of the line containing an error. Test-takers are to put a tick beside a correct line. Corrections made to an originally correct line are not to be awarded any marks. This objective marking system contributes to the reliability of the sub-test and hence enhances the test's selection function. The other indicator of a good selection function is believed to be the discrimination power of the test.

Discrimination Power as an Indicator of Good Selection

The discrimination power of the test has been regarded as an important index of the selection function of the NMET by its constructors. It is expected that the test results will not only distinguish those candidates who should be offered a place at universities from those who should not, but also that the results will make it possible to place the most promising youngsters at the most prestigious universities in China (Cheng & Qi, 2006).

The use of the discrimination power as an indicator of a test's selection function is consistent with the views on the quality of items and tests in the language testing literature (Alderson, Clapham & Wall, 1995; Henning, 1987; Hughes, 1989). Commonly used methods to measure discriminability are statistical calculations to arrive at discrimination indexes of individual items (Baker, 1989; Alderson, et al., 1995). In the present study, the discrimination power of the proofreading sub-test was examined using the discrimination indexes calculated by the NEEA, which has run statistical analyses of the test results every year since 1992. In addition, the teacher and student participants have also been invited to make judgments about the discriminability of the proofreading sub-test based on their experience of teaching/drilling with the sub-test, because it is important to know whether teachers and students are aware of the discriminating function of this sub-test and whether they think it performs this function well.

The author was aware, however, that discrimination index alone is far from being sufficient for our understanding of the selection function of a test or a sub-test. For a test to select well, the first and foremost prerequisite is its validity (Bachman & Palmer, 1996). Unfortunately, because of time constraints, no systematic investigation was conducted into the validity of the proofreading sub-test. So for the present study the selection function of the sub-test is examined only from the perspective of its discrimination power.

Washback as an Indicator of Test Quality

Washback, that is, the influence of tests or testing on teaching and learning (Alderson & Wall, 1993) has been stressed in recent years. According to Bachman and Palmer (1996), washback or impact is one of the six qualities that should be used to evaluate a language test, and it is viewed as a component of validity by other researchers (Li, 1997; Messick, 1996; Morrow, 1986).

One way to address the washback issue in empirical studies is to specify washback quality, that is, positive versus negative washback. Positive washback was demonstrated when the tests motivated students to work harder (Hughes, 1989), drew "attention to areas that had not been explicitly taught previously" (Shohamy, 1993, p. 15), caused expansion in teaching content and materials (Li, 1990), and made the teachers cover the new textbooks recommended by policy-makers (Wall & Alderson, 1993, p. 66). Negative washback effects include the facts and observations that the relevant test, rather than the curriculum, dictated what skills and knowledge were taught (Qi, 2004; Wall & Alderson, 1993), that textbooks became clones of the test (Shohamy, 1993), that tests discouraged students from putting genuine efforts into their learning (Paris, Lawton, Turner & Roth, 1991), and that a test reduced teachers' abilities to teach in ways that are incompatible with standardized testing formats (Smith, 1991).

One point needs to be made regarding the concept of washback quality. The terms *positive* and *negative washback* strike a note of value judgments, but the underlying standards by which these judgments are made are intangible and no standards have been discussed explicitly by the researchers studying the quality of washback. That certain standards have been adopted, however, can be inferred from the comments and criticisms of tests. Some researchers might be thinking of humanistic principles when they criticize tests for making students anxious (e.g., Paris et al., 1991). Others might hold the relevant curriculum as a desirable standard. When they see a curriculum narrow under the pressure of testing, they consider it to be evidence of negative washback effect (Bracey, 1987; Smith, 1991) and when teaching content expands as intended because of the test, it is seen as evidence of positive washback effect (Li, 1990). It is desirable, therefore, that further research into the quality of washback explains explicitly what is meant by positive or negative washback. In the present study, positive washback is operationally defined as "teaching and learning practices which are believed by the participants of the study to contribute to English learning."

Another concern about washback studies is that not many of the researchers have included the test-takers' and teachers' views about the quality of washback, with the study by Shohamy (1993) on the washback of an Arabic test as one of the few exceptions. Shohamy found that among the students who felt the test had affected them, 62 percent claimed that they were motivated to learn Arabic and learned more, and 38 percent reported that they were frustrated and anxious under the pressure of the test and their proficiency in Arabic did not improve. The logical conclusion is that a test affects different learners differently. It is also desirable to evaluate the washback quality of a test from the perspective of more than one stakeholder group. Including different perspectives might be conducive to more informed decision-making regarding test reform, especially if the decisions are made based on assumptions about negative washback of a test.

Research Questions

To achieve the aim of understanding how the proofreading sub-test contributes to the NMET's function as a selection tool and as a washback agent so as to inform decisions about its potential removal, the study addresses the following questions:

1   What is the function of the proofreading sub-test in the NMET as a selection tool?
2   What is the function of the proofreading sub-test in the NMET as a means of bringing about positive washback in school teaching and learning?

Answers to these questions will reveal whether the proofreading sub-test is perceived to be capable of helping the NMET as a whole to achieve its dual goals.

Methodology

Participants and Instruments

Data were collected through interviews and a questionnaire. Four NMET test constructors and two university professors were interviewed. These six interviewees were considered teaching experts because they are all experienced university professors specializing in English language teaching and research. Nine Senior III[3] teachers and nine students from nine middle schools in three different provinces were also interviewed. These provinces were chosen because a comparison of proofreading practices in their respective schools would make it possible to find out whether washback of the proofreading sub-test was thought to exist or not.

In order to demonstrate that washback exists, researchers normally collect baseline data and follow-up data to link the test in question to practices in schools. Although it was impossible to collect baseline data in the present study due to time constraints, the reforms that were happening at the time of data collection made it possible to compare washback in Province A, where the NMET paper no longer included the proofreading sub-test, with washback in Province B and C, where proofreading was still tested, so as to establish a relationship between the proofreading sub-test and the drilling of proofreading in schools, namely, washback brought about by the sub-test. The schools in each of the three provinces include one key school, one ordinary school and one poor school.[4]

Based on the interview results, a questionnaire, in Chinese, was developed with a teacher version and a student version (the differences are only in the wording). The questionnaire consists of 31 items, which were intended to obtain demographic information about the respondents; information concerning whether and how the proofreading sub-test was perceived to have affected teaching and learning; information about respondents' familiarity with the way in which the sub-test was usually set; and respondents' views on the washback quality of the proofreading sub-test and its discrimination power.[5]

The questionnaire was intended for teachers and students from five types of schools in the two provinces that still tested proofreading in the local NMET paper. The five types of schools have been classified by the local education departments according to the resources they enjoy, the quality of their teachers, and the academic level of their students, with Type One schools at the top and Type Five at the bottom. Type One schools are provincial key schools, Type Two are city key schools, and the rest are all ordinary schools. Type Five schools, however, are the poorest in terms of their resources and in all other aspects among the ordinary schools.

Data Collection and Analysis

Interview data were collected by individual interviews with an interview guide focusing on whether and how proofreading is practiced, and participants' views about the discrimination function and washback effect of the sub-test. All 24 interviews were audio-recorded and analyzed by the author. The analysis procedure was: (1) listening to each of the interview recordings for information which would help to answer the research questions and taking notes; (2) classifying the notes to find out the pattern of washback of the proofreading sub-test, participants' views concerning the washback quality, and its discrimination power.

The questionnaire data were collected from the two provinces that were still testing proofreading at the time of the present study. Student questionnaires were completed in the students' classrooms with the help of their teachers and the teacher questionnaires were mailed to them by the provincial English inspectors[6] and were completed and sent back to the inspectors by post by the teachers. The researcher then collected the copies from the inspectors.

After discarding the unusable ones (questionnaires with 50 percent or more of the items unanswered), 1,309 completed questionnaires, 398 from teachers and 911 from students, were used for data analysis with SPSS 12.0. First, the reliability of the questionnaire was tested using Cronbach's alpha and results show it is acceptable: $r = .79$ for the student questionnaire, $r = .76$ for the teacher questionnaire. Then factor analysis using principal component analysis with varimax rotation was conducted to find out whether these items tapped the variables indicated in the questionnaires. The responses from the teachers and students were treated as a group and analyzed together.

The results show that the items expressing frequency of proofreading drilling activities belong to two Factors: (1) the expected washback by test constructors and (2) the actual washback observed in school. The two activities expected by the test constructors, namely students proofreading their own and peer's writing, load high (.5 or above) on Factor 1 and four of the five items which stand for actual drilling activities (teacher lecturing on grammar rules relevant to the proofreading sub-test, on the error types tested, on test-taking strategies, and students drilling in stereotypical proofreading tests) load high on Factor 2. One item (Item 5.7) behaved unexpectedly. It was assumed to belong to actual drilling activities because it was based on one teacher's report in the interview, but it turned out to load high on Factor 1 which is taken to stand for the test constructors' expected activities. This will be discussed in the section on expected and actual washback.

The other 15 items of the questionnaires were analyzed separately from the above mentioned items because they were intended for different information. They are taken to stand for: (1) respondents' views on washback quality, (2) respondents' familiarity with error types, and (3) respondents' familiarity with test-taking strategies; and (4) respondents' views on the discrimination power of the proofreading sub-test. These variables correspond to a great extent with what was intended to be measured. But there is a discrepancy between the predicted categories and the resulting factors, i.e., some of the items which were intended to measure error types belong to the factor which was believed to be the category of test-taking strategies (Factor 3). This probably means the respondents took some of the error types as test-taking strategies. Thus it is not possible to separate their knowledge about the error types from test-taking strategies. As the reliability test and the factor analysis prove that the data can be regarded as reliable and valid, frequencies and means were extracted to be used in the discussion.

Results and Discussion

For the convenience of discussion, results are presented in relation to the two research questions. Participants and provinces are referred to as "Student A", "Teacher A", "Province A", and so on to ensure anonymity of the participants.

RQ1. What is the function of the proofreading sub-test in the NMET as a selection tool?

The proofreading sub-test is expected to contribute to the NMET's discrimination power so as to add to its function as a selection tool. The NMET constructors believe that the proofreading items test language use and discriminate better than the other items in the test, especially in ranking those candidates with high English proficiency. Proofreading is conceptualized as part of the writing construct as is described by one of the test constructors:

> We think the writing process is like this: after I've written down something, I'll read it through to see what I've missed and what mistakes I've made. We can always find something missing here and there. There are wrong uses of punctuation, words, spelling, and even incoherence, all kinds of problems. So, we know there must be moderation in writing. According to Krashen, there's a monitor. Proofreading is in fact monitoring after writing. Monitor is a type of language use ability. So we're testing this ability. (Constructor A)

In the NMET, writing is measured in the second paper which comprises the proofreading sub-test and a writing task (see Cheng & Qi, 2006 for details on the NMET papers). That task provides a hypothetical situation that simulates a real-life language-use context and asks the candidates to write a short text of about 100 words according to the content given in the input. According to Constructors A, B, and C, the writing task is more valid and authentic than the proofreading sub-test because it involves actual writing and simulates real-life writing occasions, though its rating tends to be more subjective and it probably does not make fine distinctions between the top level candidates and those whose English is above average. In comparison, the proofreading tends to be more reliable and discriminate better than the writing task because the rating is more objective, with one mark awarded for each right correction.

This observation of the discrimination power of the proofreading sub-test is confirmed by the routine statistical analyses carried out by the NEEA which show that the proofreading sub-test has functioned well in terms of its discrimination power. To take the NMET 2003 statistics for example, the proofreading section has a larger proportion of items which have achieved a higher discrimination index than items in other sections (see Cheng & Qi, 2006, p. 61).

Teachers and students also recognize the discrimination function of the proofreading sub-test based on their experience in drilling with it, despite the fact that they do not normally have access to the discrimination indexes of the NMET items. Three items in the questionnaire (Items 6.4, 6.7, and 6.9) were intended to measure respondents' beliefs about the discrimination power of the proofreading sub-test, and these three items all received mean ratings above 3 on a 5-point scale (3.79, 3.26, and 3.49, respectively). This means the majority of teachers and students tended to think that the proofreading sub-test is capable of distinguishing students with good English proficiency from those whose English levels are comparatively low. There seems to be consensus among the NMET constructors, teachers, and students that the proofreading sub-test has a strong discrimination power which in turn contributes to the NMET's selection function and this view has been supported by the relevant statistical analyses carried out by the NEEA.

RQ2. What is the function of the proofreading sub-test in the NMET as a means of bringing about positive washback in school teaching and learning?

In search of an answer to this question, we need to find out whether the proofreading sub-test produces washback, what this washback looks like if produced, and what is meant by positive washback by the test constructors, teachers, students, and teaching experts. This section is arranged according to these concerns.

Existence of Washback

The results show that the NMET proofreading sub-test does produce washback in Senior III English teaching and learning in secondary schools. Teachers teach how to do proofreading and students practice it because it is included in the NMET. In other words, the proofreading sub-test causes teachers and students to "do things they would not necessarily otherwise do" (Alderson & Wall, 1993, p. 117).

At the time the interview data were collected, Province A had replaced the proofreading sub-test with a reading-and-information transfer item. It was found that in the three schools in that province, proofreading drilling activities were stopped altogether. This was reported by the teacher and student interviewees and confirmed by an examination of the NMET preparation materials they were using. There were no proofreading items at all in those materials collected by the researcher during the interview trips there.

In the other two provinces, because the proofreading sub-test was still included in the NMET paper, proofreading was drilled in all the six schools where the interview data were collected. Also, responses to the item which asks about the average number of proofreading texts done by students since the beginning of the school year show that on average the students did two to three proofreading texts every week. Further, according to the teachers and students, they had drilled even more frequently in the previous years. To quote Teacher C:

> Proofreading is not practiced as frequently as it was last year because there is the rumor that it might be removed in the coming NMET test paper.

It is clear that the proofreading sub-test does induce washback, namely, drilling of proofreading, which is not otherwise a normal practice in Senior III teaching. When it is included in the NMET, proofreading is practiced. When it is removed from the test, it disappears from classroom teaching and learning. But what should be made clear here is that this does not mean that it is the proofreading format that produces the washback and another test format will not induce washback. The washback originates from the NMET itself, but different test formats will result in different classroom practices. The next concern is how it is practiced and whether it is practiced as expected by the NMET constructors.

Expected and Actual Washback

The expected washback of the proofreading sub-test is to make students correct their own or one another's errors in writing. As is mentioned previously, proofreading is regarded as a component of the writing process by the NMET constructors. So it was expected that students would do drafts and correct their own errors when practicing writing or help one another improve their writing scripts. To encourage such practices, the proofreading text in the NMET has been deliberately made to resemble middle school students' writings with respect to sentence structures and choices of words. The errors to be corrected in the proofreading task have been derived from the common errors made by Chinese learners (Test Constructors A, C, and D).[7] If students practice self-correction and peer-correction while practicing writing, the washback of the proofreading sub-test can be viewed as expected and positive. But unfortunately, the data of the present study show that English writing practice in Senior III fell short of this expectation (see Items 5.3 and 5.4 in Table 16.1).

The actual washback was proofreading drilling activities such as teachers discussing the error types tested, teaching students test-taking strategies, lecturing on the grammar points that are usually tested, and students doing mock proofreading sub-tests. These activities were found to be carried out in all six schools in Province B and C as was reported by the interviewees. Furthermore, it was found from the questionnaire results that drilling activities were frequent practices in other schools in these two provinces as well (see Items 5.1, 5.2, 5.5, and 5.6 in Table 16.1).

It is clear that the activities which were intended by the test constructors (Items 5.3 and 5.4) were practiced less frequently than the other activities which were more closely related to pure test preparation (Items 5.1, 5.2, 5.5, 5.6). All these items received ratings above the mid-point of 3, except Item 5.7, which was based on one teacher's interview data and which turned out to be non-representative of practices by other teachers and students. The intended positive washback did not seem to occur. Instead, teachers and students had their own ways of drilling proofreading in preparation for the NMET. To have a better understanding of the drilling, an elaboration of the error types and test-taking strategies is desirable.

The interview data reveal that the teachers and students were very familiar with the error types of the proofreading sub-test and had developed some strategies to deal with them. There is even a rhyme that has been written in Chinese to help students remember the error types and how the items were usually set. It reads to the effect that in the NMET proofreading sub-test usually one line is correct; one or two lines contain extra words that should be deleted; one or two lines are incomplete and need to have words inserted to make them correct, and six lines each contain a word that needs to be changed (一对六改三加减). Among the words that need to be changed, there are articles, nouns, adjectives, adverbs, etc. (逐句细读诊错点, 冠名形副代连介). According to the interview data, students are advised to use the error types and error distribution pattern as a checklist to check the lines one by one. After they have identified and corrected the errors they are sure of, they should regard all those lines they are not sure of as correct lines and put a tick beside each. The logic is that although there is usually only one correct line in the proofreading sub-test, the candidates will at least get one mark if they tick all the lines that they are not certain about, but they will probably get no marks at all if they make wrong corrections.

Teachers' lectures tend to include rules of errors related with nouns, verbs, adjectives, and so on and ways to correct them. For example, the students are told to first identify the nouns and verbs in a line and check if the noun is correct in terms of the singular or plural form and if the verb is in the right tense and mood. Armed with knowledge of the error types, rules of errors, and ways of correction, students practiced proofreading in a highly ritualistic way. This is further confirmed by the questionnaire data which show

Table 16.1 Frequency of Proofreading Drilling Activities, Teachers' and Students' Familiarity with Error Types and Test-taking Strategies and their Views on Washback Quality

Frequency with which Proofreading Drilling Activities were Carried Out				Teachers' and Students' Familiarity with Error Types and Distribution of the Proofreading Sub-test				Teachers' and Students' Views on Washback Quality			
Items	Cases	Mean	SD	Items	Cases	Mean	SD	Items	Cases	Mean	SD
5.6 Teacher discussing test-taking strategies	1,301	3.53	.82	6.10 One correct line	1,303	4.20	.89	6.1 Improves general English	1,303	3.40	.916
5.5 Teacher discussing error types tested	1,307	3.43	.85	6.11 An item on inter-sentence logical relationship	1,303	3.95	.80				
5.1 Teacher lecturing on grammar rules	1,306	3.34	.86	6.12 An item on verb use	1,303	4.15	.77	6.3 Improves reading	1,301	3.08	1.05
5.2 Students practise proofreading	1,304	3.21	.81	6.13 An item on noun use	1,299	3.89	.84	6.5 Improves writing	1,299	3.53	1.01
				6.14 An item on adjective use	1,301	3.62	.85				
5.7 Students keeping records of their own errors	1,308	2.61	1.19	6.15 An item on adverb use	1,301	3.58	.88	6.8 Improves grammar knowledge	1,299	3.61	.88
				6.16 Adding a word	1,301	4.00	.83				
5.3 Students proofreading their own work	1,306	2.30	1.01	6.17 Deleting a word	1,283	4.06	.79	6.20 Is harmful to English learning	1,268	2.70	1.12
				6.18 Using error types described in Items	1,300	3.68	.93				
5.4 Students proofreading peer work	1,299	1.86	.89	6.19 Ticking all the lines you're unsure of	1,299	3.93	.94				

For Items 5.1–5.7: 1, Never; 2, Occasionally; 3, Sometimes; 4, Often; 5, Very often.
For Items 6.1–6.20: 1, Strongly disagree; 2, Disagree; 3, Neutral; 4. Agree; 5, Strongly agree.

that most teachers and students are familiar with the error types and agree on the test-taking strategies (Table 16.1).

Apparently, the actual washback is far different from what was expected. Proofreading is practiced in isolation instead of being incorporated into the practice of writing. What is more, with the ritualistic practice, it does not at all resemble possible real-life proofreading of their own writing by Chinese learners of English. This, however, can be traced to the way proofreading is tested in the NMET. It seems that the NMET constructors are naïve to expect combined practice of writing and proofreading when the two are separate tasks in the NMET. This finding that teaching and learning activities tend to become clones of test items is consistent with the findings by other researchers (e.g., Shohamy, 1993). With an understanding of how proofreading was practiced in the schools, our next concern is how the participants view the washback quality of the proofreading sub-test.

Washback Quality

As it was defined earlier in this chapter, positive washback refers to teaching and learning activities that are considered to be conducive to English learning by the participants in the present study. With this criterion, the teachers, students, test constructors, and teaching experts were invited to comment on the proofreading drillings in schools in terms of whether they reflect positive washback.

Most teachers and students tended to think that the washback of the proofreading sub-test was positive in that practicing proofreading helped to improve students' general English proficiency, reading skills, writing skills, and grammar knowledge. These beliefs were confirmed by the questionnaire results (Table 16.1). It can be seen that the items representing the view that proofreading practice enhances different aspects of English learning, Items 6.1, 6.3, 6.5, and 6.8, all received ratings above 3, and the item which suggests that proofreading practice induces negative washback because it is harmful to expose learners to English with errors received a rating that is below 3 (Item 6.20). This means that these teachers and students as a group tended to view the washback brought about by the proofreading sub-test as beneficial to learning. This result is unexpected because the assumption was that teachers and students disapproved of this sub-test on the basis of its negative washback, and consequently some provinces removed the proofreading sub-test from the locally developed NMET paper.

In contrast to the teachers and students, the NMET constructors and teaching experts regarded the type of washback triggered by the proofreading sub-test as negative as was found in the interview data.[8] They were unanimous in their objection to the ritualistic drilling of the proofreading sub-test. To them, this type of practice, with the sole aim of boosting scores, contributes little, if anything, to English learning. To quote Test Constructor B:

> I think the sole purpose of this type of drilling is to raise scores. It has nothing to do with English learning. I don't think one's English can be improved by such drilling.

When asked to comment on the teachers' and learners' views about the positive washback of the proofreading sub-test in terms of its role in improving reading, writing, grammar knowledge, and general English proficiency, the test constructors and teaching experts did not seem to share any of the above assumptions on the proofreading. In their opinion, proofreading, which was unlike regular reading, made the readers focus on form but not on meaning, and thus could not be beneficial to the development of reading skills. Further, it might even reduce reading speed when over-practiced. As for writing, they thought proofreading was only one component of writing. To enhance the ability to proofread, it was best for learners to proofread their own or peers' work instead of drilling with texts filled with ritualistic and artificial errors. Concerning the view that such drilling improves learners' knowledge of grammar, the experts agreed that it was good to raise students' awareness of the structure of the language to some extent, but they also thought that too much practice of it, especially in the current way, would restrict creative learning. Students might become too worried about making mistakes to try and use what they had learned through listening and reading. As to whether proofreading enhances proficiency in general, the experts' answer was no. To quote one of them:

> Proofreading as it is used in the NMET is simply a test format. It has never been a learning activity. Other activities such as listening, reading, writing, discussion, students correcting their own writing, etc. are more efficient language learning activities. They can better improve one's English proficiency than the proofreading drills.

In summary, most teachers and students consider the actual washback brought about by the proofreading sub-test as positive, but the test constructors and teaching experts view it as negative and non-beneficial to English learning. Although they accept proofreading as a testing instrument, the test constructors do not think it is an appropriate learning activity. What they suggest is that proofreading be incorporated into writing practice and that learners correct their own errors when trying to improve drafts.

Conclusions and Implications for Policy

The main findings of the present study are that test constructors, teaching experts, and the majority of teacher and student participants agree that the NMET proofreading sub-test is efficient from a selection point of view, but opinions differ on its washback quality. Most teachers and learners in this study think favorably of the sub-test's washback effect while test constructors and teaching experts disapprove of it. The teachers and students are consistent in their attitudes towards the proofreading sub-test as they believe that it discriminates well and that drilling for it improves English learning. The test constructors, in contrast, face a dilemma. On one hand, they are aware of the strong discrimination power of the proofreading sub-test, but on the other hand, as they disapprove of the drilling carried out in schools to prepare for it, they now doubt about having the proofreading sub-test in the NMET. The two teaching experts both believe the washback effect brought about by the proofreading sub-test is harmful to teaching and learning.

Why do the participants agree on the selection function of the proofreading sub-test but differ concerning its washback effect? Unfortunately, no straightforward answer can be seen in the data collected because no questions were asked in the interviews and no items were included in the questionnaire to explore the reasons behind participants' views about whether the proofreading sub-test contributed to or harmed English learning. This is a limitation of this study.

However, it can be hypothesized that the difference is largely caused by different perspectives. The teachers and students might be more concerned about efficient preparation for the test. Since they have accumulated detailed knowledge about the proofreading sub-test, they might be confident about it and would not welcome any reform which might result in an unfamiliar new test task which in turn might cause problems in test preparation. The belief that proofreading drilling is conducive to English learning might have been the result of a superficial judgment based on the fact that proofreading activities do involve reading, some writing, and the use of grammar knowledge. In other words, many teachers and students might favor the proofreading sub-test out of inertia. On the other hand, the test constructors and teaching experts might think more of actual learning efficiency, rather than test preparation, when they examine the washback of the proofreading sub-test, as they are not under the pressure of taking the NMET like the students or helping students prepare for the NMET as the teachers are. The test constructors' and experts' knowledge of current beliefs about English learning is probably the basis upon which they evaluated the sub-test's washback effect. They may think that intense test preparation is undesirable and learning efforts and time should be invested in activities that will genuinely enhance learning.

Based on the finding that many teachers and students think favorably of the proofreading sub-test in terms of its discrimination power and washback effect, their opinions should be respected and the proofreading should be retained for the time being in order not to cause inconvenience or probably even panic in Senior III test preparation. However, minor changes need to be made so as to alter the ritualistic drilling in schools. For example, the pattern of error types and numbers can be changed. In one test, there can be one correct line and in another there might be two. Also, it is well acceptable by teachers and students that a proofreading sub-test tests two or three errors concerning the use of nouns or verbs because random errors, namely, errors which do not follow fixed rules, normally occur in real-life writing by English learners.

In the long run, however, I do think the proofreading sub-test should be removed on washback grounds. But before that, more research is needed to gain a better understanding of the individual NMET sub-tests and the NMET as a whole in terms of its selection function and washback effect in order to strike a balance so that the test will be able to successfully select qualified candidates for higher education and at the same time avoid triggering serious negative washback. After all, as is illustrated by the proofreading sub-test, it is extremely difficult, if not impossible, for a test to perform both functions well.

Notes

1. The study reported in this chapter was supported by the MOE Project of the Centre for Linguistics and Applied Linguistics of Guangdong University of Foreign Studies.
2. In 2005 and 2006, five more provinces were given the responsibility to develop their own NMET papers.
3. Senior III teachers, rather than teachers from other grades, were selected because they have to help students prepare for the NMET to be taken at the end of the school year and so they are

more concerned with the format and have a better knowledge of the philosophy of the test than teachers teaching at lower grades.
4. In China, schools fall into two main categories: key schools and ordinary schools. Key schools enjoy privileges in terms of a larger share of the educational budget, better-qualified teachers, and have permission from official education departments to enroll students before ordinary schools (Liu, 1993; Zhao & Campbell, 1995). Within the key school category, schools are further classified into provincial key schools, city key schools and district key schools which are supervised by the provincial, city, and district education departments respectively, with provincial key schools as the top level key schools and district key schools at the bottom. Among the ordinary schools some are better than others at the three levels mentioned above. Those which are ranked lowest among the ordinary schools are regarded to be poor schools by students and their parents.
5. Due to space constraints, only part of the information elicited by the questionnaire is used here. Interested readers may contact the author for a copy of the questionnaire.
6. English inspectors in China are staff members in the local education departments at various levels who are responsible for guiding and assisting teachers in teaching English, including preparation for the NMET. The provincial English inspectors are those who work in the education departments of their provinces.
7. The item writers are all English teachers. They draw on their students' errors when setting the proofreading items.
8. The teacher and student data were collected and analyzed first and the results of it, namely, how proofreading was practiced and their views on its washback were presented to the test constructors and teaching experts when they were interviewed.

References

Alderson, C., Clapham, C. & Wall, D. (1995). *Language test construction and evaluation.* Cambridge, UK: Cambridge University Press.

Alderson, J. C. & Wall, D. (1993). Does washback exist? *Applied Linguistics,* 14, 115–129.

Bachman, L. F. & Palmer, A. S. (1996). *Language testing in practice.* Oxford: Oxford University Press.

Baker, D. (1989). *Language Testing: A critical survey and practical guide.* London: Edward Arnold.

Bracey, G. W. (1987). Measurement-driven instruction: Catchy phrase, dangerous practice. *Phi Delta Kappan,* 68, 683–686.

Cheng, L. & Qi, L. (2006). Description and examination of the National Matriculation English Test in China. *Language Assessment Quarterly: An International Journal,* 3, 53–70.

Gui, S., Li, X. & Li, W. (1988). A reflection on experimenting with the National Matriculation English Test. In National Education Examinations Authority (Eds.), *Theory and practice of standardized test* (pp. 70–85). Guangzhou, China: Guangdong Higher Education Press.

Heaton, G. B. (1988). *Writing English language tests.* London: Longman.

Henning, G. (1987). *A Guide to language testing: Development, evaluation, research.* Rowley, MA: Newbury House.

Hughes, A. (1989). *Testing for language teachers.* Cambridge, UK: Cambridge University Press.

Li, X. (1990). How powerful can a language test be? The MET in China. *Journal of Multilingual and Multicultural Development,* 11, 393–404.

Li, X. (1997). *The science and art of language testing.* Changsha, China: Hunan Education Press.

Liu, Y. (Ed.). (1993). *Book of major educational events in China.* Hangzhou, China: Zhejiang Education Press.

Messick, S. (1996). Validity and washback in language testing. *Language Testing,* 13, 241–256.

Mo, Y. (2004). Guangdong sets its own university entrance examination papers this year. *Yangcheng Evening News* (February 20, p. 1). Guangzhou, China.

Morrow, K. (1986). The evaluation of tests of communicative performance. In M. Portal (Ed.), *Innovations in Language Testing* (pp. 1–13). London: NFER-Nelson.

Paris, S. G., Lawton, T., A. Turner, J. C. & Roth, J. L. (1991). A developmental perspective on standardized achievement testing. *Educational Researcher*, 20(5), 12–19.

Qi, L. (2004). Has a High-stakes Test Produced the Intended Changes? In L. Cheng, J. Watanabe & Curtis, A. (Eds.), *Washback in language testing: Research contexts and methods* (pp. 117–190). New York: Lawrence Erlbaum.

Qi, L. (2005) Stakeholders' conflicting aims undermine the washback function of a high-stakes test. *Language Testing*, 22, 142–173.

Shohamy, E. (1993). The power of test: The impact of language testing on teaching and learning. *NFLC Occasional Papers*, June.

Smith, M. L. (1991). Put to the test: the effects of external testing on teachers. *Educational Researcher*, 20(5), 8–11.

Wall, D. & Alderson, J. C. (1993). Examining washback: The Sri Lankan impact study. *Language Testing*, 10, 41–69.

Zhao, Y. & Campbell, K. (1995). English in China. *World Englishes*, 14, 377–390.

17 The Computerized Oral English Test of the National Matriculation English Test

Yongqiang Zeng, Guangdong University of Foreign Studies

This chapter introduces the Computerized Oral English test (COET;「英语计算机化口试」) of the National Matriculation English Test (NMET;「高考英语」) in Guangdong Province, The People's Republic of China and reports on the construct validation of the COET. Qualitative and quantitative analyses were employed for construct validation. The qualitative analyses are mainly based on experts' responses to a questionnaire on whether the COET sub-tests could test the oral communicative competence as intended, which is defined within Hedge's framework (2001). A total of 20 experienced English language teachers were asked to rate the questionnaire carefully and independently. According to the judgments of these experts, Part A in the COET could only elicit students' skills in pronunciation and intonation, while the other two parts could measure more competencies, such as linguistic competence, aspects of pragmatic competence and strategic competence, discourse competence, and fluency, which cover the five major competencies proposed by Hedge. In the quantitative analyses, 30 recorded performances were sampled from the population on the COET and were rated. Factor analysis was conducted, and three major factors were extracted: pronunciation and intonation, translating, and comprehension and oral production, which was consistent with the construct defined by the COET developers.

A Brief History of the NMET Oral Test

The National Matriculation English Test (NMET), originally known as the Matriculation English Test, was established in 1985 as one part of nationwide university entrance tests (see also Chapter 16). The first version of the NMET oral test was also developed in 1985 consisting of two sub-tests: pronunciation and reading-aloud, with an emphasis on the assessment of pronunciation and intonation. Though the oral test was designed only for students who intended to major in foreign languages in universities and colleges, it was a major step towards communicative language teaching in China. According to Luoma (2004), speaking is arguably the most important skill in learning a foreign language, yet it is widely recognized that speaking is a skill which is more difficult and painstaking to assess than any other skill in language testing. Consequently, language testers have made great efforts in developing and examining oral tests, trying to achieve both good validity and high reliability in their tests.

With the introduction of the communicative approach to language teaching in China, English teaching has undergone revolutionary changes, which clearly called for a reform of language examinations to accompany changes in language teaching. In 1995, a new version of the oral test was designed with more emphasis on the assessment of communicative competence. For example, the new form of the oral test used role-play as one of its test items, in which a test-taker and two examiners interacted to complete a given communicative task. The test-taker was first given 2 min to read Chinese prompts and prepare for the communicative task. To complete the task, the test-taker was required to ask Examiner A five questions to elicit certain information and then go to Examiner B to answer nine questions according to the information obtained from Examiner A. The role play lasted 4 min, and was based on face-to-face interaction for information exchange in communication (Li & Wang, 2000).

In terms of authenticity and validity, this form of oral test was believed to be better than the reading-aloud version developed in 1985. But disadvantages do exist, especially for large-scale tests like the NMET, and the limitations are quite apparent:

1   Examiners in different areas may not perceive the rating scale consistently while rating, because these examiners have different levels of English oral proficiency. So the fairness of the test can be called into question.
2   Parallel forms of the test are needed in each administration to ensure security. Equating these parallel forms is problematic.
3   Each test-taker has to be tested separately and individually in real time, so a great deal of time and money is spent on rater training, test administration, and developing and maintaining multiple parallel tests.
4   It can be very difficult to evaluate an oral interview quickly, objectively, and reliably. Thus, the examiners are working under great pressure all the time.

In short, the role play as a form of the oral test did not guarantee high reliability and applicability.

However, the development of new technologies has brought a new perspective to language teaching and testing, including some of the latest developments in oral testing, such as computer-based and computerized oral tests. As the administration of oral tests is traditionally a time-consuming and labor-intensive process, in large-scale testing programs, there appears to be a trend towards using technology-based methods of assessing oral proficiency. The Test of Spoken English (TSE), a component of the Test of English as a Foreign Language (TOEFL), is tape-mediated, i.e., the examinees are administered the test using a tape and a test booklet. However, the Computerized Oral Proficiency Instrument (COPI) developed by researchers at the Center for Applied Linguistics (CAL) in the USA employs computers to administer oral proficiency tests.

Due to the weaknesses of the role play in the NMET oral test, and in an attempt to develop a more reliable, valid and practical oral test, in 2004 the test designers in Guangdong province moved toward computer-based language testing. As part of this move, the Computerized Oral Test of the National Matriculation English Test has been in use since 2004 as a component of the National Matriculation English Test in Guangdong Province.

Introduction to the Computerized Oral English Test

The new Computerized Oral English Test (COET) in the NMET was designed for those who want to major in university foreign languages or related subjects, such as international trade and business. The test is administered in language labs, where the same test stimuli are given to each test-taker, whose responses are recorded for double-rating on a computer-based marking system. The COET claims authenticity in its task design, and high reliability in test administration and rating, with good validity for the oral test. The COET is administered once a year, and there have been over 400,000 test-takers sitting for the test since it was first used in 2004. From 2011 on, the annual population of the test-takers will increase to over 500,000.

The COET has three parts, each of which focuses on different domains of test-takers' speaking abilities. The first part utilizes imitation and reading aloud test techniques, which are intended to measure test-takers' pronunciation and intonation. The second part is a role play in which speakers' abilities to receive and comprehend information and to ask and answer questions are emphasized. The last part is an oral composition, where test-takers' comprehensive abilities in speaking are explored. The whole test lasts approximately 30 min. Detailed descriptions of each part are provided below.

Part A. Reading Aloud

This part requires test-takers to watch part of a movie or a television series with the subtitles on the screen. After watching the movie/TV series, test-takers are allowed 1 min to practice reading the subtitles, which are displayed on the screen. Then the movie/TV series is played again for test-takers to imitate. After that, the test-takers begin to imitate the speaker by reading the subtitles. The volume on the television screen is turned off, so the examiner can hear the candidate rather than the actors playing their parts and saying their lines. Test-takers' performance in this part of the COET is evaluated against two criteria: accuracy and fluency of pronunciation.

Part B. Role Play

This part requires test-takers to complete a communicative task by taking on a role while interacting with the computer, which is playing another role. For example, test-takers play the role of a student who is listening to a lecture. Test-takers ask questions about the lecture, and then answer questions from a "classmate" (a role played by the computer) who did not attend the lecture. In the administration of this part, test-takers are first required to listen for certain information, and then ask three pre-designed questions on the basis of the Chinese prompt. Twenty seconds are allowed for the preparation of each question. Immediately after asking each question, the computer, acting in a certain role in this communicative situation, offers the answer to the question. The test-takers are required to take down necessary information while listening to the answer. After asking three questions, the test-takers, acting in another role, need to answer three questions from the computer. Test-takers are given 10 seconds to prepare for their answer to each of the three questions. Test-takers' performance in this part is evaluated against two criteria: language and content, so that test-takers are required to offer necessary and appropriate information in clear and precise spoken English.

Part C. Oral Composition

This part requires test-takers to give a 2-min oral composition after watching a short silent video film. They are required to make up a story, give some comments, or describe what is going on in each scene based on what they have seen of the film. They are allowed 1 min to prepare their oral English composition before they begin to speak. Test-takers' performance in this part is evaluated against four criteria: content, language, coherence, and pronunciation, with more consideration and weight given to content and language, so that test-takers are required to offer in appropriate and well-organized English a coherent and relevant description of what they have seen of the film.

Construct Validation of the COET

According to its test designers, the NMET COET is intended to measure test-takers' ability to express their ideas in English, i.e., oral communicative competence. Two major pairs of issues frequently arise in testing, namely, validity versus reliability, and direct versus indirect methods of assessment. According to Wood (1993), if we focus more on direct methods in order to enhance validity, reliability may be threatened. On the other hand, if indirect methods are preferred for a high reliability, validity may be sacrificed to some extent. In the COET, reliability is strengthened by fair administration and rating. However, although fair administration and rating is a necessary condition, it is not a sufficient condition for validity (Bachman & Palmer, 1996). Validity, however, is of central concern to all testers (Alderson, Clapham & Wall, 1995). In order to address the issue of construct validity, we should first answer the question of what the underlying construct of the COET is, or what it is that the COET is designed to test.

The NMET, of which the COET is a sub-test, was designed in accordance with the New National Syllabus for Middle Schools (Ministry of Education of the People's Republic of China, 2002), which emphasizes the importance of communicative competence in English teaching and learning. In the current study, the question to be answered is therefore whether the COET measures students' oral communicative competence in English as a foreign language. This study, entitled *Computer-based Oral English Test (COET): Its Validation and Implementation,* was initiated in Guangdong province in 2005 and completed in 2006. The aim of the study was to provide empirical data for the construct validation and implementation of the COET. The author of this chapter was the coordinator of the study. The participants came from two universities and four middle schools in Guangdong and consisted of 20 experts on language testing, language teaching, and computer science. The group of participants was composed of four language testing researchers, 12 teachers of oral English in universities, and four middle school English teachers with at least 2 years' experience in preparing their students for the oral test in the NMET. The following is a brief report relating to the construct validation of the COET, with the main source of evidence for construct validation coming from expert judgments and factor analysis.

Expert Judgments

A logical analysis comparing test content to its underlying theory can usually give some indication of the number and nature of the constructs reflected by the test

(Wiersma & Jurs, 1990). Expert judgments are often collected to make inferences about the correspondence between a test and its underlying theory when attempting to see whether a test is a successful operationalization of a theory (Alderson et al., 1995). According to Alderson et al. experts should first be selected, then given some definition of the underlying theory, and asked to make judgments after an inspection of the test regarding its construct validity. One of the most effective ways of doing this is by establishing a rating scale which the experts use in their analysis. The expert judgments are then "used to argue for or against the use of test performance as an indicator of the theoretically defined construct that the test is intended to measure as well as to inform empirical validity inquiry" (Chapelle, 1998, p. 32). As this process is crucial to construct validation, it is important to note here that the experts involved in the judgments must be testing professionals who also know well the construct in question.

To investigate the construct validity of the COET, we first need a framework for the competence which is to be measured. Hymes (1972), Canale and Swain (1980), and later Bachman (1990) contributed a great deal to the framework of communicative competence in a broad sense, but discussions of language ability are often very general and abstract (McNamara, 1996). By comparison, Hedge's (2001) model is more specific and has some significant implications for language teaching and learning. The operational definition of oral communicative competence for the present study was therefore adapted from Hedge, who stated that competence referred to students knowing how . . .

Linguistic competence:

1   To achieve accuracy in the grammatical forms of the language
2   To pronounce the forms accurately
3   To use stress, rhythm, and intonation to express meaning
4   To build a range of vocabulary.

Pragmatic competence:

1   To use stress and intonation to express attitude and emotion, and to understand and use emotive tones
2   To learn the scales of in/formality (from informal to formal)
3   To use the pragmatic rules of language (e.g., Grice's Cooperative Principles)
4   To select language forms appropriate to topic, listener, etc.
5   To learn the relationship between grammatical forms and functions.

Discourse competence:

1   To take turns, use discourse markers, open and close conversations, and to use cohesive devices.

Strategic competence:

1   To use achievement strategies, i.e., to find another way to express oneself to enable the conversation to continue
2   To use reduction/avoidance strategies, i.e., to avoid uncertain forms or structures.

Fluency:

1 To deal with information gaps in real discourse
2 To process language and respond appropriately with a degree of ease
3 To be able to respond with reasonable speed in "real time".

(Adapted from Hedge, 2001, p. 56)

In the present study, we issued a questionnaire in Chinese which was developed on the basis of the above framework of communicative competence, in order to obtain expert opinions about what abilities are judged to be measured by the COET. In the present study, the questionnaire adopted a 1–5 point Likert scale of agreement, and 20 experts were invited to respond to the questionnaire.

Using means and standard deviation, the questionnaire aimed to illustrate general tendencies in the experts' judgments of what abilities were measured by the COET. The questionnaire had three parts, each of which included 15 questions reflecting the 15 competences identified in Hedge's (2001) framework. With respect to the variance between responses to each question, we conducted a Chi-square test on each question, but to achieve clearer results, before we conducted the Chi-square tests, we converted the 5 points of the Likert scale to 3 points, i.e., we combined the categories of "strongly agree" and "agree" into "agree", and combined "strongly disagree" and "disagree" into "disagree". "Uncertain" was retained in the Chi-square test. In this way, all of the experts' responses were converted into three categories, i.e., "agree", "uncertain", and "disagree". We interpreted a mean rating above 3.0 as showing that there is the tendency for the ability, as defined in the question, to be measured by a particular item. The results of the Chi-square tests are displayed and discussed below.

Results of Expert Opinions on Part A

Table 17.1 presents the results of expert opinions on the three parts of the COET. From the column **Part A** in Table 17.1, we can see that the mean for pronunciation (4.80), intonation and stress (3.93), and use of stress or intonation to express attitude or emotion (3.25) were rated above 3.0. The first two abilities belong to the pronunciation and intonation of linguistic competence as mentioned above, and the third one, although in the category of pragmatic competence, can also be regarded as an ability of pronunciation and intonation. All the other abilities were relatively low, ranging from 1.15 to 2.15, which suggests that they were considered by the experts as not having been measured in Part A of the COET.

A Chi-square test was applied to the responses in the 3-point scale to check whether there was a clear tendency in experts' responses to these questions. The results are presented in Table 17.2. Chi-square test results that fall at or below .05 are considered significant. Therefore, as we can see from Table 17.2, the results for all the questions except Question 5 reached the significant level ($p<.05$), indicating that experts' responses to all the questions except Question 5 showed a clear tendency, i.e., they thought that an ability was either measured or not measured in Part A.

As indicated by the number of "disagree", "uncertain" and "agree" responses in Table 17.2, all 20 experts agreed with Question 2, showing that pronunciation ability was clearly thought to be measured in Part A. Also, most of the experts (12 out of 20) agreed with

Table 17.1 Results of Expert Judgments of the Three Parts in the COET

Communicative Competence		Part A		Part B		Part C	
		Mean	SD	Mean	SD	Mean	SD
Linguistic Competence	1*Grammar	2.01	1.08	4.25	.72	4.55	
	2 Pronunciation	4.80	.41	4.05	.68	4.55	.69
	3 Intonation and stress	3.93	1.07	4.15	.59	4.05	1.05
	4 Vocabulary	1.60	.75	4.02	.46	4.82	.41
Pragmatic Competence	5 Use of stress or intonation to express attitude or emotion	3.25	1.25	3.83	.69	4.15	.67
	6 Appropriate use of formality	1.35	.59	3.71	.86	3.95	.89
	7 Use of pragmatic rules	1.30	.66	3.75	1.02	3.81	.77
	8 Appropriate use of registers	1.15	.49	3.80	.62	4.01	.79
	9 Form-function relationship	1.35	.93	4.05	.83	3.62	.75
Discourse Competence	10 Turn-taking or opening/closing a conversation, cohesive devices	1.54	.89	3.53	.95	4.15	.93
Strategic Competence	11 To prevent conversation breakdown by finding another way to express something	1.25	.64	3.85	.49	4.21	.69
Fluency	12 To avoid using uncertain forms and structures	1.45	.83	3.20	.95	3.35	1.27
	13 To deal with information gaps in real discourse	2.15	1.09	3.83	.83	3.85	.75
	14 To process language and respond appropriately with ease	1.72	1.08	3.92	.72	3.35	1.09
	15 Reasonable speed of response	1.85	1.04	4.10	.85	4.00	.73

* The numerical numbering refers to the questions in the questionnaire. For example, 1 refers to Question 1 in the questionnaire. The expression such as "Grammar" indicates the abilities stated in the questionnaire questions.

Table 17.2 Chi-square (χ^2) Test of Experts' Responses to the Questionnaire

Questions	Part A						Part B						Part C					
	DA	U	A	χ^2	df	p	DA	U	A	χ^2	df	p	DA	U	A	χ^2	df	p
1	15	2	3	15.73	2	.00	0	3	17	9.80	1	.00	0	2	18	12.81	1	.00
2	0	0	20*				1	1	18	28.94	2	.00	0	2	18	12.81	1	.00
3	2	6	12	7.64	2	.02	0	2	18	12.83	1	.00	2	4	14	12.42	2	.00
4	17	3	0	9.81	1	.00	0	2	18	12.82	1	.00	0	0	20			
5	6	4	10	2.82	2	.25	1	4	15	16.34	2	.00	0	3	17	9.81	1	.00
6	19	1	0	16.20	1	.00	0	6	14	3.21	1	.07	1	5	14	13.33	2	.00
7	18	2	0	12.82	1	.00	0	6	14	3.21	1	.07	1	5	14	13.33	2	.00
8	19	1	0	16.21	1	.00	3	4	13	9.12	2	.01	1	3	16	19.92	2	.00
9	18	0	2	12.82	1	.00	2	5	13	9.71	2	.01	1	8	11	7.92	2	.02
10	17	2	1	24.10	2	.00	4	4	12	6.43	2	.04	1	4	15	16.31	1	.00
11	18	2	0	12.83	1	.00	0	4	16	7.23	1	.01	0	3	17	9.80	1	.00
12	16	4	0	7.22	1	.01	4	8	8	1.62	2	.45	4	5	11	4.32	2	.12
13	13	4	3	9.16	2	.01	1	6	13	10.91	2	.00	0	7	13	1.83	1	.18
14	16	3	1	19.91	2	.00	3	3	16	19.91	2	.00	5	7	8	.74	2	.71
15	15	3	2	15.76	2	.00	1	3	16	19.91	2	.00	0	5	15	5.01	1	.03

Questions 1–15 refer to the 15 questions in each **Part A, B** and **C** of the questionnaire. DA, Disagree; U, Uncertain; A, Agree.
* No Chi-square was calculated for questions 2 in **Part A** and 4 in **Part C** as all 20 experts agreed in their responses to this question.

Question 3, indicating that intonation and stress was also thought to be tested in Part A. However, although Question 5 had a mean rating score higher than 3.0 (see Table 17.1), the Chi-square test showed that there was no clear tendency that the experts agreed with the question ($p = .25$). This suggests that experts were not sure whether the ability to use stress and intonation to express attitude or emotion was in fact measured in Part A.

The conclusion which can be drawn from the experts' opinions is that Part A mainly measures students' abilities with respect to pronunciation and intonation/stress. The results were not surprising, considering that this kind of test—reading aloud (including repetition)—is usually intended to measure students' pronunciation and intonation (Underhill, 1987).

Results of Expert Opinions for Part B of the COET

The column **Part B** in Table 17.1 gives the means and standard deviations for experts' responses to Part B. All the means of the responses to Part B were above 3.0, with the lowest mean rated at 3.20, indicating that this part of the COET test was thought to measure many more abilities than Part A. Most means of the responses that were above 4.0 belonged to linguistic competence, with grammar rated at 4.25, intonation/stress at 4.15, pronunciation at 4.05, and vocabulary at 4.02. However, other abilities, such as fluency (4.10) and pragmatic competence involving knowing the relationship between forms and functions (4.05), and conversation strategies (3.85), were also considered by the experts to be tested by this part of the COET.

The Chi-square test (Table 17.2) shows that all of the responses reached the significant level, except Question 6 ($p = .07$), Question 7 ($p = .07$), and Question 12 ($p = .45$). This means that there was no tendency for agreement or disagreement on the part of the experts concerning Question 6, 7 and 12, indicating that experts were not sure whether appropriate use of formality (Question 6), use of pragmatic rules (Question 7) and the ability to avoid using uncertain forms and structures (Question 12) were measured in Part B of the COET. Abilities in the other questions were thought to be measured in Part B, as indicated by the means in the column **Part B** in Table 17.1 and the number of "disagree", "uncertain" and "agree" responses in Table 17.2. The results show that experts thought Part B tested most of the abilities in Hedge's (2001) communicative competence framework. More specifically, linguistic competence, discourse competence, and fluency were thought by the experts to be measured in Part B, whereas pragmatic competence and strategic competence were thought to be only partly measured, as some of the abilities were thought not to be measured in Part B.

Results for Part C of the COET

Experts' responses to the questions on Part C, the oral composition, are shown in the column **Part C** in Table 17.1, which shows that all the means were above 3.0, with the lowest mean being 3.35. All the abilities relating to linguistic competence were given high ratings—grammar with a rating of 4.55, pronunciation 4.55, intonation and stress 4.05, and vocabulary 4.82. The other competencies were all rated approximately 4.0, somewhat lower than those for linguistic competence, but still generally higher than in Parts A and B of the COET.

A Chi-square test was conducted on the responses for Part C (see Table 17.2). As we can see from the table, Questions 12, 13, and 14 did not reach the level of significance, indicating that there was no clear tendency in experts' responses to these questions. In other words, experts were not sure whether Part C of the COET measured the ability to avoid using certain forms and structures, part of strategic competence, the ability to deal with information gaps in real discourse, part of fluency, or the ability to process language and respond appropriately with ease, also part of fluency. As indicated by the means in the column **Part C** in Table 17.1 and the majority of "agree" responses in Table 17.2, all of the other abilities were thought by experts to be measured in Part C.

In summary, in the experts' opinion, grammatical competence, pragmatic competence and discourse competence were all measured in Part C, i.e., all the abilities that belonged to these competencies were thought to be tested in Part C. Strategic competence and fluency, however, were thought to be only partly measured in Part C according to the experts.

Overview of Expert Opinions on All Three Parts of the COET

From the analyses of each part of the COET, we can reach several conclusions concerning the experts' judgments on what the COET measured. First, Part A of the COET, in the experts' opinion, primarily measured pronunciation and intonation. Second, Part B and Part C measured all of the competences to some extent. More specifically, among the five competencies identified in our communicative competence model (Hedge, 2001), linguistic competence was thought to be measured in both Part B and Part C. Pragmatic competence was measured in Part B and Part C. Discourse competence was thought to be measured in both Part B and Part C. Strategic competence was also taken to be measured in these two parts, although the experts were not sure about whether one of the two abilities, the ability to avoid using uncertain expressions, was tested or not. It is important to bear in mind that although the experts did not show a clear tendency as to whether some abilities were tested or not in Part B or Part C, these abilities were not thought to be unmeasured in these two parts. In fact, although not statistically significant, these abilities tended to have mean ratings near 4.0, indicating that the experts may have thought that they were measured in the two parts. So we can reach the conclusion that although Part A was only thought to test pronunciation and intonation, both Part B and Part C of the COET were thought to a great extent to measure test-takers' communicative competence, which means that the test appears to be testing what it is intended to test.

Factor Analysis

To further demonstrate the relationship between the three sub-tests of the COET, we conducted a factor analysis for each part of the COET. As described earlier in this chapter, the COET consists of three sub-tests, i.e., reading aloud (Part A), role play (Part B), and oral composition (Part C). Part B, role play, includes six items: three items involving asking questions and three for answering questions. Therefore, altogether there are eight items in the COET. Factor analysis of varimax rotation was conducted for these items. After varimax rotation, three factors were extracted in this analysis. Meanwhile, the scree plot showed that the eigenvalues of three factors were above 1.0, also suggesting that these three factors contributed the majority of an explanation of the total score variance. The results are generally consistent with what the test designers of the COET claimed to test, three parts for three different aspects of the underlying construct of speaking or oral communicative competence.

The three factors can clearly be seen. The first factor has substantial loadings on Part A, B4, B5, B6 and Part C, which means that these five components have relatively large correlations with each other, though Part A has a much higher loading on Factor 3. B1 and B3 have high loadings on Factor 2, which indicates that these two belong to a larger domain. Surprisingly, B2, which is supposed to belong to Factor 2 together with B1 and B3, was extracted into Factor 3, with Part A. The argument we put forward interpreting the factors is as follows:

Factor 1: The largest loadings are on answering questions and oral composition. This factor is labeled "comprehension and oral production".
Factor 2: The largest loadings are on asking questions. This factor is thus labeled "interpreting".
Factor 3: The largest loadings are on reading aloud. This factor is labeled "pronunciation and intonation".

The results of factor analysis further confirmed our hypothesis concerning the construct of the oral test, which consists of three main sub-tests. This analysis demonstrates that the COET appears to test what it claims to test.

Implications

The three sub-tests in the COET reflected the underlying construct that the COET intends to measure, i.e., oral communicative competence as defined in Hedge's (2001) framework. The expert judgments on the questionnaire and the quantitative analysis confirmed that the COET, in spite of its low degree of interactiveness, tests many aspects of oral communicative competence by using a combination of these three sub-tests.

Computerized language tests, including computer-based and computer adaptive language tests, have attracted attention from language testers for only a decade or so (Choi, Kim & Boo, 2003). During those years, most attention has been paid to the comparability between paper-based language testing and computerized language testing. Receptive-response items, such as multiple-choice and true-false questions, can be switched to computer-based tests with relative ease, whereas the more productive-response questions, such as oral interview and composition, are much more difficult to develop with computers (Brown, 1997). However, although it is painstaking, it is not impossible, as is shown by this study. The successful development of the COET has made it possible to introduce computer-based oral tests into high-stake, large-scale tests like the NMET in China.

Computerized or tape-mediated oral tests are semi-direct tests in nature. Unlike direct tests such as face-to-face interviews, they do not require extensive training for test administrators. In such test elicitation, all test-takers respond to the same audio (or video) pre-recorded stimuli and to explicit instructions heard through the headphone or seen on the screen in a language laboratory. Large numbers of test-takers can be tested at the same time, and responses can be recorded and rated by raters later, eliminating the need for an immediate, rushed rating (Jones, 1985). Also, as such semi-direct tests do not require a well-trained examiner to administer the test either, the taped test performance can be sent to remote testing sites (Jones, 1985), making such a test particularly useful for an enormous country like China.

In general, as Heaton (1991) stated, the use of language labs has made it possible to administer more reliable oral tests to large numbers of students in a relatively short time. The oral test administered in a language lab promotes reliability based on its standardization and objectivity and improves test rating and management. But its disadvantage is that it is not authentic: students speak to a computer instead of a real person; there is little if any interaction with others; and there are no opportunities to switch roles or ask for repetition as in live conversation (Underhill, 1987). Therefore the speech delivered by the students is clearly a kind of monologue (Luoma, 2004).

Computerized oral tests are the result of the development of advanced, new computer technology, and thus they are a brand-new test mode requiring more research. As mentioned previously, semi-direct oral tests, such as computerized oral tests like the COET, involve unidirectional interaction. However, according to Luoma (2004), such tests can cover some aspects of interactive speaking, so it cannot be argued that computerized or tape-mediated oral tests cannot test oral communicative competence. It is a matter of degree, i.e., to what extent these tests can test oral communicative competence, since we know that even a live face-to-face oral interview cannot cover all aspects of test-takers' communicative competence, and any oral test, by definition, cannot be a completely "real-life" situation.

One thing that needs to be recognized, however, is that the constructs of semi-direct oral tests and face-to-face interviews are somewhat different because of the test modes adopted in these two tests. As Stansfield and Kenyon (1992) stated, both face-to-face interviews and semi-direct oral tests achieve a high degree of validity as tests of general oral language proficiency, but some "inherent differences of a theoretical nature" between these tests exist (p. 121). As pointed out previously, Luoma (2004) distinguishes between these two testing modes by calling them "spoken production" and "spoken interaction". There are, indeed, some differences between the performances elicited by these different test modes. These, however, cannot prevent us from concluding that the COET, as a semi-direct oral test, can elicit test-takers' various communicative abilities. What needs to be borne in mind is that few tests are completely communicative and most oral tests only have some elements of communicativeness, even in the case of a live, face-to-face interview format. As long it is accepted that the impetus to use semi-direct tests is to test large numbers of test-takers more reliably and fairly, we need to be willing to accept the new test methods as a good substitute for oral interviews.

The successful development and implementation of the COET has direct implications for language testing as well as for language teaching and learning. First, in addition to its high reliability, the COET, as a new test method, appears to measure to a great extent what it claims to measure, namely, oral communicative competence. Language testers and testing researchers can reassure test stakeholders that it is both a valid and a reliable oral test.

Second, regarding English teachers and learners, some basic skills could be given more attention in order to build a more solid foundation for speaking, such as reading aloud or imitation. However, role-play and oral composition may be more desirable activities to practice, as they reflect more communicative competence. But English teaching and learning should not only be centered on these three tasks, and more communicative activities, such as real life information transfer between test-takers or in an interview, should also be involved in learning and teaching in order to improve oral communicative competence.

Third, the results from this validation study of COET have a number of implications for test developers. The developers of the COET appear to have been successful in developing this new test, which appears to be reliable and valid; the challenge for the test developers, however, is to design some more comprehensive and more communicative tasks for the COET to further promote communicative language teaching in China. Since oral tests may have a great washback effect on English teaching and learning, test developers of the COET need to be extremely aware of its washback effect. One important consideration is to give the oral test more communicative elements by combining more tasks in the test, or to make group discussions or real life interactions between test-takers available. Since some test-takers might use expressions such as "pardon" or "sorry, I did not catch you", which is also a kind of communicative competence, the rating scale of the COET may recognize the use of such expressions by asking raters to give a certain score indicating that students' competence with such expressions has been recognized. Thus, test-takers' communicative competencies could be better presented.

In addition, visual information is missing in the COET, since test-takers' performance is recorded on audiotapes. Therefore, non-verbal communication, such as eye contact, body language, or facial expression cannot be recorded. One solution would be to use videotapes in order to capture more information regarding test-takers' non-verbal performances, which could help raters to judge test-takers' oral communicative competence more fairly.

References

Alderson, J. C., Clapham, C. & Wall, D. (1995). *Language test construction and evaluation*. Cambridge, UK: Cambridge University Press.

Bachman, L. F. (1990). *Fundamental considerations in language testing*. Oxford: Oxford University Press.

Bachman, L. F. & Palmer, A. S. (1996). *Language testing in practice*. Oxford: Oxford University Press.

Brown, J. D. (1997). Computers in language testing: Present research and some future direction. *Language Learning & Technology*, 1, 44–59.

Canale, M. & Swain, M. (1980). Theoretical bases of communicative approaches to second language teaching and testing. *Applied Linguistics*, 1, 1–47.

Chapelle, C. A. (1998). Construct definition and validity inquiry in SLA research. In L. F. Bachman and A. D. Cohen (Eds.), *Interfaces between second language acquisition and language testing* (pp. 32–70). Cambridge, UK: Cambridge University Press.

Choi, I. C., Kim, K. S. & Boo, J. (2003). Comparability of a paper-based language test and a computer-based language test. *Language Testing*, 20, 295–320.

Heaton, J. B. (1991). *Writing English language tests*: Fourth impression. London, UK: Longman.

Hedge, T. (2001). *Teaching and learning in the language classroom*: Second impression. Oxford: Oxford University Press.

Hymes, D. (1972). On communicative competence. In J. B. Pride & J. Holmes (Eds.), *Sociolinguistics*. Harmondsworth: Penguin.

Jones, R. L. (1985). Some basic considerations in testing oral proficiency. In Lee, Y. P. (Ed.), *New directions in language testing*. Oxford: Pergamon Institute of English.

Li, X. & Wang, Y. (2000). Testing oral English on a mass scale: Is it feasible?—The oral component of the MET in China [Special Issue]. *Hong Kong Journal of Applied Linguistics*, 5, 160–186.

Luoma, S. (2004). *Assessing speaking*. Cambridge, UK: Cambridge University Press.

McNamara, T. (1996). *Measuring second language performance*. Harlow: Longman.

Ministry of Education of the People's Republic of China (2002). *New National Syllabus for Middle Schools*. Beijing: Beijing Normal University Press.

Stansfield, C. W. & Kenyon, D. M. (1992). The development and validation of a simulated oral proficiency interview. *Modern Language Journal*, 76, 129–141.

Underhill, N. (1987). *Testing spoken language*. Cambridge, UK: Cambridge University Press.

Wiersma, W. & Jurs, S. G (1990). *Educational measurement and testing* (2nd ed.). Boston: Allyn and Bacon.

Wood, R. (1993). *Assessment and testing: A survey of research*. Cambridge, UK: Cambridge University Press.

18 The Hong Kong Certificate of Education

School-Based Assessment Reform in Hong Kong English Language Education

Chris Davison, The University of New South Wales,
Liz Hamp-Lyons, The University of Hong Kong

School-Based Assessment (SBA) is increasingly being promoted in the Asian region as a more valid, reliable, and equitable form of assessment, and as an integral part of the development of a more outcomes-oriented curriculum. As part of its major overhaul of curriculum and assessment in 2005, the Hong Kong Examinations and Assessment Authority (HKEAA) commissioned the authors to design, implement, and evaluate a School-Based Assessment component as part of the Hong Kong Certificate of Education Examination (HKCEE) in English Language. This chapter reports the preliminary findings of a 2-year longitudinal study, funded by the HKEAA, of the implementation of the new assessment scheme in 8 Hong Kong secondary schools, exploring some of the issues and problems involved in moving English language teachers and their school communities from a traditional norm-referenced to a standards-based assessment system.

Introduction

In 2005, the Hong Kong Examinations and Assessment Authority (HKEAA) introduced a School-Based Assessment (SBA) component into the Hong Kong Certificate of Education Examination (HKCEE) in English Language to align assessment more closely with the current English Language teaching syllabus (Curriculum Development Council, 1999) as well as with the proposed new Senior Secondary curriculum (Education and Manpower Bureau, 2007). The SBA English component seeks to provide a more comprehensive appraisal of Form 4–5 (Grade 9–10-equivalent) learners' achievement by assessing learning objectives which cannot be easily assessed in public examinations whilst at the same time enhancing teaching and learning. In-class performance assessment of students' authentic oral language skills using a range of tasks and guiding questions and the use of teacher judgments of student performance using common assessment criteria are innovative aspects of the new School-Based Assessment scheme.

This initiative marks an attempt to move from traditional, norm-referenced externally-set and assessed examinations towards a more student-centred, standards-based assessment that draws its philosophical basis from the *assessment for learning* movement (Assessment Reform Group, 1999; Black, Harrison, Lee, Marshall, & Wiliam, 2003). School-based assessment is increasingly being promoted in the Asian region as a more valid, reliable, and equitable form of assessment, but many schools and their communities are skeptical about the relevance and acceptability of such approaches being imported into a very different culture and educational system without sufficient consultation or adaptation for the Chinese learner, arguing that traditional conceptions of learning, teaching, and assessment are more appropriate to so-called Confucian-heritage cultures, especially in an increasingly competitive educational environment. Other educational researchers point to Hong Kong's dismal track record in implementing assessment reform (Adamson & Davison, 2003; Carless, 2005; Yung, 2001, 2002), exacerbated by large class sizes teachers' limited professional autonomy and assessment experience, and students' relatively low levels of English language skills, even in some English-medium schools.[1] However, Holliday (1994) argues that conflicts in curriculum innovation projects are inevitable because educational environments are constructed from a variety of interconnected cultures. According to Holliday (1994), it is less misleading and more useful to understand the conflicts in terms of what he calls "professional-academic cultures" rather than in terms of "national culture profiling" (p. 111). He points out such "relationships are extremely complex whether working across a national culture divide or within the same national culture," (p. 113), with many problems caused by researchers underestimating the difficulties.

Drawing on the preliminary findings of a 2-year longitudinal study of the implementation of SBA in a range of Hong Kong secondary schools, this chapter explores teachers' changing attitudes and practices as they move from a traditional norm-referenced to a standards-based assessment system. The chapter concludes that despite initial concerns about excessive workload and a marked lack of teacher assessment readiness, many aspects of this particular Hong Kong English language assessment initiative are being accepted and implemented effectively in a wide range of Hong Kong schools, although the effects on the English language outcomes of learners are not yet known.

The Hong Kong Assessment Context

Hong Kong schools have long been dominated by a traditional examination culture (Hamp-Lyons, 1999). Studies of the impact of earlier changes in the Hong Kong external examination system in oral English language (e.g. Andrews, 1994; Andrews, Fullilove, & Wong, 2002; Cheng, 1997, 2005) found that changes to summative assessment did not automatically lead to improvement in learning, as the teacher and school mediated the nature of the change. As Andrews et al. have described, in 1994 in response to university concerns about spoken English levels among undergraduates, a speaking component (an individual oral presentation based on a text, followed by group discussion) was added to the HKAL. Andrews et al. (2002), drawing on King (1997), report that the 1994 changes "produced 'negative washback' as well as positive washback, the former resulting from teachers' perceptions that the new oral format was too difficult", which King claimed led to ". . . students, encouraged by their teachers, . . . resort[ing] to memorising lists of set phrases to cope with most of the situations encountered in the oral tests" (p. 210). In a follow-up study, Andrews et al. (2002), found the oral examination had affected students' spoken output, but mediated through exam-related published materials, resulting in fairly superficial learning outcomes, "familiarisation with the exam format, and the rote-learning of exam-specific strategies and formulaic phrases" (p. 220).

Studies of the implementation of other assessment innovations such as the Target-oriented Curriculum in Hong Kong primary schools (e.g. Cheung & Ng, 2000; Carless, 2004; Adamson & Davison, 2003) also found that any change in teacher assessment practice was difficult, severely constrained by traditional school culture and by teacher, parent, and student expectations. Earlier studies of the assessment readiness of Hong Kong Form 4–5 (S4–5) English language teachers by the authors (Davison, 2004, 2007a; Hamp-Lyons, 2007) identified a number of factors affecting teachers' assessment attitudes, beliefs, and practices, including a lack of clarity about the concept of school-based assessment, low levels of confidence in their own professional knowledge and skills, concerns about fairness, and the acceptance of such alternative assessment by the wider school community, especially more traditional test-oriented parents. Such concerns are not unique to Hong Kong teachers, having been raised by researchers in English language education (Hamp-Lyons, 2001; Rea-Dickins, 2007; Teasdale & Leung, 2000) and in school assessment generally (Black, 2001; Black & Wiliam, 1998; Cheah, 1998; Stobart, 2005). However, in Hong Kong, teachers' assessment readiness is seen as even more problematic given teachers' extremely heavy workload, reliance on textbooks, rigid timetabling structures, hierarchical patterns of interaction, and the widespread coaching/tutorial school culture (Hamp-Lyons, 1999).

As consultants, we wanted the SBA initiative to have a positive influence on teaching and learning, and be taken up in meaningful ways by English language teachers. In designing the initiative we drew on the *assessment for learning* principles that had been adopted curriculum-wide in Hong Kong education policy documents (Curriculum Development Institute, 2002) and which are being implemented progressively in a wide range of senior subjects. *Assessment for learning* can be defined as "all those activities undertaken by teachers and/or by their students, which provide information to be used as feedback to modify the teaching and learning activities in which they are engaged" (Black & Wiliam, 1998, pp. 7–8). *Assessment for learning* is based on the idea that pupils will improve most if they understand the aim of their learning, where they are in relation to this aim, and how they can achieve the aim or close the gap in their knowledge: "For any assessment the first priority is to serve the purpose of promoting students' learning" (Black et al., 2003, p. 2). *Assessment for learning* is significantly different from traditional examinations in the role it offers to the teacher as assessor of their own students' learning and as judges of whether each student has met the expected standards of the subject. As the SBA was designed to be used for both formative and summative purposes, teachers are also encouraged to link the SBA to student self and peer assessment, teacher feedback, and enhanced teaching and learning (SBA Consultancy Team, 2006a).

The HKCEE English School-Based Assessment Component

The SBA component is conducted over 2 years of schooling, contributing 15 percent towards students' final English scores.[2] It involves the assessment of English oral language skills, based on topics and texts drawn from a program of independent reading/viewing ("texts" encompass print, video/film, fiction and non-fiction material). Students choose at least three texts to read or view over the course of 2 years, keeping a logbook or brief notes, and undertaking a number of activities in and out of class to develop their independent reading, speaking and thinking skills. For assessment, they participate in several interactions with classmates on a particular aspect of the text they have read/ viewed, leading up to making an individual presentation or group interaction on a specific text (for a summary of the assessment requirements, see http://www.hkeaa.edu. hk/DocLibrary/SBA/CE-Eng-Requirements-0604.pdf).

Assessment tasks, developed or adapted by the teacher, can vary in length and complexity, giving students multiple and varied opportunities to demonstrate their oral language abilities individually tailored to their language level and interests. To ensure that the oral language produced is the student's own work, not the result of memorization without understanding, certain requirements or "conditions" must be followed, including students being assessed by their usual English teacher, in the presence of one or more classmate(s). Teachers can ask the students questions as appropriate in order to prompt or extend the range of oral language produced and/or to verify the students' understanding of what they are saying.

Students are assessed according to a set of assessment criteria, consisting of a set of descriptors at each of six levels across four domains—*pronunciation and delivery, communication strategies, vocabulary and language patterns,* and *ideas and organization.* Teachers are encouraged to video or audio record a range of student assessments to assist with standardization and feedback, involving the students as much as possible. During the class assessments, which might span a number of weeks, individual teachers at the same level are encouraged to meet informally to compare their assessments and make adjustments to their own scores as necessary. Such informal interactions give teachers the opportunity to share opinions on how to score performances, and how to interpret the assessment criteria. Near the end of the school year, there is a formal meeting of all the English teachers at each grade level, chaired by the SBA Coordinator in each school, to review performance samples and standardize scores. Such meetings are critical for developing agreement about what a standard means, i.e., *validity,* consistency in and between teacher-assessors, i.e. *reliability,* public accountability, and professional collaboration/support. At the end of each year, there is a district-level meeting for professional sharing and further standardization. Each SBA Coordinator is encouraged to take a range of typical and atypical individual assessment records (and the video or audio recordings) and the class records for sharing. Once any necessary changes are made, the performance samples are archived and the scores are submitted to the HKEAA for review. Maintaining notes of all standardization meetings and any follow-up action is also encouraged so schools can show parents and the public that it has applied the SBA consistently and fairly. The HKEAA then undertakes a process of statistical moderation[3] to ensure the comparability of scores across the whole Hong Kong school system.

The SBA initiative marks a significant shift in policy as well as in practice for the Hong Kong educational community; thus, the provision of appropriate teacher training material and support was an important consideration in the implementation process (SBA Consultancy team, 2006a). A professional development package was developed, including an introductory DVD and booklet, and two training CD-ROMs. In addition to the appointment of school-level SBA coordinators, 39 district-level group coordinators, mostly serving teachers, were employed to coordinate training, standardization, and moderation sessions. All teachers were also encouraged to complete a 12-hour supplementary professional development program with comprehensive course and video notes on DVD (SBA Consultancy Team, 2006b) in their first year of SBA teaching.

The HKEAA also funded the authors to conduct a 2-year longitudinal study of the implementation of SBA in a range of Hong Kong schools, the preliminary findings of which form the remainder of this paper.

The Longitudinal Study

The longitudinal study of the setting, implementation, marking, and moderation of the new School-Based Assessment component of the English Language Examination over 2005–07 was commissioned by the HKEAA in December 2005, with a view to informing planning for the inclusion of School-Based Assessment within the new Hong Kong Diploma of Secondary Education that will commence in 2009–10. The study used both quantitative and qualitative methods of data collection and analysis, including regular questionnaires of all teachers, students, and other key stakeholders, including the Principal and head of the English panel, from a representative range of schools in Hong Kong, complemented by focus group interviews and observational samples of teaching-and-assessing sequences. In this chapter, we focus on the teacher questionnaire data from eight schools/groups of English teachers in the first and final occasions of data collection in February–March 2006 and March–April 2007[4] in order to capture any changes in teachers' beliefs, attitudes, and knowledge over a full year of innovation implementation.

There were five Chinese-medium and three English-medium schools in the sample, with a range of different banding and geographical areas ranging from the more affluent areas of Hong Kong island and the highly urbanized Kowloon peninsula to the largely rural and new settled areas of the New Territories. The teachers also varied considerably in term of demographic profile and experience, with ages ranging from early 20s to late 50s, and one with 30+ years of teaching experience.

The questionnaire was the same for all rounds of data collection, although the numbering of the items was slightly different. The data reported below will be a comparison of teachers' views in the first and last rounds of data collection, indicated as occasion 1 ($n = 38$) and occasion 2 ($n = 35$) in the tables. The questionnaire consisted of three main sections: personal and school information; teachers' views on their own and their school's preparation and implementation of the HKCEE English Language School-Based Assessment components, and their views on common concerns; and teachers' perceptions of the effects of School-Based Assessment on students and teachers. Teachers were asked to indicate their responses on a 6-point Likert scale, in which 1 represented *strongly disagree* and 6 represented *strongly agree*, with 3.5 the neutral mid-point. The questionnaire results were then analyzed using SPSS and the means and standard deviations of the teachers' views on the various sections of the questionnaires were tabulated and tested for significance using chi square. In all rounds, the questionnaires had space for additional comments to be written in at the conclusion of each major substantive questionnaire item. These open-ended comments enabled respondents to provide judgmental, qualitative comments that they felt could not be fully represented through the Likert scaled questionnaire items. The number of written comments for each item was tallied, and the comment itself was recorded. Where comments were essentially identical, this was represented by a multiplier against it (e.g., "'too much pressure' × 3" represented three comments that there was too much pressure). Descriptive statistics, together with Chi-square test results, are presented below for comparison purposes, and the key concerns and issues are also identified and discussed.[5]

Findings: Teachers' Views of the SBA Initiative

Over a 12-month period—from the second semester of the first year of SBA implementation up to the same point a year later—the quantitative analysis of the teacher questionnaire data suggests that many aspects of this particular Hong Kong English language assessment initiative are being accepted and implemented,[6] with generally more positive attitudes towards SBA and rising confidence among teachers in many areas, albeit with areas of concern.

Teachers' Views on their Own Preparation for SBA

As Table 18.1 shows, on the first occasion of questionnaire data collection, teachers were rather neutral about their preparation for SBA. In the data collected 1 year later, despite

Table 18.1 Teachers' Views on their Preparation for SBA

14/16. *Your views about your preparation for School-Based Assessment: I think that I . . .*		*Occasion 1**			*Occasion 2*[†]		
		n	*Mean*	*SD*	*n*	*Mean*	*SD*
14a/16a	have a good understanding of the schedule, content and processes of School-Based Assessment	38	3.97	1.241	35	4.57	.979
14b/16b	have a good understanding of the underlying assessment philosophy of School-Based Assessment	38	3.92	1.148	35	4.69[‡]	.796
14c/16c	have had sufficient opportunity to attend professional development on School-Based Assessment	38	3.89	1.226	35	4.17	1.014
14d/16d	have had sufficient opportunity to discuss School-Based Assessment with other teachers	38	3.71	1.160	35	4.26	.980
14e/16e	have had sufficient opportunity to develop and/or adapt School-Based Assessment tasks for my students	38	3.58	1.056	35	4.11	1.132
14f/16f	have had sufficient opportunity to discuss the processes and scoring criteria for School-Based Assessment with my students	38	3.66	1.072	35	4.23	.942
14g/16g	have sufficient knowledge, skills and confidence to do the assessments properly	38	3.92	1.282	35	4.46	1.039
14h/16h	am able to give sufficient feedback to students	38	4.21	1.044	35	4.43	1.065
14i/16i	need additional time (e.g., lunch time, after school) to implement School-Based Assessment properly	38	4.84	1.001	35	4.89	1.051

* Occasion 1 indicates the data collected in February–March 2006.
† Occasion 2 indicates the data collected in March–April 2007.
‡ There is a significant association between the frequency of responses and the time at which data were collected: ($p \leq .05$): $\chi^2 = 12.212$; $p = .016$.

widespread concern from teachers about excessive workload and an initial lack of teacher assessment readiness, we see strong, positive changes on all items in this category, except for the last item, where we see teachers somewhat less concerned that SBA will demand extra-curricular time. The item with the greatest positive change, and the only one with a significant chi-square result, is 14b/16b, "I have a good understanding of the underlying assessment philosophy of School-Based Assessment." Although most of the changes across occasions have not reached the level of statistical significance, the results in this section suggest that the professional development support and school-based opportunities for discussion about students' performances and about the SBA process have been effective, and that teachers have grown more confident as users of SBA and feel more able to provide the necessary support to their students.

Teachers' Views on their School's Preparation for SBA

Table 18.2 summarizes teachers' responses when asked about their own school's preparation for SBA. On the first occasion, teachers had reported feeling that their school was less than adequately prepared (as demonstrated by a mean of less than 3.5 across all items) in almost all areas except the provision of technical equipment. However, 1 year later, teachers' views of their school's preparation are much more positive. In particular, teachers' views relating to whether their school has given parents and students enough

Table 18.2 Teachers' Views on their School's Preparation for SBA

15/17. *Your views about your school's preparation for SBA: Our school…*		Occasion 1*			Occasion 2†		
		n	*Mean*	*SD*	*n*	*Mean*	*SD*
15a/17a	has collected sufficient books for School-Based Assessment	38	3.45	1.267	35	3.63	1.031
15b/17b	has collected sufficient non-print materials for School-Based Assessment	38	3.18	1.136	35	3.54	1.010
15c/17c	has collected sufficient resource material and references about School-Based Assessment for teachers	38	3.26	1.057	35	3.66	1.027
15d/17d	has suitable recording equipment for School-Based Assessment	38	3.82	1.270	35	3.91	1.292
15e/17e	has given parents and students enough information about School-Based Assessment	37	3.38	1.255	35	4.14‡	.912
15f/17f	has made appropriate timetabling arrangements for School-Based Assessment	38	3.32	1.491	35	3.86	1.089
15g/17g	has provided sufficient technical support for School-Based Assessment	37	3.51	1.239	35	4.00	1.029
15h/17h	has given teachers sufficient meeting time to plan and discuss student assessments	37	3.32	1.082	35	4.06‡	.906
15i/17i	has established effective arrangements to monitor and evaluate the implementation of School-Based Assessment	37	3.14	1.058	35	3.86	1.033

* Occasion 1 indicates the data collected in February–March 2006.
† Occasion 2 indicates the data collected in March–April 2007.
‡ There is a significant association between the frequency of responses and the time at which data were collected in Occasion 1 and Occasion 2 ($p \leq .05$): 15e/17e, $\chi^2 = 11.146$, $p = .049$; 15h/17h, $\chi^2 = 11.056$, $p = .050$.

information about SBA (15e/17e) have changed significantly, perhaps partly due to the HKEAA English subject team running many more district-level seminars, and partly due to the release of pamphlets and a CD-rom for parents, a very important step, given Hong Kong parents place great importance on their child's education, and may resist educational change because they do not understand it will benefit them. Another area where significant change can be seen relates to "the availability of meeting time to plan and discuss student assessments," which was a substantial concern on the first occasion (item 15h/17h), but probably ameliorated by the efforts to encourage teachers to interact within and across schools.

Teachers' Views on the Implementation of SBA

As Table 18.3 shows, when teachers were asked about the implementation of SBA principles and processes at the beginning of this study, they were least confident that students' speaking skills could be assessed effectively within the normal classroom (lowest means among all items in this table), and were concerned that SBA might result in unfair judgments of students' speaking skills. However, although teachers have become more confident that classroom assessment is workable, their response is still not very positive (Item 16a/18a: 3.41 to 3.80), nor is the change significant. With regards to the fairness of SBA, teachers' attitudes have become slightly more positive (Item 16d/18d), although this needs to be closely monitored. On other aspects of the SBA implementation, their views are also positive, although the changes over the year are not dramatic. The area

Table 18.3 Teachers' Views on the Implementation of SBA

16/18. Your views about the implementation of School-Based Assessment: I think that...	Occasion 1*			Occasion 2†		
	n	Mean	SD	n	Mean	SD
16a/18a	students' speaking skills can be assessed well in the normal classroom	37	3.41	1.117	35	3.80	1.302
16b/18b	it is good that students have more than one opportunity to be assessed	37	4.49	1.044	35	4.63	.910
16c/18c	School-Based Assessment can be incorporated into the regular curriculum	37	3.81	1.175	35	4.03	1.248
16d/18d	School-Based Assessment will result in fair judgments of each student's level of speaking skill	37	3.57	1.237	35	3.74	1.146
16e/18e	meetings of all teachers involved in School-Based Assessment at the school level are essential	37	4.41	.985	35	4.57	.979
16f/18f	meetings of School-Based Assessment coordinators across a range of schools are essential	37	4.03	1.236	35	4.26	1.094
16g/18g	students can make adequate video- or audio-recordings of School-Based Assessment	37	3.59	1.166	34	4.12	1.094
16h/18h	the statistical moderation of School-Based Assessment scores by the HKEAA is essential	36	4.31	1.238	34	4.44	1.133

* Occasion 1 indicates the data collected in February–March 2006.
† Occasion 2 indicates the data collected in March–April 2007.

of least change is Item 16h/18h concerning statistical moderation: this is not surprising since at the time of this study teachers had not yet had the chance to see this put into practice and judge its effects on their students, their schools, and themselves.

Teachers' Views on the Potential Problems with SBA

As Table 18.4 shows, when teachers were asked at the beginning of this study about potential problems with SBA, the strongest response was on Item 17b: "there is too much administrative work involved in the SBA" (mean of 5.08). One year into implementation, this had declined slightly, to a mean of 4.83. To some extent, given the teachers' unfamiliarity with SBA, it is inevitable that it should be perceived as an administrative burden, and the level of concern should fall further as the innovation is institutionalized. Table 18.4 also shows that two important concerns relating to trust have shown significant positive change across the year: Item 17a/19a, where teachers' distrust of their peers' proper conduct of SBA has lessened significantly: and Item 17f/19f, "Students and parents may not trust teachers' assessments" where the concern has also lessened significantly. Given collaboration is not common practice in Hong Kong schools, the change in Item 17a/19a is encouraging, since it suggests that teachers are becoming much more confident that the processes put in place for SBA are trustworthy. A serious concern for teachers at the beginning of SBA was that they might face direct criticism

Table 18.4 Teachers' Views on the Potential Problems of SBA

17/19. Your views about the potential problems of School-Based Assessment: I think that...		Occasion 1*			Occasion 2†		
		n	Mean	SD	n	Mean	SD
17a/19a	some teachers may not follow the official guidelines properly when conducting School-Based Assessment in their classrooms	37	4.27	.693	34	3.44‡	1.186
17b/19b	there is too much administrative work involved in the School-Based Assessment	37	5.08	.894	35	4.83	1.071
17c/19c	the effectiveness of School-Based Assessment will be undermined by the tutoring and coaching culture in Hong Kong	37	4.35	1.160	34	4.32	1.121
17d/19d	students may be able to memorize responses/performances and reproduce them for the School-Based Assessment	37	4.30	1.309	35	4.17	1.150
17e/19e	teachers may not have the knowledge and skills to implement School-Based Assessment properly	37	3.89	.936	35	3.31	1.132
17f/19f	students and parents may not trust teachers' assessments	37	3.81	1.411	35	2.77‡	1.285
17g/19g	teachers will have trouble integrating School-Based Assessment into their regular teaching	37	4.16	1.118	35	3.91	1.269

* Occasion 1 indicates the data collected in February–March 2006.
† Occasion 2 indicates the data collected in March–April 2007.
‡ There is a significant association between the frequency of responses and the time at which data were collected in Occasion 1 and Occasion 2 ($p \leq .05$): 17a/19a, $\chi^2 = 16.647$, $p = .005$; 17f/19f, $\chi^2 = 13.562$, $p = .019$.

from parents; the change here suggests that the supports put in place for teachers, and the information given to parents, are having the desired effects. This section of the questionnaire is the one where we see most change in teachers' beliefs, attitudes, and knowledge, with two items of statistically significant positive change. However, teachers are still somewhat concerned about the potential of the tutorial school/coaching culture to undermine SBA effectiveness, and the (probably related) possibility that students may memorize responses and produce them in SBA assessments.

Teachers' Views on the Effects of SBA on Students

Table 18.5 summarizes teachers' responses to the items relating to the effects of SBA on students. The data from the beginning of the study suggested rather mixed views in this area: teachers appeared somewhat hopeful that SBA would help students to improve their speaking skills, and provide stronger students with a challenge, but they were concerned that SBA might disadvantage weaker students, increase students' workload, and have a negative effect on students' attitudes to using English. In the data collected a year later (but before teachers knew their students' SBA results), we can see that teachers' views on whether SBA will lead to improved speaking skills, identify students' strengths and weaknesses, and challenge students with higher speaking abilities have remained stable.

Table 18.5 Teachers' Views on the Effects of SBA on Students

18/20. Your views about the effects of School-Based Assessment on students: I think that School-Based Assessment . . .		Occasion 1*			Occasion 2†		
		n	Mean	SD	n	Mean	SD
18a/20a	will help improve students' reading skills	37	3.78	1.228	35	3.97	1.361
18b/20b	will help improve students' speaking skills	37	4.16	1.143	35	4.20	1.324
18c/20c	will help students to become more independent learners	37	3.84	1.093	35	3.80	1.256
18d/20d	will challenge students with higher speaking skills to their full extent	36	4.25	.996	35	4.20	1.324
18e/20e	will help shy or nervous students to gain higher marks	37	3.38	1.163	35	3.66	1.282
18f/20f	will provide students with a more natural assessment experience than the current CE English oral exam	37	3.76	1.116	35	3.86	1.264
18g/20g	will motivate students and give them an interesting assessment experience	37	3.68	1.002	35	3.83	1.098
18h/20h	will disadvantage students with lower speaking skills	37	4.11	1.242	34	3.24	1.281
18i/20i	will give a fairer assessment of students' speaking ability than the current CE English oral exam	37	3.68	1.082	34	3.76	1.257
18j/20j	will help identify student strengths and weaknesses in speaking	37	4.03	1.040	35	4.00	1.057
18k/20k	will have a negative effect on students' attitudes to using the English language	37	2.86	1.058	35	2.66	1.110
18l/20l	will increase students' workload	37	4.57	1.094	35	3.97	1.294
18m/20m	will make students more nervous	36	3.67	1.095	35	3.31	1.367

* Occasion 1 indicates the data collected in February–March 2006.
† Occasion 2 indicates the data collected in March–April 2007.

However, teachers are now less likely to feel that SBA will increase students' workload or make them more nervous (as indicated by the lower means on occasion two on these items, and that they are very much less likely to feel that SBA will disadvantage students with lower speaking skills). This is an interesting finding given exams have traditionally been designed to discriminate among the higher ability levels, leaving many less successful students indistinguishable at the bottom or off the performance charts. A follow-up analysis of the student data in this study will hopefully reveal more students from "lower banding" schools are motivated to improve their English in the assessment system.

In regard to whether SBA can motivate students, whether it provides a more natural assessment experience, whether it helps shy or nervous students or helps them become more independent learners, and whether it gives students a fairer assessment experience, teachers' attitudes have become slightly more positive. But nearly all of these changes across a year of SBA implementation are small and no real pattern emerges, apart from the large change in teachers' views about the suitability of SBA for students with lower English proficiency. To clarify these rather ambiguous results, we quote one of our teacher participants: "SBA has not successfully or dramatically increased their ability but it does provide more opportunities for them to present opinions with better confidence, for the SBA lessons have provided a mode of learning that is close to giving private tutoring in small groups." Clearly, the attitudes of teachers are still in flux in terms of how SBA is affecting and will affect their students, perhaps because teacher at this stage had not seen any moderated results.

Teachers' Views on the Effects of SBA on Teachers

Table 18.6 summarizes teachers' views about the effects of SBA on themselves. When SBA was first mooted, teachers' immediate concern was that it would lead to much heavier

Table 18.6 Teachers' Views on the Effects of SBA on Teachers

19/21. Your views about the effects of School-Based Assessment on teachers: I think that the School-Based Assessment . . .	*Occasion 1**			*Occasion 2†*		
	n	*Mean*	*SD*	*n*	*Mean*	*SD*
19a/21a will encourage teachers to implement assessment for learning	36	3.64	1.018	34	3.76	1.103
19b/21b will encourage teachers to promote extensive reading	37	3.92	.954	35	4.06	1.110
19c/21c will encourage more professional sharing within schools	37	3.95	1.026	35	4.08	1.222
19d/21d will encourage more professional sharing across schools	37	3.81	1.076	35	3.80	1.208
19e/21e will encourage teachers to think of assessment in a new perspective (e.g., to plan for self/peer and other alternative assessment activities)	37	3.73	.932	35	4.20	1.132
19f/21f will provide other professional development opportunities for teachers	37	3.78	1.004	35	3.86	1.287
19g/21g will increase teachers' workload	37	5.65	.716	35	4.86	1.309

* Occasion 1 indicates the data collected in February–March 2006.
† Occasion 2 indicates the data collected in March–April 2007.

workloads. This same response is seen in our data on the first occasion of questionnaire administration, where there is a very high mean response on the last item (19g: "Will increase teachers' workload"). However, the data from one year later show that teachers' concern has declined considerably (from 5.65 to 4.68), although workload is still their greatest concern overall. Teachers have also become slightly more positive about the various SBA-related professional sharing and development opportunities. The largest increase is on Item 19e/21e: "will encourage teachers to think of assessment in a new perspective (e.g. to plan for self/peer and other alternative assessment activities)", which might be seen to be an effect of the professional development courses (SBA Consultancy Team, 2006b). However, none of these changes is significant; and the data cannot show any explanation of why teachers' views in some areas have become so much more positive, yet their views of SBA's effects on themselves remain very cautious.

Teachers' Own Voices in Questionnaire Comments

Given the very short timeline for implementing SBA and Hong Kong teachers' general lack of sophisticated assessment understanding (Yung, 2006), it is not surprising that some teachers have a somewhat negative or an ambivalent attitude towards it. In open-ended comments on the questionnaire at the beginning, teachers commented that "it disrupts the syllabus", "an extra paper to take care of in addition to the already difficult four papers", "too much pressure". Such comments show a lack of understanding of the principles of SBA as a form of *assessment for learning*, to be integrated into classroom instruction; yet since the innovation is not merely of a new assessment system, but also of a new teaching and assessment philosophy, the relatively cautious, even skeptical attitude adopted by many teachers in this study to a number of aspects of the initiative is not surprising.

Many of the teachers' concerns in the initial stages of the implementation process related to practical issues and concrete support (Davison, 2007a, 2007b). One issue that was raised frequently at the beginning was the need for more technical support, resources and equipment, and this issue also came through in the open-ended comments on the first occasion questionnaires in the longitudinal study: "Pressure in terms of worries regarding the lack of support from school. There is much hindrance in buying/ordering readers/viewing materials especially because of the lack of funds." Also in these first questionnaires' open-ended comments, there were negative references to the short lead-in time for the introduction of SBA, the lack of financial resources to support it, the lack of teacher training/professional development, and the need for materials to integrate SBA into the curriculum. The words "unclear/not clear" occurred fairly frequently, for example: "Great pressure: resources/guidelines on implementation not clear enough. It gives me a strong impression that EMB itself does not know clearly about it." However, these comments grew less frequent over the data collection period, and there are none in the open-ended comments on the teacher questionnaire at the end of the first year of implementation, suggesting these problems had been addressed. However, even in the data collection in March–April 2007, after three terms of working with SBA, some teachers were still expressing discomfort with implementing certain aspects of SBA, and some (a fairly small number) were still asking for professional development or more support.[7]

Teachers' overriding concerns seemed to relate to time, with many comments relating to timetabling problems or curriculum crowding beyond the individual teacher's control. The implementation of a classroom practice-oriented form of assessment in a "traditional" school subject like English raises some problems that are not found, or found less often, in laboratory subjects such as biology and chemistry, where some lessons are longer, and where active groupwork is a norm. At this stage, teachers clearly perceive the introduction of SBA as adding to their time pressure. This is understandable in the early stages of implementation of any classroom, thus it may be too soon to draw any conclusions. However, several positive changes do appear to be emerging that can offset the added pressure on teachers' and students' time, with more teacher comments about increased time that have a positive 'spin' to them, for example, "Spending more time on video-taping; Spending more time on sharing views and teaching students how to read." In this and some other comments the sense is that the added time is being spent on worthwhile activity.

More positively, the results also indicate that SBA is beginning to permeate the English teaching culture in at least some schools. Even in open-ended comments in the first round of teacher questionnaire data, we saw that some teachers were able to recognize the intentions and potential of SBA, for example: "There has been a major change in my role as a teacher. I've been actively involved in helping my students to improve their learning, helping them to understand the assessment criteria, and providing feedback on how they can do better," "It provides an opportunity to urge students to read, view, and speak." However, later in the year this trend was more obvious, as exemplified in the comments below from teacher 'L', describing changes in her practices over the year:

> L: I am also teaching this year's S3, and in this year's S3, we're trying to incorporate SBA in the curriculum, i.e., we try to include some films or some texts related to the same theme as we go on. And in that case I think students could have a better relationship of what they are viewing in class or what they are doing in class and then they could have a larger exposure of what are some of the reading texts included they can get in touch with for the SBA in future. I think in this way, teachers will feel more comfortable with SBA, not a separate thing that we are to deal with.

Another trend which emerged during the implementation process was for teachers to comment about changes and improvements in the teacher–student relationship: "Enhance the relationship with my students!", "Get more chances to know my students, get more chances to motivate and give orientation to students", "It has increased the magnitude of my oral communication with my students". For Hong Kong secondary teachers, with their large classes and more formal interaction, this enhanced communication is a very positive sign.

Although teachers are far less certain at this stage about SBA actually improving students' oral language skills, a number of teachers did comment that SBA increased students' opportunities for exposure to real English, and this was borne out by comments that students were more confident in their oral English and more motivated to read and speak in English, and the increased student workload created by SBA is offset by benefits to students' language learning.

There were also several comments indicating a positive change in teachers' attitudes to working together, important as for the innovation to work in the long-term, teachers must learn to trust each other and be willing to work together. Hopefully, these positive signs of teacher–teacher interaction, enhanced communication with students, and willingness to develop professionally will become more frequent as both teachers and students overcome the burdens of the changes and the perceived added workload and adjust to a different way of working together.

Conclusion

The introduction of this school-based approach into the assessment of the oral English of Form 4 and 5 learners in Hong Kong has occurred as part of a policy shift towards *assessment for learning* principles, and was specifically motivated by the belief that SBA would enable a more comprehensive appraisal of learners' achievement and enhance students' capacity for self-evaluation and life-long learning. The preliminary analyses of the longitudinal study data suggest that despite teachers' initial concerns about increased workload, and in contradiction to the preconceived skepticism of many schools and their communities about the relevance and acceptability of such progressive approaches for the Chinese learner being imported into a very different culture and educational system without sufficient consultation or adaptation (Marton, 2000), SBA is beginning to take hold in the English language curriculum. As we saw in Table 18.1, teachers' perceptions of their own understanding of the underlying assessment philosophy of School-Based Assessment improved significantly during this period. Convincing teachers of the worth of the change is critical to its becoming embedded into educational practice and if teachers are to be convinced that it is worthwhile they must understand it well. In educational innovation terms there are some encouraging early indicators of change. Empirical evidence of parents' increased willingness to accept in-class assessment of their own child's English was not available from the longitudinal study due to lack of a sufficient sample of parents, but the significant finding discussed in connection with Table 18.2, that teachers are much more confident that their school has given parents and students enough information about School-Based Assessment, is indirect evidence that a concerted effort to inform and involve parents by the education authorities, partly through the school and the class teacher, is having success. Hong Kong parents see it as their responsibility to take an active and often interventionist role in their child's education: this is the positive side of what is often seen as a negative effect of so-called 'Confucian heritage cultures' on the Chinese learner. Over the 2 years of the study, it has become clear that in addition to professional development for teachers it is essential to provide substantial and substantive information to parents.

Another encouraging sign is the teachers' perceptions of a modest but perceptible improvement in students' learning attitudes. The longitudinal study was not designed to evaluate change in students' levels of oral language performance, and the effects on English language outcomes will not be known for some years. However, early examination of qualitative data from students in the larger study suggests that students' understanding of speaking is growing more sophisticated, that they are able to reflect on their own performances and the need for further improvement, and that although they perceive SBA as more "work" for them as well as their teachers, many of them value what they gain from this kind of learning, suggesting that so-called "Asian" cultures may actually be more open to change than is often assumed.

Acknowledgment

We would like to thank Mrs Christina Lee, the HKEAA, and the participating teachers and schools for their extensive assistance with this study. We are also grateful for the constant encouragement and support of our research team at the University of Hong Kong, in particular our Project Officer Wendy Leung, who helped so much with the data collection and analysis.

Notes

1. There are approximately 480 government and aided secondary schools in Hong Kong, officially classified into two groups: Chinese-medium (CMI) and English-medium schools (EMI), although a significant number of CMI schools switch to English at the beginning of Form 4 to prepare their students for entry to the English-medium university sector. Schools are also informally classified to according to the predominant ability "banding" of the students they enroll: Band 1 (highest) to Band 3 (lowest).
2. See Choi & Lee (Chapter 5) for a full description of the other components of the English examination.
3. It is difficult to justify statistical moderation from a theoretical perspective, given SBA and the external examination are measuring different things under very different conditions, but it is considered essential to ensure public confidence in the examination system is maintained, while allowing the HKEAA to be more innovative in its assessment practices (see HKEAA website: http://www.hkeaa.edu.hk/doc/tas_ftp_doc/CE-Eng-StatModerate-0610.pdf).
4. The data relating to students, parents, and other key stakeholders and in-depth case studies of the experiences of specific teachers will be reported elsewhere.
5. Inevitably, over the course of a year some teachers had left and some had joined each school so the data cannot be completely matched.
6. Whether or not the implementation is truly effective is a different question, which is being pursued by in-depth analysis of the qualitative data of this study, especially through video-recordings from classrooms, and in other studies being carried out by the authors with colleagues at the University of Hong Kong.
7. The professional development courses are still being run 3–4 times a year for teachers who have not yet done them or who are moving into teaching at this level for the first time.

References

Adamson, B. & Davison, C. (2003). Innovation in English language teaching in Hong Kong primary schools: One step forwards, two steps sideways. *Prospect, 18*(1), 27–41.

Andrews, S. (1994). The washback effect of examinations: Its impact upon curriculum innovation in English language teaching. *Curriculum Forum, 4*(1), 44–58.

Andrews, S., Fullilove, J. &Wong, Y. (2002). Targeting washback: A case-study. *System, 30,* 207–223.

Assessment Reform Group. (1999). *Assessment for learning: Beyond the Black Box.* Cambridge: University of Cambridge School of Education. Retrieved November 11, 2005, www.assessment-reform-group.org.uk/CIE3.pdf

Black, P. (2001). Formative assessment and curriculum consequences. In D. Scott (Ed.), *Curriculum and assessment.* Westport, CT: Ablex Publishing.

Black, P. & Wiliam, D. (1998). Assessment and classroom learning. *Assessment in Education: Principles, Policy & Practice, 5,* 7–74.

Black, P., Harrison, C., Lee, C., Marshall, B. & Wiliam, D. (2003). *Assessment for learning*. New York: Open University Press.

Carless, D. (2004). Issues in teachers' re-interpretation of a task-based innovation in primary schools, *TESOL Quarterly*, 8, 639–662.

Carless, D. (2005). Prospects for the implementation of assessment for learning. *Assessment in Education: Principles, Policy & Practice*, 12, 39–54.

Cheah, Y. M. (1998). The examination culture and its impact on literacy innovations: The case of Singapore. *Language and Education*, 12, 192–209.

Cheng, L. (1997). Does washback influence teaching? Implications for Hong Kong. *Language and Education*, 11, 38–54.

Cheng, L. (2005). *Changing language teaching through language testing: A washback study*. Cambridge, UK: Cambridge University Press.

Cheung, D. & Ng, D. (2000). Teachers' stages of concern about the target-oriented curriculum. *Education Journal*, 28(1), 109–122.

Curriculum Development Council (1999). *English Language Education Secondary Syllabus*. Hong Kong, China: Hong Kong Government Printer.

Curriculum Development Institute. (2002). School policy on assessment: Changing assessment practices. Retrieved May 14, 2008, http://cd.edb.gov.hk/basic_guide/BEGuideeng0821/chapter05.html

Davison, C. (2004). The contradictory culture of classroom-based assessment: Teacher assessment practices in senior secondary English. *Language Testing*, 21, 304–333.

Davison, C. (2007a). Views from the chalkface: School-based assessment in Hong Kong. *Language Assessment Quarterly: An International Journal*, 4, 37–68.

Davison, C. (2007b). Different definitions of language and language learning: Implications for assessment. In J. Cummins & C. Davison (Eds), *International Handbook of English language teaching*, Volume 1 (pp. 533–548). Norwell, MA: Springer.

Education and Manpower Bureau. (2007) Senior Secondary Curriculum and Assessment Guides (Final version): English Language Key Learning Area. Retrieved March 24, 2008, http://www.edb.gov.hk/FileManager/EN/Content_5999/eng_lang_final.pdf

Hamp-Lyons, L. (1999). Implications of the "examination culture" for (English language) education in Hong Kong. In V. Crew, V. Berry & J. Hung (Eds.), *Exploring diversity in the language curriculum* (pp. 133–141). Hong Kong: Hong Kong Institute of Education.

Hamp-Lyons, L. (2001). Fairness in language testing. In Kunnan, A. J. (Ed.), *Fairness and validation in language assessment* (pp. 99–104). Cambridge, UK: Cambridge University Press.

Hamp-Lyons, L. (2007). The impact of testing practices on teaching: Ideologies and alternatives. In J. Cummins & C. Davison (Eds.), *The International Handbook of English language teaching*, Volume 1 (pp. 487–504). Norwell, MA: Springer.

Holliday, A. (1994). *Appropriate methodology and social context*. Cambridge, UK: Cambridge University Press.

King, R. (1997). Can public examinations have a positive washback effect on classroom teaching? In P. Grundy (Ed.), *IATEFL 31st International Annual Conference Brighton, April 1997* (pp. 33–38). London: IATEFL.

Marton, F. (2000). Afterword: the lived curriculum. In Adamson, B., Kwan, T. & Chan, K.K. (Eds.), *Changing the curriculum: The impact of reform on primary schooling in Hong Kong*. Hong Kong: Hong Kong University Press.

Rea-Dickins, P. (2007). Classroom-based assessment: Possibilities and pitfalls. In J. Cummins & C. Davison (Eds.), *The International Handbook of English language teaching*, Volume 1 (pp. 505–520). Norwell, MA: Springer.

SBA Consultancy Team. (2006a). *2007 HKCE English examination: Introduction to the school-based assessment component* (2nd ed.) Hong Kong: HKEAA.

SBA Consultancy Team. (2006b). *Professional development for the school-based assessment component of the 2007 HKCE English Language Examination.*

Stobart, G. (2005). Fairness in multicultural assessment systems. *Assessment in Education: Principles, Policy & Practice*, 12, 275–287.

Teasdale, A. & Leung, C. (2000). Teacher assessment and psychometric theory: a case of paradigm crossing? *Language Testing*, 17, 163–184.

Yung, B.H.W. (2001). Examiner, policeman or students' companion: Teachers' perceptions of their role in an assessment reform. *Educational Review* 53(3), 251–260.

Yung, B.H.W. (2002). Same assessment, different practice: Professional consciousness as a determinant of teachers' practice in a school-based assessment scheme. *Assessment in Education* 9(1), 101–121.

Yung, B. (2006). Assessment reform in science: Fairness or fear. Norwell, MA: Springer.

Part V

The Link between Test Validity and Validation, and Test Use and the Consequences

Conclusion and Beyond

19 The Impact of English Language Assessment and the Chinese Learner in China and Beyond

Liying Cheng, Queen's University
Andy Curtis, The Chinese University of Hong Kong

We started this book in Chapter 1 by acknowledging the long examination tradition dating from ancient China and the enormous number of Chinese Learners learning English and taking English tests inside and outside China. We will end the book in this final chapter by discussing the implications of these facts and figures and by aiming to provide some directions for future work in the area of English language assessment with Chinese Learners. This chapter will first bring together the main points from the discussions of each of the previous chapters, including the implications and consequences of the extensive use of large scale assessment/testing in China and the current trend(s) which may indicate where assessment/testing will go in the future.

The Valued Examination-driven Context

This book has been structured in such a way that the readers can situate the discussions of the Chinese Learner in relation to English language assessment within a historical, social, political, and economic context in China (see Chapters 1 and 2). Throughout the book, we can see the essential role that examinations have played and continue to play in Chinese society—being successful in examinations is the key to succeed in study, work and life. On the other hand, we can also see the rather 'unquestionable' status examinations enjoy in these societies—being regarded as a fair (just) means by which to select and to teach, and as a road to success. Traditionally, Chinese society in general has accepted the function of testing as a fair indicator of students' academic success. Consequently, teachers and students follow the testing in their teaching and learning and/or make passing of the test the goal of their teaching and learning. In this sense, academic success is narrowly defined as the learning required to pass a test. That is the main reason why the University Entrance Examination to Higher Education (UEEHE) is often nicknamed the "Footslog Bridge" [独木桥]—the only route to academic success via a long and laborious walk or march, although there are many ways to reach higher education in mainland China, such as via the Self-Taught Higher Education Examination System (STHEE) and the various Admission Tests to Higher Education for Adults (ATHEA), as discussed in Chapter 3. This combination of the importance of examinations and societal acceptance of examination has created a highly-valued, highly-selective, rather narrowly-defined examination-driven context which has influenced the lives and the education (teaching and learning) of generations of Chinese Learners.

An important aspect and a distinctive feature of this book is that it has based an understanding of English language assessment in China on the theoretical framework of Assessment Use Argument (AUA) (Bachman & Palmer, in press), in which an attempt is made to link test validation and test consequences from the point of views of both test developers and test-users. However, it is important to point out that within the Chinese context, sometimes the test-developers are also the test-users, and/or the other way around. Therefore, the definition of test-developers and test-users is blurred. In this sense, the link between the two needs to be bridged in order to answer the fundamental questions in assessment such as why, what, how and whom to assess, so the impact and consequences of our assessment practices can be beneficial to our stakeholders.

Chapters 3–6 thus provide a holistic view of English language assessment (including foreign language assessment) from the four major test organizations in China. These chapters present a panoramic overview of English language test developments in China over the past 50–60 years. These chapters also demonstrate the complex political, historical, social, and educational contexts within which their test developments have been created and developed. From these chapters, we can see a close relationship between educational development and test development in China which can help us to appreciate the importance of the background context for any test development. In this context, testing and training (teaching) go hand in hand, and testing serves and drives teaching and learning at the same time. For example, in Chapter 5, the authors point out that:

> The conduct of oral examinations is both costly and labor-intensive, but if speaking skills are not examined, they are not likely to be taught. This reflects the ingrained examination-oriented culture in Hong Kong. The Authority sees its natural role in taking on this responsibility. (p. 74)

One of the main reasons for this close relationship is the fact that these Chinese test developers are also university professors and/or researchers working closely together within national and local educational organizations. In this way, the Chinese situation is conceptually different from major testing organizations, such as Educational Testing Service (ETS) and Cambridge ESOL.[1] It is, then, natural that test developers in China make use of the valued function of testing in Chinese society to bring about positive washback into teaching and learning (see also Cheng, 2005; Cheng & Qi, 2006; Li, 1990). The same use of testing is also evident in international language testing (see Wall & Alderson, 1993) and in educational measurement (Madaus, 1990; Popham, 1987).

Chapters 7–12, from the point of view of test-users, illustrate another important piece of the Assessment Use Argument (AUA) framework. Chapters 7, 8 and 9 report on Chinese test-takers taking three major international English language tests, i.e. the TOEFL, the IELTS, and the MELAB tests. These chapters not only provide a comparative view of Chinese test-takers in relation to the global test-taking population, but also take a closer look at sub-groups of Chinese test-takers, e.g., those from mainland China, Hong Kong, and Taiwan. In this sense, these chapters situate Chinese test-takers within the broader international context and provide details of test-takers educated in three different Chinese teaching, learning, and assessment contexts. Through these chapters, we can develop a better understanding of how Chinese Learners compare internationally, and gain a greater understanding of the unique characteristics of these Chinese Learners in their English language development.

Chapters 10, 11, 12, on the other hand, report on tests developed and administered in specific Chinese contexts. The introduction of the Public English Test System (PETS) in mainland China is one important step towards catering for the massive, various, and public needs of English language assessment beyond formal educational institutions. The development of the Graduate School Entrance English Examination (GSEEE) is a direct response to the rapidly-growing postgraduate education in mainland China over the past 30 years. This chapter further illustrates some of the struggles and challenges that test-takers must go through in order to meet the national entrance requirements. The vast geographical regions over which the test-takers are spread and their uneven education developments in relation to the national uniform requirements provide major challenges related to the question of how we can address the issue of fairness—also commonly used in China to mean 'justice'—for a test of this nature. In this GSEEE chapter, we also see the rapidly-expanding testing coaching business which caters to the needs of test-takers passing the national GSEEE test, but which may also distort the nature of English language teaching and learning—a phenomenon commonly appearing when the testing stakes are high (Chau, 2008). Chapter 12 critiques a more recently developed but extremely important test of English, the General English Proficiency Test (GEPT), in Taiwan. The chapter offers an exemplary attempt to look at the aspect of the test development and test use employing the Assessment Use Argument (AUA) framework.

Chapters 13–18 bring the empirical research piece to the Assessment Use Argument (AUA) framework, as each of the chapters provides an empirical study with test-takers in a unique testing/assessment setting. All six of these chapters focus on test-takers, except for Chapter 18, which focuses on teachers. Chapter 13 discusses the oral performance of Chinese test-takers in relation to two other groups of test-takers and explored potential cultural-specific and/or test-driven elements that these Chinese test-takers brought with them into their test performance. Chapter 14 reports on a study exploring the relationship between test-takers' beliefs about the CET and their test performance, with Chapter 15 set in the context of CET where the authors investigated the assessment environment students experienced in their teaching and learning of the College English course. Chapters 16 and 17 deal with the NMET—the national university entrance test and the most high-stakes test for the largest groups of Chinese Learners in mainland China. Chapter 16 reports on a washback study of the proofreading sub-test of the NMET, whereas Chapter 17 is a validation study of the oral sub-test of the NMET. Between these two chapters, we can see the efforts made by the test-developers and test-users in their attempts to build an instrument not only serving as an effective selection instrument, but also a test that can potentially positively guide the teaching and learning of English at secondary school level in mainland China. Chapter 18 reports on a study conducted with a group of teachers of English in Hong Kong secondary schools to understand their initial reactions and responses to the newly introduced school-based assessment into the Hong Kong Certificate of Education Examinations in English. The chapter presents an intriguing case of how teachers react to an assessment change moving from assessment *of* learning to combine assessment *for* learning where teacher assessment is counted—for the first time in the educational history of Hong Kong—as part of students' final scores in their secondary school leaving examinations in English.

All together, the chapters in this book present a holistic view of the English language assessment situation within the Chinese context. The book, most of all, addresses these issues in relation to the Chinese Learner. A number of major recurring themes have emerged from the previous chapters of this book, of which some of the main themes are presented here.

Dual Assessment Functions: Selection and Teaching

As mentioned above, the unique role academics played in test development in China has added to the blurring of the distinction between test-developers and test-users, which can be seen in the CET, NMET and GSEEE contexts. For example, the National College English Testing Committee (NCETC) consists of 25 Chinese university professors whose research areas focus on English language teaching and testing. This is also true for the early test development of the NMET where test-developers (professors working in universities) had the clear intention to use the test to positively influence the teaching and learning of English in Chinese secondary schools (see Cheng & Qi, 2006). Therefore, it is natural for those involved to be concerned about both the quality of the test (validation) as well as the influence of the test on teaching and learning (consequences). However, the efforts to serve these two somewhat competing functions—selection and teaching— are difficult to realize in reality and in practice. The well-intended washback may not be realized when the purpose of the test is primarily selective.

In addition, due to the high-stakes selection function of these tests, an increasing number of institutions or coaching schools have sprung up across China. As mentioned above, Chapter 11 pointed out that the need for coaching programs/schools has given rise to "professional"[2] test instructors/coaches as well as to a considerable volume of coaching materials and a large number of coaching schools, thus creating sizeable business opportunities for those involved, but in many ways polluting the test scores and distorting the nature of English language teaching and learning.

It is therefore widely acknowledged in the Chinese context that the English testing system (as well as English teaching and learning) needs to be further enhanced in terms of its quality. More empirical research needs to be conducted to provide evidence for the validity of the tests and to understand the intended and unintended consequences of the tests. The impact of the two national tests—the NMET and the CET—on the teaching and learning of English in China is particularly evident and continues to be much debated.

The Size that Counts

Internationally, Chinese Learners have always been the largest first language (L1) group of the global TOEFL candidate population and the third largest L1 group of the IELTS test-takers. For the past 10 years, the proportion of Chinese TOEFL candidates accounted for, in most years, more than 20 percent of the global TOEFL candidate volume (see Chapter 7). Domestically in mainland China alone, more than 27 million Chinese university students are learning English and taking English tests (http://www.hnedu. cn/). It is important to note that this figure does not include learners at the school level, where students start to learn English around Grade 3 in China (see Cheng, 2008), nor does this figure include learners in Hong Kong and in Taiwan. As rightly pointed out in Chapter 4 (p. 44), the test-taker population of the College English Test "has become the world's largest for any test of English as a Foreign Language (EFL)". In the June 2008 test administration alone, 7.7 million of test-takers sat the College English Test. Taking all the tests and test-takers discussed in this book into consideration, it is no exaggeration to say the Chinese Learners are one of the largest group of learners learning English and taking English tests in the world today, and such a large group of learners/test-takers deserve considerable research in the English assessment and testing field.

Lessons to be Learned

As pointed out in Chapter 7 (p. 102), "the general Chinese TOEFL population, in particular the candidates from the Chinese Mainland, clearly and consistently outperformed the overall world TOEFL population in the first 10 years [1995–2005] under study. However, the performance of the Chinese Mainland group, which forms the majority of the [entire] Chinese candidate population, appears to have weakened during the 2005–07 period based on the test results of the TOEFL iBT administrations." Interestingly, perhaps importantly and perhaps not coincidentally, this was when the TOEFL iBT introduced a full range of integrated testing in all four skills—including speaking. The same situation can also be seen from the test performance of Chinese test-takers on the IELTS exam—also an integrated test of the four major language skills—where Chinese test-takers lagged behind test-takers worldwide—particularly in speaking and writing. Comparatively, Chinese test-takers appear to have an upper hand when it comes to discrete-point testing items, e.g. on the MELAB. As was pointed out in Chapter 9, the means of MELAB part scores and final scores among Chinese test-takers were higher than the means of the whole test-taker population, except for the speaking test. Although the MELAB's discrete-item testing formats may lack authenticity, interactiveness, and practicality in language use, this testing feature seems to have favored Chinese Learners, who have had a great deal of experience with multiple-choice examinations in China and who have received much more input on linguistics-related knowledge but less on pragmatics-related knowledge while they were learning English in China.

The strength and weakness of Chinese Learners' English language performance on these tests have mirrored the teaching and learning of English in China which are driven by many years of discrete-point and multiple-choice testing during these learners' schooling. The CET, NMET, and GSEEE still adopt multiple-choice as one of their major testing formats.

What kinds of Chinese Learners have we produced over the many years of such multiple-choice testing (and teaching) practices where one choice is the correct answer? What is the impact of such educational practices on these learners' life-long learning inside and outside China? This is an important challenge for both the testing and teaching communities to reflect on in China (Cheng, 2008) and in other parts of world with increasing numbers of Chinese Learners in tertiary education (Cortazzi & Jin, 2004). As can be seen from this book, large-scale multiple-choice testing still dominates the Chinese English assessment context, a fact which needs to be fully realized of within the testing and teaching field in China and elsewhere outside China. In this way, we can understand the consequences and the impact of such large-scale testing practices on Chinese Learners.

Another promising aspect we have seen is that school-based assessment has been introduced into Hong Kong secondary school teaching and learning as part of the Hong Kong Certificate of Education Examinations in English. The revised secondary school English curriculum in mainland China (Ministry of Education, 2005) has also suggested alternative and diversified forms of assessment such as peer- and self-assessment. Furthermore, a number of teacher training seminars and workshops were conducted on classroom assessment practices—an attempt to combine assessment *of* learning with assessment *for* learning into the teaching and learning of English within the Chinese contexts. Two of the recent examples are as follows: The first was a 3-day workshop supported by the International Language Testing Association (ILTA), held in March 2008 at the Guangdong University of Foreign Studies (workshop details can be found at: http://www.clal.org.cn/ltworkshop/index.htm). The major goal of the workshop was to provide Chinese secondary school English teachers with the necessary knowledge, skills, and experiences so they can better understand the impact of large-scale testing on their teaching and their students and so they can orient their classroom assessments to promote the learning of English, rather than let the testing formats become the formats of their own teaching and be blindly driven by the test scores of their students. This workshop also raised these teachers' awareness so they can assess for the learning of their students. The second example was a pre-LTRC workshop in June 2008 on *applying school-based assessment for learning in a formal examination system*. This workshop framed school-based assessment within assessment *for* learning, outlined the key components of the English oral SBA, and provided participants with the opportunity to use the assessment criteria to assess a range of samples of oral language use (http://www.sis.zju.edu.cn/sis/sisht/english/ltrc2008/pre_workshop1.html).

Clearly, then, there appear to be many lessons still to be learned about English language assessment and the Chinese Learner, especially if, as noted in the Preface to this collection, China comes to be one of the driving forces in English language teaching and testing globally. However, the many lessons learned and presented in this volume will, we believe, provide a solid foundation on which to build a better understanding in the future.

Notes

1. According to its website, "founded in 1947, ETS develops, administers and scores more than 50 million tests annually—including the TOEFL® and TOEIC® tests, the GRE® General and subject Tests and *The Praxis Series*™ assessments—in more than 180 countries, and at over 9,000 locations worldwide" (http://www.ets.org/). Also according to its website, "Cambridge ESOL offers the world's leading range of certificates for learners and teachers of English— taken by over 2 million people in 130 countries. They help people gain entrance to university or college, improve job prospects or measure progress in English" (http://www.cambridgeesol.org/).
2. Although these people do this work as an income-generating job or business, they are not "professional" in the sense of training, qualifications or experience.

References

Bachman, L. F. & Palmer, A. S. (in press). *Language Assessment in the Real World.* Oxford: Oxford University Press.

Chau, M. (2008). *Learning to write essays or teaching to crack tests: An empirical study investigating the washback and impact of TOEFL test-preparation in China.* Paper presented at the 30th Language Testing Research Colloquium, Hangzhou, China.

Cheng, L. (2005). *Changing language teaching through language testing: A washback study.* Studies in Language Testing: Volume 21. Cambridge, UK: Cambridge University Press.

Cheng, L. (2008). The Key to Success: English Language Testing in China. *Language Testing,* 25(1), 15–38.

Cheng, L. & Qi, L. (2006). Description and examination of the National Matriculation English Test in China. *Language Assessment Quarterly: An International Journal,* 3(1), 53–70.

Cortazzi, M. & Jin, L. (2004). *Changing practices in Chinese cultures of learning.* Keynote address at the Responding to the Needs of the Chinese Learner in Higher Education Conference, University of Portsmouth, England.

Li, X. J. (1990) How powerful can a language test be? The MET in China. *Journal of Multilingual and Multicultural Development,* 11(5), 393–404.

Madaus, G. (1990). The distortion of teaching and testing: High stakes testing and instruction. *Peabody Journal of Education,* 65(3), 29–46.

Ministry of Education. (2005) *New Senior English Curriculum for China* [普通高中英语课程标准 (实验)]. Ministry of Education, Beijing, The People's Republic of China.

Popham, W. J. (1987). The merits of measurement-driven instruction. *Phi Delta Kappa,* 68, 679–682.

Wall, D. & Alderson, J. C. (1993). Examining washback: The Sri Lankan Impact Study. *Language Testing,* 10(1), 41–69.

Contributors

Qingsi Liu works as a subject officer in the Test Development of Foreign Languages of the National Education Examinations Authority (NEEA), Beijing, China.

Yan Jin is Professor of Applied Linguistics at the School of Foreign Languages, Shanghai Jiaotong University, Shanghai, China.

Chee-cheong Choi joined the Hong Kong Examinations and Assessment Authority when it was established in 1977 and retired as Secretary General of the Authority in August 2004.

Christina Lee is the General Manager of the Assessment Development Division of the Hong Kong Examinations and Assessment Authority.

Antony John Kunnan is Professor of TESOL at California State University, Los Angeles, USA.

Jessica R. W. Wu is Head of Testing Editorial Department of the Language Training and Testing Center (LTTC), Taiwan.

David D. Qian is Associate Professor and Deputy Director of the Research Centre for Professional Communication in English at the Department of English, The Hong Kong Polytechnic University.

Janna Fox is Associate Professor and Director of the Language Assessment and Testing Research Unit within the School of Linguistics and Applied Language Studies at Carleton University, Ottawa, Canada.

Xiaomei Song is a doctoral candidate at the Faculty of Education, Queen's University, Ontario, Canada.

Jianda Liu is Professor in the National Key Research Center for Linguistics and Applied Linguistics at Guangdong University of Foreign Studies, Guangzhou, China.

Lianzhen He is Professor of English at the School of Foreign Languages, Zhejiang University, Hangzhou, China.

Viphavee Vongpumivitch is Assistant Professor in the Department of Foreign Languages and Literature at National Tsing Hua University, Hsinchu, Taiwan.

Yang Lu is Associate Professor of English and now the Examination Officer for Mandarin Chinese Programmes in the University of Nottingham, UK.

Jing Zhao is a doctoral candidate in the program of Quantitative Research, Evaluation, and Measurement (QREM), School of Educational Policy and Leadership, The Ohio State University, USA.

Xiaoying Wang is Associate Professor at the School of English and International Studies at Beijing Foreign Studies University, Beijing, China.

Luxia Qi is Professor of English at Guangdong University of Foreign Studies, Guangzhou, China.

Yongqiang Zeng is Professor in Faculty of English Language and Culture, Guangdong University of Foreign Studies, Guangzhou, China.

Chris Davison is Professor of Education and Head of School at the University of New South Wales, Sydney, Australia.

Liz Hamp-Lyons is Professor of English Language Assessment at the University of Bedfordshire, UK.

Index

Printed in the USA/Agawam, MA
October 27, 2011

562069.001